THE WESTERN CHURCH
IN THE LATER MIDDLE AGES

The Western Church

IN THE LATER MIDDLE AGES

Francis Oakley

Cornell University Press

ITHACA AND LONDON

First published 1979 by Cornell University Press.
First printing, Cornell Paperbacks, 1985.
Fourth printing, 1991.

International Standard Book Number (cloth) 0-8014-1208-0
International Standard Book Number (paper) 0-8014-9347-1
Library of Congress Catalog Card Number 79-7621
Printed in the United States of America
Librarians: Library of Congress cataloging information appears on the last page of the book.

⊗ The paper in this book meets the minimum requirements of the American National Standard for Information Sciences—Permanence of Paper for Printed Library Materials, ANSI Z39.48-1984.

Memoriae
W. F. F. GRACE
Doctoris

CONTENTS

PREFACE

In this book I try to address the history of the fourteenth- and fifteenth-century church in its own terms, conscious not only of discontinuities but also of continuities with the earlier medieval experience. By so doing I hope to have avoided the distortions and refractions that occur when that history is seen too obsessively through the lens of the Reformation.

After an opening chapter focused on the ecclesiastical institution, delineating the broad movement of papal history and establishing a basic chronological framework, the approach is topical rather than strictly chronological, reaching back, at need, to identify the deeper roots of some critical late-medieval development or forward, where desirable, to identify its subsequent legacy. In the final chapter, by switching to a biographical approach, I hope to have brought to life some of the movements and developments of the period and to have illustrated both their interrelations and their disjunctions. In an Epilogue I return briefly to the complex of problems surrounding the antecedents of the Reformation that historians have found so vexing and at the same time so very intriguing.

The footnotes I have striven to limit in both number and length. With the exception of citations to works printed in collected writings and essays in collective volumes, the citations in those footnotes are given in abbreviated form. Full titles and locations may be found alphabetically arranged by name of author or editor in the Bibliography.

I acknowledge with gratitude the many debts I have incurred in the course of preparing and writing this book. For the patience, efficiency, and good humor with which she handled my repeated demands on the Interlibrary Loan Service, I thank Lee Dalzell of the Williams College Library. For their work on one or another of the drafts through which the manuscript passed I thank three excellent typists: Constance Ellis, Cathryn Rowan, and Julie Peterson. For grants from the Class of 1900 Fund toward the cost of preparing the manuscript for the press I thank the president and trustees of Williams College; for the award of the Summer Fellowship in 1974 that enabled me to spend a fruitful month amid the incomparable holdings of the Folger Shakespeare Library in Washington, D.C., I thank the director and trustees of that institution. For their willingness to read the manuscript in whole or in part and to give me the benefit of their help, criticism, and advice, I thank my fellow historians and friends: Steven Ozment of Harvard, Brian Tierney of Cornell, and James Wood of Williams. For preparing the Index I thank Brian Oakley. Nor would these acknowledgments be truly complete if I failed to express my gratitude to those who first introduced me to the history of the medieval church—to my tutors of Oxford days, Trevor Aston of Corpus Christi College and J. R. L. Highfield of Merton, and to my old schoolteacher, the late W. F. F. Grace, who, by an alchemy one can only admire without being able to emulate, aroused in me as in many another sixth-former at St. Francis Xavier's College, Liverpool, an abiding love for things historical. It is to his memory that this book is dedicated.

F. O.

Williamstown, Massachusetts

THE WESTERN CHURCH
IN THE LATER MIDDLE AGES

INTRODUCTION

The fourteenth century had other aspects . . . which seem
paradoxical until they are viewed in connection with the
general course of human history, in which the ebb and flow
of the life of nations is seen to depend on higher laws, more
general purposes, the guidance of a Higher Hand. . . .
Weak as is the fourteenth century, the fifteenth is weaker
still; more futile, more bloody, more immoral; yet out of it
emerges, in spite of all, the truer and brighter day, the
season of more general conscious life, higher longings, more
forbearing, more sympathetic, purer, riper liberty.
                                          —WILLIAM STUBBS

When he wrote these words more than a hundred years ago, it was
the political and constitutional history of England that Bishop Stubbs
had in mind. For his contemporaries and immediate successors, however, the same words could equally well have applied, both in their
gloomy conviction of decline and the countervailing hint at benign
providential movement, to the history of the English church during
the same period. By the closing decades of the nineteenth century,
most historians were no longer disposed to regard the entire history
of the medieval church as one of gross superstition, moral turpitude,
and religious degradation. But the strictures withheld from the English church of the High Middle Ages continued to be applied,
with scarcely mitigated force, to the later medieval church. It is hardly surprising, then, that in their accounts the preoccupations of the
Reformation Parliament should cast backward across the centuries

15

immediately preceding so very long a shadow. Nor is it surprising that beneath the confused alarms and clumsy maneuverings of these centuries the same historians should detect the working of an immanent dialectic, the complex interactions of a series of movements and events flowing remorselessly in the direction of the Act in Restraint of Appeals and the final breach with Rome. "We have now to trace," wrote W. W. Capes in 1900,

> the growth of a spirit of opposition to ecclesiastical pretensions, which had different rallying cries as time went on, and often changed its objects and methods of attack. At first it was a question mainly of privileges and material rights; there was no talk of doctrine or church practice. The movement may be called anti-clerical at times, as it questioned the status and privileges of ecclesiastics. . . . Later on it was not so much anti-clerical as anti-papal, for it was felt more and more keenly on all sides that the aggressions of the Court of Avignon disorganized the national Church, robbed responsible patrons of their rights, drained off vast sums to be spent on alien objects, and paralysed the administrative powers of the bishops.[1]

Capes was a sober historian, who, unlike some of his contemporaries, does not give the impression of having been on nodding terms with Providence. But that does not prevent him from finding manifestations of the underlying spirit of opposition to which he refers in phenomena as diverse as open defiance of episcopal authority, town-gown riots at Oxford, attacks on monasteries and convents, the pillaging of churches, and rioting for charters of liberty at St. Albans and Canterbury. Nor does it prevent him from detecting expressions of that spirit above all in the Wycliffite movement and in the anti-papal legislation of the fourteenth century—the several statutes of Provisors and Praemunire, destined after 1393, he tells us, "to rank henceforth as the great bulwark of the independence of the National Church."[2]

About this approach to the history of the later medieval church in England much was of specifically English origin—not least the stubborn underlying conviction (present indeed in Capes though ex-

1. Capes, p. 61.
2. Ibid., p. 12.

pressed more forcefully by some of his contemporaries) that that
church had "from the first been a National Church, as regards its
inherent life and independent attitude, as well as its intimate and
peculiar relations with the State."[3] But there was also much about
the approach that was of less insular provenance—notably the sense,
widespread among church historians in general, that by the fourteenth and fifteenth centuries the medieval church "had reached the
term of its natural development" and that those centuries were of
interest mainly because "they were the age which nursed the Reformation."[4]

Thus a more than symbolic significance was attached to the "outrage of Anagni," the abject humiliation of Pope Boniface VIII in
September 1303 at the hands of mercenaries under French leadership
and in French pay. That outrage, it was felt, degraded not just the
pope but also the papacy itself. Indeed, its occurrence was nothing
less than "a symptom of its [the papacy's] inner dissolution."[5] The
insult at Anagni, the subsequent transfer of the papacy from Rome
to Avignon and its prolonged residence there, the emergence of the
nominalist theology, the retreat from the externals of religion reflected in the mysticism of Germany, the Netherlands, and England,
the onset of the Great Schism, the rise in the conciliar movement
of opposition to the pretensions of Rome, the more radical undermining by Wycliffe and Hus of the whole hierarchical order of the
church—all of these and more were seen as a series of interrelated
developments leading inexorably to the final onset of the Protestant
Reformation. One simply embarked at Anagni on the tides of destiny,
it seems, to be swept forward with irreversible momentum over seas
scattered with the wreckage of thirteenth-century hierocratic ambitions, to arrive at one's destination on October 31, 1517, with
Luther's hammer strokes ringing in one's ears.

The passage of time, of course, has eroded much of the confidence
with which such views were once held. In the historiography of the
later medieval church complexity reigns now as king. But if his-

3. Hunt, pp. vi–vii.
4. Sohm, pp. 103–7; I cite the English translation, pp. 135–39.
5. Ibid.

torians of the English church have moved long since to kick the habit of reading history backward from the break with Rome, historians of the late-medieval church at large, and especially those concerned with doctrinal or theological developments, have been much less consistent in their efforts. As a result, the Protestant Reformation contrives still to cast a surprisingly long shadow backward.

This attitude is at once more readily comprehensible and less distressingly anachronistic than might be supposed. The Reformation involved a doctrinal upheaval of truly formidable dimensions and one that called urgently and immediately for historical explanation. The impulse to equip Luther with appropriate late-medieval forerunners, therefore, was one felt already in his own lifetime, and by his Catholic adversaries as well as his Protestant apologists.[6] Thus, in the judgment rendered on the ninety-five theses by the Faculty of Theology at Paris and published in April 1521, Luther's views were linked with those of a whole series of previous troublemakers—among them the Waldensians, the Wycliffites, the Hussites, and the Brethren of the Free Spirit—and he was accused of trying "to restore the doctrines of the aforementioned heretics."[7] And writing to Erasmus in 1523, Cuthbert Tunstall, bishop of London, said of the new Lutheran ideas: "It is no question of pernicious novelty; it is only that new arms are being added to the great crowd of Wycliffite heresies."[8]

On the Protestant side, likewise, the notion of Luther's medieval forerunners—picked up early and bent to the exigencies of Protestant polemics by Philipp Melanchthon (1497–1560)—was given its most explicit expression by the Lutheran controversialist and historian Flacius Illyricus (1520–75), and, for the English-speaking world, its most influential formulation in John Foxe's *Book of Martyrs*. By the seventeenth century, the tradition of the forerunners was well established in the Protestant camp. By the nineteenth century it had be-

6. See Oberman's interesting essay "The Case of the Forerunner" in his *Forerunners*, pp. 1–49, on which much of this paragraph is based.
7. "Determinatio Theologiae Facultatis Parisiensis super doctrina Lutherana hactenus per eam revisa," in Argentré, 1: pars. 2, 365.
8. Citing from Dickens, p. 37; Latin text in Allen, ed., 5:292.

come an historiographic cliché. And in mid-century Karl Ullmann provided the classic formulation in his monumental *Reformers before the Reformation*, laying great stress on the contributions of such fifteenth-century theologians as John Pupper of Goch (d. 1475), John of Wesel (d. 1481), and Wessel Gansfort (d. 1489).[9]

Ullmann was by no means the last prominent historian to adopt this approach. As time wore on, however, it fell increasingly into disfavor and scholars became less reluctant to concede Luther's fundamental originality. Nevertheless, if in the present century the particular quest for Luther's forerunners has forfeited much of its respectability, the general concern with the antecedents of the Reformation has lost none of its urgency. Protestants are still tempted to see in the religious and ecclesiastical turmoil of the fourteenth and fifteenth centuries above all signs and portents of the greater upheaval to come.[10] And Catholic scholars have become inclined increasingly to agree with them, to regard the period as a regrettable one distinguished by a "movement away from the church," by "theological confusion," and by a "fatal lack of Catholic clarity" in doctrinal matters.[11] Indeed, for the proud career of Christian thinking in the Middle Ages it was "journey's end," the period that witnessed "the decay of scholasticism," one marked by "doctrinal confusion," by the rise to prominence of the "radically unCatholic" Ockhamist system, by "the utter corruption of Christian thought which nominalist theology represented."[12] This was a theology, we are assured, that the great scholastic thinkers of the High Middle Ages would scarcely have recognized. Although it was undoubtedly the theology in which Luther was trained and which he sought finally to overthrow, it has

9. Ullmann, *Reformatoren vor der Reformation* (1841–42). The English translation appeared in 1855.
10. Thus Spinka, *Advocates* (1953), p. 16: "The continuity and interdependence of the entire reform movement from the breakdown of Scholasticism [in the late thirteenth century] to the Reformation of the sixteenth century is obvious." Cf. Léonard, 1:7–33.
11. Lortz, *How the Reformation Came*, p. 107; idem, *Reformation in Germany*, 1:75, 156.
12. In order of citation, Gilson, *History*, p. 528; Denifle, 1:522, 587; Lortz, *Reformation in Germany*, 1:196; Bouyer, p. 164; Van der Pol, pp. 38–40.

to be admitted that in so doing he was breaking with "a Catholicism that was no longer Catholic."[13] And although church historians of less obtrusively confessional bent have been less flamboyant in their formulations, they, too, have sometimes been apt to see the big discontinuities as having occurred already in the late thirteenth century, to perceive the religious and ecclesiastical life of the fourteenth and fifteenth centuries as no more than an epilogue to the history of medieval Christianity, something to be treated briefly or more superficially and imprecisely than earlier centuries. They have frequently been tempted, in effect, to concede the later Middle Ages to the Reformation historians.[14]

Under these circumstances it is not too surprising that the Reformation continues to loom large in the thinking of those concerned with the history of the late medieval church, or that they do not always resist the temptation to see an inordinate amount of that history as pointing in the direction of the sixteenth-century Reformers. But although this approach enables them to bring some order and clarity to a period of notorious complexity, and although, in the present state of research, no comparably unified vision is ready at hand, it must still be insisted that the historiographic price being paid is too high. And for three main reasons.

In the first place, and in general, to adopt the approach is also in some measure to endorse the practice of reading history backward; that is, to run the risk of viewing the religious and ecclesiastical history of the fourteenth and fifteenth centuries too selectively and of subordinating its complexities too rigidly to the alien problematic of a later era. Whatever the discontinuities of the late thirteenth century, they can hardly compare with those that marked the religious life of north and northwestern Europe in the sixteenth century.

13. Lortz, *Reformation in Germany*, 1: 200; cf. Denifle's remark (1: 536) to the effect that Luther, being formed intellectually in the Ockhamist tradition, lacked "training in a sound theology."

14. This is certainly true of two brief accounts of medieval church history that are widely used in U.S. classes: Baldwin, *Mediaeval Church*, and Russell, *History of Medieval Christianity*. It is true also of the excellent longer account by Knowles and Obolensky, *The Christian Centuries*, II, which devotes only about sixty of roughly five hundred pages to the fourteenth and fifteenth centuries. The contributions, however, of such scholars as Rapp, Moeller, Pantin, and Hay are cast in a different mold.

It is clearly more appropriate, then, to follow the course pursued by Pantin in approaching the history of the late-medieval English church: to choose "to tackle the problem from the other end, and to ask ourselves, how does the fourteenth century grow out of the thirteenth century? In what respects is it a logical continuation or a mishandling of opportunity? A climax or an anti-climax?"[15]

In the second place, even if one is not squeamish about reading history backward, it must still be insisted that to read it backward solely from the ideas and activities of the magisterial Reformers—or, as is so often the case, from those of Luther alone—is misleadingly restrictive. Radical Reformation and Catholic Reformation alike also had their medieval antecedents. To ignore them is to mistake the complexity of the Reformation era itself, the continuities that bound it to the life of the preceding centuries, and the discontinuities that separated it from that life.

In the third place, to allow the Protestant Reformation to bulk too large in one's thinking about the later Middle Ages may also be to mistake the very shape of European history. It is certainly to ignore the case Ernst Troeltsch made for understanding the Reformation as fundamentally "medieval" in its spirit, preoccupations, and inspiration, and for seeing the Enlightenment, instead, as the great watershed of modernity. By the same token, it may also be to decide for Dilthey and to view the Reformation as the great divide, as having sponsored the critical break with the earlier medieval past and the decisive departure in the direction of modernity.[16] More damagingly, it may well be to make that decision in ignorance, without a conscious effort to address the competing points of view. The problem is not that in this venerable debate a decision for Dilthey *cannot* be defended. The point, rather, is that it *should* be defended.

---

15. Pantin, p. 2.
16. Succinct statements by Dilthey and Troeltsch of their positions can conveniently be found in Spitz, *Reformation*, pp. 8–27. For current thinking on the issue, see the papers printed in Oberman, ed., *Luther and the Dawn of the Modern Era*, especially Gerhard Ebeling, "Luther and the Beginning of the Modern Age," pp. 11–39. In that same volume (p. 127, n. 1), William J. Bouwsma draws attention to the little-known fact that Troeltsch himself at the end of his life retreated somewhat from his "medieval" interpretation of Reformation theology.

CHAPTER 1 · PROBLEMS OF ORDER: ECCLESIASTICAL GOVERNMENT IN TRANSITION

Behold, Reverend Father, at dawn of the vigil of the Nativity of the Blessed Mary just past, suddenly and unexpectedly there came upon Anagni a great force of armed men of the party of the King of France and of the two deposed Colonna cardinals. Arriving at the gates of Anagni and finding them open, they entered the town and at once made an assault upon the palace of the Pope. . . . Sciarra [brother of the deposed Colonna cardinals] and his forces broke through the doors and windows of the papal palace at a number of points, and set fire to them at others, till at last the angered soldiery forced their way to the Pope. Many of them heaped insults upon his head and threatened him violently, but to them all the Pope answered not so much as a word. And when they pressed him as to whether he would resign the Papacy, firmly did he refuse—indeed he preferred to lose his head—as he said in his vernacular: "E le col, e le cape!", which means: "Here is my neck and here my head!" Therewith he proclaimed in the presence of them all that as long as life was in him, he would not give up the Papacy. Sciarra, indeed, was quite ready to kill him, but he was held back by the others so that no bodily injury was done the Pope.
    —WILLIAM HUNDLEBY

As the great turning point in the history of the late-medieval church, the traditional choice of Boniface VIII's pontificate (1294–1303) and "the outrage of Anagni" (September 7, 1303) is not without its advantages. A few years later, it is true, the arrival in Italy of the German emperor-elect, Henry VII (1308–13), was still in itself enough to promote turmoil throughout the peninsula. Dante, writing enthusiastically in what he called "the first year of the most auspicious passage of the sacred Henry into Italy," was moved to refer to him as "the king of the earth, and minister of God," and even to affirm that "when the throne of Augustus is vacant, the whole world goes out of course."[1] A few years later still, Pope John XXII (1316–34), claiming the right to pass definitive judgment on the validity of the imperial election, was still bold enough to excommunicate Lewis of Bavaria, Henry's imperial successor, for refusing to accept that claim. Such formulations and gestures, however, were redolent of an age that was already slipping away. With it were fading not only the imperial dreams of the German kings and the pretensions of the popes to some sort of temporal supremacy in Christendom, but also the whole universalist ideal that had proved in the West to be one of the most enduring Roman imperial legacies. In his clash with the powerful national monarchies of France and England, Boniface VIII had come into collision with forces antipathetic both to papal temporal pretensions and to the very ideal of universalism itself. And the events at Anagni serve as well as any other (and certainly more dramatically than most) to symbolize the type of transition that was occurring.

The choice of Anagni, then, does indeed have its advantages. They are more than offset, however, by the degree to which that choice directs attention to the papal claim to exercise authority in temporal matters and away from the peculiar characteristics pertaining, during the Middle Ages, to ecclesiastical jurisdiction in general. This latter is an issue less obvious, perhaps, but one of more profound and enduring significance. Those advantages are more than offset, too, by the concomitant tendency to endow the period in ecclesiastical history preceding Anagni with attributes of hope, vigor, and zeal, while burdening the two centuries following it with characteristics of weariness, decadence, and despair. Such qualities were certainly manifested often enough by the ecclesiastical life of the late Middle Ages. But the problems confronting the church in the fourteenth and fif-

1. Toynbee, ed., VI and VII, pp. 67–68, 77, 100, 105.

teenth centuries cannot properly be understood without some comprehension of the more ancient and fundamental disabilities under
which the medieval church had labored long before the pontificate of
Boniface VIII, as well as some sense of the deterioration in the position of the papacy during the half-century before the start of his
pontificate. Jurisdictional peculiarities, long-term disabilities, and
short-term disadvantages must all be addressed before we turn to the
complexities of fourteenth- and fifteenth-century ecclesiastical life.

Ecclesiological Fundamentals

About the conditions prevailing in the primitive apostolic church
the possibility of anything approaching complete historical agreement is exceedingly remote. But it is becoming something of a commonplace today to acknowledge that the New Testament authors
appear to have resisted in considerable measure the temptation to
understand their own organizational structures in terms applicable
also to secular organisms. Thus they eschewed most of the more
obvious words available in the Greek vocabulary of politics in favor of
a new term—*diakonia*, "service." Whereas the rejected words expressed "a relationship of rulers and ruled" and conveyed "overtones
of authority, officialdom, rule, dignity, or power," *diakonia* did not.
Instead, bearing connotations of self-abasement and used by the
New Testament authors to denote service to one's fellows, it suggests
a conception of ecclesiastical office as ministerial, as grounded in love
for others, contrasting sharply with secular notions of office as
grounded in power and in law.[2]

With the growth in the number and size of the Christian communities, however, there developed a tendency to assimilate this
peculiarly New Testament conception of office to the more generally
familiar, less demanding and administratively manageable *political*
pattern of thought. By 313, when Constantine granted toleration to
Christians, bishops had already for some time been acting as arbi-
trators, administrators, and legislators in the churches under their

2. Küng, pp. 388–93, 398.

supervision. But they had been doing so as leaders of private societies whose membership was no less voluntary than is that of modern denominational churches and chapels or of such comparable social organizations in the modern world as universities and trade unions. These were societies that concerned directly only one area of human life, and the decisions of their leaders attained binding force only in the degree to which they succeeded in touching and molding the consciences of the faithful.

It was the fundamental importance of the "Constantinian revolution" and of the later disintegration of Roman imperial power in the West that they succeeded in engineering a radical change in this whole state of affairs. By the fifth century, with the transformation of Christianity from the proscribed creed of a minority to the official religion of the empire, ecclesiastical authority, supported increasingly by the public force of the imperial administration, was itself becoming political and coercive and was beginning to reach out into areas that today are regarded as pertaining to the state. During the centuries that followed, these developments persisted, and, as overt paganism died out or was suppressed, the distinction between spiritual and temporal became blurred; church membership and membership in the state gradually became coterminous. By the end of the eighth century, from its beginnings as a voluntary, private organization, the church had blended into the *respublica christiana*, an all-inclusive and coercive society that was neither voluntary nor private. Over that Christian commonwealth, until the latter years of the eleventh century, at least, the holders of the revived imperial office—the Carolingians and their German successors—could claim more convincingly than anyone else, and in matters religious as well as temporal, to wield supreme authority.

The Gregorian reformers finally launched a frontal assault against the ancient tradition of "pontifical kingship" reflected by this state of affairs. Nevertheless, Gregory VII (1073–85), by laying claim to a jurisdictional authority superior to that of emperors and extending even to the right to deprive them of their titles, revealed himself to be responsive to the allures of that tradition. For a while in the twelfth century, when appeals from the decisions of lower courts began to flood into the papal court, it appeared that in its judicial aspect papal jurisdiction was destined to embrace a system of appeals not just from ecclesiastical courts but from secular courts as well. Royal opposition and the development of secular law quickly foreclosed that possibility.[3] But that limitation notwithstanding, the popes of the High Middle Ages emerged in no small measure as sacral monarchs, true medieval successors of the Roman emperors, claiming many of the attributes of those emperors and using some of their titles, surrounded by their ceremonies, wearing their regalia, and showing by the mid-thirteenth century little hesitation about invoking the most secular of sanctions against those powers that seemed seriously to threaten their imperial position.

By the time of Boniface VIII, nevertheless, however forcefully reiterated in theory, such essentially temporal claims were already teetering in practice on the edge of bankruptcy. Far more important for an understanding of the problems of late-medieval ecclesiastical life is the profound effect of the developments we have been describing on the very notion of ecclesiastical office itself. The major effect had been the displacement of the New Testament terminology by an essentially political vocabulary drawn from Roman law and the concomitant corrosion of the New Testament understanding of the ministry by a vision of very alien provenance. By the seventh century the word *jurisdictio* had been taken into canonistic usage from Roman law and over the following centuries it was used intermittently to denote the general administrative activity of ecclesiastical government. By the thirteenth century, with the immense growth of papal governmental activity promoted by the Gregorian reform and by papal leadership of the crusading movement, and with the great contemporaneous revival of legal studies, canon lawyers were distinguishing the power of ecclesiastical jurisdiction (*potestas jurisdictionis*)

3. See Southern, p. 146. In 1215 the Fourth Lateran Council, seeking to contain the flood of appeals to Rome, attempted to make a clear distinction between the competencies of the secular and ecclesiastical courts and warned the latter against attempting to extend their jurisdiction at the expense of the former. See Alberigo et al., p. 229, Const. 42.

from the sacramental power, or power of order (*potestas ordinis*), which priests and bishops possessed by virtue of receiving the sacrament of order. Within that power of jurisdiction, in turn, they distinguished a double modality, one pertaining to the internal and the other to the external forum. The former (*potestas jurisdictionis in foro interiori*) concerned the domain of the individual conscience; it was a power exercised through the sacrament of penance, it was exercised only over those who voluntarily submitted themselves to its sway, and it was directed to the private good. This was not the case, however, with the power of jurisdiction in the public sphere (*potestas jurisdictionis in foro exteriori*), which was a coercive power pertaining to a public authority, exercised even over the unwilling and directed to the common good of the faithful. Unlike the powers wielded by ecclesiastical bodies either today or in the pre-Constantinian era, it was a truly governmental power. And it remained such long after the specifically temporal claims of the papacy began to lapse into desuetude.

From the end of the thirteenth century, then, when the decline of universal empire and the rise of national monarchs had begun to sponsor a shift in the meaning attached to *respublica christiana*, it became increasingly common to distinguish the international church from the secular states within the boundaries of which it functioned and to treat it as a separate entity, juridically self-sufficient and autonomous. To this entity now the term "Christian commonwealth" came to be attached, and along with it the related terms "ecclesiastical commonwealth," "ecclesiastical polity," "ecclesiastical kingdom," and so on. So that by the late Middle Ages the church had come finally to regard itself as a "perfect society"—indeed, as the Kingdom of God on earth—over which presided a papal monarch in whom reposed, the canonists commonly argued, the fullness of jurisdictional power (*plenitudo potestatis*).

In all of these developments, and especially as they pertain to the papacy, two interrelated factors stand out as fundamental. We have already looked at the first—namely, the profound impact upon ecclesiastical law and institutions of the Roman empire, which was felt most directly in the last centuries of the ancient world and again dur-

ing the course of the twelfth-century renaissance. The second factor
to be considered is the enduring significance of the initiatives taken
during the late eleventh century by Gregory VII and his reforming
successors.

Anyone prone to minimize the essential continuity of late-medieval
papal history with that of the earlier period would find it a sobering
experience to glance at the twenty-seven blunt propositions of the
Dictatus papae, the famous document that was entered in the papal
register in March 1075. Those propositions not only reflect the thinking of Gregory VII himself but also provide the key to the principal
directions of papal policy right through into the fourteenth century.
Several of them—notably the unprecedented claim that the pope
could depose emperors[4]—point in the direction of the development
of papal claims to temporal power that peaked in the thirteenth century. And in the others—for example, the claim that the pope could
depose or reinstate bishops, or, if necessary, transfer them from see
to see[5]—we can see adumbrated that drive to exercise the fullness of
papal jurisdictional power over the provincial churches that was to be
pushed so vigorously by Alexander III in the twelfth century and
Innocent III and Innocent IV in the thirteenth, but reached its peak
only in the fourteenth century after the papal curia had been settled
at Avignon.

Scarcely less revealing, however, are the silences of the *Dictatus
papae*. What Gregory and his followers actually did succeeded, for
good or ill, in laying down the main lines of papal endeavor for the
remainder of the medieval period, but what they left undone goes a
long way toward explaining much that is otherwise inexplicable about
papal policy in the late Middle Ages. It also helps explain the fundamental and enduring weaknesses of the medieval church and the difficulties with which subsequent reformers had again and again to
grapple. Whatever the success of the Gregorians in reducing the degree of direct royal and imperial control over episcopal appointments
(and they could not eliminate it), they did little to undercut that

---

4. Art. 12. See Ehler and Morrall, eds., pp. 43–44.
5. Ehler and Morrall, eds., arts. 3, 5, 13, 25.

whole system of noble proprietary control over churches, which, under the influence of barbarian custom and feudal institutions, had grown up during the early-medieval centuries and spread throughout Western Europe until it embraced most of the parish churches and a goodly portion of the monasteries, too. The fundamental significance of this failure lies less in the further measure of lay control it left standing—for churches had come to be owned outright by bishops and monasteries as well as by kings and nobles—than in the permanent impact it had on the notion of ecclesiastical office. To this point we have been stressing the degree to which, in the centuries following the Constantinian era, the church had been politicized, and, with it, the categories of its structural self-understanding. It is the enduring significance of the proprietary-church system that it effected a further transformation of the notion of ecclesiastical office, a further departure from that found in the New Testament.[6]

What was involved was a blurring of the crucial distinction that the Romans had made and that we ourselves make between the holding of office and the ownership of property. This mingling paralleled a comparable development in secular political life and is reflected in the medieval use of a single word—*dominium*—to denote both proprietary right and governmental authority.[7] It is reflected also in the use of the word "benefice," drawn from the vocabulary of feudalism, to denote a spiritual office. Just as churches had come to be conceived of as pieces of real property, to be bought, sold, inherited, or granted out as a sort of fief, so too their incumbents had come to be regarded as quasi-feudal dependents and their offices as *beneficia* or rewards. The canonists of the twelfth century did succeed in substituting for the notion of outright ownership that of the possession of certain legal

6. There has been much disagreement among historians about the origins of the proprietary church. Despite its overemphasis on Germanic origins, the best introduction to the subject is still the inaugural address at Basel of Ulrich Stutz, *Die Eigenkirche*. An English translation of this classic statement is in Barraclough, ed., *Mediaeval Germany*, 2:35–70.
7. Whereas Roman lawyers had used the word solely to denote proprietary right and we ourselves use its derivative "dominion" to denote authority of a governmental type.

rights in a church, notably the *jus patronatum*, the right of choosing the incumbent and bestowing the benefice upon him. But in the latter half of the century those same canonists, when they sought to classify according to the categories of the revived Roman law the accumulated body of rules concerning the disposition of benefices, took a fateful step. They classified them as belonging not to public law but to private[8]—not, that is, to the branch of law concerned with the public welfare and enforced in the interest of the common good, but to that branch pertaining to the protection of proprietary rights and enforced in the interest of the private suppliant. Hence the persistent, almost instinctive, tendency of medievals, clergy and laity alike, to conceive of the benefice in overwhelmingly material terms, to regard ecclesiastical office less as a focus of duty than as a source of income or an object of proprietary right.

As a result, it was to the benefice that underfinanced kings, princes, and popes alike felt free to turn when, burdened with increasingly onerous and expensive governmental tasks, they had to find the wherewithal to remunerate and reward the growing bureaucracies upon whose diligent service their administrations depended. Hence the "widespread system of sinecurism, absenteeism, and pluralism" that characterized late-medieval ecclesiastical life, in which the actual pastoral duties were discharged by hired substitutes. "If we wanted to imagine a modern equivalent to this system," Pantin has suggested,

> we should have to suppose a cabinet minister, for instance, instead of drawing a salary, holding the headship of three or four colleges at Oxford and Cambridge, the professorships, let us say, of Roman Law, Forestry, Gynaecology, and Classical Archaeology at various other universities, Directorships of Education in several counties, and the headmasterships of two or three of the more expensive public schools, drawing the revenues of all these offices, and performing the duties by deputy. Such a picture will give us some idea of how an important official in the medieval Church or State was provided for.[9]

8. In this connection see Barraclough, *Papal Provisions*, p. 83, who stresses the importance of Alexander III's decretal, X, 2, 13, c. 7; in Friedberg, ed., 1:282–83.
9. Pantin, p. 36.

The Emergence of the French Affiliation

Just as it is important to keep these long-term disabilities in mind when approaching church history of the fourteenth and fifteenth centuries, it is necessary to be aware of some short-term disadvantages. The chief disadvantage was the deterioration in the position of the papacy that occurred in the latter years of the thirteenth century, without which the humiliation of Boniface VIII would have been inconceivable.

As early as 1245, during the First Council of Lyons, disturbing signs of trouble to come appeared.[10] That council, it is true, like its great predecessor the Fourth Lateran Council of 1215, bore witness to the pope's supreme legislative authority, and did so in striking fashion. Despite some misgivings,[11] it also witnessed the solemn judgment and deposition of the Emperor Frederick II, whose combination of the imperial title with the kingship of Sicily and whose assertion of authority in Lombardy successive popes had seen as a threat to their own territorial independence at Rome. No bishop rose to the emperor's defense. The disposition of the kingdom of Sicily was left to the pope and that of the imperial title was left to the electors. With the death first of Frederick in 1250 and then of his son Conrad in 1254, an unparalleled interregnum of almost a quarter of a century ensued in the empire.

In some ways, no doubt, the outcome was a great triumph for the papacy. But distressing signs pointed to a gloomier future: the Council of Lyons met during a six-year exile of pope and curia not only from Rome but also from Italy; it was forced to hear a formal appeal from its sentence to the judgment of a future pope and future general council; and it received a protest from a group of English noblemen against the papal grant of English benefices to Italians. Though unsuccessful, this protest is particularly significant. It came in the con-

---

10. Signs evident in the interesting account given by Matthew of Paris in his *Chronica Majora*; ed. Luard, 4:430–73. See especially pp. 440–44 for the English letter of complaint to the pope against the extortions of the curia.
11. Ibid., pp. 432–56.

text of other grievous complaints from such unimpeachable sources as Louis IX of France (1226–70) and Robert Grosseteste, bishop of Lincoln (ca. 1168–1253), concerning the burdens that increasing papal taxation and provision of candidates to benefices were imposing on the provincial churches. Complaints, indeed, were being voiced about the mounting disorder in the whole traditional system of episcopal government caused by the increasing centralization of ecclesiastical administration in Rome. For well over a century the clergy of the local churches had by and large welcomed the extension of papal control into the provinces, and by their own petitions and appeals had done much to stimulate and accelerate that process. Nor did they necessarily cease to do so now; throughout the fourteenth and fifteenth centuries they continued to bombard the curia with petitions for privileges, preferments, and exemptions. But from this time on, evidence of clerical opposition to papal policy increases—evidence of bodies of clergy so disgruntled as to be willing, in moments of critical tension, even to side with their rulers against the pope.

Far from disappearing, then, the problems already evident at the time of the First Council of Lyons grew in seriousness during the remaining years of the thirteenth century. And in a very real sense the island of Sicily proved to be the rock on which the imperial papacy of the High Middle Ages was shipwrecked. Innocent IV had secured the desired condemnation of Frederick II, but the papally sponsored "crusade" against the emperor and the continuers of his Hohenstaufen dynasty drew little support and aroused serious doubts about the responsiveness of papal policy to truly spiritual needs. The installation in 1266 of Charles of Anjou, Louis IX's brother, as King of Sicily— the work of a French pope who had once served the Capetian dynasty —did not improve the situation. Charles proved just as anxious as Frederick II before him to establish a foothold in northern Italy, and he revived the old Hohenstaufen dream of conquering the Byzantine Empire.

If the first of these aims threatened the territorial independence for which earlier popes had so ruthlessly fought, the second imperiled the reunion between the Greek Orthodox and Latin churches for which they had so persistently striven. Such a reunion was actually achieved by Gregory X (1271–76) and proclaimed in 1274 at the Second Council of Lyons. It was, admittedly, a shaky affair right from the start. But, even so, the moral prestige of the papacy was hardly enhanced when Martin IV (1281–85)—another pope who had risen in the service of the French king and was very much, it seems, an Angevin creature—proved willing to sabotage it altogether by excommunicating the Byzantine emperor and backing Charles of Anjou's plans to conquer Constantinople. Still less was that prestige enhanced by Martin's further willingness—after Charles's Sicilian subjects had revolted and offered the crown to Peter, king of Aragon —to pronounce Peter deposed, to encourage Philip III of France to take possession of his kingdom, and to preach a crusade against Aragon to achieve that end.

It is one of the ironies of this whole uninspiring stretch of history that the tendency of so many popes of the late thirteenth century to support Angevin ambitions and side with what they took to be French interests did not strengthen the old papal alliance with France. Quite the contrary, in fact. If the success of the crusade against Frederick II had done much to disillusion Europeans in general with the quality of papal leadership, the failure of the crusade against Aragon did even more to disillusion the French in particular. Philip III died on the way home from the crusade; the reign of his successor was marked by increasing coolness toward papal policies; and, as we have seen, it was the French—for centuries the faithful allies of Rome—who finally launched the attack that so many historians have regarded as signaling the downfall of the medieval papacy.

They could hardly have launched that attack, however, had there not been a significant deepening in the discontent caused by the increasing centralization of ecclesiastical government in Rome. Much of that discontent can be traced to the expedients to which the popes were driven by the need to finance their crusades—increases in direct taxation of clerical income and intensified interference in the process of ecclesiastical preferment. But part of it can be traced also to the disgruntlement of the secular clergy at the disorder generated in the normal diocesan administration by the privileges and exemptions that the popes had heaped upon the Franciscan and Dominican friars. Their dissatisfaction had found influential theoretical expression during the 1250s at the University of Paris, where secular and mendicant masters has embarked upon a vigorous exchange of polemical writings on the subject. For their part, the more radical or "Spiritual" wing of the Franciscans were alarmed at the degree to which their order, by being drawn into the network of the ecclesiastical establishment, was being lured away from the apostolic ideal and the life of poverty envisioned by its founder.

Meanwhile, at Rome itself, the fulcrum upon which the whole machinery of ecclesiastical government pivoted, the college of cardinals, was riven by feuding between the representatives of the local Roman nobility, notably between the Orsini and Colonna families. As a result, the latter part of the thirteenth century was punctuated by a series of very difficult papal elections and by scandalously long vacancies in the papal office. And it was in the wake of a particularly long vacancy lasting from April 1292 to July 1294 that matters came to a head. They did so with the onset of two particularly significant but singularly ill-juxtaposed pontificates—those of Celestine V (July–December 1294) and Boniface VIII.

It was a case of the wrong men in a crucial role at wholly the wrong time and in quite the wrong sequence. A deadlock created by the rivalry of Orsini and Colonna led the cardinals to turn to an eighty-year-old outsider, the devout Benedictine hermit Peter of Morrone, whose name the Franciscan general, Malabranca, had suggested. The reluctant accession of Peter as Celestine V was greeted with rapture by the Spiritual wing of the Franciscans and with glee by Charles II, Angevin ruler of what we must now call the Kingdom of Naples. The Spirituals saw in him the "angel pope" awaited by those who had embraced the apocalyptic ideas attributed to the abbot Joachim of Fiore. Charles II saw rather a chance to divert the papal authority to the support of the Angevin cause. This chance he did not miss. He was able to prevail upon Celestine to make his residence at Naples rather than at Rome and, before Celestine's abdication in December 1294, certainly influenced his decision to include among the twelve new cardinals he created no less than seven Frenchmen, four of them subjects of Charles II from the Angevin Kingdom of Naples itself.

Celestine resigned his high office amid signs of mounting administrative chaos. But it was less governmental confusion than Celestine's manifest unworldliness and the fact that a papal abdication was unprecedented that made the task confronting his successor so very difficult. And Boniface, apart from his advanced years, was in almost every way a marked contrast to his predecessor. Capable and hardheaded, he was suspected already of having had a hand in Celestine's abdication and, after 1296, in his death, too. Even his unquestionably positive achievements generated problems for him. Thus the regulations he introduced to counteract the disorder and dissension promoted in diocesan government by the extensive privileges and exemptions previously granted to the mendicant orders, while they were carefully and impartially framed, nonetheless alienated many of the friars. Similarly, the improvements he wrought in papal fiscal administration, along with his concomitant success in suppressing disorder and extending his control and property holdings within the papal states, led him into conflict with the Colonna interests.

That conflict proved fatal. It led first to Boniface's harsh measures of 1297, excommunicating the two Colonna cardinals, James and Peter, and depriving them of their rank. It led next to the Colonna memorandum questioning the legitimacy of his title, charging him with grave sin, and calling upon the rulers of Christendom to have a general council sit in judgment upon him. It led finally to something of a coalition of forces between the deprived cardinals, now out for revenge, and the counselors of the French king, already locked in combat with Boniface on the issue of royal taxation of the French clergy. Although capable and hardheaded, Boniface was also a formidably stubborn old man, committed to what was by now an anachronistically high notion of papal authority and to a vigorous implementation of the jurisdictional and fiscal rights that flowed from it.

The destruction of the Hohenstaufen and the onset in mid-century of the great interregnum had marked the end of any truly effective imperial authority. But although the old imperial threat to papal independence had been vanquished, there was no lack of potential new threats to replace it. Had Boniface had the eyes to see the situation as clearly as we can see it in retrospect, he would have realized that by his own day the power, prestige, and pretensions of the English and French monarchs had risen to such a degree that they posed a threat not only to each other but also to the smooth operation of the whole machinery of jurisdictional and fiscal control over the universal church that the papacy had constructed during the course of the previous two centuries. Boniface, however, did not have the eyes to see. He did not realize the nature of the threat posed by the new national monarchies, and the policies he adopted were fated rather to heighten than to assuage the dangers that now confronted him.

Hostilities between England and France broke out in 1294, and neither Edward I nor Philip IV, harassed by the costs of war, was willing to tolerate Boniface's untimely assertion that in the absence of papal permission he lacked the right to tax the clergy in his kingdom (*Clericis laicos*, 1296). In the prevailing mental climate, with public opinion in the two kingdoms favoring the monarchs and significant numbers of clergy inclining to support them, too, threats of excommunication proved to be of no avail. The prestige of the papacy had fallen too low to permit the successful deployment of such spiritual weaponry—so low, indeed, that in 1297 Boniface was forced to compromise on the question of taxation. So low, too, that a subsequent clash—touched off four years later when Philip prosecuted a French bishop on a trumped-up charge of treason—led to the final confrontation. Boniface issued his ringing affirmation of his own supreme authority in the bull *Unam sanctam* (1302). The deprived Colonna cardinals then renewed their coalition with the advisers of the French king and called for a general council to judge the pope. Finally came the extraordinary chain of events leading up to the assault upon Boniface at Anagni, his escape, and his death only a month later.

The very independence of the papacy was now threatened by French policy and by the extremes to which, in pursuit of that policy, Philip's close advisers were willing to go. Much therefore depended upon the moves that Boniface's immediate successors chose to make. Those successors, however, turned out to be pliant men who preferred not to risk the type of defiance that might well have mobilized support on their behalf across Europe. The second of them, indeed, may have owed his election to French influence. As archbishop of Bordeaux, Clement V (1305–14) had been a vassal of Edward I of England in his capacity as duke of Aquitaine; but he was a subject, nonetheless, of the French king, and his pontificate was punctuated by a series of compromising concessions to French wishes. Not least of these concessions were his exoneration of Philip's agents for their actions against Boniface and his scandalous suppression of the order of Knights Templar at the Council of Vienne (1311–12). Even more damaging was the degree to which he built up French influence in the college of cardinals.[12] So, too, his failure even to visit Rome: in 1309, after four years of peregrination in southern France, he took up residence at Avignon—not at that time French territory but divided from France only by the river Rhône. Clement did not transfer the seat of the papal curia from Rome and there is no reason to think that he regarded his move to Avignon as in any way permanent. But it is customary to date the beginning of the Avignonese papacy from that year.

Avignon and the Monarchical Papacy (1309–77)

It was Petrarch—poet, humanist, fervent Italian patriot, vitriolic critic of the worldliness and moral turpitude of the papal court, disappointed aspirant to a bishopric—who did most to attach the expression "Babylonian Captivity" to the Avignonese period, implying thereby a tragic exile of the papacy from its proper home and its scandalous subordination to the exigencies of French royal policy.

Much support for his point of view can be found in the literary

---

12. As well as the speed with which he did so. Thus, of the ten cardinals whom he created in December 1305, nine were French—four of them nephews of his. This step, along with subsequent promotions in 1310 and 1312, reduced the Italian element to a very definite minority. See Mollat, *Popes at Avignon*, p. 6.

sources of the day—especially in the English, German, and above all Italian chronicles—though not, understandably enough, in their French counterparts. Until the voluminous materials preserved in the Vatican archives were made accessible to scholars some ninety years ago, it was customary for historians to base their views uncritically on "the malevolent accounts of contemporary chroniclers, and the tendentious writings of Petrarch, St. Catherine of Siena and St. Bridget of Sweden." Thus, they portrayed an Avignonese papacy— morally corrupt, financially extravagant, administratively tyrannical —as "the source of the greatest evils for the Church, and, in the last analysis, the chief cause of the great schism of the West."[13] Few, I imagine, would now deny that the very existence in 1378 of a well-established alternative capital at Avignon (with half the curia still, indeed, in residence there) helped make schism feasible. Apart from that, however, the work of the revisionists during the last half century and more has done much to modify, if not always successfully to transform, the traditionally negative picture of the Avignonese papacy. It has done so with reference to the three features of that papacy customarily represented in the darkest of hues: the matter of the French affiliation; the personal moral character of the pontiffs themselves; the growing centralization and absolutism of the ecclesiastical government.[14]

For those eager to minimize the extraordinary nature of the Avignonese phase in the history of the papacy, it has become customary to stress how much time the popes of the two centuries preceding it had spent away from Rome in other parts of Italy, and how much time such popes as Innocent IV and Gregory X (1271–76), who actually left Italy, had spent in France.[15] There was, in fact, nothing

13. Ibid., pp. xiii, 343.
14. For a brief account of these changes in interpretation, see Guillemain, "Punti di vista." Mollat and Guillemain have made the most important contributions to these changes. See especially Mollat, *Popes at Avignon*, and Guillemain, *Cour pontificale*.
15. Thus it has been said, as the result of a calculation frequently repeated, that "in the two hundred and four years from 1100 until 1304, the popes spent one hundred and twenty-two years away from Rome and eighty-two in Rome: that is forty years more away from Rome than in it" (Mollat, *Popes at Avignon*, p. xii, citing L. Gayet, *Le Grand Schisme d'Occident* [Florence, 1889], p. 3).

particularly unusual about popes' choosing to reside away from Rome. More unusual, but still not unprecedented, was their choosing to reside beyond the borders of Italy. Truly striking, however, was the duration of their absence from Rome and Italy—which extended through no fewer than seven pontificates—and the fact that they established a more or less itinerant curia in a fixed location and (eventually) in more or less permanent quarters outside Italy. This was a very serious and wholly unprecedented step. As such, it was not taken without considerable hesitation. However strategically located Avignon was as a potential capital for the world of Latin Christendom, and however safe, convenient, even ideal a place of residence when compared with the rigors of Rome, there is little to indicate that any pope before Benedict XII (1334–42) had resigned himself to making his permanent residence there. Throughout his long pontificate, John XXII (1316–34) made do with quarters in the episcopal palace that he had occupied in his younger days as bishop of Avignon, and the various departments of his curia had to function in buildings scattered around the town. The papal archives were allowed to molder at Assisi, where they had been since 1304. It was left for Benedict XII to signal a change of heart when, in 1336, he began the building of the papal palace, a fortress designed to house not only the pope's immediate household but also the offices of the curia, and to which, in 1339, he had the archives transferred.

It seems clear in retrospect that this change of heart, this decision to make Avignon the permanent residence of the papacy, reflected changes in the situation in Italy—as also did the later decision to return to Rome. Conditions in Italy in general and at Rome in particular, unsettled already at the end of Boniface VIII's pontificate, had become so turbulent in the wake of the emperor Henry VII's foray across the Alps that John XXII realized it would require a major military effort at pacification to render feasible any return to Rome. That effort he had undertaken, expending on the project during his pontificate no less than 63 percent of the papal revenues. By the time of his death, however, his armies had failed to achieve their goal and his Italian policy lay in ruins. Thus, in deciding to make the papal residence at Avignon permanent, Benedict XII was accepting the harsh corollary of his predecessor's failure in Italy. His own policy of papal appeasement, however, did nothing to slow the erosion of papal authority in the papal states, and his four successors returned, as a result, to the militant policy of John XXII.[16] This time the huge expenditures of papal treasure were not made in vain. The renewed interest of the popes in returning to Rome can be partially attributed to the Anglo-French truce, the concomitant threat posed by hordes of unemployed mercenaries, and the resulting deterioration in the security of Avignon. Cardinal Gil Albornoz's successful reconquest and reorganization of the papal territories during the 1350s even more fully explain the change in conditions that made the return possible. In 1350 Clement VI's own legate, Anneboldo di Ceccano, narrowly avoided assassination during his jubilee pilgrimage to Rome. In 1367, however, Pope Urban V himself was able to return for a short period of time, and in 1377 his successor, Gregory XI, returned on what promised to be a more permanent basis.

Given these circumstances, the prolonged residence at Avignon, however unprecedented, does not in itself support the traditional charges of slavish subordination to the wishes of the French crown. Nor, despite the fact that all seven Avignonese popes were French, do the policies that most of them actually pursued. What one sees instead—at least after the close of Clement V's harassed pontificate —is something of a return to the pro-Angevin and generally pro-French policy that had been so marked a feature of the late-thirteenth-century papacy, a revival of the sense, so painfully violated during the pontificate of Boniface VIII and his two successors, that France was the papacy's natural ally and the French king the natural leader of the renewed crusading effort in the East that most of these pontiffs sought (unsuccessfully) to promote. It is this strengthened affinity, then, rather than any "servility" in their relationship with France, that explains the partiality of these pontiffs to the French cause during the Hundred Years' War as well as the extent and variety of the finan-

16. Clement VI (1342–52), Innocent VI (1352–62), Urban V (1362–70), Gregory XI (1370–78).

cial aid that several of them extended to the French kings. Such aid certainly surpassed that granted to the rulers of other nations. But so too did the revenues the papacy drew from France surpass those drawn from any of the other countries of Latin Christendom. Of the thirty-one tax collectories established by the Avignonese curia, no fewer than fifteen were situated in the French kingdom, which by 1328 was the source of half the papacy's total revenue.[17]

The evidence suggests, then, that the Avignonese papacy was not so abjectly submissive to French royal pressure as Italian, English, and German contemporaries alleged it to be or as propagandists and historians were later to assume. It was, nonetheless, during a period of intermittent Anglo-French war and of renewed papal conflict with the German emperor, overwhelmingly French in complexion—indeed, as seen in the light of modern research, more overwhelmingly so than may well have been apparent at the time. Thus, of the 134 cardinals created by the 7 Avignonese popes, 112 were French. Of the remaining 22, 14 were Italian and 2 English. None were from Germany. Again, though large numbers of Italian curialists appear to have moved to Avignon, they were increasingly outnumbered by the French. Of those whose nation of origin can be established, 1,552 (70 percent) were French as against 521 (23.6 percent) Italian. The Empire and England accounted, respectively, for only 69 (3.1 percent) and 24 (1 percent).[18]

These are startling figures. They make it clear that it would be foolish to attribute to the sacred college or to the papal curia during the Avignonese era any really faithful representation of the diversity of the universal church. Just how foolish, indeed, becomes clearer still when these figures, further analyzed, reveal that all 7 Avignonese popes, 96 of the 112 French cardinals they created, and almost half of the curialists whose native dioceses we know came from Languedoc. No minor point, this last, for anyone concerned with the alleged

---

17. Renouard, pp. 73, 104.
18. I base these figures (and those cited later) on the careful calculations of Guillemain, *Cour pontificale*, pp. 441–80 and 700–702; see also the helpful maps 5, 7, and 8. The department in which the most crushing preponderance of French personnel occurs (85.6 percent) is that of domestic services (including the kitchens).

submissiveness of these popes to the will of the French monarch. It is well to be reminded, after all, that so many of these men—popes, cardinals, curialists—hailed from a region that had long enjoyed a distinct cultural identity, that they were not Frenchmen at all in any modern sense of the term, and that "John XXII could not read, without the help of a translator, the letters which Charles IV sent to him and which were written in the language used at Paris."[19] No minor point, either, for those concerned with our second issue—the moral stature of the Avignonese pontiffs—because still further analysis of the figures uncovers the remarkable degree to which they preferred to confer the cardinalate or curial office upon those they best knew, upon churchmen from their own native regions (Quercy, Gascony, and above all Limousin), and, in the cases of Clement V, John XXII, and Clement VI, upon members of their own family circles.

The nepotism of these three pontiffs is very marked indeed: Clement V, for example, raised five members of his family to the cardinalate. But in his case, as also in that of John XXII, nepotism reflects above all the need to build up a faction of supporters on whose loyalty he could truly rely. Nor did nepotism necessarily imply an extravagant or luxurious mode of life. Clement V, it must be admitted, was wildly extravagant, and Clement VI's magnificence of style and easygoing generosity is summed up well in the reply he was allegedly accustomed to give to those who reproached him for it: "My predecessors did not know how to be pope."[20] But John XXII was of simple habits and unostentatious life; so was Benedict XII. And the frugality of Urban V's life went far beyond that imposed upon all of Clement VI's Avignonese successors by the burden of debt from Clement's excesses, exacerbated by the grinding demands of the Italian campaigns. Like Benedict XII before them, all three of those successors, moreover, were men of reforming instinct. It is in the pontificate of Clement VI alone that one can discern at the papal court truly convincing evidence of the profligacy, dissipation, and luxury of life that came to be associated with the Avignonese papacy *tout court*.

19. Guillemain, "Punti di vista," p. 187; cf. Mollat, "Jean XXII."
20. Baluzius, *Vitae*; ed. Mollat, 1:298.

This being so, the explanation for the enormous freight of contemporary criticism heaped upon the Avignonese papacy must be sought elsewhere than in the personal characteristics or moral stature of these men. Moreover, the overwhelmingly French complexion of that papacy, however relevant to English, German, or Italian complaints, sheds little light upon those charges emanating from France itself. The underlying reason, then, must be sought in what these popes actually did—especially in the policies pursued by John XXII during what was the most significant of these pontificates and in the extension of that whole structure of administrative centralization and fiscal exploitation pursued so persistently throughout this period.

Capable administrator though he was, John XXII's stubbornness and inflexibility did much to diminish his effectiveness as a policy maker. The death of the emperor Henry VII had been followed by a double election, with Lewis of Bavaria and Frederick of Habsburg both laying claim to the title. After the battle of Mühldorf (1322), however, Lewis was clearly triumphant. John's stiff-necked refusal to recognize that fact, his claim that the imperial throne was still vacant, and his subsequent decision (in the teeth of opposition within the sacred college) to excommunicate Lewis together provoked a great deal of hostility in Germany. At the same time, his equally imperious intervention in the Franciscan controversy concerning apostolic poverty succeeded in broadening the base and deepening the bitterness of that hostility, leaving to his successors a formidable legacy of rancor, despair, and alienation from the policies and procedures of the ecclesiastical establishment.

Early in the history of the Franciscan order difficulties had inevitably arisen concerning the interpretation of the Rule, which included, in imitation of the life of Christ and the apostles, the obligation of individual and collective poverty. Gregory IX (1227–41) had sought to solve the problem by the bull *Quo elongati*, which not only permitted the reception and employment of money on behalf of the friars by "spiritual friends" but also distinguished between the ownership (*dominium*) and simple use (*usus facti*) of goods, and asserted that the friars, neither individually nor in common, actually enjoyed ownership of the goods that they used. In 1245 Innocent IV had gone a stage further and definitely laid down the principle that the ownership of goods left for the use of the friars was vested in the Holy See; in 1279 and 1312 this interpretation was confirmed by the decretals *Exiit qui seminat* of Nicholas III (1277–80) and *Exivi de paradiso* of Clement V.

Such a solution admittedly failed to satisfy the Spiritual wing of the order, which became increasingly the focus of dissent and the subject of persecution. Under the firm rule of the Franciscan general Michael of Cesena, however, the opposition of the most extreme zealots had largely been crushed, and the order was enjoying a period of comparative tranquillity at least, when, after an inquiry instituted in 1321, John XXII adopted a stand that did more than alienate the fanatic minority, splitting the order and driving Michael of Cesena himself into opposition and exile. In the two bulls, *Ad conditorem canonum* (December 1322) and *Cum inter nonnullos* (1323), John denied the legal validity of the distinction between *dominium* and *usus facti* when applied to goods consumed by use and, further, condemned as heretical an assertion recently made by the chapter general of the order at Perugia (May 1322)—namely, that Christ and the apostles owned no property either individually or collectively.

If John's policy toward Lewis of Bavaria was unwise, still less fortunate was the one he adopted toward the Franciscans, fueling a long and acrimonious controversy that ranged against him, as well as Michael of Cesena himself, the great English Franciscan philosopher William of Ockham (d. 1349). But it was the juxtaposition of the two policies that was truly disastrous. In condemning the doctrine of apostolic poverty, John appeared to many to be turning his back upon the New Testament itself. The Franciscans were not reluctant to accuse him of heresy, nor did Lewis hesitate, when in 1328 he descended on Rome, to declare John deposed as a heretic and to sponsor a Franciscan as antipope. Not long after, Michael of Cesena and Ockham took refuge at Lewis's court, where, along with the radical Italian antipapalist Marsilius of Padua (ca. 1275–ca. 1343), they mounted against pope and papacy a formidable campaign of propaganda. They revived the old antipapal gambits of Philip IV's publicists (such as the appeal to a general council), and they ventured also into much more radical territory, leaving behind a veritable mine of arguments against what the papacy and ecclesiastical establishment had come to be in their own day and would continue to be until the end of the Middle Ages.

In framing their arguments, these critics and others understandably made much of John XXII's alleged heterodoxy.[21] But their criticisms bit much deeper and were of more enduring significance when they focused on and responded to the great and ever widening gulf between the simplicity of the apostolic church, as they intuited it, and the triumphantly rationalized and increasingly bureaucratized structure of central government in the church of their own day. To the development and articulation of that structure the Avignonese contribution was immense. The curial staff, which had numbered about two hundred under Nicholas III and three hundred under Boniface VIII, grew to over six hundred, a level at which it stabilized until the eighteenth century. Systematized and reorganized by John XXII, this enlarged curia became above all a great fiscal machine. It was designed to make up for the loss of revenues from the papal states and to extract from the provincial churches in the most orderly and efficient way the vast sums of money most of these popes needed to finance their Italian wars. It served other ends, too, notably the vindication, at the expense of the episcopal hierarchy, of direct papal jurisdiction over those churches. But, then, the exercise of jurisdiction usually carried its financial rewards; and the centrality of their concern with the whole fiscal organization is perhaps best illustrated by the willingness of three popes as different in character, aims, and personality as John XXII, Benedict XII, and Clement VI to continue in office from 1319 to 1347 the same papal chamberlain, Gasbert of Laval, one of whose primary responsibilities during those years was the articulation and improvement of that organization.

21. In a series of sermons preached in 1331–32, John ventilated a novel view concerning the Beatific Vision, which he was later to withdraw when it was condemned by the theologians of the University of Paris.

The specific situation and burdens of the Avignonese popes may have suggested the need to develop the central administrative apparatus of the church, and the establishment of a sedentary curia in permanent quarters at Avignon may have provided the opportunity. Nevertheless, it is important always to remember that the institutional logic they were following was one long since established. It was the logic that had led their predecessors to lay claim to the fullness of that *potestas jurisdictionis in foro exteriori*—the governmental power in which all prelates shared—and to commit themselves in their day-to-day administration to so vigorous a vindication of that claim as to provoke complaints from the provincial churches as early as the First Council of Lyons. More specifically, if we are properly to understand the "fiscalism" for which the Avignonese popes and their successors were so roundly condemned in their own day and so persistently criticized since, it is important also to recall both the extent to which ecclesiastical office had already been politicized and the degree to which it had been "materialized"—transformed, that is, into an object of proprietary right.

Like all other rulers in the Middle Ages, secular as well as ecclesiastical, the popes had traditionally been expected to "live of their own." They were to support themselves and their administrative machinery on the customary revenues accruing to them from the papal territories in central Italy, from the kingdoms that were vassals of the Holy See, and from the churches, abbeys, and exempt ecclesiastical foundations that were under its protection. As the popes came to undertake more extensive governmental tasks, as ecclesiastical administration came increasingly to be centralized in the Roman curia (a process similar to contemporaneous developments in the monarchies of Europe), such customary revenues proved to be as inadequate to their needs as were traditional sources of income to the needs of their royal and princely counterparts. Already at the start of the thirteenth century, in the context of the crusading movement, Innocent III (1198–1216) had laid the foundations for a papal system of taxation, securing agreement to the notion that all benefices should be expected to contribute a percentage of their revenues to the support of the crusade. That percentage had come usually to be fixed at one-tenth, and such tithes continued to be demanded in the fourteenth century. The actual income they produced, however, was by now greatly diminished and in any event could hardly be relied upon as a regular source of revenue. What was needed, especially with the weakening of control over the papal territories, was the establishment of some sort of regular general tax. The fathers assembled at the Council of Vienne, however, had been hostile to that idea, and the Avignonese popes, already struggling to cope with a substantial reduction in revenue from their Italian possessions and soon to be confronted with the enormous expenditures required to recover them, were left to exploit and extend the remaining sources of income.

Those sources of income were of uneven promise, considerable complexity, and great diversity. They ranged from visitation fees to the *jus spolii* (the right, under certain conditions, to take possession of the goods of an ecclesiastic), from charitable subsidies requested of groups of clergy to profits of one sort or another accruing from the fees or fines imposed by papal courts.[22] Common to many sources of revenue, however, and certainly to most of those systematically exploited by the Avignonese pontiffs, was some connection with the benefices, major or minor, which the pope himself claimed the right to fill. The Gregorian reformers had striven hard, though not with complete success, to contain lay interference in the realm of ecclesiastical appointments, and, whatever the degree of influence exerted by kings, to ensure that the normal and formal procedure for filling major benefices (bishoprics and abbacies) should be canonical election by the cathedral chapters or monastic communities. Appointment to minor benefices, both sinecures (*sine cura*) like cathedral canonries and parish rectorships with cure of souls, they left where it had been before—in the hands of bishops, who could nominate to canonries and to deaneries, and in those of lay or clerical patrons, who could place their candidates in parishes or chaplaincies.

Bodies of electors, however, whether canons or monks, were im-

22. Lunt, *Papal Revenues*, gives a useful listing and analysis of these various types of revenue, along with documentary illustration.

mune neither to internal faction nor to external pressure, and the papacy by virtue of its higher jurisdictional power was frequently called upon (or tempted) to intervene and settle disputes either by arbitration or by direct nomination. As early as the twelfth century the popes had intervened to supersede the rights of normal electors or patrons and to "provide" their own candidates to ecclesiastical positions. Indeed, the distinguished theologian Peter Lombard (d. 1160) had been one of the first to benefit from this procedure. For the interested parties such interventions were often desirable because they were authoritative; for the popes themselves they were desirable because they carried with them enhanced influence over the higher clergy along with the promise of new sources of revenue. They tended, accordingly, to multiply, as did comparable interventions to provide papal candidates to minor benefices. But it was on a rising tide of petitions from interested parties and would-be provisees that the whole system gathered momentum, and it was only after 1265 that the papacy began to regulate it by means other than the appeal to judicial precedent. In that year, declaring that "the plenary disposition of churches, honours, and dignities, and other ecclesiastical benefices is recognized to pertain to the Roman Pontiff," Clement IV in the bull *Licet ecclesiarum* affirmed as an ancient and laudable custom the exclusive right of that pontiff to nominate candidates to all benefices vacated by ecclesiastics who died while employed at the *curia* or present at the papal court (*vacantes apud sedem apostolicam*).[23]

The first general reservation may well have done no more than place a long-established custom on firm legal ground and it seems not to have generated any immediate increase in the number of "papal provisions" actually made. That was certainly not the case with the subsequent extensions of such general reservations. Thus Boniface VIII in 1295 extended the notion of *vacantes in curia* to include those dying within two days' journey from Rome; Clement V reserved for papal provision the benefices of all bishops consecrated at the curia; John XXII, Benedict XII, and Urban V went further still. Indeed, after Urban's extension in 1363 of reservations to include all patriarchates,

23. *Liber Sextus*, 3:4, 2; ed. Friedberg, 2:1021.

archbishoprics, and bishoprics, as well as all monasteries and convents above a stipulated income level, a system had been created whereby the pope had the right to provide to all major benefices and to a very large proportion of those minor benefices that were in the gift of clerical patrons.[24]

All this represented an immense and systematic intensification in the exercise of the pope's jurisdictional power. It is frequently difficult to compute with certainty the precise numbers of provisions involved, but Guillemain's careful calculations for the eight years of Benedict XII's pontificate (1334–42) reveal a total of 4,002 provisions and expectations (that is, provisions to benefices not yet vacant) issued—by any standards a massive intervention in the realm of collation to benefices. The more so, it should be noted, in that it actually reflected a slackening in the tempo of provision after the intense centralizing activity of John XXII. And after Benedict's death the pace was to pick up once more and become increasingly rapid.[25]

What percentage of these interventions reflect the desire of the popes to respond to the great waves of petitions from the provinces that inundated the papal court or to satisfy the wishes of kings and princes to furnish their own ministers or favorites with benefices is not clear. Nor is it clear how many of them reflect the need of the popes to make suitable financial arrangements for the members of their own growing bureaucracy. But whatever the case, for every provision that successfully installed a papal candidate in a benefice (by no means all did), some financial benefit accrued sooner or later to the papacy. These benefits ranged from the *jus spolii*, already mentioned, or the income from benefices reserved to the pope that stood vacant, to the two great benefice taxes: first, the "services" paid by all prelates holding bishoprics or abbacies worth more than one hundred florins per annum and amounting to about one-third of that annual income, and second, the annates, a substantial portion of the first year's revenue of those benefices conferred by papal provision but worth less than one hundred florins. With the progress of administra-

---

24. Care was normally taken to avoid encroaching upon the rights of lay patrons.
25. See Guillemain, *Politique bénéficiale*, pp. 129–41.

tive centralization and the concomitant extension of the system of papal provision, the relative importance of those benefice taxes also mounted. In fact, by the end of the Avignonese era they had come to constitute about one-half of the total revenues of the papacy.

A system of this sort clearly could not have operated without widespread clerical support, and such support was later on to manifest itself at the Council of Constance (1414–18), when reformers raised the question of provisions. If that system presupposed the treatment of benefices primarily as property, the law itself endorsed that presupposition. If it set aside the older rights of clerical electors or patrons, many of whom had become increasingly subservient to corrupting aristocratic influences, it opened up, as university authorities quickly realized, opportunities for advancement to educated men whose lack of social standing would, in the view of those electors or patrons, have made them ineligible for office. If, in the case of the minor benefices, it did not guarantee certain possession and the avoidance of litigation, it still offered the best route to security of title. If, finally, in the case of the major benefices, it interfered with the old procedure of canonical election, it avoided in return the confusion and disarray provoked with such tiresome regularity by disputed elections. Complaints, therefore, at least in countries with which the pope's policies were not at odds, tended characteristically to come either from disgruntled patrons or from disappointed candidates for ecclesiastical preferment.

But not always. For the system of papal provisions entailed its own corruptions, and in many ways did so progressively. Presupposing the material conception of the benefice, that system nourished accordingly the stubborn abuses of pluralism (accumulation of several benefices in the hands of one man) and nonresidence. Attempts were made to curb such abuses, but the wars, plagues, and deteriorating economic conditions of the fourteenth century ran counter to such reforms. These external conditions caused severe drops in the revenues from landed estates and made more frequently necessary a combination of benefices to produce the requisite income. Moreover, although the system of papal provisions had grown largely in response to the need of individual petitioners, by the mid-fourteenth century it had become an essential feature of the whole centralized administrative machinery implementing the wishes of a monarchical papacy, which was distinguished increasingly by the lack of institutional restraints on the exercise of its power. By that time also it had been transformed into a system vigorously and not always fastidiously exploited in the furtherance of the pope's political objectives and the satisfaction of his financial needs. And, as the years of schism were to show, the more crushing those needs, the less fastidious the mode of exploitation.

None of this, of course, was calculated to assure thoughtful Christians, clerical or lay, that they could afford entirely to ignore the criticisms of established ecclesiastical structures voiced so noisily, so intemperately, and occasionally at such unconscionable length by the Franciscan dissidents or by the propagandists of Philip IV and Lewis of Bavaria. It was, after all, in the context of papal leadership both of the crusading movement and of reform that the papacy had begun to exercise the fullness of jurisdictional power in the church. But already by 1291, when the last Christian stronghold in Palestine fell to the Muslims, the crusading movement had become moribund, and long before that the leadership in the drive for reform had passed out of papal hands. The cry for change, heard already at the first and second councils of Lyons, had swelled at the Council of Vienne into the far-reaching program of reform "in head and members" laid out by William Durand, bishop of Mende, in his *De modo concilii generalis celebrandi*. This program called, in effect, for the reversal of the whole trend toward the centralization of ecclesiastical government in Rome and a return to the ancient regime of ecclesiastical synods and strong independent bishops. But nothing had come of it, and Vienne turned out to be the last in the series of general councils begun and dominated by the reforming papacy of the High Middle Ages. Dissidents might call for the convocation of a general council, but it was not until 1409 that another was to assemble, and then without papal summons and under extraordinary circumstances of great crisis.

In the absence of a council, the sponsorship of reform and the imposition of restraint on the exercise of papal power would have to come from some other quarter. But although secular rulers were not averse to toying with that role, they usually did so for diplomatic reasons, in the attempt to put pressure on the pope to further their own aims. The fact is, of course, that the whole papal system could hardly have operated without their complicity and their ability to bend it to serve their own ends. While not disposed, then, to concede in principle to papal jurisdictional claims, they did not refrain from sharing in practice the proceeds accruing from the implementation of that jurisdiction.

Thus, the kings of France and England both received a large share of the tithes levied on the churches within their respective kingdoms —a share amounting in England over the years 1301–24 to about £230,000, and set in 1330, for example, at 50 percent of the particular subsidy being raised in that year: "a convenient arrangement," as Pantin has said of the English case, "by which the pope incurred the odium and the king got the money."[26] Similarly, those kings were by no means reluctant to seek, in lieu of the salaries they could not afford to pay, papal provisions to bishoprics and minor benefices for their ministers. English historians, as we saw in the Introduction, used once to make much of the statutes of Provisors (1351) and Praemunire (1353). Those measures, however, were less "the bulwark of the independence of the National Church" than sophisticated pieces of weaponry added to an already well-stocked legal armory, making it even easier for the king to increase his own ecclesiastical patronage while still contriving to pose "as a defender of the rights and liberties of English churchmen against the Papacy."[27] That is, should he actually choose to enforce the statutes. Should he not—as was frequently the case—they remained available nonetheless, as powerful inducements to ensure the pope's willingness to provide the candidates whom the king nominated.

By the end of the Avignonese era, it is true, there were already

---

26. Lunt, *Financial Relations*, 1:366–418; 2:75. Pantin, p. 79.
27. Pantin, p. 84.

indications that rulers were becoming dissatisfied with such de facto arrangements, or at least with the share in the ecclesiastical spoils that the popes had hitherto been willing to concede to them. During the following half century, the strain of war, plague, and deepening economic depression moved many of them to assert a greater and more direct measure of control over the national and territorial churches within their jurisdictions—but only, again, under the extraordinary conditions of schism and the unprecedented degree of papal weakness generated by that cleavage within the church.

In the meantime, the college of cardinals remained the only other instrumentality capable of imposing limits on papal power and of sponsoring reform. Any driving concern with reform it may have felt at this time it succeeded in keeping well under control. But the involvement of the cardinals in the government of the universal church had been deepening ever since the eleventh century, when the election of popes had become their exclusive prerogative. Already in 1289 Nicholas IV had granted to them no less than half the revenues that the Roman church possessed at that time.[28] By the beginning of the fourteenth century their independent power was formidable, their financial strength impressive, the perquisites attached to their position multitudinous. The state of affairs at Avignon encouraged them to insist increasingly on what they considered to be their rightful share in the spoils accruing from papal financial policy; it also strengthened their determination to guarantee more effectively their fluctuating involvement in the framing of papal policy, perhaps even to transform it into a constitutional right. That determination found notable expression in 1352, during the vacancy after the death of Clement VI, when they drew up and swore to the first known electoral capitulation affirming both the fiscal and governmental rights of the college. If the papal conception of the shape of church government was unquestionably monarchic, theirs was becoming increasingly oligarchic. Tensions mounted accordingly—the more so in that many of them served as the paid advocates of secular rulers, lobbying at the curia on behalf of the policies of their patrons. "So long as

28. Lunt, *Papal Revenues*, 1:26–27.

policy, aims and interests of popes and cardinals were identical," Walter Ullmann has said, "there was no reason for resistance on the part of the latter."[29] Once they diverged, however, trouble was to be expected.

In 1378 they did diverge, in the wake of the first papal election since the return of the papacy to Rome, that return itself achieved despite the reservations expressed by many in the sacred college. But the anticipated trouble attained unexpectedly serious proportions— nothing less, in fact, than the outbreak of what has since come to be known as the Great Schism of the West. And it was in the context of that scandalously protracted schism that cardinals, councils, and kings—all three—succeeded in coming together to cooperate, if not in effecting reform, at least in imposing their will on the rival claimants to the papal office.

The Great Schism and Its Aftermath (1378–1449)

Historians concerned with the critical events of 1378 have been more than usually fortunate in the quality and amount of relevant source materials surviving from that time.[30] But in an area of historical investigation across which later theological disputes have always cast particularly long shadows, the availability of evidence has not been enough to secure harmony of interpretations. This is readily comprehensible. Although the story of the events of 1378 is simple enough in its broad outlines, in its detail it is extremely complex and has been hotly disputed. The detail, unfortunately, proved to be determinative at the time and has since continued to be the focus of disagreement.

It was in 1377 that Gregory XI had finally been persuaded to bring

29. Ullmann, *Origins*, p. 7.
30. Speaking with special reference to the group of manuscripts in the Vatican archives known as the *Libri de schismate*, K. A. Fink comments that "no other occurrence of this period left behind such an amount of written material" (Jedin and Dolan, eds., 4:402). Given Fink's well-attested familiarity with the Vatican sources and the authoritative nature of his own contributions over the years to our understanding of the history of the schism and its aftermath, a special value attaches to his brief sketch of that history in Jedin and Dolan, eds., 4:401–25, 448–87.

the papacy back to Rome. He had done so despite opposition from some of his cardinals and the threat to his life posed by the hostility of the Roman nobles. By the time of his death, in March 1378, he had repented of the move and had decided to return to Avignon. After his death the Roman populace was gripped by the fear that such a move might still take place.

As a result, the conditions under which the papal election took place were far from ideal. Six cardinals had been left behind at Avignon to supervise the considerable part of the curial apparatus that continued to function there. Of the sixteen present for the election, one was Spanish, four were Italian, and eleven were French. The French, however, were divided along regional lines, and when the election took place in April it was accompanied by rioting outside the conclave and suspicion and dissension within. It ended very quickly, amid scenes of considerable confusion, with the choice of an outsider, the archbishop of Bari, a compromise candidate who took the title of Urban VI (1378–89). The Roman mob had clamored noisily for the election of a Roman. The cardinals, unwilling to accede to that demand but divided among themselves and also (they were later to claim) in fear for their lives, had been forced for the first time in over half a century to choose a non-French pope. The archbishop of Bari was not a Roman, but he did enjoy the triple advantage of being an Italian, a subject of the Angevin ruler of Naples, and a curial official who had served long and faithfully at Avignon. While the fact of his nationality might appease the Romans, it seemed reasonable to expect that he would also be subservient to the cardinals. His subsequent behavior, however, did not vindicate such hopes, and his treatment of the cardinals—violent, erratic, abusive, suggestive even of insanity—led to a rapid worsening of relations with them.

In May and June 1378 all the cardinals except the four Italians left Rome for Anagni, where they would be beyond papal control. There, in August, they publicly repudiated Urban's election, claiming it had taken place under duress and was therefore invalid. Finally, on September 20, joined now in conclave by the three surviving Ital-

ian cardinals (who had abandoned Urban in July),[31] they proceeded
to elect in his place Robert of Geneva, one of themselves, who assumed the title of Clement VII (1378–94). After failing in an attempt to seize Rome, Clement departed from Italy in May–June
1379 and took up his residence at Avignon.

Since neither of the rival claimants proved able to displace the other
or to command the allegiance of all the Christian nations, the schism
they engendered was far more serious than its numerous predecessors
in the West had been. Despite all the efforts of churchmen and temporal rulers to end it, it endured for almost forty years. Both claimants
went on to appoint whole new batches of cardinals; both obdurately
refused, either individually or concurrently, to withdraw. Loyalties
quickly hardened, and as the years went by their rival curias strove
to perpetuate their claims. Benedict XIII was elected in 1394 to succeed Clement VII at Avignon, and Boniface IX, Innocent VII, and
Gregory XII, in 1389, 1404, and 1406 respectively, to succeed
Urban VI at Rome. The outcome was the development within the
church of widespread disorder and an exceedingly grave constitutional
crisis.

Much of the blame for this development has customarily been
placed upon the national and dynastic animosities then prevailing in
Europe as well as upon the growing ambitions and pretensions of the
cardinals. There is much to be said for this point of view. The territorial composition of the two "obediences," Roman and Avignonese,
was in large part predictable on the basis of previous political and
diplomatic alignments. Thus England and much of the Empire sided
with Urban, and France, Scotland, and Castile with Clement. Similarly, the resentment that the cardinals had betrayed at Urban's immediate and ill-tempered assaults upon their dignity, their privileges, and their opulent style of life is very well attested.

Recent studies of the disputed election and its background con-

---

31. Though they abstained from actually voting. The fourth Italian, Tebaldeschi,
had died on September 7, but not before affirming the legitimacy of Urban's election.
See Ullmann, *Origins*, pp. 62–63.

verge, nevertheless, on the conclusion that the doubts later expressed by the cardinals about the validity of Urban's title have to be taken more seriously than once was usual.[32] The uncertainty caused by violence outside the conclave and fear within was admitted at the time. Because of it, the Italian cardinal Orsini had abstained from voting in the conclave; within two days of the election, its validity was being questioned at Rome itself.[33] Those who argued, then and later, for the legitimacy of Urban's title based their case not on the facts of the election itself but on the subsequent behavior of the cardinals (not excluding Orsini)—their participation in his coronation, their performance of homage to him, their delay in challenging the validity of his election, and so on. Přerovský, however, has emphasized their real and growing doubts about the sanity of the new pope and the extent to which such doubts were justifiable.[34] Emphasized, too, has been the degree to which their behavior at Rome in the two weeks following the election was the result of coercion and fear and fell short, therefore, of constituting any genuine "tacit consent." Toward the end of April 1378 Cardinal Pedro de Luna is reputed to have said that "if the pope or other Romans found out that I or some other member of the Sacred College had doubts about his election, none of us would escape."[35] And with the official letters about Urban's election that the cardinals sent to the rulers of Europe, the wording of which had sometimes to be approved by the pope himself, they sent also secret messages that undercut the position they were officially adopting.[36]

This being the case, however real their other motives, the cardinals clearly had some valid grounds for questioning the legitimacy of

32. Notably Seidlmayer and Přerovský. Cf. the succinct remarks in Fink. Ullmann's *Origins*, the most recent account in English, though it too accords serious consideration to the objections of the cardinals, marks something of an exception to this trend. There is also a careful and nuanced account by E.-R. Labande, in Delaruelle et al., 1:3–44.

33. Přerovský, p. 42.

34. Ibid., pp. 65–69, 182–90.

35. "Nam si ipse vel alii Romani scirent quod ego vel aliquis ex dominis meis dubitaremus de sua electione, nullus nostrum evaderet" (Baluzius, *Vitae*, ed. Mollat, 2:701).

36. Fink, p. 338; Seidlmayer, pp. 243, 288.

Urban's claim to be pope. Similarly, however convenient such questioning may have been to their own political interests, those rulers who aligned themselves with Clement VII were able to do so with reasonably good conscience, though sometimes only, it should be noted, after considerable hesitation. Not even Charles V of France rushed to recognize Clement, and it certainly appears improper to infer that that monarch had come to an understanding with the dissident cardinals at the time of the second election. Similarly, it was only after extensive hearings at both Avignon and Rome and as the result of a lengthy judicial process that the Kingdom of Castile declared for Clement.

Thus, however desirable a clear solution to this vexing problem may be, the historical evidence simply does not permit one to insist on the exclusive legitimacy of Urban's title to the papacy (and, therefore, of the titles of his successors in the Roman line), although this has often been done.[37] It should be remembered that not only the Urbanists had the support of dedicated Christians, clerical or lay. Whereas St. Catherine of Siena (ca. 1347–80) supported Urban, St. Vincent Ferrer (1350–1419) supported Benedict XIII. Men at the time, it seems, were in a state of "invincible ignorance," and so too, as Mollat insists, are we. The best we can do is to recognize that after April 8, 1378, there was one man with a doubtful claim to the papacy and after September 20, 1378, there were two.

The impact of this unprecedented state of affairs was, of course, far-reaching and immense. Apart from the spiritual anxiety and distress of conscience that it generated in the minds of thoughtful Christians everywhere, it resulted also in a great deal of administrative confusion and jurisdictional conflict. Those religious orders organized on a truly international basis had to be split into two, and in the borderlands of the empire, where the line between the two obediences was fluctuating and unclear, the schism spawned divisions within such dioceses as Cambrai, and related dissension invaded even

---

37. Usually, I would suggest, on anachronistic grounds that are theological or canonistic rather than truly historical. For this point and its consequences, see Oakley, *Council over Pope?*, pp. 111–26.

cathedral chapters and individual monastic houses. Moreover, even after the lines had been fairly clearly drawn, calculating rulers showed a distressing tendency to switch obediences. Thus, in Italy, Naples and Bologna, for example, oscillated in their allegiances; in the Spanish peninsula, Portugal switched in 1381 from Clement to Urban; in the British Isles, as late as 1406 the Welsh prince Owen Glendower went over to Benedict XIII.

The disruption of the central administrative machinery of the papacy was even more traumatic. It led to a crippling (if understandable) strain on the whole fiscal system erected with such care by the Avignonese pontiffs but now, along with the urgently needed revenues it had been designed to channel into the papal treasury, divided into two. There is a great gap in the Vatican archives where one would expect to find the documents for these years of the Roman *camera apostolica*, and that gap has been said to reflect very faithfully a "total abdication of the central administration" in the larger and geographically more scattered Roman obedience.[38] Hence we know little about the financial situation of the Roman pontiffs except for the degree to which they had to rely on such hand-to-mouth financial expedients as the sale of privileges, offices, indulgences, and property, as well as on a hastily improvised administrative structure incapable even of supervising the frequently questionable activities of their tax collectors.

The Avignonese pontiffs, on the other hand, inherited the archives, the treasury, and most of the trained curial officials of Gregory XI. Despite the smaller size of their obedience and the loss of revenue from the papal states, they maintained, accordingly, a smoothly functioning administrative machine that succeeded in furnishing Clement VII, at least, with a revenue somewhat greater (according to Favier's calculations) than half of that accruing to Gregory XI. But they did so at the price of raising the "fiscalism" of the Avignonese papacy to its peak and of taxing at levels geared to the more favorable economic

38. Favier, p. 698. So crippling is this lack of documentation that in this lengthy study Favier abandoned the attempt to cover both obediences and finally concentrated on Avignon alone (see p. 5).

conditions of an age long since gone. These were truly crippling levels that failed to take into account the deleterious impact of war, plague, and an economic slump that had by now reached fairly massive proportions. Hence, as early as 1392, the protest of the French clergy against a tenth levied by Clement VII and in 1398 their willingness at the Third Council of Paris to lend their support to what was essentially a *royal* withdrawal of obedience (and therefore of revenues) from Avignon. Hence, too, the deepening reaction on the part of provincial churches elsewhere, driving them away from the bankrupting "protection" of the rival pontiffs and into the welcoming arms of monarchs and princes whose ecclesiastical policies were rarely dictated by considerations of unambiguously religious character.[39] And in the intricate diplomacy surrounding the repeated attempts to bring the schism to an end those monarchs and princes were destined to play a very large role.

Apart from efforts by the two pontiffs to settle the issue by force of arms (the so-called *via facti*), hope centered initially on the possibility of some successful arbitration between the two claimants and still more on the possibility of assembling a general council representing the entire church to render a judgment on the validity of the contested elections. This latter view, sponsored originally by the Italian cardinals in the months immediately following Urban's election, was given forceful expression by St. Vincent Ferrer in Aragon, at Paris in 1379–81 by the German theologians Conrad of Gelnhausen (ca. 1320–90) and Henry of Langenstein (ca. 1330–97), as also (somewhat more tentatively) by their younger French colleague Pierre d'Ailly (1350–1420). The "conciliar movement" was something of a reality, then, right from the beginning of the schism, although the pressure that the French king successfully exerted on the University of Paris in order to make it align with Clement quickly led to a bracketing of conciliarist views there.

As time went on, however, members of both obediences came to

---

39. For France and England, see P. Ourliac in Delaruelle et al., 1, especially p. 305, where he notes that the cathedral-priory of Canterbury had to devote 46 percent of its revenues to meeting papal and royal imposts.

regard both claimants as sharing more or less equally the responsibility for protracting the schism, and support shifted accordingly to what was known as the *via cessionis*, a plan that envisaged the renunciation of both claims by the rival pontiffs and the subsequent combination of the two colleges of cardinals to elect a new and universally accepted pope. This shift was particularly marked in the years after 1394, when the cardinals at Avignon, on the death of Clement VII, ignored the pleas of the French king and insisted on proceeding to the election of a new pope. These were years of mounting pressures on behalf of the *via cessionis*, pressures exerted on the Roman pope by the German rulers and on his Avignonese rival by the French king—the latter going so far in his attempts to coerce an abdication as to embark in 1398 on a unilateral national withdrawal of obedience from the pope.

This attempt failed, as did all subsequent efforts to promote the *via cessionis*, but the years of seemingly barren diplomacy bore unexpected fruit toward the end of 1408 in the revival of the idea of a general council. This became a feasible alternative when the collapse of a final round of negotiations between the Roman and Avignonese popes led the French clergy to renew their withdrawal of obedience from Avignon and led disgruntled cardinals from both camps to forswear allegiance to their pontiffs. Gathering together at Leghorn and addressing themselves to the secular rulers and bishops of both obediences, the cardinals summoned a general council of the whole church to meet in Italy. When this action began to draw widespread support, the rival pontiffs in desperation assembled their own councils at Perpignan and Cividale respectively. But both of these councils (and especially the latter) were poorly attended. Neither, certainly, could boast of the impressively ecumenical character of the general council that opened at Pisa on March 28, 1409, which was better attended than the two councils of Lyons and that of Vienne had been.

This council of Pisa enjoyed the support of the greater part of Christendom. It was attended by four patriarchs, twenty-four cardinals, more than eighty archbishops and bishops (with more than another hundred represented by proxies), more than a hundred abbots (nearly two hundred more sent their proctors), the generals of the mendicant orders and of most other religious orders, several hundred theologians and canonists, and representatives of thirteen universities, of many cathedral chapters, and of most European princes (the kings of the Spanish peninsula and the German king Rupert were notable exceptions).[40] When the two rival pontiffs refused to cooperate with the council, the assembly declared itself to be canonically constituted and an ecumenical council and then embarked on a careful legal process directed against the two popes. It culminated on June 5, 1409, with the formal deposition of both as notorious schismatics and heretics—a sentence signed by no fewer than twenty-four cardinals.[41]

In proceeding thus, the council fathers followed the generally accepted canonistic teachings of the day that a pope who deviated from the true faith or who was guilty of notorious crimes that scandalized the church and were therefore tantamount to heresy was liable to judgment by the church and even to deposition. They also followed a widespread and well-established canonistic opinion to the effect that, while in such a legal process the cardinals had certain powers of initiative, the body competent to proceed to judgment was the general council. Certainly, the greater part of Christendom seems to have regarded their action as valid, as it did the unanimous election by the cardinals from both obediences of a new pope, Alexander V. The Roman and Avignonese pontiffs were left with drastically reduced obediences, and their survival may have been assured only by the death of Alexander V in 1410 and the succession of John XXIII (1410–15)—by the most favorable of estimates a man of unpraiseworthy life and a less than worthy candidate for the high office into which he was thrust.

What actually emerged from the Council of Pisa, nevertheless, was the addition of a third line of claimants—a clearly intolerable situa-

40. See Fink, in Jedin and Dolan, eds., 4:418.
41. Ibid., p. 422. Cf. the useful collection of translated documents concerning the council in Crowder, pp. 41–64.

tion, which led in 1413 to the summoning of the Council of Constance, itself so well attended that it was undoubtedly the greatest ecclesiastical assembly of the whole Middle Ages.[42]

John XXIII himself convoked the council in December 1413, but he did so with extreme reluctance and only after considerable pressure from the emperor-elect, Sigismund, who was to play a prominent role throughout the conciliar proceedings. For John, the council was to be simply a continuation of the Council of Pisa, and he hoped with the support of the multitudinous Italian bishops to secure another condemnation of his rivals and renewed confirmation of his own papal title. Those hopes were dashed, however, when, within a few months of the opening of the council in November 1414, the northern Europeans insisted that voting be by conciliar "nations"—eventually five in all—each casting a single vote in the general sessions regardless of the number of its members.[43] The council then proceeded, early in 1415, to take up the problem of the schism, and quickly concluded, despite general recognition of the legitimacy of the Council of Pisa and of John XXIII's election, that the only hope for success lay in the resignation of that pope along with the two rivals deposed at Pisa. Eager to bring pressure to bear on John XXIII in order to secure

42. In his *Chronicle of the Council of Constance*, the contemporary writer Ulrich Richental, who had a taste for (sometimes rather fanciful) statistics, listed as being in attendance, in addition to Popes John XXIII and Martin V and a host of other officials temporal as well as spiritual, 5 patriarchs, 33 cardinals, 47 archbishops, 145 bishops, 93 suffragan bishops, 132 abbots, 155 priors, 217 doctors of theology, 361 doctors of both laws, 5,300 "simple priests and scholars," more than 3,000 merchants, shopkeepers, craftsmen, musicians, and players, and more than 700 "harlots in brothels"—these last to be distinguished from those "who lay in stables and wherever they could, beside the private ones whom I could not count." Trans. from Mundy and Woody, eds., pp. 84–190 at 189–90. Cf. the useful collection of translated documents on the council in Crowder, pp. 65–145.

43. The five were the French, the Italian, the German, the Spanish, and the English. These "nations," like the nations of the medieval universities, were combinations of nationalities. Thus, the "English" nation included the Irish and the Scots, the "German" included the Poles, Czechs, Scandinavians, and others. Debate took place in the separate meetings of the nations and in a special "steering committee," which was made up of representatives from each nation. From July 1415, the college of cardinals, as a corporate body comparable to the nations, was permitted to cast a single vote in the general sessions of the council.

his cooperation, the assembly began to focus attention on the alleged notorieties of his life.

Over the course of the next three years, until its dissolution in April 1418, the council embarked on many projects and took some very important actions—notably the condemnation of the teachings of Wycliffe and Hus, the condemnation of tyrannicide, and the promulgation of a series of reform measures, the most significant of which was the decree *Frequens*.[44] None of these conciliar achievements, however, can vie in importance with the successful termination of the schism and the election of a pope the validity of whose title was accepted by the whole church.

Intimidated by threats that his alleged misdeeds called for a public investigation, John XXIII played for time by letting it be known that he would indeed be willing to yield up his office. At the same time he planned in secret to flee from the council and thereby to disrupt its activities. His plan very nearly succeeded. His flight to Schaffhausen on March 20, 1415, caused great alarm and confusion among the council fathers. Had not Sigismund rallied them, the assembly, in the absence of the pope who had convoked it and the validity of whose title most recognized, might well have disintegrated. But as it became clear that John was unlikely to return and was probably going back on his pledge to resign, the determination of the fathers to proceed was strengthened and their sentiments became increasingly conciliarist. As a result, at the fifth general session on April 6, 1415, the council formally promulgated the famous superiority decree, *Haec sancta synodus*, the main section of which reads as follows:

> This sacred synod of Constance . . . declares, in the first place, that it forms a general council, legitimately assembled in the Holy Spirit and representing the Catholic Church Militant, that it has its power immediately from Christ, and that all men, of every rank and position,

44. In accordance with the central provision of that decree general councils were to assemble regularly in the future, the first after the lapse of five years, the second after a further interval of seven years, and, thereafter, every ten years. For the text, see Alberigo, pp. 414–15; English trans. in Crowder, pp. 128–29.

including even the pope himself, are bound to obey it in those matters that pertain to the faith, the extirpation of the said schism, and to the reformation of the said Church in head and members. It declares also that anyone, of any rank, condition or office—even the papal— who shall contumaciously refuse to obey the mandates, statutes, decrees or instructions made by this holy synod or by any other lawfully assembled council on the matters aforesaid or on things pertaining to them, shall, unless he recovers his senses, be subjected to fitting penance and punished as is appropriate.[45]

This decree continues to be a controversial one, but there can be little doubt that the subsequent activity of the council was grounded in the claims it advanced.[46]

On May 17, 1415, John XXIII was taken prisoner. On May 29 he was deposed—not, it should be noted, because the council questioned the legitimacy of his title, but because it had tried him and found him guilty of simony, perjury, and other forms of scandalous misconduct. This sentence he did not challenge. Less than two months later, Gregory XII, the Roman pope already deposed at Pisa, offered to resign if he were permitted to convoke the council himself, thus legitimating it in his own eyes and in the eyes of his followers. By so doing, of course, he could also claim to have received from the council at least tacit confirmation of the legitimacy of the Roman line of popes. The council fathers were aware of this possibility, but their overriding objective was unity, they had his promise to resign, and they were even less disposed to make a fuss about a formality that very few of them took seriously than they had been the previous year when they treated the ambassadors of both Gregory XII and Benedict XIII as official papal delegates rather than merely as private Christians— despite the fact that they themselves endorsed the sentences of Pisa and recognized John XXIII as legitimate pope.

45. Alberigo, p. 385.
46. See de Vooght, *Pouvoirs du concile*, and the essays in Franzen and Müller, *Konzil von Konstanz*, as well as Franzen, "Council of Constance." For the contributions of de Vooght, Küng, Gill, Jedin, Franzen, Hürten, Pichler, Riedlinger, Brandmüller, and Tierney to the continuing debate about the dogmatic status of *Haec Sancta*, see Oakley, *Council over Pope?*, pp. 105–41, and de Vooght, "Controverses sur les pouvoirs du concile," two summary statements in which most of that literature is analyzed, criticized, or commented upon.

At the fourteenth general session of the council, therefore, held on July 4, 1415, Gregory's bull of convocation was read and his resignation accepted. His Avignonese rival, who finally lost the support of the Spanish kingdoms in December 1415, proved to be more stubborn. Indeed, surrounded by a tiny coterie of adamant supporters, Benedict persisted in his claim to be the one true pope right up to his death in 1423. But by then events had passed him by. On July 26, 1417, long after the members of his obedience had declared their adherence to the council, he was judged guilty of "perjury, heresy, and schism" and declared deposed. Less than a year later, after a protracted wrangle on the issue of which should take precedence, reform or the election of a new pope, the latter won out. An enlarged body of electors, including deputies from each conciliar nation as well as the cardinals from all three of the former obediences, went into conclave to choose a new pope. With the election on November 11, 1417, of one of the cardinals of the Roman obedience who had adhered to the Council of Pisa and who now took the title of Martin V (1417–31), the years of doubt were over. The church had at last an unquestionably legitimate pope and the Great Schism was at an end.

The conciliar movement, however, was not. The schism had been ended only because a general council had formally claimed to be the legitimate repository of supreme power in the church on certain crucial issues, had been able and willing to enforce that claim, and, in the decree *Frequens*, had been careful to set up constitutional machinery to impede any reversion to papal absolutism. This machinery was to prove less effective than doubtless they had hoped, but clearly not so ineffective as Martin V may have wished. In accordance with the provisions of *Frequens*, Martin summoned a new council to meet in 1423 at Pavia, transferred it to Siena, and then in March 1424, without having himself put in an appearance, peremptorily dissolved it before it had really succeeded in getting its teeth into the task of reform. Seven years later, again in accordance with *Frequens* but this time only under pressure, he convoked another council to meet at Basel, appointing Cardinal Cesarini (d. 1444) president and giving him the power to dissolve it. Shortly thereafter he died. When the council opened in 1431, it did so under his successor, Eugenius IV

(1431–47), a much less capable and decisive man, and under very unpromising circumstances. The college of cardinals was undergoing something of a reaction to Martin V's authoritarian administration, and the assembly in general bore an enormous freight of reforming expectations.

The fate of the Council of Basel (1431–49) was in large measure determined by two great external issues: the Hussite wars and the quest for reunion with the Greek Orthodox church. Nevertheless, the "great matter" of the council was still the constitutional question of the relationship of pope to general council.[47] One might have assumed that this matter had been settled at Constance—both by the theoretical pronouncements of the council and by the action it had taken. But its failure to achieve any really thoroughgoing reform of the church and especially of the curia, the unwillingness or inability of Martin V himself to implement such a reform on his own authority, his ambivalence and that of Eugenius toward the conciliarist constitutionalist claims, and their attitude of "business as usual" when it came to operating the central administrative machinery of the church— all of these factors helped engender among the ecclesiastics assembled at Basel a deep suspicion and fear of papal intentions. They helped intensify, too, a growing reaction against the papal claims to a plenitude of power and against the centralized mechanisms of papal administration as they had developed over the two previous centuries.

It was Eugenius who precipitated the crisis. Because he was opposed to the council from the start, and because Martin V had reached an agreement with the Greeks to hold a council of reunion on Italian soil, Eugenius was not eager to prolong the life of the Basel assembly. On December 18, 1431, despite the opposition of some of the cardinals, he published in consistory a bull dissolving the council. But he had misjudged the mood both of the council fathers and of the cardinals, fifteen of whom (out of a total of twenty-one) now sided with the council. He had also misjudged the priorities of Cardinal Cesarini.

47. See the useful collection of translated documents on the council in Crowder, pp. 146–81.

In the wake of a crusade against the Hussites that had met with disastrous defeat, Cesarini had committed Basel to vital negotiations with
the moderate party of the victors. These negotiations were now threatened by the papal bull of dissolution. When it arrived, therefore, he
joined with the council fathers in refusing to obey the pope. Deadlock
ensued, and, as support for the pope dwindled and as men of the
stature of Cesarini and Nicholas of Cusa (1401–64) rallied to the
council, it proceeded to reaffirm conciliar principles and ultimately
to put them into practice.

Given the circumstances prevailing, it is hardly surprising that in
1432 the council chose to republish the decree *Haec sancta*. But in the
following years, it devoted its energies not only to the struggle with
the pope but also to the negotiation of a Hussite settlement and to
reform of the church "in head and members." It was the conclusion of
an agreement with the Hussites that finally brought the pope to heel.
That settlement was greeted with great relief in Germany and eastern
Europe, enhancing the council's prestige and making the pope's opposition to its activities well-nigh indefensible. On December 15,
1433, therefore, he capitulated. In the bull *Dudum sacrum* he declared
his earlier dissolution of the council invalid and proclaimed that the
council's activity had been legitimate all along.

What had been achieved, is turned out, was a truce rather than
any final settlement. At the time, it may well have seemed to the
conciliarists that their victory was complete. Their own conception of
meaningful reform in the church proved, however, to be their un-
doing. Although they managed to take one or two steps to promote
reform of the lower clergy and discussed many more measures, the
bulk of their effort was directed to reform of head rather than of members. And that reform was concerned mainly with curtailing papal
financial resources and limiting papal administrative powers. Against
such measures Eugenius protested in vain. Not until 1437 was he able
to impose his will, and then only because the council by its actions
had begun to forfeit the support of some of its most distinguished
participants.

By that time "the representatives of the lower clergy, the chapters and the universities, and the horde of doctors, had long ago gained an overwhelming ascendancy at Basle, while the bishops were withdrawing from a Council which, after creating a curia of its own, was deeply involved in the business of allocating prebends."[48] As a result, when, on September 18, 1437, Eugenius transferred the council to Ferrara, which the Greeks had accepted as the site for the council of union, a significant minority of the council membership, which included Cesarini, Nicholas of Cusa, and other luminaries (and which Eugenius was quick to dub the *sanior pars*), obeyed the decree. In January 1439, allegedly because of the threat of plague, the assembly was transferred once more, this time to Florence.

In the meantime, the majority that had stood fast at Basel went on to proclaim the superiority of council over pope to be an undeniable article of faith, to declare Eugenius IV deposed as a heretic, and to elect in his place Duke Amadeus of Savoy. He took the name Felix V (1439–49), won support in Switzerland and Austria and from several universities, and benefited from the declared neutrality of France and Germany. But it was a blunder on the part of the Basel rump council thus to have precipitated a new schism within the Latin church, especially when the papal council of Florence had succeeded only four months previously in ending the ancient schism between Greeks and Latins, a happy event promulgated in July 1439 in the union decree *Laetentur coeli*. Both events, certainly, worked to ensure the final victory of Eugenius IV's policy—though it was his successor, Nicholas V (1447–55), who reaped the benefit of that victory. The deepening radicalism of the conciliarists did little to bolster their flagging fortunes, and on April 7, 1449, after France had followed the example of Germany in renouncing its neutrality and rallying to the side of the Roman pope, Felix V resigned. On April 25 the Council of Basel (transferred a year earlier to Lausanne), having been permitted the formality of electing Nicholas V, decreed its own dissolution.

48. Jedin, *History*, 1: 19.

The Restoration Papacy and the Era of National Churches
(1449–1517)

Though the conciliar theory outlived the ignominious ending of
Basel, the conciliar movement—the great attempt to engineer a constitutional revolution in the church—is usually regarded as having
met its decisive defeat at that time. The popes of the restoration era
emerged once more as monarchs of a distinctly absolutist stamp, but
monarchs now equipped, in the formulations of the decree *Laetentur
coeli*, with the first conciliar definition of the Roman primacy. This
definition Jedin has described as "the *Magna Carta* of the papal restoration." [49] It was later to serve as the basis for the solemn definition
promulgated by the First Vatican Council in 1870 as part of its dogmatic constitution *Pastor aeternus*. But the road from *Laetentur coeli*
to *Pastor aeternus* was neither direct nor untroubled. Although the
papacy had triumphed over the conciliar movement, it had done so at
the price of accepting—helping sponsor, even—what amounted to
a constitutional revolution of a different type, and one that was determinative for the history of the papacy in particular and the Roman
Catholic church in general right down to the nineteenth century.

Even before the outbreak of the schism some secular rulers had
begun the process of asserting their jurisdiction in an increasingly
direct fashion over the provincial churches falling within their territorial boundaries. They were thereby reversing a tide that had been
flowing in the opposite direction ever since the eleventh century,
when the Gregorian reformers had mounted their campaign to lib-
erate the provincial churches from royal or imperial control. The

49. Ibid., pp. 19–20. The crucial portion of *Laetentur coeli* runs as follows: "We
define that the holy Apostolic See and the Roman Pontiff hold the primacy over the
whole world, that the Roman pontiff himself is the successor of Peter, prince of the
Apostles, that he is the true vicar of Christ, head of the whole Church, father and
teacher of all Christians; and [we define] that to him in [the person of] Peter was given
by our Lord Jesus Christ the full power [*plenam potestatem*] of nourishing, ruling and
governing the universal Church; as it is also contained in the acts of the ecumenical
councils and in the holy canons" (Alberigo, p. 504).

process was particularly well advanced in England, where the kings had become adept at marshaling national antipapal feeling in order to bring pressure to bear on the papacy to concede them an ever larger share of the collations to English benefices and of the taxes levied on the English church.[50]

But it was above all the schism that gave so many other rulers their chance—most directly those who, like the kings of Aragon and Navarre or Giangaleazzo Visconti, duke of Milan, at one time or another adopted a position of neutrality between the two obediences, but also those who joined in the 1398 withdrawal of obedience from the Avignonese pontiff. France was an outstanding beneficiary, and it has been cogently argued that, in voting for the withdrawal of obedience at the Third Council of Paris, even the French clergy cherished no illusory hopes of freedom and realized full well that they were expressing "nothing but consent to a royal policy." That policy involved "a major constitutional action, a re-organization of the ecclesiastical life of the country," one that placed the king at the head of the Gallican church, thereby leaving it, after the five years of subtraction, "fully integrated into the French realm."[51]

The years of schism, then, marked a critical phase in the disintegration of what had been under papal leadership and government a genuinely international church into a series of what were, de facto if not de jure, national and territorial churches dominated by kings, princes, and the rulers of such city-states as Venice and Florence. Those years set a pattern that rulers were to follow throughout the fifteenth century in their efforts to gain control of their churches. In 1477 Lorenzo de' Medici remarked that apart from the scandal involved there was much to be said for having three or four popes instead of one, and during the earlier part of the century the rulers of Latin Christendom saw similar opportunities in the confusion en-

50. See McKisack, pp. 272 ff. She acknowledges (p. 274, n. 1) her indebtedness to the unpublished Oxford dissertation of J. R. L. Highfield, "The Relationship between the Church and the English Crown, 1348–78" (1950).
51. Kaminsky, "Politics of France's Subtraction of Obedience," pp. 368, 396–97. He adds: "Papal government could never be the same again."

gendered by the struggle between Eugenius IV and the Council of Basel. In 1438, in the Pragmatic Sanction of Bourges, Charles VII of France, with the support of the French clergy, adopted in modified form several of the council's decrees affirming conciliar supremacy, abolishing annates, restricting appeals to Rome, and limiting the papal rights of collation to benefices, and gave them the force of law in France. The German electors did something similar in the *Acceptatio* of Mainz; so too, in 1439, did the Visconti ruler of Milan. Although the Pragmatic Sanction and like instruments were not at all systematically enforced, they were persistently used as a means to blackmail the pope into conceding a more favorable share of the ecclesiastical spoils.

The fifteenth century witnessed the parceling among the secular rulers of Europe of the pope's sovereign authority over the church, or, better, a frequently renegotiated division of that authority between pope and rulers. The concordats that Martin V had concluded in 1418 with the several conciliar nations at Constance reveal the type of variation that was to persist in such accommodations, the pope making his most damaging concessions in the concordat with England and retaining his traditional fiscal and administrative rights most effectively in the concordats with Italy and Spain. These variations simply reflect differences in the balance of power between the pope and the several rulers concerned. By the end of the century, accordingly, with the emergence of a unified and powerful Spanish state, it became necessary to concede to the Spanish crown a very far-reaching control indeed over the life of the Spanish church. What is surprising, however, is the extent to which Eugenius IV was willing to promote this whole process of establishing rulers as masters of their respective churches so long as those rulers were willing to withdraw support from the conciliar idea and from the threat of reform in head and members that went with it. Possession of the actual substance of power mattered less, it seems, than the enjoyment of a theoretically supreme authority in the universal church.

It was with the substance of power, however, that the money went. The era of councils and the damaging concessions made to kings and princes entailed a grievous diminution in the size of the revenues flowing from the church at large into Rome. The nature of the records available permits only highly conjectural estimates of papal income for the years after Constance. Partner has been able to calculate, however, that whereas Gregory XI's annual income on the eve of the schism averaged between 200,000 and 300,000 cameral florins, that of Martin V in the year 1426–27 amounted to about 170,000 cameral florins. More significant, however, is the fact that whereas only about a quarter of Gregory's revenues came from the papal states, almost a half of Martin's reduced income emanated from that source.[52] To Martin V himself, and even more to the popes of the era of restoration, the implications of this state of affairs seemed clear: if they were to enjoy any independence of action at all, it was extremely urgent that they make themselves masters of their own territories in Italy.

This policy came very much to the fore during and after the pontificate of Nicholas V, with the ending of the Council of Basel, and, as a result of the Peace of Lodi (1454), the achievement of a balance of power within Italy. The substance of power over the provincial churches having passed out of their hands, the popes of the restoration era—however grandiose their theoretical position as supreme pontiffs of the universal church and however much men paid lip service to that position—concentrated their attention increasingly on pacifying and protecting their own Italian principality. To do so they had to involve themselves in the complex diplomacy and ever shifting coalitions required by the need to maintain the balance of power in Italy, to stave off the threat of French and Spanish intervention in the politics of the peninsula, and to diminish the impact and contain the extent of that intervention when they failed. And the success of their efforts is reflected in the gradual reconstruction of the city of Rome, in the magnificence of the Renaissance papal court, in the degree of general financial recovery to which this splendor gave witness, and in the fact that by the pontificate of Sixtus IV (1471–84) the papal state was itself producing at least 64 percent of the total papal revenues.

52. Partner, *Papal State*, pp. 153–54; see also idem, "The 'Budget' of the Roman Church," in Jacob, ed., *Italian Renaissance Studies*, pp. 256–74.

Appropriately enough, it was during the pontificate of Sixtus that Italian superseded Latin as the language of the curia.

The endeavours of Pius II (1458–64) had made it clear that such efforts at territorial consolidation were not necessarily incompatible with an active concern for the twin tasks of reforming the church and uniting Christendom in a great crusade against the infidel—the ancient goals in pursuit of which the medieval papacy had risen to greatness.

But even apart from their moral stature or lack thereof, the role and preoccupations of an Italian prince were not such as to promote re-form-mindedness in his successors. The question of reform inevitably raised (as the electoral capitulations of the cardinals reveal) their failure to adhere to the provisions of *Frequens* and the chilling memory of the desperate struggle for survival that Eugenius IV had had to wage against the Council of Basel. Despite the outcome of that strug-gle, the idea of the council was not dead. During the latter half of the fifteenth century appeals from the judgment of the pope to that of a general council were frequent. And despite the understandable pro-clivity of their princely rivals to use such appeals as diplomatic sticks with which to beat the popes, the canonists defended the procedure, and against it such popes as Pius II, Sixtus IV, and Julius II railed in vain.[53]

When examining problems of ecclesiastical government in this period, one is understandably tempted to focus on the dubious per-sonal morality of some of the popes themselves; to note, for example, their predilection for nepotism, and to chart the simoniacal intrigues that went into the elections of Innocent VIII (1484–92), Alexander

53. For a listing and discussion of appeals to a general council after Pius II's prohibi-tion, see Picotti, 33ff.; Jedin, *History*, 1:67, n. 4, cites some further instances and notes that Picotti "does not adequately distinguish between the appeal to the Council as a legal procedure and the demand for a Council and its convocation." But it is clear that an altogether exaggerated importance has been accorded to Pius II's bull *Exe-crabilis* (1460), prohibiting the "execrable abuse" of appealing to a council. (There is a translation in Crowder, pp. 179–82.) It was regarded at the time, and during the subsequent half-century and more, not as any definitive or binding judgment but simply as the reaction of one faction. Even Pius II's papal successors do not appear to have regarded it as authoritative and it was not widely disseminated. Cf. Jedin, *His-tory*, 1:66–68.

VI (1492–1503), and Julius II (1503–13). And, brooding about the two last, one is led to wonder perhaps at the circumstances that placed in succession upon the papal throne an urbane but unreconstructed philanderer and a gifted but bellicose diplomatic and military adventurer. A better grasp of what was at stake, however, may perhaps be gained by glancing in conclusion at the nature and achievement of the Fifth Lateran Council (1512–17), the last of the pre-Reformation general councils, and at the events leading up to its convocation.

That such a council should have been convoked at all is by no means to be taken for granted. An extraordinary contingency was required to overcome Julius II's distaste for the idea of the council, which he shared with both his predecessors and his successors. The contingency was the sudden transformation of what had seemed like a blunted diplomatic weapon into a potent ecclesiological threat—nothing less, in fact, than the independent convocation by opposition cardinals (one Italian, two Spanish, two French) of the would-be general council that has gone down in history as the *conciliabulum* of Pisa (1511–12). That those cardinals, appealing to the decree *Frequens*, should have taken such a step reflects not only their own disgruntlement with Julius II (and, indeed, with his predecessor, too) but also the persistence of the old curialist "oligarchic" tradition into the era of papal restoration and the veritable struggle for power that had raged between the college of cardinals and the popes during the latter years of the fifteenth century. In this struggle the efforts of the cardinals had been somewhat less than successful, and had the French king withheld his active support, it is as hard to imagine their risking the convocation of the council as it is to imagine its successful assembly.

Louis XII's wish to promote such a council is explicable entirely in terms of his political ambitions in Italy and the attempts of Julius II to thwart them. Early in 1510, in an abrupt reversal of his earlier policy, Julius had thrown in his lot with the opponents of the French presence in Italy; and Louis now sought, with the complaisance of the emperor Maximilian I and the help of the cardinals of the opposition, to encompass his ruin. Not surprisingly, the council turned out to be a small and almost entirely French affair. It did little more than reissue the Constance decree *Haec sancta synodus* and pronounce Julius II to be suspended from office. Indeed, its major achievement was to provoke the pontiff into attempting to take the wind out of its sails by himself convoking the Fifth Lateran Council. In that attempt he was wholly successful; the first half-dozen sessions of the council were occupied almost exclusively with the condemnation of the activities of the Pisan assembly, the proscription of those who persisted in adhering to it, and the reconciliation of those who had abandoned it. Under such circumstances Louis XII changed tactics and after Julius's death in 1513 indicated that he was open to some sort of mutually satisfactory accommodation with Julius's successor, Leo X (1513–21).

In its organization and procedures the Lateran Council was very much a papal council, poorly attended by all except the Italian bishops, summoned to counteract the effect of the French exploitation of conciliar theory, and punctuated by anxious attempts to contain that theory. Even in convoking it, Julius II sought to prevent any misunderstanding of his action by pointing out that the decree *Frequens* had long since lapsed into desuetude and that, even if it had not, circumstances would have rendered it inapplicable in his own day.

Again, scenting presumably a whiff of "episcopalism" about it, Leo X rejected outright a modest proposal of the assembled bishops to establish an episcopal "sodality" or "fraternity" to protect their common interests (*episcopalis societas, confraternitas, sodalicium*).[54] With the concurrence of the cardinals, he imposed a "perpetual silence" on the whole idea. Even more tellingly, Leo and his successor moved to destroy the particular alliance that had always threatened to give the conciliar idea teeth and had recently succeeded in doing so—the alliance between the most vigorous proponent of conciliarism, the Faculty of Theology at Paris, and the ruler most frequently tempted

54. These are the words that occur in the documents. See Baronius et al., vol. 31, ann. 1516, nos. 1–4 (citing Paris de Grassis); also Hefele and Hergenröther, vol. 8, app. H. and J., pp. 845–53. For a discussion of this interesting proposal and for the arguments supporting the interpretation of *Pastor aeternus* proffered below, see Oakley, "Conciliarism at the Fifth Lateran Council?," pp. 452–63.

to exploit it, the French king. They destroyed it in the fashion that had become classic—by reassuring the king that he had more to gain by aligning himself with the pope and turning his back on the conciliar idea than by trying to use it as a diplomatic weapon. The strong card held by the popes was the very strength of Francis I's Italian ambitions and his sure sense that, military victories notwithstanding, he could hardly hope to realize those ambitions if he had to confront the implacable hostility of the papacy.

The outcome was the Concordat of Bologna (1516), which, while it formally conceded to the French king the right to nominate to nearly all the bishoprics, abbacies, and major benefices in his kingdom, was not "the unqualified triumph for the French monarchy which it has generally been acclaimed to be."[55] It was bitterly opposed both by the Parlement and by the University of Paris on the grounds that it restored annates, permitted the resumption of appeals to Rome, and conceded the superiority of the pope's authority to that of a general council.[56] So far as royal control over the French church is concerned, the concordat may have done little more than regularize and extend it somewhat within clearly defined limits and in return for some important concessions—or, at least, would have done little more than that had Francis I fully honored its provisions.

Certainly, whatever the price Leo X actually paid by agreeing to its terms, he appears to have thought it worthwhile, for in return, after all, he secured the abrogation of the Pragmatic Sanction of Bourges, the base from which for so long the French conciliarists had been able to operate with impunity, and as a result the restoration of annates and the removal of restrictions on appeals to Rome. That same year, in the bull *Pastor aeternus*, the Lateran Council was able to declare the Pragmatic Sanction null and void and to declare that the Roman pontiff alone, inasmuch as he had "authority over all councils," possessed "full right and power to convoke, transfer, and dissolve councils."[57]

55. See Knecht, p. 31.
56. Ibid., pp. 27–29.
57. Text in Alberigo, p. 618.

Contrary to what has so often been said, and especially in the wake of the First Vatican Council, this bull did not attempt to repudiate, either explicitly or implicitly, the Constance superiority decree *Haec sancta synodus*. Even at this late date, it seems, to have attempted to do so would have been to go too far.[58] Certainly, the Gallican theologians discerned no such intent in the bull. For them, on matters conciliarist, it was business as usual. In March 1518 the Faculty of Theology at Paris, by way of protest against the compromising concordat of 1516, did not hesitate to follow the traditional route and to appeal to a future general council. By that time, of course, the Lateran Council itself had been dissolved, and with it the hopes for the long-awaited reforms that its opening session had helped excite. By that time, too, Martin Luther had disseminated his ninety-five theses. In November 1518, in anticipation of the papal sentence, Luther himself appealed from the judgment of the pope to that of a future general council. In his appeal, ironically enough, he drew the legal sections from the text of the earlier appeal launched by the theologians of Paris.[59] In March 1521, to compound that irony, those same theologians issued their *Determinatio*, branding Luther's central doctrines as heretical and furnishing him with a truly formidable genealogy of heretical forebears. The die, it seems, was cast.

58. Though such a move was certainly not regarded as redundant at the time. Ferdinand the Catholic of Spain, in the instructions he gave to his representatives at the council, explicitly suggested the need for a formal repudiation of *Haec sancta* (see Doussinague, app. 50, 539).
59. The two appeals are compared in Thomas, *Concordat*, 3:72–74.

CHAPTER 2 · MODES OF PIETY: LITURGICAL, MYSTICAL, MONASTIC, POPULAR

And therefore whatso thou be that coveytest to come to contemplation of God, that is to say, to bryng forthe soche a
childe that men clepyn in the story Beniamyn, that is to say,
sight of God: than schalt thou use thee in this manner. Thou
schalt clepe togeders thi thoughtes and thi desires, and make
thee of them a chirche, and lerne thee therin for to love only
this good worde Jhesu, so that alle thi desyre and thi thought
be onely sette for to love Jhesu, and that unsesyngly, as it
may be here, so that thou fulfille that is seyde in the psalme:
'Lorde I schal bles thee in chirches,' that is in thoughtes and
desires of the love of Jhesu. And than, in this chirche of
thoughtes and desires, and in this onehead of studies and of
willes, loke that alle thi thoughts and thi desires and thi
studyes and alle thi willes be only set in the love and the
preisyng of this Lorde Jhesu, withouten forgetyng, as fer
forth as thou maist by grace and as thi freelte wil suffre, ever
more mekyng thee to preier and to counsel, pacyently
abidyng the wille of oure Lorde, unto the tyme that thi
mynde be ravisched aboven itself to be fed with the faire
foode of aungelles in the beholdyng of God and godly
thinges. So that it be fulfilled in thee that is wretyn in the
psalme: 'Ibi Beniamyn adol[es]entulus in mentis excessu.'
That is: 'There is Beniamyn, the yonge childe, in ravesching
of mynde.' Amen.
—"TRETYSE OF THE STODYE OF WYSDOME"

If by piety we mean the stance of the faithful before God as it is expressed not only in the struggle to avoid sin and to attain virtue but

also in meditation, prayer, adoration, worship, and the longing for union with the divine, then a particular message is conveyed by the quotation above (itself a fourteenth-century reworking of a twelfth-century text).[1] It may be taken to signal that the late eleventh and twelfth centuries form the watershed of late-medieval piety.[2] In Chapter 1 it was argued that the subsequent career of the ecclesiastical institution was largely determined by what the Gregorian reformers did and what they left undone. In relation to the subsequent development of medieval piety a similar importance attaches to the new departures made during roughly the same period by such spiritual pacesetters as St. Peter Damiani (1007–72), St. Bernard of Clairvaux (1090–1153), and Richard of St. Victor (ca. 1123–73), as well as to those enduring modalities of the spiritual life left virtually untouched. The Reformation historian, his senses sharpened by exposure to later conflicts, is often apt to scent novelty in aspects of fourteenth- and fifteenth-century spiritual life where none perhaps exists. But the medievalist likewise, lulled even in fifteenth-century works by the reassuring patter of references to Augustine and Jerome and Cassian and Bernard, is sometimes tempted to attribute to medieval piety a degree of stability that scrutiny of its history cannot in fact sustain. The stretch of history involved is a long one. That it was marked by some discontinuities no one, I imagine, would question. That the most important of those discontinuities, however, and the ones in many respects determinative for the whole texture of late-

1. "Tretyse of the Stodye of Wysdome," in Hodgson, ed., *Deonise Hid Divinite*, pp. 45–46, ll. 10–15. This work, attributed to the anonymous author of the *Cloud of Unknowing*, is a translation-paraphrase of the *Benjamin Minor* of Richard of St. Victor (d. 1173). The passage cited incorporates materials added by the Middle English writer that do not occur in the Latin.

2. In two recent studies, Giles Constable has documented the popularity of twelfth-century spiritual writings on the later Middle Ages, and, developing the insights of André Wilmart, M.-D. Chenu, and others, has argued for "an affinity of religious temperament between this age and the twelfth century"; see "Twelfth-Century Spirituality," pp. 31–32. He concludes that "in religious history, unlike intellectual history, the four centuries from the twelfth to the sixteenth must be seen as a whole and that the turning point in medieval religious history . . . falls in the late eleventh and twelfth centuries . . ." (ibid., pp. 49–50). Cf. his "Popularity of Twelfth-Century Spiritual Writers," in Molho and Tedeschi, eds., pp. 5–28.

medieval piety, should have occurred already in the early-medieval centuries and again during the late eleventh and twelfth centuries may well be less clearly apparent. With those earlier centuries, then, we must begin.

Liturgical and Devotional Premises

In any discussion of Christian piety the initial focus should properly be not the private prayer life of Christians as individuals or as members of voluntary subgroupings but rather the liturgy, that whole range of worship "which is officially organised by the church, and which is open to and offered by, or in the name of, all who are members of the church."[3] The celebration of the Eucharist has always constituted the very heart of liturgical worship, but the understanding of the Eucharistic action and the mode of its performance have scarcely been stable. Central to the performance and the understanding of the Eucharist in both primitive and patristic eras, however, was its corporate nature. It was an action not simply of the priesthood but of the whole community of the faithful. For its fulfillment it required that all orders—bishop, priests, deacons, subdeacons, acolytes, and laity alike—properly perform their own particular, "liturgy." Moreover, the action itself was not really understood in temporal terms as a repetition by a man or group of men of Christ's historic sacrifice or as merely a memorial to that sacrifice. More mysteriously, in that the church was itself conceived quite literally as the body of Christ (indeed, as the "true" body or "body of the whole Christ"—*verum corpus, totius Christi corpus*), the action was itself trans-temporal. It was one in which Christ, the high priest, and the faithful of his church, united in one body as head and members and by their very action intensifying that union, offer to the Father that very body under the form of bread and wine,[4] re-presenting thereby the one sacrifice of Christ—or, better, "energizing" that one sacrifice. As St. John Chrysostom put it toward the end of the fourth century in

3. Dix, p. 1. Though I have also consulted Klauser and Jungmann, the following paragraphs are most heavily dependent upon Dix's fine book.
4. See Dix, p. 248.

a fashion typical of the early commentators: "We do not offer a different sacrifice like the high-priest of old, but we ever offer the same. Or rather we offer the *anamnesis* of the sacrifice."[5] And the word *anamnesis*, it should be noted, conveyed something akin to an active "reliving" rather than a merely passive remembering.

This conception of the Eucharist—in the context of which metaphysical questions concerning the precise nature of Christ's physical presence understandably did not arise—survived the transition from the comparative simplicity of private worship to the imperial grandeurs of public ceremonial undergone by the eucharistic act in the wake of Constantine's grant of toleration to Christianity and its subsequent ascent to the status of an official religion and civic cult. Down to the thirteenth century, indeed, the original conception of the Eucharist found something more than routine echoes in the formulations of theologians, and its memory remained embedded in some of the liturgical texts themselves until it was brought to light once more during the course of the last hundred years. As early as the fifth and sixth centuries, however, a certain erosion had set in, and by the onset of the religious "revolution" of the late eleventh and twelfth centuries a critical transformation, which that revolution did nothing to undo, had already long since been completed.

The transformation reflected changes both practical and theoretical. On the practical side were the marked increase in the number and importance of the prayers to be said by the clergy alone (fourth century); the rapid and catastrophic decline in the frequency of lay communions and the concomitant fading of the people's offertory (fourth and fifth centuries onward); the appearance in the West and growing dominance of the "low mass," or Eucharist not sung by bishop, priests, deacons, and people but said by a single priest assisted by a solitary minister (sixth century onward); the emergence of independent vernacular languages and the final incomprehensibility of the Latin liturgy to the great mass of Europeans (eighth and ninth centuries); and the contemporaneous shift to recitation of the canon in an

5. Chrysostom, *Homiliae XXXIV in Epistolam ad Hebraeos*, Hom. XVII, 3, in Migne, ed., *PG*, 63:131. Cf. Dix, p. 243, whose translation I cite. For the meaning of *anamnesis* in the New Testament, see Kettell and Friedrich, eds., 1:348–49.

inaudible whisper and removal of the celebrant to the front of the altar where he could no longer face the people. All of these changes contrived to transform the Eucharist from a corporate liturgical act in which laity and clergy alike participated into an exclusively priestly liturgy, something the priest did on behalf of lay people, themselves reduced progressively from "doers" to "hearers and seers" and, finally, to "seers" only. To complete the preconditions necessary for the liturgical phenomena characteristic of the late Middle Ages it remained only for a certain monastic practice, already established by the eighth century, to spread in the following centuries among the secular clergy and eventually to reshape the rite of the mass as publicly celebrated. The practice was that whereby those monks who were also priests celebrated daily, and often simultaneously on separate side altars, masses that were "private," that is, without any congregation.

These practical changes were accompanied by (and perhaps helped to stimulate) an enormously complex series of interrelated theoretical shifts. At their most profound, these shifts involved a diminution in the sense of the organic connection between Christ and his church and also, therefore, between Christ's sacrifice of himself and the church's eucharistic action. More obviously, they involved a stress on the more purely temporal and sacerdotal nature of the eucharistic action, a tendency to align it with the unambiguously *historical* moment in Christ's redeeming activity (with the Passion rather than the Resurrection or Ascension). A tendency also to see it as in some mysterious sense a *repetition* of that historical sacrifice and to attribute to the priestly consecration alone what had originally been regarded as the work of the eucharistic action as a whole—namely, the making present of Christ in his body and his blood.

These alterations in the meaning attributed to the Eucharist, coupled with the practical changes already outlined, led to the formation of a fundamentally new pattern of liturgical thinking and behavior. The controversies concerning the metaphysical relation of Christ's body and blood in the sacrament to the physical elements of bread and wine which raged on and off from the ninth to the eleventh centuries also contributed to that process.[6] Within the new pattern each mass came to be regarded as in some sense a repetition of Christ's original sacrifice on Calvary, a fresh sacrifice generating its own individual quantum of grace, a sacrifice that, simply by virtue of their possession of holy orders, priests and priests alone could offer, applying its merits in accordance with their own chosen intentions to petitioners or benefactors, present or absent, living or dead.

That pattern was clearly signaled in the early Middle Ages by a significant Frankish interpolation in the old Roman text of the canon of the mass.[7] Having undergone considerable intensification during the centuries that followed, it was to endure until the end of the Middle Ages, and in Catholic Europe to the Council of Trent and beyond. It may be said to have been particularly congruent with the conditions of religious life from the seventh to the eleventh centuries, when the characteristically Christian preoccupation with the personal relationship of the individual soul to God was to a striking degree submerged in the collective rhythms of a devotional life that was external rather than internal, public rather than private, communal rather than personal.

So strong was this bent, indeed, that even the monks—those products of what at the start had been a nonclerical, unambiguously sectarian, and intensely private quest for personal sanctification— were transformed into a class of professional clerical intercessors. They became the dischargers of an onerous round of corporate worship, performing in choir the successive phases of the Divine Office, inter-

6. Thus, as Dix points out (p. 621), "the first treatise on this problem in theological history" was the *De corpore et sanguine domini*, written about 840 by Ratramnus.

7. "Together with Thy servant N. our Pope [and N. our bishop and all the orthodox and the worshipers ⟨who are⟩ of catholic and apostolic faith] remember Thy servants and handmaids N. and N. and all who stand around, whose faith is accepted of Thee and whose devotion known [for whom we offer unto Thee, or] who offer unto Thee this sacrifice of praise, for themselves and all who are theirs. . . ." (cited by Dix, p. 501). Dix comments (p. 501, n. 1) that the bracketed clauses are later Frankish interpolations into the authentic Roman text and adds: "In the Roman idea it is *the people themselves* who are the offerers; in the Gallican interpolation it is the priest who offers *for* them."

ceding with God in their masses on behalf of the rest of society, and completing as substitutes the burdensome penances that their aristocratic benefactors felt themselves unable to discharge. They were, in fact, the "soldiers of Christ," by their ceaseless round of prayer struggling against the swarming evils that threatened their society. To that calling professional competence and commitment were central; the quest for individual perfection, however, was by no means a necessary motivating force.

During these early-medieval centuries, more than ever before, the monasteries molded the spirituality of the church at large. And the most striking characteristics of that spirituality were its public, impersonal, communal, even "heroic" qualities: its worship of a God who was seen above all as mighty lord of the universe and terrifying judge of man, of a Christ portrayed even on the cross as triumphant king, royal Christ reigning in glory, heavenly analogue of the greatest of earthly kings. It is understandable that when change came, the monasteries functioned as spiritual pacesetters for the church at large. During the course of the eleventh century there began to appear within the world of Benedictine monasticism a certain uneasiness with the established order of religious living: a restless desire for a more evangelical or apostolic mode of life, a yearning once more for greater solitude and heightened poverty, for an existence geared less to the needs of the community at large than to the disciplined exploration of those profound depths of the soul wherein the individual seeker could hope to encounter the divine.

The teachings of St. Peter Damiani south of the Alps and to the north those of Hugh (d. 1141) and Richard of St. Victor, of Ailred of Rievaulx (d. 1167), and, above all, of St. Bernard of Clairvaux were at the same time a manifestation of that yearning and a response to it. So, too, were the flurry of monastic reform and the appearance of new monastic orders in the latter part of the eleventh century and the first part of the twelfth. Particular emphasis should be placed upon the spread of reformed congregations of canons regular following the so-called Augustinian rule (to one of which Hugh and Richard of St. Victor belonged) and upon the founding and rapid proliferation of the Cistercians, the order that St. Bernard himself joined and upon which he placed the imprint of his own dynamic spiritual vision.

It is, then, to the impact of an originally monastic impulse, to the example of the Cistercians in particular, and to the work of St. Bernard above all that we must ascribe the dissemination across Europe during the twelfth century of a different type of spirituality— more emotional, more personal, more private, more preoccupied with individual will and inner piety than that generally cultivated in the great age of Benedictine monasticism that had now drawn to a close. The interior life of the committed individual, the hunger of the soul for the divine, the longing to be "immersed completely in that sea of endless light and bright eternity,"[8] the tender and compassionate devotion to Christ's sacred heart and holy name, to his human life and suffering and to that of his blessed mother—such themes, if not altogether novel, became dominant in a way that they had not been before.

These were the themes that the new mendicant orders of the thirteenth century, and especially the Franciscans, took as their own. Through their example, their spiritual direction, popular preaching, and "third order" (which opened even to lay folk a life of evangelical and penitential dedication), the Franciscans made themselves felt everywhere as a vital spiritual force, bringing the new, more personal and emotional piety, and the simple religious devotion that went with it, into the homes of the comparatively unchurched city dwellers of Europe.

During the thirteenth and fourteenth centuries, at a time when the public corporate structures of the church, monastic as well as secular, were entering a period of troubles and confusion, this new type of more individual and affective piety continued to flourish and even to put forth new shoots. Without it, and certainly without the great spiritual achievement of the Augustinian canons, the Cistercians, and the Franciscans, the great flowering of mysticism in the fourteenth century and the emergence of the *devotio moderna* in the fifteenth

8. The words cited are those of St. Bernard of Clairvaux, *De diligendo Deo*, chap. 10; from Petry, ed., p. 65.

would have been inconceivable. Without it, too, it would be difficult really to comprehend many of the attitudes and practices that came to characterize the popular piety of those centuries. But it must also be insisted that without one great weakness in that spiritual achievement it would be equally difficult to comprehend some of the qualities characteristic of all three of the spiritual developments to which we have just referred. That great weakness reflected the failure to reverse the process that, over the centuries, had transformed the practice and understanding of the Eucharist.

Upon that other great segment of the church's liturgical worship, the Divine Office, the spiritual revolution of the late eleventh and twelfth centuries certainly did have its effect. It encouraged the individual participant to view the performance of the office less as the discharging of an external ritual function than as what it had originally been intended to be: an occasion to evoke and express a personal interior devotion. Nor did the Eucharist go altogether unaffected. The introduction during the twelfth century of the elevation of the host at mass; the institution during the thirteenth century of the feast of Corpus Christi and processions of the Blessed Sacrament; the growth during the fourteenth and fifteenth centuries of the practice of exposing the previously consecrated eucharistic Species for public adoration in an *ostensarium* or monstrance; a contemporaneous increase, however modest and regional, of the frequency with which the laity actually received communion—all of these practices bear witness to a deepening of devotion to the mystery of the Eucharist. But in its individualism, its concentration on the priestly consecration, its sense that in the sacrament alone one encounters the true body of Christ, its preoccupation, therefore, with seeing and adoring the consecrated Species, this devotion was light-years away from the primitive and patristic view of things. It assumed as its very foundation the transformation that had occurred in the late-antique and early-medieval centuries.

In a marvelously quotable passage in his *Defence of the True and Catholic Doctrine*, Archbishop Cranmer (1489–1556) asked:

What made the people to run from their seats to the altar, and from altar to altar, and from sacring (as they called it) to sacring, peeping, tooting and gazing at that thing which the priest held up in his hands, if they thought not to honour the thing which they saw? What moved the priests to lift up the sacrament so high over their heads? or the people to say to the priest "Hold up! Hold up!"; or one man to say to another "Stoop down before"; or to say "This day have I seen my Maker"; and "I cannot be quiet unless I see my Maker once a day"? What was the cause of all these, and that as well the priest and the people so devoutly did knock and kneel at every sight of the sacrament, but that they worshipped that visible thing which they saw with their eyes and took it for very God?[9]

Few readers would be likely to miss the element of parody in this description. But most would be disposed to see in it an accurate witness to one very striking characteristic of Catholic piety on the eve of the Reformation. And properly so. Always provided, of course, that that characteristic is taken for what it truly was: no late-medieval novelty, indeed, but the mature dividend of a legacy from a much more distant era.

The Flowering of Mysticism in the Fourteenth Century

It is a commonplace among the classic writers of the Christian tradition, and one echoed by Jean Gerson (1363–1429), chancellor of the University of Paris, at the start of the fifteenth century,[10] to distinguish three ways in which man can attain to a knowledge of God. First, as Paul suggests (Rom. 1:20), we can do so by applying the powers of our natural reason to the things of the world that manifest his creative activity. This way was traditionally called *natural* theology. Second, we can do so by scrutinizing his own revelation of himself as reported to us in the Scriptures. This way was *dogmatic* theology. Third and more mysteriously, it is possible for the devout soul

---

9. Cranmer, "An Answer to . . . Stephen Gardiner," in Cox, ed., 1:229.
10. See his *De mystica theologia speculativa*, Cons. 2; ed. Combes, pp. 7–8.

to be so "ravished above itself" as to achieve direct, intuitive, ecstatic experience of God. Dom David Knowles has said:

> Such at least is the traditional teaching of the Church, reinforced by the express declarations of theologians and saintly Christians throughout the centuries from the days of the apostles to our own time. This knowledge, this experience, which is never entirely separable from an equally immediate and experimental union with God by love, has three main characteristics. It is recognized by the person concerned as something utterly different from and more real and adequate than all his previous knowledge and love of God. It is experienced as something at once immanent and received, something moving and filling the powers of the mind and soul. It is felt as taking place at a deeper level of the personality and soul than that on which the normal processes of thought and will take place, and the mystic is aware, both in himself and in others, of the soul, its qualities, and of the divine presence and action within it, as something wholly distinct from the reasoning mind with its powers. Finally, this experience is wholly incommunicable, save as bare statement, and in this respect all the utterances of the mystics are entirely inadequate as representations of the mystical experience, but it brings absolute certainty to the mind of the recipient. This is the traditional mystical theology, the mystical knowledge of God, in its purest form.[11]

Whereas natural and dogmatic theology, the first two of these ways, were pursued with great vigor by the scholastic theologians during the quickening in intellectual activity that occurred in the High Middle Ages, the third was very much the beneficiary of the great awakening of spiritual life in the late eleventh and twelfth centuries. During those centuries the monastic histories of the Cistercians and Augustinian canons are punctuated by evidences of the revival of mystical religion. So, too, in the thirteenth century is that of the Franciscans. In the writings of St. Bernard and the Victorines, moreover, and in St. Bonaventure's masterpiece, the *Itinerarium mentis in deum* (1259), the mystical way found notable and extremely influential expression. But it was the fourteenth century that saw the greatest flowering of medieval mysticism, above all in Germany and

11. Knowles, *English Mystical Tradition*, pp. 2–3.

the Netherlands but also in England and, though to a much lesser degree, in Italy.

Although the Victorines had responded to the quickening philosophical currents of their day, they, like St. Bernard, had written in the context of a revitalized monastic piety, addressing themselves both explicitly and implicitly to a monastic readership of rather restricted nature. The mystics of the fourteenth century, on the other hand, not all of them members of monastic orders and writing usually in the vernacular rather than in Latin, were responding to a much more variegated clientele. Evelyn Underhill has said that "mysticism only becomes articulate when there is a public which craves for the mystical message."[12] The very existence and nature of that broader clientele attests to the continuing penetration into European society of a deeply interior piety capable of stimulating even outside the cloister that "naked entente directe unto God" required of those who aspired to cast themselves adrift on "the boundless sea of the Divinity."[13]

Thus, in Italy, though St. Catherine of Siena became affiliated with the Dominican Third Order, she was clearly an independent spirit and certainly no cloistered one, neither the product of a traditional monastic formation nor concerned in the *Dialogue* or the multitudinous letters that she dictated (for she was illiterate) to communicate with a merely monastic readership. She was, in fact, an activist, addressing herself to popes and cardinals in particular and to the Christian world in general. This last cannot be said of the English mystics of the period, for all appear to have been solitaries and the counselors of solitaries. But that itself implies withdrawal not only from the world at large but from the smaller world of monastic community as well. Thus, although Walter Hilton (d. 1396), author of *The Scale of Perfection* and other works, was an Augustinian canon, there is evidence to suggest that he had become a solitary

12. Underhill, p. 54.
13. The phrases cited occur, respectively, in *Cloud of Unknowing*, ed. Hodgson, p. 28, ll. 8–9 (also p. 58, ll. 15–16), and in Jan van Ruysbroeck's *De Gheestelike Brulocht*, trans. Colledge, p. 124.

when he wrote at least some of those works and that he wrote the first part of *The Scale* for the encouragement and guidance of a particular anchoress. Similarly, the anonymous author of *The Cloud of Unknowing* (flourished ca. 1380) was probably a solitary or hermit and *The Cloud* was addressed to another solitary. More strikingly, Richard Rolle (ca. 1300–1349), the hermit of Hampole and prolific author of English lyrics, letters, and commentaries as well as several Latin treatises, appears at no time of his life to have been either monk or priest. He addressed many of his writings to devout people in general, clerical and lay, thereby gaining for his work an enduring popularity that lasted right through into the sixteenth century. And of Julian of Norwich (1342–ca. 1416) it need only be said that she was a devout laywoman who, at the age of thirty and while still living at home with her mother, experienced a series of visions or "shewings" that transformed her life, leading her to become a recluse and years later, in an attempt to communicate what she had experienced and to convey its meaning, to write (or dictate) her *Revelations of Divine Love*.

The case of the great German mystics—Meister Eckhart (ca. 1260–1328), John Tauler (ca. 1300–1361), and Henry Suso (ca. 1295–1366)—is somewhat different. All three were Dominican friars usually discharging in their sermons and writings pastoral responsibilities toward nuns belonging to Dominican convents in the Rhineland. That context is itself revealing. The thirteenth century—a time when women, it seems, were beginning to live longer than men and to outnumber them[14]—had seen a veritable explosion in the number of women seeking a life of religious dedication, and the many new convents founded (Strasbourg alone had seven Dominican convents) proved inadequate to cope with the demand. In the towns of Germany and the Netherlands, therefore, the convents came to be surrounded by communities of Beguines, which continued to proliferate at an extraordinary rate into the early fourteenth century. The Beguines were religious women who belonged to no monastic order, lived in accordance with no official rule, took no formal vows,

14. Herlihy, especially pp. 6–7.

but, while continuing to pursue ordinary occupations, committed themselves to a community life of simplicity and celibacy. Like the comparable "Beghard" communities of laymen that came into existence during the same period, the Beguines were only minimally connected with the ecclesiastical authorities, and they were frequently suspected of heresy. And although ecclesiastical suspicions ran well ahead of the facts, as they so often did, heretical or quasi-heretical opinions undoubtedly did find a home in some communities. One such opinion, a mystical doctrine asserting the possibility of total unification in this life with the godhead and the concomitant redundancy of the ordinary sacramental ministrations of the church, it seems proper to attribute, in the light of their own writings, to the heretics known as the Brethren of the Free Spirit.[15]

In such suspicious circumstances, the ecclesiastical authorities were concerned to provide for religious bodies of women the type of skilled pastoral guidance that only an educated clergy could give. By decree of Pope Clement IV (1267) and of the German Dominican provincial (1286–87) the pastoral care of Dominican convents for women was entrusted to the theologians of the order. All three of the great German mystics of the fourteenth century were called upon to undertake such responsibilities. In their tracts and sermons, accordingly, they responded to the special needs of their charges, attempting to express the most profound speculations in the vernacular tongue and to relate what they were saying to the practical day-to-day exigencies of the devout life. Their efforts were so focused that the late Herbert Grundmann identified as the prerequisite for the emergence of "the complicated phenomenon" known as "German" mysticism this confluence of "Dominican theology and care of souls, vernacular preaching, feminine piety, and the special place that Germany occupied in the religious movements of the thirteenth and fourteenth centuries."[16] Nevertheless, it would be proper to note that Eckhart, Tauler, and Suso addressed themselves also to wider and

15. Though other, more exotic, doctrines and practices were attributed to them by their persecutors.
16. Grundmann, *Religiöse Bewegungen*, p. 527.

more varied audiences, preaching to Beguines and the laity at large. Suso was in correspondence with the Rhineland group of lay reformers and mystics who called themselves the Friends of God and from whose circle was later to emerge the compilation published by Luther under the title *A German Theology*. Additionally, Jan van Ruysbroeck (1293–1381), the greatest of the Flemish mystics, though he eventually became prior of a community of Augustinian canons, was for most of his life a secular priest, attempting in the vernacular writings that he addressed to laity and clergy alike to respond to that deep thirst for guidance in the life of the soul that had become widespread in the Flanders of his day.

The appearance in the fourteenth century of so distinguished and extensive a number of mystics bears witness to the wide dissemination during the two preceding centuries of the more individual and interior piety cultivated especially by the Cistercians and Franciscans, but it would be improper to give the impression that their teachings were at all uniform. No less improper, indeed, than it would be impossible in brief compass and in an intelligible fashion to convey the full range and variety of their thinking. But it has become something of a commonplace among historians to distinguish between two fundamental traditions of Christian mysticism.

The first tradition, espoused by the Cistercians and Franciscans and exemplified above all by such men as St. Bernard of Clairvaux and St. Bonaventure, responded to the Augustinian stress on will and love. The second, espoused by the Dominicans and best exemplified by Eckhart and Tauler, responded especially to the Neoplatonic strand in the thinking of St. Thomas Aquinas, to the newly available writings of the sixth-century Syrian monk whom we know as Pseudo-Dionysius, and to the further access opened to Neoplatonic ideas in 1264 by William of Moerbeke's translation of the *Institutio theologica* of Proclus (d. 485). The former is seen as a tradition of *affective* mysticism, locating in the will the movement of the questing soul toward encounter with God and understanding that encounter as an ecstatic communion of wills, human and divine. The latter tradition is envisaged as a more speculative, essentialist mysticism, locating in the intellect the movement toward encounter with the divine and understanding that encounter as the surging of like toward like, an ecstatic penetration into the supreme intelligence, a veritable union of essence in which the human is absorbed into God, like the spark returning to the fire, the drop of water merging with the wine.[17] The former tradition is portrayed as unambiguously orthodox; the latter, because of its pantheistic overtones, as suspect of heterodoxy. Less persuasively, perhaps, the former is labeled as characteristically Christocentric in its orientation, the latter as more remotely theocentric.

There is much to be said for this classification.[18] It provides a framework within which one can readily comprehend the suspicion of heterodoxy against which Eckhart, Tauler, Suso, and even Ruysbroeck had to contend, and suggests intriguing possibilities of correlation with a more universal typology recently proposed with Indian mysticism in mind but responding also to stages in psychological development.[19] Nevertheless, however tempting, that traditional classification still presents us with some serious difficulties. They have been variously identified.[20] On the one hand, the will clearly plays a more important role than that classification would suggest, even in the most essentialist of mystics such as Eckhart. Some scholars have found it possible, indeed, to argue (though not, I think, convincingly) that Tauler's understanding of the mystic encounter was not that of a union of essence but of a conformity of wills. On the other hand, in the work of mystics who are commonly classified as "affective," such as St. Bonaventure, the place of knowledge and intellect

17. On this and related images, see Lerner, "Image of Mixed Liquids."
18. Which Oberman endorses, though with suitable qualifications (*Harvest*, pp. 326–40).
19. Larson, "Mystical Man in India," an interesting article that attempts to go beyond the traditional historical or phenomenological approaches and to build on the anthropological and psychological insights of Erich Neumann and Erik Erikson. In particular, it contrasts the "unitive mystical experience," involving a sense of the bliss of undifferentiated unity and symbolized by the oneness of infancy, with the "copulative mystical experience," to which the presence of the "other" is essential and which is symbolized by the relationship of marriage and adult sexuality.
20. For a discussion of the relevant literature, see Ozment, "Mysticism, Nominalism, and Dissent," in Trinkaus and Oberman, eds., p. 68 and n. 1.

is not necessarily marginal. Nearly all of those mystics found it helpful to draw upon Neoplatonic ideas, whether directly from Latin
translations of Proclus and Plotinus or indirectly via the writings of
Pseudo-Dionysius or, indeed, via St. Augustine himself. And a work
as influential as the *German Theology* turns out to combine themes that
fit into both the "speculative" and "affective" traditions.

More disturbingly, however, though in so elusive an area of discourse the point can be advanced only with diffidence, too rigid an
insistence on the distinction between speculative and affective mysticism will serve us ill if it disposes us to miss the degree to which the
traditional "Augustinian" preoccupation with love and will so often
set the terms on which Neoplatonic ideas were absorbed by the writers of mystical works. Thus, the two Victorine authors who were very
influential in mediating the thinking of Pseudo-Dionysius to the late-
medieval world—Richard of St. Victor in the twelfth century and
Thomas Gallus, abbot of St. Andrew's at Vercelli, in the thirteenth
—reshaped that thinking by substituting for the characteristically Greek and Neoplatonic preoccupation with the role of intellect
in the mystical ascent the more traditional Augustinian emphasis on
will and love both in the life of contemplation and in the final ecstasy
of communion with God. The influence of Richard of St. Victor on
late-medieval mysticism needs no emphasis, but it should perhaps be
pointed out that Gallus was the author both of a commentary on
Pseudo-Dionysius and of the Latin translation on which the author of
The Cloud of Unknowing, for example, depended in making his own
English version of Pseudo-Dionysius's *De mystica theologia* and also in
coming to terms with the thought of that author.[21] Thus, if in *The
Cloud* itself he insists that the words of Pseudo-Dionysius "wilen
clearly aferme al that I have seyde or schal sey,"[22] the mystic union

21. Thus, in the prologue to his translation (which he entitles *Deonise Hid Divinite*),
he says that "in translacioun of it, I have not onliche folowed the nakid lettre of the
text, bot for to declare the hardness of it, I have moche folowed the sentence of the
Abbot of Sainte Victore [Thomas Gallus], a noble and a worthi expositour of this same
book" (in Hodgson, ed., *Deonise Hid Divinite*, p. 2, ll. 8–12).
22. Hodgson, ed., *Cloud*, p. 125, ll. 13–14, a comment to which the author refers in
the prologue to *Deonise Hid Divinite* (ed. Hodgson, p. 2, ll. 5–8).

envisaged by that book is unquestionably a union of will and love "for onli love may reche to God in this liif, bot not knowing." [23]

In all of this, it may be suggested, if we avoid too exclusive a preoccupation with the high intellectualism of Eckhart and his Dominican followers, we can see at work in late-medieval mysticism (and despite the renewed infusion of Neoplatonic modes of thought) a force that had persistently made itself felt whenever philosophical views of Greek provenance had come into contact with the nonphilosophic understanding of the human and the divine enshrined in the pages of the Bible. It was a force massively at work in the thinking of even so ardent a Neoplatonist as Augustine; it was a force that had set a limit to Aquinas's absorption of Aristotle; it was a force that made its presence felt most dramatically in the thinking of Duns Scotus (ca. 1266–1308), William of Ockham (ca. 1285–1349), and the nominalist philosophers and theologians who became so prominent in the intellectual world of the fourteenth and fifteenth centuries. Perhaps more surprisingly, it was a force that left its mark also on the rather somber vision of man framed by such luminaries of Italian Renaissance thought as Petrarch, Coluccio Salutati (1331–1406), and Lorenzo Valla (1405–57). And what was it? Nothing other, in fact, than the biblical doctrine of creation and the notion of a transcendent and omnipotent divinity that it presupposed.

No matter how open to philosophies of Greek provenance Christian thinkers imagined themselves to be, they undermined the very foundations of those philosophies when they attempted to combine them, as repeatedly they did, with the biblical God of power and might. He could not be identified in characteristically Greek fashion with the rational order of an eternal cosmos in which man himself partook, but was instead a transcendent God of power and unimpeded will upon whose inscrutable decision that order, the universe itself, and all its human denizens were radically contingent.

Given this fact, there is much to be said for a recent attempt to bracket the difference between speculative mysticism and affective

23. Hodgson, ed., *Cloud*, p. 33, l. 11. Cf. Knowles, *Mystical Tradition*, pp. 66–69.

mysticism, to understand the late-medieval mystics, instead, within a common conceptual framework based on a crucial distinction that attained great prominence among the scholastic theologians of the late Middle Ages, especially among those of the nominalist persuasion.[24] The distinction between the absolute power of God and his ordained power (*potentia dei absoluta, potentia dei ordinata*) reflected the determination of medieval theologians to affirm the freedom and omnipotence of God and the ultimate dependence upon his untrammeled will of his creation, of the moral norms imposed on man, and of the whole sacramental and ecclesiastical machinery. Current research is making it clear that the distinction was itself susceptible of more than one meaning. The meaning that came to the fore in the late Middle Ages, which is sometimes signaled in the texts by the substitution of the word "ordinary" for "ordained" (*potentia ordinaria* for *potentia ordinata*), and which is in question here, is the distinction between the way in which God ordinarily acts—in accordance, that is, with the particular order (natural, moral, ecclesiastical) he has actually chosen to establish—and those extraordinary acts of untrammeled omnipotence in which he sets aside or acts apart from that order.

This distinction is relevant to the understanding of medieval mysticism because, as Ozment explains,

> in the practical terms of medieval religious life and theological debate, the *potentia Dei ordinata* was simply the church with her orthodox doctrines and sacraments, which embodied God's "revealed will." And the *potentia Dei absoluta* was that sphere of divine freedom above and beyond this chosen system of salvation. Concretely, the former represented the "establishment"; the latter the permanent possibility of historical novelty.

And "mysticism in the late Middle Ages," he goes on to suggest, "can be called a commonsense science of a presently active *potentia Dei*

---

24. For this attempt, see Ozment, "Mysticism, Nominalism, and Dissent," in Trinkaus and Oberman, eds., pp. 66–92; also Ozment, *Mysticism and Dissent*, especially pp. 1–60.

absoluta." The Bible tells us that on the road to Damascus God broke through the normal willed regularities of the order of salvation to convert Paul, and the mystical thinker's "most basic building block is the biblical witness to God's sovereign freedom to operate beyond what he himself has established as normative."[25] Whatever their persuasion and however they construed the mystic encounter, all such thinkers believed that in the profounder reaches of the soul there exists an ineluctable orientation to the divine, a "spark of the will" (*synteresis voluntatis*), a "peak of the mind" (*apex mentis*), a "ground of the soul" (*Seelengrund*), a receptacle that only God can fill, "an eternal hunger," as Ruysbroeck described it, "that shall never be appeased."[26] And it is here, in the moment of mystic communion, with a "steryng of love—that is the werk of only God,"[27] and in an omnipotent departure from the covenanted and corporate regularities of his order of salvation, that God establishes an immediate and direct contact with the individual soul.

Of this direct, noninstitutional, and quintessentially individual encounter with the divine much was to be made later on by Sebastian Franck (d. ca. 1542), Thomas Müntzer (d. 1525), and other radical reformers of the sixteenth century, who plundered the writings of the late-medieval mystics in an anxious quest to justify direct and personal revelations superseding not only the doctrinal traditionalism of Rome but also (and more alarmingly for their Protestant contemporaries) the purified scripturalism of Wittenberg, Zurich, and Geneva.[28] Their emphasis, however, should not dispose us to view the late-medieval mystics as in this respect necessarily their forerunners. Even if their own orthodoxy was sometimes suspect, those mystics were fundamentally men and women of the church, themselves the products of her disciplines, urging upon their disciples the reception of her sacraments, warning them against the seductions of those she

25. Ozment, *Mysticism and Dissent*, p. 2.
26. Ruysbroeck, *Spiritual Espousals*, 2:xxi; trans. in Colledge, p. 140.
27. Hodgson, ed., *Cloud*, p. 62, l. 2.
28. See Ozment, *Mysticism and Dissent*, pp. 14–16. Cf. Hegler, p. 13, for an earlier assertion of a link between the views of Franck and those of the late medieval mystics.

had branded as heretics, defending even on some debatable issues the integrity of her public authority, and sharing, several of them, in the exercise of that authority.

The point could be illustrated at length. In the struggle between John XXII and Lewis of Bavaria, both Tauler and Suso sided with the pope. As provincial of the Saxon province of his order from 1303 to 1311, Eckhart was deeply involved in ecclesiastical administration; he was also an ardent believer in the efficacy of frequent communion.[29] In the struggle against mystical heterodoxy in the Brussels region, Ruysbroeck campaigned, it seems, with great vigor. And so on. But perhaps the classic statement that Julian of Norwich made in describing her visions or "shewings" will suffice:

> I am not good because of the shewing, but only if I love God the better. . . . And I am sure that there are many that never have shewing nor sight except of the common teaching of Holy Church, who love God better than I. . . . [I]n all things I believe as Holy Church preacheth and teacheth. For the faith of Holy Church, of which I had understanding beforehand and which, I hope by the grace of God, I will fully keep in use and in custom, stood continually in my sight. It was my will and meaning never to accept anything that could be contrary thereto. With this intent and with this meaning I beheld the shewing with all my diligence. For in all this blessed shewing I beheld it [the sight and the faith] as one in God's meaning.[30]

There is no reason for us to doubt the sincerity of such affirmations. But the fact remains that their contemporaries did not always take them at face value—at least in the case of the more speculative Rhineland mystics. And that fact is not wholly irrelevant to the emergence in the Low Countries of the type of piety that was known as *Devotio moderna*.

Monastic Piety and the *Devotio moderna*

The "new devotion" was of modest origins. It stemmed from the struggle of Geert Groote (1340–84), son of a draper in the small com-

---

29. See e.g., Eckhart, *Talks of Instruction*, no. 20; trans. in Blakney, pp. 27–30.
30. In Walsh, pp. 61–62.

mercial town of Deventer in the eastern Netherlands, to find a mode of religious life congruent with his own highly personal spiritual instincts. A master of arts of the University of Paris, he had pursued higher studies in theology, medicine, and law, and, though not in priestly orders, had obtained several benefices when, at some point after 1370, he encountered his moment of truth. At that time, under the influence of an old friend, Henry Eger, prior of the Carthusian monastery of Monnikhuizen, he withdrew to that house for a period of reading and reflection, steeping himself in the spirituality of the Rhineland mystics and especially of Ruysbroeck, whose supporter and disciple in many ways he became. His own aspirations, however, became neither clearly monastic nor fully mystical.[31] They involved a life of service in the world and partook of a combination of cautious practicality in spiritual matters and uncompromising rigor in the realm of morality. In the ten years between 1374 and his death, having disposed of his benefices and of some of his property and accepted ordination as a deacon (he thought himself unworthy of the priesthood), he embarked upon a life of personal austerity and public rigor, preaching in the region around Deventer and the neighboring towns of Kampen, Zwolle, and Windesheim, attacking immorality and the heresy of the Free Spirit but reserving what were perhaps his sharpest barbs for monks who held too lightly their vows of poverty and secular clerics tainted with simony or guilty of concubinage. The very vigor of his onslaught stimulated a clamor of opposition that led indirectly to the bishop's eventual withdrawal of his license to preach—a decision from which Groote appealed to the pope but which he respected and which was still in force when he died in 1384.

Before his death, however, he had turned his house in Deventer over to a community of religious women and given them an order of life in accordance with which they were to remain laywomen, taking no vows and adopting no habit, working for a living and striving to pursue in common a life of service to God. From this community grew

---

31. Cf. his "Conclusa et Proposita, non vota in nomine domini," in Pohl, 7:97: ". . . malum esset etiam propter contemplationem pietatem et justitiam quod per aliam fieri non posset deserere et proximi utilitates pias."

the later Sisters of the Common Life. Similarly, the nucleus of the future Brothers of the Common Life had emerged under his direction in the group of laymen pursuing a common life at the vicarage of Florens Radewijns (1350–1400), the only one of his immediate disciples whom Groote had encouraged to take priestly orders. Finally, in 1387, in establishing at Windesheim a community of Augustinian canons, Radewijns acted upon an idea that Groote had died too soon to realize, making available a fully monastic life for those among the brothers who felt called to that state.

By the end of the fifteenth century, houses of all these groups— Brothers and Sisters of the Common Life and Augustinian canons of the Windesheim congregation—had multiplied and were to be found throughout the region that now forms Holland and Belgium, in the Rhineland in general, and across a good part of western Germany as well. And in both types of community, nonmonastic as well as monastic, was cultivated, developed, and preserved the mode of piety to which the Windesheimers[32] Thomas à Kempis—of Kempen— (1380–1471) and John Busch (1399–1479) themselves attached the name *Devotio moderna*. The new devotion found its most notable and extraordinarily influential expression in the collection of four books that it now seems safe to attribute to Thomas à Kempis and that is known under the title *The Imitation of Christ*. By using the name *Devotio moderna*, these men reveal that they themselves assumed that there was something new and distinctive about their form of spirituality. Unfortunately, neither they nor their successors quite succeeded in pinpointing wherein that novel and distinctive character consisted, and historians have naturally felt impelled to remedy that failure.

Until quite recently, the general tendency was to emphasize the element of novelty and, with much flourishing of the *Imitation of Christ*, to portray the *Devotio moderna* very much as a harbinger of things to come. Thus it has been seen to reflect a disgusted turning away from the arid and convoluted speculations of the nominalist

32. I use this expression to refer not simply to those who belonged to the house at Windesheim but to all the Augustinian canons belonging to the Windesheim Congregation.

theology ("What availeth a man to reason high secret mysteries of
the Trinity, if he lacks meekness, whereby he displeaseth the Trinity?
. . . I had rather feel compunction of heart for my sins, than only to
know the definition of compunction" [*Imitation*, I, 1; p. 4]).[33] Or it
has been considered a cultivation in corporate fashion, as it were, of
the mysticism of the fourteenth-century Rhinelanders and especially
of Ruysbroeck ("Betwixt Almighty God and a devout soul there are
many ghostly visitings, sweet inward consolations, much heavenly
peace, and wondrous familiarity of the blessed presence of God"
[*Imitation*, II, 1; p. 59]). Or, again, it has been found to foster Christian humanism (no fuel, admittedly, in the *Imitation* for this). It has
even been seen as emphasizing an interior and individualistic piety
that tends to bypass the external sacramental mediation of the church
and points in the direction of the Protestant Reformation (only in the
fourth book of the *Imitation* is the Eucharist discussed). At the same
time, it has also been portrayed as involving a stress on a lively,
meditative piety to which the eucharistic ministrations of the church
were absolutely central and which flowed right on into the Catholic
Reformation of the sixteenth century (the fourth book of the *Imitation*
treats of nothing else: "It is a great mystery; and great the dignity of
priests, to whom it is granted that is not granted to Angels. For only
priests that be duly ordained in the Church have power to sing Mass
and to consecrate the Body of Christ" [*Imitation*, IV, 5; p. 236]).

A somewhat livelier sense of the historical context in which the
Devotio moderna emerged and flourished, a more intensive scrutiny of
the lives and writings of those who sustained it, and a much more
acute sense of its development across time have brought most of these
claims into question.[34] Thus there is not much to be said for seeing
in it any marked reaction to nominalism as such. Though it is by
no means a central motif in his writings, Groote himself does appear

33. These and all subsequent references to the *Imitation* are given to the translation of
Richard Whytford (1556), ed. Raynal.
34. See especially Post, *Modern Devotion*. It should be noted that this book—the
summa, as it were, of revisionist work on the subject—is not simply a translation of
the same author's earlier *De Moderne Devotie, Geert Groote en zijn stichtingen* (Amsterdam, 1940; repr. 1950), but a different and much more extensive work.

to have rejected the nominalist theory of knowledge. There is some reason, however, to doubt that many of his followers would even have known what that theory was. It was not, apparently, of interest to them. Their rejection was of a different sort; it was a rejection of everything that would hinder or distract from a rigorous life of interior devotion and loving imitation of Christ. That rejection included higher education, academic theology, and, indeed, the study of "anything which does not refresh the soul."[35] The brothers were not given university educations. From those of their reading lists that have come down to us not only the nominalist authors are missing, but the scholastic theologians in general. In their reading they applied themselves, instead, to the fervent scrutiny of the Scriptures and of such spiritual writers as St. Augustine, Richard of St. Victor, St. Bonaventure, and, above all, John Cassian (d. 434)—author of those great classics of ascetic literature the *Institutiones* and *Collationes*. With this general attitude of reserve toward higher education, of course, it would have been odd if the brothers had exercised any great leadership in the introduction of humanist ideas into northern Europe. The tendency, therefore, has been to downgrade their contribution in this respect, to point out that until about 1480 their involvement in teaching went no further than the exercise of pastoral care over the schoolboys attending the neighboring city schools, especially those lodging in their hostels whom they would often try to help with their lessons. In the early days, indeed, the brothers required any teacher who entered their ranks to relinquish his teaching post as incompatible with his religious profession. Only at the end of the fifteenth century, it turns out, did they move to set up a few schools of their own and to permit individual brothers to teach at such city schools as that at Deventer, which Erasmus attended between 1478 and 1483, but which was certainly not under their control. All of this, it seems likely, was too little and too late to enable them to play any major or determinative role in the introduction of humanism into northern

---

35. Thus Lubbert ten Bosch, "Collecta quaedam ex devotis exercitiis domini Lubberti," in Pohl, 7:265–66. Cf. Post, *Modern Devotion*, p. 258.

Europe, and their once much-vaunted part in this process has become
of late, therefore, very much a *quaestio disputata*.

More surprisingly, perhaps, their reputation as cultivators and dis-
seminators of the spirituality of the Rhineland and Flemish mystics
has been challenged, and decisively so. Reader and admirer of Ruysbroeck Groote himself certainly was. But if he thought well enough of
some of Ruysbroeck's works to translate them, he was nervous that
others might not properly be understood by the uninstructed, and he
explicitly stated his antipathy toward those would-be mystics of his
own day who were willing to speculate loosely about the union of
human and divine and to preach that "whatever God is by nature, that
we can become through grace." [36] His disciples would seem to have
taken that nervousness and antipathy as their point of departure and
ended by ignoring the Rhenish and Flemish mystics altogether. None
of them appear on the reading lists, not even Ruysbroeck, and R. R.
Post has argued that of all the "New Devotionalists" only the Windesheimers Henry Mande (d. 1431) and Gerlach Peters (d. 1411) can be
said to have espoused a full-fledged mysticism. [37] Certainly, Thomas
à Kempis does not do so in the *Imitation*. Intense individualists in
their piety these advocates of the *Devotio moderna* certainly were, and
the *Imitation* can furnish ample evidence for that claim, but it was an
individualism moving wholly within the ambit established by the
potentia Dei ordinata. It was a religious individualism, in other words,
that did not reach beyond (let alone call into question) and, in effect,
presupposed that whole sacramental and ecclesiastical system of salvation which Catholic orthodoxy proclaimed to be of divine ordination.

That conclusion, of course, is directly relevant to any attempt to
relate the *Devotio moderna* to the teachings of the Protestant Reformers. One should not ignore the fact that among those of the Brothers
and Sisters of the Common Life and of the Windesheimers who actually encountered Lutheran ideas, the overwhelming majority appear

36. ". . . et quicquid Deus est per naturam, hoc nos efficimur per gratiam," in Mulder, Ep. 31, p. 136. Cf. Leclercq et al., pp. 513–14.
37. Post, *Modern Devotion*, pp. 331–42.

to have reacted to them with characteristically conservative aversion. The amount of criticism heaped upon the brothers, especially in their early days, makes it altogether too easy to assume that there *must* have been something at least implicitly heterodox about them and to miss how very orthodox their commitments were and how fundamentally traditional their ways. Even the most respectable of Beguines and Beghards had had to struggle hard to avert ecclesiastical hostility, and the brothers, as Groote had himself foreseen, were forced to do likewise. At the same time that the mendicant orders felt themselves attacked by the brothers' rejection of begging, the diocesan clergy were reluctant to hand over to them the cure of souls in the houses of the sisters. But when at the Council of Constance the Dominican Matthew Grabow took up his accusations against both brothers and sisters, they found powerful and unimpeachable protectors in the persons of Cardinal Pierre d'Ailly (1350–1420) and his former pupil Jean Gerson. The condemnation that the council handed down was directed, therefore, not at the Brethren but at Grabow.

Finally, it is simply incorrect to classify as representatives of the *Devotio moderna* the theologians John Pupper of Goch and Wessel Gansfort, both of them sufficiently suspect in their doctrinal views to have been regarded as "Reformers before the Reformation." Despite allegations to the contrary, Pupper appears to have had nothing to do with either the brothers or the Windesheimers, and though Gansfort respected their ideals and had fairly extensive contacts with them, he never entered their ranks and certainly did not learn his theology from them. Both were university men, pursuing the type of interest in scholastic theology eschewed by the Devotionalists. And the same must be said of another theologian, Gabriel Biel (d. 1495), who joined the brothers only late in life and was unique in combining a university professorship at Tübingen with the office of prior of the brothers at Urach.

So far as anticipations of the Reformation are concerned, then, we are left very much with the alleged tendency of the Devotionalists to bracket or bypass the sacramental mediations of the visible church, to turn away from the externalities of religion so prominent in their own day in order to pursue instead a life of interior devotion. Despite repeated affirmations of such charges, however, surprisingly little can be said on their behalf. So far as ecclesiastical authority is concerned, the attitude of the Devotionalists was unimpeachable. Like Tauler and Suso before them, the brothers, sisters, and canons of the Utrecht diocese accepted exile from 1426 to 1432 rather than breach the interdict that the pope had imposed upon that diocese as a result of a disputed election. Their faith in ecclesiastical authority was such, indeed, that they appear to have made sure that they acquired the indulgences attached to so many of the prayers they said. Thus, writing in 1503, a brother from the Harderwijk house emphasizes the value during the canonical hours of bowing the head at the *Gloria Patri*: not only can it serve to revive the attention, it is also required if the indulgences are to be secured.[38]

Given these facts, it is appropriate also to accept only with the severest of reservations any notion that the Modern Devotionalists ignored the externals of religion. Their concern, rather, was to try to ground such "works" in the good intentions that were vital to their fruitfulness. Vigils, images, the rosary, indulgences—these, it seems, they accepted as a matter of course, and if we are prone to recall the assertion of the *Imitation of Christ* that "they that go much on pilgrimage be seldom thereby made perfect and holy" (*Imitation*, I, 23; p. 45), perhaps we should also recall that Thomas à Kempis was a monk committed to the ideal of stability, writing specifically for monks pursuing the contemplative life, and persistently concerned to exclude or downgrade anything not conducive to that life. Indeed, we would do well to recall in general the degree to which the context of the *Devotio moderna* was monastic or quasi-monastic and to remember what that meant. For the Windesheimers it meant, in fact, an enclosed life differing from that of other monasteries mainly in the rigor of their customs and observance and in the fact that they had restored manual labor (in the guise of book copying) to its ancient place in the daily routine. One of their primary and most time-

38. Ibid., pp. 400–401.

consuming occupations was the singing in choir of the canonical hours. Unlike the canons, the brothers took neither vows nor habit and exercised pastoral duties both among the schoolboys attending the local schools and among the sisters. But their mode of religious life was otherwise not so very different. If, as a community, they sang only part of the hours, they prayed the rest. Much of their devotion, like that of both the canons and the sisters, centered on the daily mass, communion being received, in the monastic fashion of the day, every other week and on major feast days. When the author of the *Imitation* downgraded the veneration of relics (he did not reject it), he did so, after all, not in a void but in explicit comparison with the worth of devotion to the Eucharist—for "Thou, my Lord God, my Lord Jesus Christ, God and Man, are here wholly present in the Sacrament of the Altar, where the fruit of everlasting health is had plenteously, as oft as Thou are worthily and devoutly received" (*Imitation*, IV, 1; p. 225).

The intensely private and individualistic nature of this eucharistic devotion has often been remarked. In the absence, however, of any attempt to recover the more corporate patristic understanding that had been lost so many centuries earlier, it is hard to envisage what other form that devotion could well have taken, apart from that of trying to move beyond the merely ritual observance of externals and of using the mass as an occasion to stimulate and deepen through meditation what was essentially an inward piety.[39] In this, as in all their practices, the Devotionalists were concerned not to reject the traditional externalities of medieval religion but through assiduous application, meditation, and the removal of worldly distractions to infuse them for the individual practitioner with a rich interior significance—one hinging, characteristically, on the life and example of Christ and designed to foster a tender piety toward his humanity. In

---

39. Thus *Imitation*, IV, 2; p. 230: "Therefore thou oughtest always with a new renewing of mind to dispose thee to it, and with a well-advised and a deep consideration to think on this as new and as pleasant a joy and comfort when thou singest Mass or hearest it, as if Christ the same day first entered into the womb of the Virgin, and were made Man, or if He the same day suffered and died upon the cross for the health of mankind."

this, too, as in so many of their practices, they must be judged to have looked backward to the type of piety developed and disseminated by the Cistercians and Franciscans before them (and which they, indeed, continued to deepen) rather than forward to anything specific to sixteenth-century Protestantism. If they are to be said, indeed, to have looked forward to anything at all, it must surely have been to the piety certainly of Erasmus, perhaps also of the Catholic Reformation.[40] For whatever one makes of the alleged influence upon Ignatius of Loyola's meditational method of the *Rosetum*, or *Rosary of Spiritual Exercises*, written by the Windesheimer John Mombaer (d. 1501), Ignatius is said to have esteemed the *Imitation of Christ* above all other devotional writings, and the spiritual affinity is clear enough.

We are left with the question of what was distinctive about the *Devotio moderna*. By no means easy to answer, the question is best approached by an attempt to locate and understand the new devotion and the institutions that sustained it in the history of monasticism and of monastic piety. In this connection Vandenbroucke has suggested the existence of a certain analogy between the conditions prevailing in the monastic world in the last years of the twelfth century and of the fourteenth century.[41] The suggestion is a fruitful one. By the end of the twelfth century the traditional type of monastic life was no longer satisfying either the needs of the church at large or the aspirations of all those who aspired to a life of more than ordinary religious commitment. In this context surfaced the twin impulses that led on the one hand to the multiplication of communities of Beghards and Beguines and on the other to the creation of the great international orders of mendicant friars. By the end of the fourteenth century, in turn, the Beghard and Beguine movement was in decline and the friars had lost their earlier vitality. And in that context surfaced the impulse that produced Geert Groote and led to the emergence of the *Devotio moderna*.

But that impulse, it should not be forgotten, discharged itself

40. The reference, of course, is to Erasmus's religiosity, *not* to his scholarly interests.
41. In Leclercq et al., p. 489.

along more than one line. In the first place, it sparked the move leading to the foundation at Windesheim of a monastery of Augustinian canons regular and in the course of time to the foundation or co-option of other monasteries that came to be grouped together in the Windesheim congregation. On the face of it a rather conservative move, reverting to a form of monastic life that predated the appearance even of the mendicant orders and was nourished, if the reading lists do not deceive us, on a very traditional diet of scriptural and devotional reading.[42] And yet it was these Windesheimers who produced most of the literature that we associate with the *Devotio moderna*.

There is nothing paradoxical about this. At the end of his great study of the monastic and religious orders of medieval England, Dom David Knowles identifies the following as prominent among the factors contributing to the relaxation of religious life in the majority of English monasteries: the increasing frequenting of universities by the monks, occasioning prolonged absences from the cloister and calling for a variety of dispensations and privileges; the relaxation of the Rule in relation to fasting, abstinence, the possession of private property, and other matters of daily life; the lack of the type of purposeful and satisfying daily occupation that the copying of books had once provided; and the failure to develop any sort of spiritual method or meditative practice going beyond the spiritual stimulus provided by the liturgy or by the prayerful reading of the Scriptures, the fathers, and the great spiritual writings of the twelfth century.[43]

A comparison with the practices of the Windesheimer houses is instructive. There none of the destructive factors was at work: none of the canons were sent to university; the Rule was maintained in all its rigor; the copying of books was pursued with a degree of intensity, commitment, and concentration that had few parallels in earlier centuries; from the start a persistent attempt was made to cultivate a deep interior piety by using the little things of daily life as stimuli to brief meditations or "ruminations" on the life of Christ, and, over the

---

42. Thus Post, *Modern Devotion*, p. 322, stresses the marked impact of John Cassian upon the spirituality of Florens Radewijns.
43. Knowles, *Religious Orders*, 2:456–68.

course of time, a shift occurred to the more systematic and methodical
techniques of meditation that find expression in Mombaer's *Rosetum*.[44] The most novel thing in all of this was, if anything, the degree
to which the Windesheimers succeeded in holding on to a bitter-
sweet sense of how very great had been the fervor of their monastic
predecessors "in the beginning of their religion" and of how very
quickly that "first fervor" could be lost—hence their own dogged determination that "the desire to profit in virtue" should not fall asleep
in them" (*Imitation* I, 18; p. 29). Because of that determination they
came to assume throughout their region a position of leadership in the
"Observantine" movement of monastic reform that made itself felt across Europe during the late fourteenth and fifteenth centuries and in
more than one of the monastic and religious orders.

In the second place, the Devotionalist impulse led to the appearance of the Brothers and Sisters of the Common Life. With their initial willingness (in the case of the brothers) to mix clerics and layfolk
in a single community, their initial lack (in the case of both brothers
and sisters) of formal vows and distinctive habit, their commitment
nonetheless to lives of celibacy, obedience, individual poverty, and
possession of goods in common, they may be said to have carved out
new middle ground somewhere between the positions of the traditional monastic orders and those of the Beghards and Beguines. The
sisters, it is true, both individually and as communities, betrayed a
persistent tendency to move toward the adoption of a fully monastic
status. That tendency was not lacking among the brothers, either, for
many of whom a period of life in a brother house served as a prepara-
tion, testing ground, or way stage en route to the cloister. But for
most of them their choice of way of life was a distinctive one, more
moderate, more experimental, more hesitant even. It was a choice
that conveys a humble sense that the higher peaks of the spiritual life
might well not be for them, that it was preferable to make the ascent
step by cautious step and to take it day by routine day than to reach too
high, as had so many religious before them, only to fall so very low. It

44. Though they too, as Constable reminds us ("Twelfth-Century Spirituality," pp.
47–48), had their roots in the twelfth century.

was a choice, accordingly, that was a good deal less secure for the community as a whole, which, unlike a monastery, did not possess the coercive legal power to force back a brother who chose to leave, but was more responsive, despite its undoubted rigor, to the weakness of the individual brother whose life was simply not to be bent to the maintenance of lifelong vows he might find himself unable to sustain. As one of them wrote in 1490, addressing himself to this very issue of coercion:

> We are not Religious, but we wish and strive to live in the world religiously. . . . Since, moreover, our way of life issues and has issued from a core of devotion, it would be unfitting for us to establish so many and so burdensome obstacles [*dispendia*] to reputation, peace, tranquillity, concord and chastity. For there is a great difference between our voluntary life as Brothers and the rules, statutes and irrevocable necessity governing those who are Religious. If their monasteries go to rack and ruin through the presence of unstable and undisciplined monks, how much sooner, therefore, would the life of the Brothers be destroyed by the coerced presence of increased numbers of such rebellious and unstable members.[45]

Within the framework established by that choice, however, and under urban conditions a good deal more distracting and certainly closer to the secular rhythms of ordinary daily life, they set out to cultivate very much the same type of meditative and intensely inward piety as that of their monastic cousins. Their success made their example an unusually compelling one, especially when, having become an almost wholly clerical body, they began to discharge pastoral duties among the boys attending the urban schools. It was in the hostels established by the brothers for those schoolboys that many a future priest or monk discovered his vocation, and their influence on the religious life of northwest Europe grew in time to be enormous. But "influence" is a deplorably flexible word, and before turning to the more "popular" levels of that religious life, we should call to mind the *caveat* that Post issued at both the beginning and the end of his study of the *Devotio moderna*. "One must not take it for granted," he said,

---

45. "De coercendis inconstancie filii," in Doebner, ed., p. 113.

"that everyone who showed any signs of piety at the end of the Middle Ages, or who was assumed to be devout, belonged to the Modern Devotion."[46]

Popular Piety at the End of the Middle Ages

Delaruelle's remark that "we are better informed about the abuses of the fifteenth century than we are about the virtues of the thirteenth"[47] relates with particular force to our knowledge of the religious sensibilities of the broader masses of city and country dwellers. About the modes of piety prevalent among the less articulate strata of society throughout the Middle Ages we know very much less than we do about the spirituality of the elites. And although we are increasingly better informed in this respect for the later Middle Ages than for the earlier period, that fact generates its own problems. As the evidence continues to accrue—evidence concerning the quality of popular preaching, the survival in the villages of magical and quasi-pagan practices, the activities of confraternities, the nature of legacies left for religious purposes, the means of religious instruction, the range of liturgical and paraliturgical rites, the dissemination of popular devotional literature—it is hard to know what to make of it all, what to compare it with, from what perspective to view it.

The problem is exacerbated not only by the existence of regional and local variations but also by the fact that so much of what we have come to know has been gleaned from the exhortations of such popular preachers as St. Bernardino of Siena (d. 1444); the propaganda of such would-be reformers as Pierre d'Ailly and Nicholas of Clémanges (d. 1437); the proposals of such reform groups as the compilation known as the *Capitula agendorum*, which emanated from Parisian reforming circles on the eve of the Council of Constance; and the criticisms recorded during visitations like the notable one Nicholas of Cusa (1401–64) undertook as papal legate to the Germanies in 1451–52, or those conducted during the same century by St. Antonino and

46. Post, *Modern Devotion*, pp. xi, 676.
47. Delaruelle et al., 1:xi. Cf. the remarks of Hay, pp. 72–73.

others in Tuscany and in the diocese of Bologna by Niccolò Albergati (who even "found it necessary to reiterate an injunction of one of his predecessors that no one could celebrate mass who was not ordained as a priest").[48] Valuable though such sources are, they naturally focus on what was going wrong, on what their authors wished to denounce in the current religious scene as abuses or corruptions. We are left accordingly, with the problem of deciding how prevalent such abuses really were and whether they represent a downward trend in the quality of religious life or an upward shift in the level of clerical expectations.

A similar difficulty attaches to any use one might be tempted to make of insights and information gleaned from the strictures the Protestant Reformers heaped upon the religious practices of their medieval forebears. Having broken with the old church, they can scarcely be expected to have wanted to represent its customs and ceremonies in a favorable light. Indeed, understandably eager to denounce the more palpable abuses in late-medieval religious life, they were almost as quick to condemn some of the less incontestably pernicious practices—deriding, for example, as "feeding upon the dead" (*Totenfresserei*) the traditional rounds of masses for the deceased.[49] Many were willing to portray in similarly derisive light the very sacramental ministrations of the church. Thus the confessional became "a schooling in sin"; the sacrament of confirmation "plain sorcery, devilry, witchcraft, juggling, legerdemain, and all that naught is"; the Roman mass itself "nothing better to be esteemed than the verses of the sorcerer or enchanter."[50]

In handling the growing bulk of evidence concerning the popular piety of the late Middle Ages, one is tempted to assimilate the more

---

48. Hay, pp. 56–57. The text of the *Capitula agendorum* is printed in Finke, 4:548–83. Finke endorses the traditional but improper ascription of the compilation of this work to d'Ailly.
49. See Ozment, *Reformation in the Cities*, p. 95; also pp. 111–16, for a discussion of Pamphilius Gegenbach's popular versified play *Die Totenfresser* (1521), in which the sacristan says to the priest: "I like dead people better than fighting and screwing / They are our food and drink."
50. Ozment, *Reformation in the Cities*, p. 53; Thomas, *Religion and the Decline of Magic*, pp. 53, 56.

novel aspects of what we now know to familiar patterns long since laid down, to take one's cues from the compelling unified picture of religious life in France and Burgundy that Johan Huizinga painted over half a century ago in his *Waning of the Middle Ages*, a powerfully evocative picture in which superstition, irreverence, and mechanical formalism are tinted with the hues of morbidity, overripeness, decay.[51] Certainly there is enough and more to render plausible such an approach. This was an era set apart from the century preceding it by the onset of widespread famine and economic depression, by the recrudescence of prolonged and devastating warfare, and, from 1347 onward, by the repeated and traumatizing visitations of plague. It was an era set off from most that had gone before and all that were to follow (with the chastening exception of the twentieth century) by the incidence of death on an unimaginably massive scale. Small wonder, then, that it was an era during which spiritual activities were often pursued in an atmosphere of "pitched religious excitement"[52] and religious feelings frequently expressed in extreme and violent form. Small wonder, too, that religious phenomena that smack to us of the pathological periodically surfaced.

Most dramatic among these phenomena were the numerous companies of flagellants that made their appearance contemporaneously with the first ravages of the Black Death. They rose with apparent spontaneity, amid scenes of frenzied popular acclaim, in Austria, Bohemia, Germany, the Netherlands, and elsewhere. Composed mainly of laymen concerned to atone for their own sins and to assuage the inexplicable wrath of God, these itinerant bands, sometimes several hundred strong, pledged themselves to obey a "master" and committed themselves to a mode of life and a ritual performance that appears to have varied little from place to place. They confessed their sins to the master, avoided their wives, eschewed all dealings with women, flagellated twice a day in public and once during the night in private, and undertook to pursue the whole grim regimen for a fixed

---

51. See especially *Waning*, pp. 124–181.
52. Ozment, *Reformation in the Cities*, p. 20, citing Gertrud Rüchlin-Teuscher, pp. 37, 163.

period of thirty-three and a half days in commemoration of Christ's earthly life. The atmosphere generated by their gruesome activities seems usually to have been one of great solemnity and heroic intensity, evoking sentiments no less of hope and exaltation than of horror, fear, and awe:

> The men beat themselves rhythmically with leather scourges armed with iron spikes, singing hymns meanwhile in celebration of Christ's Passion and of the glories of the Virgin. Three men standing in the centre of the circle led the singing. At certain passages—three times in each hymn—all would fall down "as though struck by lightning" and lie with outstretched arms, sobbing and praying. The Master walked among them, bidding them pray to God to have mercy on all sinners. After a while the men stood up, lifted their arms towards heaven and sang; then they recommenced their flagellation. If by any chance a woman or a priest entered the circle the whole flagellation became invalid and had to be repeated from the beginning. . . . The flagellants did their work with such thoroughness that often the spikes of the scourge stuck in the flesh and had to be wrenched out. Their blood spurted on to the walls and their bodies turned to swollen masses of blue flesh.[53]

As the fourteenth century witnessed the appearance of such groups seeking through their excesses in self-torment to expiate the sins of the world, it witnessed also, and under comparably disturbed circumstances, the appearance of marauding anti-Semitic mobs and the quickened circulation of legends about hosts allegedly profaned by Jews. It was a century during which millenarian expectations of one sort or another continued to surface, and, along with the two centuries following, it witnessed a great intensification in the belief in witchcraft and sorcery. It was a time marked everywhere by a compulsive preoccupation with death, dying, and the dead, a time when crowds pressed daily into the churchyard of the Innocents at Paris, there to gape at the painting of the dance of death in the cloisters or at the skulls and bones prematurely displaced from their last resting places by the incessant demand for fashionable burial space and piled high in

53. Cohn, pp. 133–34.

charnel houses open to the curious gaze.[54] If the pain of Christ's passion rather than the glory of the Resurrection or the hope of Pentecost stood always in the foreground (and it was at this time that the "Stations of the Cross" began to become a popular devotion), so too man's suffering and death, the fear of hell and the torments of purgatory, appear to have moved the imagination more powerfully than the hope of his resurrection. *Timor mortis conturbat me* was more than merely a lyric refrain. Concern with the need to provide for death sponsored a veritable boom in books on the *ars moriendi* and the four last things as well as a vogue in performances of the *danse macabre*, in which a dancer representing a dead person or Death itself comes forth again and again to lead away men and women of all walks and stages of life—pope and king, bishop and beggar, bourgeois and bride. And from around this time we can trace the appearance and proliferation of the two-leveled type of "transitomb," which showed beneath the tranquil image of the serene deceased in all of his or her earthly panoply the parallel effigy of a grinning, worm-ridden, decaying corpse.[55] Hardly surprising that one town crier whose words were included in the records could pace the streets at dead of night proclaiming: "Wake up, wake up, you who sleep, and pray God for the souls of the dead, whom he wants to forgive."[56]

Pray for the dead of course they did, and for themselves too, piling pilgrimage upon pilgrimage in their anxious search for an ultimate security, accumulating relics and indulgences, multiplying masses and saints, creating votive masses for special needs (there was a mass of Job against syphilis), charging a swarm of minor saints with the most refined and gross of specialties (St. Blaise with the cure of throat ailments, St. Roche with the prevention of plague, St. Fiacre with the relief of hemorrhoids—this last a devotion that Henry V would apparently have liked to see flourish in England). The concern to provide

54. Huizinga, *Waning*, pp. 148–50.
55. On which see now Cohen.
56. The reference is to the town crier of Troyes in the early sixteenth century; see A. N. Galpern, "The Legacy of Late Medieval Religion in Sixteenth Century Champagne," in Trinkaus and Oberman, eds., p. 148.

for elaborate funerals and repeated anniversary masses bulks large in the wills and last testaments of the period, leading to the creation in the English chantries of veritable mass factories and elsewhere to the multiplication of altars, mass endowments, and "mass priests" without cure of souls, whose function it was to meet the demand. Some of the numbers involved are staggering. Henry VII (1485–1509) of England provided for no fewer than ten thousand masses to be said for the repose of his soul; ordinary merchants were quite capable of aspiring to the hundreds; confraternities strove regularly to look after the similar needs of their own members. The Elisabethkirche in Breslau was able to keep 122 priests scrambling for the use of 47 altars in their attempts to discharge the sole duty for which their positions had been endowed.[57]

It was a sort of "arithmetical piety" that gave "almost a magical value to mere repetition of formulae."[58] As such, it was understandably prone to generate a number of outright abuses and to spawn some very odd practices that conspired unwittingly to make nonsense of the liturgy. The parlous economic situation and the instability of monetary values, which threatened to render legacies inadequate to support the requisite numbers of mass priests, led to the undignified practice of having as many endowed masses as possible sung or said immediately after death rather than being spread out over the years. The pressure of time led to such abuses as the so-called boxed or curtailed masses, with "one Mass . . . sung to the offertory or to the Sanctus, then continued as a low Mass while at another altar a second Mass was begun."[59] The greed for the acquisition of stipends led to the proliferation of "dry" masses, brief services from which was omitted the whole canon of the mass.

When one adds to these abuses the superstitions connected with the use of indulgences, images, relics, and the Eucharist itself, the picture takes on even darker hues. The fear of the torments of purgatory that led some to procure the privilege of a *confessionale* (making it possible

57. For some other examples, see Delaruelle et al., 2:775–76.
58. Wood-Legh, p. 312.
59. Jungmann, 1:131.

for their confessors to extend to them on their deathbed the consolation of a plenary indulgence) led others, despite ecclesiastical disclaimers, to believe that even without being sorry for their sins or confessing them to a priest they could purchase with an indulgence the remission of their guilt as well as the punishment due for their misdeeds. More alarmingly, it seems to have led others to think that with an indulgence they could purchase a license to sin freely and safely in the future.[60] Stories abound of allegedly bleeding hosts and of consecrated hosts profanely used to promote fertility and to cure sick animals. In the fifteenth century the cult focused on the liquefaction of the blood of St. Gennaro at Naples appears to have attained its peak.[61] The popular yearning to see the body of Christ that led priests at mass to prolong or repeat the elevation of the host overflowed also into the superstition that to have seen the host in the morning would preserve one from death for that day. Similar superstitions clustered around the viewing of relics and of the image of St. Christopher. In rural areas, as Toussaert has argued in his detailed analysis of religious sentiment in the maritime zone of Flanders, they were buttressed by the survival of outright pagan practices and half-Christianized rites and by the prevalence of a fundamentally magical religious vision.[62] A gloomy picture it may well be, but what one makes of it depends very much on what one brings to it, and it may be suggested that by bringing the wrong things to it we have tended somewhat to misread it—in two major ways.

In the first place, we have approached many of these phenomena with too active a sense of their novelty or of their distinctively late-medieval character. The only partially successful struggle of ecclesiastical authorities to stamp out pagan practices and beliefs was by no means unique to the fourteenth and fifteenth centuries. The early-medieval *Penitentials* down to the *Penitential* of Burchard of Worms in the early eleventh century reflect the very high priority given to that

---

60. Hence the formula that appears on some indulgences of the day, warning that whoever thinks that the indulgence permits him to sin without fear will lose it; see Delaruelle et al., 2:811, n.7.
61. Thomas, *Religion and the Decline of Magic*, pp. 34–35; Hay, p. 90.
62. Toussaert, especially pp. 361–71.

struggle; reports of bishops and missionary preachers in seventeenth-century France reveal that, despite the effort of centuries, the struggle was still going on. Nor was Protestant Europe exempt. In Britain, pilgrimages "were made to the famous well of St. Winifred at Holywell throughout the seventeenth century. . . . When a man was found dead at the well in 1630 after having made scoffing remarks about its supposed powers a local jury brought in a verdict of death by divine judgment."[63] Similarly, the dismay evident in the visitors' report on Lutheran Wiesbaden in 1594 indicates that not even the catechetical diligence and educational enthusiasm of the Lutheran reformers had been enough to carry the day.[64] But indications do suggest that the long struggle had not been entirely without effect, that latter-day ecclesiastics now saw impermissible paganisms in practices that their predecessors would have tolerated, that the slow seepage of Christian ideas into the rural areas had at least had the effect of clothing pagan substance with Christian form. Late-medieval country folk in France may well have expected much of their local saints and highly prized local relics when a drought needed to be ended or the crops saved, but in sixteenth-century Sweden, a country much more recently evangelized, the peasants still assumed it appropriate to place that burden on their king, as if, he complained, "he were a god and not a man."[65]

Similarly, although the impact of war and of the Black Death undoubtedly intensified the preoccupation with suffering and death and heightened the sense of tender pathos surrounding Christ's passion (it was around this time that we first encounter in art the motif of the Pietà), it certainly did not create them. That preoccupation and that sense had been growing ever since the emergence of a more inward and

63. Thomas, *Religion and the Decline of Magic*, p. 70.
64. Strauss, pp. 30–63. He concludes (pp. 61–62) that "the evidence of the visitation protocols supports the view . . . that the operative religion of country folk, and perhaps of many city-dwellers as well, had much less to do with the doctrines of established Christianity than with the spells, chants, signs and paraphernalia of ancient magic lore and wizardry, the cult of which flourished unaffected by the imposition of new or old denominational creeds."
65. Otto Höfler, "Der Sakralcharakter des germanischen Königtums," in *Sacral Kingship*, p. 681.

affective piety in the late eleventh and twelfth centuries. Nor did they disappear when the conditions of life improved. The miseries of purgatory continued to be feared; anniversary masses continued to be endowed; the exercise of charity continued to embrace not only the living but also the dead. In his *Supplication of Souls* (1529) Sir Thomas More himself portrayed the souls in purgatory as beseeching the living for masses and prayers:

> If ye pittie the blind, there is none so blinde as we, which are here in the darke, saving for sightes unpleasaunt and lothsome, til some cumfort come. If ye pitte the lame, ther is none so lame as we, that neither can creepe one foote out of the fyre, nor have one hand at libertie to defende our face fro the flame. Finally, if ye pittie anye man in payne, never knew ye payn comparable to ours; whose fyre as farre passeth in heate all the fyres that ever burned upon earth, as the hottest of al those passeth a feyned fyre paynted on a walle. If ever ye laye sicke, and thought the nyghte long and longed sore for daye, while every houre seemed longer than fyve, bethynke you than what a long night we selye soules endure, that lye slepelesse, burning and broyling in the darke fyre one long night of many dayes, of many wekes, and some of manye yeres together.[66]

A. G. Dickens cites this passage to make the point (and rightly so) that the "dogmatic and detailed emphasis upon the horrors of Purgatory and the means whereby sinners could mitigate them" was "no mere cult of the vulgar." And with More we are into the sixteenth century. One can add that the upheavals in Catholic life engineered by the Second Vatican Council should not blind us to the fact that More's intense concern with the well-being of the souls in purgatory was not necessarily alien to the older modalities of Catholic life in the twentieth century.

Something similar can be said about the liturgy. In that realm, as we have seen, the critical changes that made the consecration of the mass the focus, the action the priest's, the sacrifice a repetition, the benefit a quantity, the number a consideration—these changes had long since occurred. It was left for the late-medieval churchmen only

---

66. More, pp. 337–38. Cf. Dickens, pp. 5–6.

to draw out the logic of those changes to its conclusion and to rationalize the whole process. This they did by developing a theology in accordance with which "the value of the Mass is a limited one, so that the smaller the number for which it is offered so much the greater is the profit accruing to each individual," and by multiplying masses accordingly.[67] On the other hand, they also responded affirmatively to the wish to see and adore the host—building tabernacles in which it could be reserved between masses, constructing *ostensaria* or monstrances in which it could be exposed (even throughout the celebration of the mass), conducting paraliturgical services and processions centering on benediction by or exposition of the sacrament. The Catholic or Counter-Reformation pruned the more bizarre excrescences and the ranks of the mass priests were ultimately thinned. In these respects, however, as in others, the spirituality of the Counter-Reformation era was very much in continuity with the late Middle Ages.

In the second place, in making our judgments about the quality of popular religious life during the late Middle Ages, we have perhaps been somewhat guilty of intruding our own sensibilities upon those of a very different era. Grisly though they may seem to us, double-decker transitombs, it turns out, did not represent merely a *memento mori* for the living, but also (and rather) represented an "expression of hope for the salvation of the soul of the deceased"; in the course of time, they came to symbolize too the Christian faith in the resurrection of the body.[68] To be a member of a company of flagellants (*disciplinati*), at least in calmer times, was not necessarily a sign of mental aberration; one might just be unusually pious. Certainly, to be admitted to the Company of San Domenico, one of several companies of *disciplinati* in fourteenth-century Siena, one had to be at least twenty years old and a working artisan, to be interviewed by the priest, to attend mass daily,

67. Iserloh, "Wert der Messe," p. 62. The view expressed is that of Pierre d'Ailly, who in this follows Robert Holcot's view.
68. Cohen, p. 181. Cf. Jankofsky for a similar line of argument concerning not only the iconography of the tombs but also the debate between corpse and worms in the poem he is analyzing. There the dead lady engages in debate with the worms devouring her body and they serve to awaken in her "spiritual insight and hope for eternal felicity" (p. 138).

go to confession twice monthly, receive communion four times a year, and to pledge oneself to the practice of mutual charity with one's fellows. Similarly, for those of appropriately balanced disposition, indulgences could function not as reinforcement to a piety of mechanical formalism but rather as a modest incentive to prayer, and anniversary masses could function not as *Totenfresserei* but rather as a proper and reassuring extension to the dead of love for one's neighbor.[69]

Despite all their stress on an inward individual piety, the Brothers of the Common Life, it should be noted, rejected neither of those practices; the *consuetudines* of their houses at Zwolle and Hildesheim show them to have been willing even to accept from benefactors foundations for masses; they betray, in this respect, no striking difference in attitude from that displayed by other priests and monks of the time. So, too, with pilgrimages. Such churchmen as St. Bernardino of Siena and Nicholas of Cusa could criticize their abuse, but they often involved a risk to personal safety and were not necessarily lightly undertaken or widely scorned. When the band of thieves that had been terrorizing the Norfolk country folk around Paston village in the mid-fifteenth century learned that a man whom they had robbed and taken captive to their boat was a pilgrim, "they gave him money," Agnes Paston tells us, "and set [him] again on the land."[70] At the other end of the scale, Margery Kempe of Lynn, in the same county (ca. 1373–ca. 1439), no true mystic perhaps but clearly a woman of more than formal piety, embarked on extended pilgrimages to Compostela in Spain, to Italy, and to the Holy Land. Even for Chaucer, we should perhaps recall, not every pilgrim on the road to Canterbury was a Pardoner or a Wife of Bath.

We need to be sure that the understandable temptation to focus on the bizarre, to assimilate religious life in general to the ecclesiastical confusion of the era, and to view both as a falling away from the achievements of the High Middle Ages does not blind us to intimations of the spread of a deeper and more inward piety even in those

69. On this last issue I would refer to the provocative article of Natalie Zemon Davis, "Some Tasks and Themes in the Study of Popular Religion," in Trinkaus and Oberman, eds., pp. 307–36, on which I have drawn at more than one point.
70. Cited in Bennett, pp. 210–11.

things that seem indicative of an external and formalistic religion. Neither in that era nor later is the preoccupation with apparitions and pilgrimages, for example, necessarily to be taken as a sign of growing superstition and religious decay. In late-nineteenth-century Ireland, certainly, the emergence of the shrine of Knock as a popular focus of pilgrimage came at a time of deepening religiosity, more widespread education, and improved religious instruction.[71] Again, while we may feel an instinctive sympathy with Cranmer's condescension toward the widespread popular desire to see the host, a late-medieval cleric breathing a very different theological atmosphere might well be disposed to view it rather as a heartening sign of deepening piety. The *capitoli* of one of the new confraternities for boys in fifteenth-century Florence require the members, among other things, to make confession once a month, to go to communion together on the feast of St. John, and to attend mass daily "or at least to try to see the body of Christ."[72] And Ambrogio Traversari (d. 1439), humanist and master general of the Order of Camaldoli, was loud in his praise for the success of such confraternities in forming youths of exemplary moral character. Even Nicholas of Cusa, who as papal legate to Germany tried to suppress the pilgrimage to the bleeding host of Wilsnack, recognized in such practices the evidence of a great hunger for the divine and ordered those whom he dispensed from pilgrimage vows to visit and venerate the Blessed Sacrament in their parish churches, for there God truly dwelt.

The scope of Nicholas of Cusa's reforming visitation and the appearance at this time of such confraternities for boys are themselves worthy of note. The latter reflects that growing concern with the

71. Larkin. Cf. the remarks of Pantin, p. 259, in relation to the religious 'life of Margery Kempe of Lynn: "The interesting thing to notice is that these manifestations of popular piety, like image-worship and pilgrimages—the very things that the Lollards attacked, and that may seem to a modern observer to take a childish or superstitious form—were to a devout person like Margery not a hindrance but a direct help and stimulus to a more spiritual devotion. There seems in fact to be a direct connexion between the use of images and the practice of meditation in the later Middle Ages."
72. See Richard C. Trexler, "Ritual in Florence: Adolescence and Salvation in the Renaissance," in Trinkaus and Oberman, eds., pp. 200–264 at 209–12.

moral and religious formation of the young that found expression also in the writing of manuals for confessors geared specifically to help them respond to the spiritual needs of youth, in the apostolate of the Brothers of the Common Life among the schoolboys of the Netherlands, in the aspiration of Savonarola (d. 1498) to marshal the spiritual energies of the young boys of Florence (the *fanciulli*), in the concern of Gerson for the religious education of the boys of the Notre-Dame choir school in Paris and his insistence in the teeth of criticism that such a ministry was by no means beneath his dignity as chancellor.

Indeed—in a period that remained too devoted to earlier medieval practice in its failure to provide in any systematic fashion for the theological and pastoral training of the secular clergy or for the catechesis of the children—the sheer range, quantity, and variety of the instrumentalities geared in some degree to the moral and religious formation of the lower clergy and laity must be regarded as impressive. These instrumentalities ranged from the increasing attention given to the sacrament of penance to the public performance of the *danse macabre*, the Mysteries, and the great passion plays (these last by no means devoid of doctrinal content); from the initiation by St. Vincent Ferrer in 1399 of the great preaching missions that took him and St. John Capistrano (d. 1456) across much of Spain and France, St. Bernardino of Siena across Italy, and John Brugman (d. 1473) across the Germanies, to the publication of an abundance of preaching manuals, Bible paraphrases and translations into the vernacular, spiritual biographies, books of instruction setting forth Christian doctrine and morality in summary form, Books of Hours for devotional reading at mass, and so on. Even if the vernacular versions of the Bible that circulated during these centuries were accessible only to the literate minority, they were accessible in French, German, Italian, English, Spanish, and Czech and included a Castilian rendering of the Old Testament translated directly from the Hebrew. Similarly, the *Lay Folk's Mass Book*, which was translated from a French original, circulated in fifteenth-century England in several regional dialects. And the titles of some of the books of popular instruction—such as the German *Spiegel der Laien* (*Mirror for the Laity*)—reveal that they were intended not as clerical aids but for the direct edification of the laity.

Of all these instrumentalities, and others to which I have not referred, the sacrament of penance and the manner in which priests were encouraged to administer it are especially worthy of attention. The seriousness with which theologians and canonists took that sacrament in the late Middle Ages can be gauged by the impressive number of "aids" they wrote to help confessors discharge their responsibilities, both the simpler and more "popular" sort and the more formidable and encyclopaedic *summae*. As examples of the former, one may cite the influential little manual that formed the second part of Gerson's *Opus tripartitum* and the first part of the *Oculus sacerdotis* (ca. 1326–28), written by the pastor and canonist William of Pagula, some passages from which the mystic Richard Rolle admired enough to incorporate into one of his own treatises.[73] In the latter category are the *Summa confessorum* of the theologian John of Freiburg (ca. 1290) and the *Summa* of Angelus Carletus de Clavasio (1480–90), generally known by their nicknames, respectively the *Joannina* and the *Angelica*.

The basic purpose of these *summae* was to convey to confessors— and through them to the faithful, who were required to confess at least once a year—what their faith required of Christians, the laws by which the church had sought to lend specificity to those requirements, and the sanctions she had attached to those laws in order to secure their observance. Among their characteristic features two have recently been emphasized. The first: the evident trend, as time went on, in the direction of placing the emphasis within the sacrament on the role of priestly absolution rather than on the penitent's sorrow for his sins—in the direction, therefore, of the Scotist teaching that "absolution, by virtue of the [sacerdotal power of the] keys, justifies by turning an attrite into a contrite man, unless he interposes an obstacle." The second, that what was involved here was not simply the imposition of norms of conduct enforced by external legal sanctions, but

73. See Pantin, pp. 196–97, who says of William, "He reminds us that . . . we must not dismiss the canonists as a race of soulless administrators." See also Boyle.

rather a process of socialization, an attempt to insert those norms into the arena of conscience so that the internal sanction of guilt would do the enforcing. What the "summists" were trying to do, in effect, was "to help ecclesiastical authorities get catalogues of forbidden behavior thoroughly internalized." [74]

These *summae* reveal clearly enough what the clerical leadership was trying to promote. How effective their efforts were is, of course, extremely hard to judge. But given the stirrings of reform evident in the late fourteenth and fifteenth centuries, it seems permissible to suspect that by the eve of the Reformation the process of socialization they were seeking to sponsor was shaping the conscience of more and more of the faithful. [75] Certainly, the degree of confidence in the church's mediatorial and sacramental ministrations presupposed by the first of the two features to which attention has been drawn was presupposed also by the intensive investment of the laity in the construction of chapels, altars, and chantries, in the accumulation of indulgences, in the endowment of masses. Similarly, a successful internalization of values of the type the "summists" sought to promote is very evident in the methodical scrupulosity of the New Devotionalists. But of how many more?

Conditions of religious life in Germany during the latter part of the fifteenth century may not have been representative of those in Europe as a whole; there is some reason to believe that the Germans of that period may have been more obviously devout than the Italians, [76] the French, or even the English. Nevertheless, in the context of the values and objectives reflected in the *summae confessorum*, a particular interest

74. Thomas N. Tentler, "The Summa for Confessors as an Instrument of Social Control," along with the comments of L. E. Boyle and Tentler's response, in Trinkaus and Oberman, eds., pp. 103–37. The words quoted occur on pp. 112 and 137. Cf. the full analysis in Tentler, *Sin and Confession*. For the "summists," and for the "attritionism" of the later Middle Ages, which, he believes, gives witness to "a total confidence in the sacramental order of the Church," see also Delaruelle et al., 2:656–64.

75. Note the comment of Tentler, *Sin and Confession*, p. 53: "The most traditional picture of the Reformation emphasizes the immorality or inadequacy of the clergy. But the massive attempt to instruct clergy and laity on the proper way to confess indicates—as any biography of Luther must show—that the church may not have been doing too badly, but rather too well."

76. See the analysis of Hay, especially pp. 49–90, 108–9.

attaches to the arresting conclusion of Bernd Moeller that religious life in Germany in the last decades before the Reformation was marked, on the one hand, by a thoroughgoing commitment to the authority of the church and, on the other, by an increasing intensity of piety. "In my opinion," he says, "one could dare to call the late fifteenth century in Germany one of the most churchly-minded and devout periods of the Middle Ages."[77]

Though such a claim runs directly counter to the more negative assessment popularized especially by Lortz, it echoes in updated form similar claims advanced in the nineteenth century.[78] Nor has it failed to win the support of contemporary scholars. But agreement concerning the intensity and vitality of late-medieval piety, although it may end one debate, can serve also to ease the way to the posing of other and more difficult questions concerning the *quality* of that piety. Asserting, in fact, that "the evidence suggests a flawed and unsatisfying piety," Ozment, for example, has argued that "the first Protestants attacked the medieval church for demanding too much, rather than too little, from laymen and clergymen, and for making religion psychologically and socially burdensome, not for taking it too lightly." Furthermore, and, in view of the claims adduced earlier for the influence of the *summae confessorum*, closer to home, he has also argued that "at no point did these apologists feel that they had greater justification for their criticism than at the point of the sacrament of penance and confession."[79]

How accurate their assessment of that sacrament was remains, of course, a matter of dispute. If sacramental penance did indeed pro-

---

77. Moeller, "Frömmigkeit," p. 30; trans. in Ozment, *Reformation*, p. 51. Speaking of Europe more generally, Moeller says elsewhere: "Die Grundeinstellung der Laienschaft gegenüber der Kirche war Devotion. Bereitschaft zur ernsten oder eifervollen Ausschöpfung der von ihr angebotenen Heilsmöglichkeiten, hoffenden oder unrühiges Hilfesuchen angesichts der bedrängenden Fragen des Lebens" (*Spätmittelalter*, p. 36).

78. Lortz, *Reformation in Germany*; idem, *How the Reformation Came*. Contrast, e.g., Janssen. Cf. the historiographical discussions in Moeller, "Probleme des Kirchlichen Lebens in Deutschland vor der Reformation," in Jedin, Probleme der Kirchenspaltung, pp. 11–32, and Ozment, *Reformation in the Cities*, pp. 1–22.

79. Ozment, *Reformation in the Cities*, pp. 21–22, 50.

mote religious and moral discipline by the inculcation of guilt and the consequent imposition of psychological burdens, it was also intended to reconcile the penitent sinner, to promote psychological relief by offering him "a relatively accessible and routine means of consolation." [80] If the rigorous examination of conscience that it demanded did carry with it the danger of encouraging "scrupulosity," of molding a hypersensitive conscience prone to torment itself with imagined failings and an overanxious search for sins, the medieval theologians were well aware of that danger, viewed scrupulosity as itself a spiritual vice, and advocated remedies for it. There are those, Gerson said, who "always have a scruple that they are not yet properly confessed. They exhaust themselves and their confessors with repeated confessions, especially of light and unimportant sins. . . ." To all of these alike, he adds, "should be given the counsel to trust not in their own justice but in the pure mercy of God; and as they overestimate their own negligence, so let them also exaggerate the infinite mercy of God." [81]

Johannes von Staupitz appears to have voiced almost identical sentiments later, when as monastic superior and spiritual guide he in turn was struggling to assuage the crippling anxieties from which the young Luther sought release. [82] It was in vain, of course, that he did so. He failed to convince his adamantly scrupulous protégé, and the Reformers went on to attack the medieval institution of sacramental penance, seeing it as an instrument of torment and anguish of spirit rather than as a medium of consolation and hope. That they did so, however, should not betray us into assuming that they "simply articulated the reactions of sensitive Christians throughout Europe." [83] Staupitz himself, to whom Luther so often acknowledged his spiritual indebtedness, maintained to the end of his life his own commitment to a traditional understanding of the sacrament, and, the Protestant challenge notwithstanding, "the consoling power of sacramental

80. Tentler, *Sin and Confession*, p. 348.
81. Gerson, *De remediis*, in Dupin, ed., 3:585C–586B; trans. in Tentler, *Sin and Confession*, p. 77.
82. Bainton, pp. 54–56.
83. I follow here the illuminating discussion in Tentler, *Sin and Confession*, pp. 349–70. The words quoted appear at p. 366.

penance" continued to touch the hearts of many of fervent spirituality throughout the Catholic world.[84] If, then, the type of disciplined and churchly piety that the late-medieval *summae confessorum* and similar instrumentalities sought to inculcate among clergy and laity alike is to be brought into relationship with sixteenth-century reforming movements, that relationship must properly be understood as one of continuity as well as discontinuity, no less as a positive inspiration to the forces of Catholic renewal than as a negative stimulus to the initiatives of Protestant reform.

84. Steinmetz, *Misericordia Dei*, pp. 97–104; Tentler, *Sin and Confession*, p. 366.

CHAPTER 3 · CURRENTS OF THOUGHT: THEOLOGICAL AND DOCTRINAL DEVELOPMENTS

And, "The Word was made flesh and dwelt among us." If the Word was not ashamed to be born of men, should man be ashamed to be born of God? Saying "He gave them power to become sons of God" does not at all mean, as Pelagius dreamed, that He gave them power to become sons of God by preceding works of merit. It is inconceivable that St. John should contradict his Lord, who said, as John himself reports, "No one is able to come unto me unless the Father who sent me draws him."
—THOMAS BRADWARDINE (ca. 1290–1349)

There is a distinction between compulsory necessity and unfailing necessity [that is, consistency]. With God compulsory necessity has no place, but an unfailing necessity is appropriate to God because of His promise, that is, His Covenant, or established law. This is not an absolute but rather a conditional necessity. According to God's established law the pilgrim who does whatever he can to dispose himself for grace always receives grace. However, if He should choose to, God could deviate from His law for someone other than the pilgrim or the devil. Then, however much such a person [with whom God has not made His Covenant] might dispose himself for grace, he would not receive it. Man's disposition does not require the giving of grace except by congruency, because grace surpasses every natural act; it is impossible for man to fully merit (*de condigno*) through any natural act.
—ROBERT HOLCOT (ca. 1300–1349)

131

Indeed no one is saved by works but entirely by grace. For if salvation is attributed to merits then there will be no grace but justice, nor grace freely given but conceded in a certain way to the necessity of justice. . . . It is nevertheless in our will where we direct the acts that we do and to will or not to will itself in whose liberty is the fall of sin, God most justly not exhibiting his mercy; and the reason of merit is by God Himself conceding grace through infinite clemency.

—COLUCCIO SALUTATI (1331–1406)

Although the principles governing inclusion in the hallowed pages of Denzinger's *Enchiridion symbolorum, definitionum, et declarationum de rebus fidei et morum* are clearly theological and canonistic rather than historical, the paucity of space devoted in that work to the fourteenth and fifteenth centuries (not much more than that allotted to the Tridentine documents alone) is a reasonably accurate index to the amount of formal activity on the part of the ecclesiastical magisterium during those centuries.[1] Amid the archaeological litter of half-forgotten and sometimes puzzling condemnations, one or two documents, it is true, stand out as possessing historic significance—*Cum inter nonnullos* (1323), for example, John XXII's catastrophic condemnation of the Franciscan doctrine of apostolic poverty, and *Laetentur coeli* (1439), the Council of Florence's bull of union with the Greek church, a document dear to the ultramontane theologians of the modern era because of its definition of the Roman primacy. But more significant than such magisterial pronouncements on doctrinal matters were the currents of theological controversy that eddied about them.

Notable among these currents were the novel explorations of the relationship between Scripture and tradition stimulated by contemporary debates about such controverted doctrines as apostolic poverty and the Immaculate Conception. Also remarkable were the wide-ranging discussions about the nature of the church that bulked so

1. Denzinger devotes pp. 278–353 to the fourteenth and fifteenth centuries, pp. 363–427 to the decrees of the Council of Trent.

large in the theological and canonistic discourse of the time, pointing not only in the direction of *Laetentur coeli* but also of *Haec sancta synodus* (1415), the Constance decree on conciliar supremacy. Of greatest significance was the intense preoccupation with the interrelated questions of sin, grace, free will, justification, and predestination, which, for the first time since the fifth century, became the dominant focus of theological dissension, intruding themselves upon the attention of scholastic theologian and Italian humanist alike, and finding but inadequate and one-sided expression in the official condemnations of Wycliffe and Hus. The quotations opening this chapter illustrate the range of late-medieval opinion on these fundamental theological questions, opinion marked by contrasts only slightly less sharp than those between the essentially Pelagian "religion of works" so evident at the level of popular devotion and the contemporaneous mystic sense of having encountered the divine through a "steryng of love—that is the werk of only God."[2]

Augustine and Pelagius Revisited

Over the course of the last half century or so, the strengths and weaknesses of late-medieval scholastic thinking in general and of its nominalist branch in particular have become the focus among scholars of mounting interest and growing disagreement. So, too, has the question of the continuity or discontinuity of that thinking with the scholastic philosophy and theology of the thirteenth century. Most would now concur in finding undesirable the older historical approach that sought anachronistically to comprehend the diversity and novelty of late-medieval thought in terms of earlier scholastic disputes between epistemological realists and nominalists. William of Ockham (ca. 1285–1349) was thus seen in opposition to Duns Scotus (ca. 1265–1308) in very much the same way as the early nominalist Roscelin (d. ca. 1125) had been placed in opposition to the famous realist William of Champeaux (ca. 1070–1121). Beyond that point, how-

2. *Cloud of Unknowing*, ed. Hodgson, p. 62, l. 2.

ever, general agreement is not easy to come by. Some scholars still persist in measuring late-medieval nominalist theology against the exacting but anachronistic standard of thirteenth- (or sixteenth-) century Thomism and finding it, accordingly, wanting. Others of more revisionist bent sometimes lump together as alleged advocates of a single "traditional interpretation" historians of widely differing concerns with whom they find themselves in real or imagined disagreement.

However understandable such attitudes are, they remain distressing. The currents that run through late-medieval philosophy and theology are both multiple and complex; they are also of varying provenance. In the present state of research an accurate synoptic vision seems likely to exceed our capacities for some time. It would seem prudent therefore candidly to admit that the nature of one's particular historical concern—whether with logic, epistemology, ethics, natural philosophy, or soteriology—is likely to frame the perspective from which one views late-medieval thinking as a whole. As our own interest at this point is fundamentally with theories pertaining to the process of salvation, we might do well to make our first approach to late-medieval theology less with the experience of the thirteenth century in mind than with that of the fourth and fifth centuries. For it was St. Augustine of Hippo (354–430), and especially the Augustine who reacted so vehemently against what he took to be the views of the Pelagians, who set the terms in which medieval (and, indeed, postmedieval) debates on the relationship between nature and grace were subsequently conducted.

To say this, however, is not necessarily to say that Augustine's teaching on nature and grace was identical, as it stood, with the norm of medieval orthodoxy on that issue. Augustine reacted against Pelagius's (ca. 354–ca. 418) fundamentally optimistic appraisal even of fallen man's moral capacities, against his unquestionable minimization of the role of divine grace in the process of salvation, and against his alleged conviction that it was possible for man in the freedom of his will and by his own natural powers to avoid sin and attain perfection in this life. Augustine's opposition led him to state his own doctrine in its harshest and most uncompromising form. He was disposed already by the moral and spiritual struggles of his earlier life to stress the devastating impact of original sin on the souls of all of Adam's descendants and the consequent inability of fallen man, without divine help, to put his free will to any moral use other than to do wrong. Now he was moved to assert not only the necessity of divine grace in the process of salvation but also its irresistible nature. As a result, he was moved further to insist upon a particularly uncompromising doctrine of predestination, whereby God based his dread decision not upon any foreknowledge of the degree of moral responsibility with which men contrive to lead their lives, but upon a secret and inscrutable justice that transcends the categories of any merely human equity. In the terminology of later centuries, that is, he was led to subscribe to a doctrine of predestination *ante praevisa merita* rather than *post praevisa merita*.

This harsh doctrine the medieval church proved unable wholly to digest. "Pelagianism" was roundly condemned in 418 at the Council of Carthage, and again in 431 at the Council of Ephesus. But although the authoritative position adopted in 529 by the Council of Orange and subsequently endorsed by Pope Boniface II (530–32) was certainly shaped by Augustine's views, it did not reflect an equally favorable response to all of them. Endorsed was Augustine's emphasis on the devastating and enduring impact of Adam's original sin on the religious and moral capacities of all his descendants. Endorsed, too, was the assertion that without some prior gift of divine grace man can do nothing to please God, since even the desire to believe presupposed the prevenient workings of the Holy Spirit. But there was no mention of irresistible grace, and the idea that God has predestined some men to damnation was roundly condemned. It clearly lay within man's power, therefore, to spurn the divine advances, and it was suggested only a little less clearly that man retained some power freely to cooperate with God's grace and by such cooperation to do at least something to further his own salvation.

The doctrinal norm bequeathed to medieval orthodoxy by the Council of Orange, then, was fundamentally of Augustinian inspiration and was regarded as such at the time, but it left some room, nevertheless, for the play of competing interpretations. Certain boundaries had been established, and in response to doctrinal probings they were reaffirmed more than once—as, for example, in the twelfth century, when the Council of Sens (1141) condemned the view that "free will as such suffices to perform something good," and the Council of Rheims (1148), on the other hand, denounced the opinion that "apart from Christ there is no meritorious human action."[3] But the intense debates of the ninth century and again of the fourteenth and fifteenth centuries (and, indeed, of the sixteenth and seventeenth centuries as well) underline the fact that legitimate disagreement had by no means been banished from the territory falling within those established doctrinal boundaries. Disagreements, moreover, often took the form of dissension concerning the precise import of Augustine's own views. The overall governing terms remained persistently Augustinian, but differences in temperament and theological concerns made for differing formulations. Again and again, for example, the essentially pastoral and missionary concern of the Pelagians, which led them so to emphasize human responsibility and the efficacy of natural human effort in the process of salvation,[4] also touched medieval thinkers. As a result, they were prompted to seek under the canopy of divine grace an enlargement of the arena wherein human effort can achieve merit. Again and again, too, the fundamentally confessional urge that had moved Augustine to acknowledge the impulsion of divine grace at every critical juncture in his own life (and to pray "all my hope can only be in [God's] great mercy"[5]) moved others. Hence they were led to elaborate confessional theologies that so stressed the providential role of divine grace in the process of salvation as to leave little room for the play of human freedom and responsibility. Thus on the very eve of the Reformation, the German theologian Gabriel Biel produced a theology of such markedly pastoral orientation that Luther accused

---

3. See Oberman, *Forerunners*, p. 130.
4. As Coelestius, the disciple of Pelagius, is reported to have said, "If I ought, I can."
5. Augustine, *Confessiones*, 10:29 (ed. Rouse, 2:148); cf. 10:31, 32, 35 (2:156–59, 164, 180).

him of "pelagianizing." [6] And shortly afterward his fellow countryman Johann von Staupitz (d. 1525), Luther's mentor and monastic
superior (from whom, he once said, he "received everything"), developed a theology of such persistently confessional orientation as to
make "grace and not nature, mercy and not justice, hope and not
fear . . . the constant themes of his message." [7]

So far, so good. For a more precise understanding of the complex
forces shaping the late-medieval discussion of these issues, however, it
is necessary, even at the risk of some confusion, to probe a little deeper. Though it is not always immediately apparent, and although Augustine himself addressed the issues separately and at different points
in his life, two matters were at stake: the sovereign initiative of divine
grace in the order of redemption and the sovereign omnipotence of
God in the order of creation. We have seen that an overriding
preoccupation with divine grace led Augustine in his writings against
the Pelagians to an uncompromising emphasis on the doctrine of
predestination and the irresistibility of grace. A firm commitment to
God's omnipotence had earlier led him in his *De libero arbitrio voluntatis* to insist, in the teeth of widely held countervailing views, that
man had indeed been endowed at the creation with freedom of will
and the ability not to sin.

In the name of overriding necessity and the universal sway of ineluctable fate, the views that Augustine had opposed had either qualified the freedom and moral responsibility of man or altogether denied
them. And it is no accident that the Manichaeans, Gnostics, and other
pagans who had espoused such views were thinkers to whom the biblical and patristic doctrines of divine omnipotence and creation *ex nihilo*
were irremediably alien. Only an omnipotent God, after all, unlim-
ited by any external or rival force and therefore radically free, could be
regarded as capable of endowing the creature he had made in his own
image and likeness with an attribute as godlike as freedom. [8] Nor is it

6. See Oberman, *Harvest*, p. 55, n. 77.
7. Steinmetz, *Misericordia Dei*, p. 131; for Luther's statements of indebtedness to
Staupitz, see p. 2.
8. Cf. Gilson, *Spirit*, pp. 108–27.

an accident that the early opponents of Augustine's predestinarian teaching should accuse him of reintroducing in Christian guise the type of heathen fatalism that he himself had earlier rejected.[9] Against that classical fatalism it had been the persistent concern of the earlier apologists for Christianity to affirm the freedom and responsibility of man. And that concern had been part of the prior and more fundamental struggle to vindicate in the teeth of pagan incomprehension the freedom and omnipotence of the transcendent Creator-God who had made him.

The point deserves emphasis. In the historic encounter between Athens and Jerusalem, between the Greek philosophical tradition and religious views of biblical provenance, the great stumbling block had been (and necessarily remained) the difficulty of reconciling the personal and transcendent biblical God of power and might, upon the free decision of whose will the very existence of the universe was contingent, with the characteristically Greek intuition of the divine as limited and inner-worldly and of the universe as necessary and eternal—or, to put it somewhat differently, with the persistent tendency of the Greek philosophers to identify the divine with the immanent and necessary order of an eternal cosmos.[10]

If Augustine himself had succeeded in effecting an accommodation with the Platonic and Neoplatonic versions in which the Christians of the ancient world encountered the Greek philosophic tradition, it was an accommodation by no means devoid of serious internal tensions. Those tensions mounted in the course of the twelfth and thirteenth centuries, when the treaty had, as it were, to be renegotiated and a far more difficult accommodation reached with full-scale philosophical systems of Arab-Aristotelian amalgam. Teaching not only the eternity of the universe but also its necessity, those systems confronted Christian thinkers with the picture of a determined world in which

---

9. See Faustus Reiensis, *De gratia libro duo*, 1:16 (*CSEL*, 21:49–50); cf. Pelikan, 1:320.

10. For discussions of this point and its implications, see the essays gathered in O'Connor and Oakley, eds.

everything had to be what it was and which permitted no room for the play of free will either in God or in man. Not even the subtle philosophical and theological diplomacy of Aquinas could fully succeed in convincing his contemporaries that such an accommodation was truly possible without the abandonment or radical modification of beliefs so fundamental to Christianity as to be nonnegotiable. And during the century following his death in 1274, while the attempt to harmonize reason and revelation was certainly not abandoned, it was pursued more cautiously and with much less confidence than heretofore in the effective reach of human reason.

The need for such caution was signaled in 1277 by the condemnations issued by the bishop of Paris and the archbishop of Canterbury, proscribing a whole series of philosophical propositions, including some advanced by Aquinas himself. In the wake of those condemnations a theological reaction set in, which stimulated a widespread concern to vindicate the freedom and omnipotence of God at the expense, if need be, of the ultimate intelligibility of the world. There was a tendency, therefore, common to thinkers of very diverse stamps, to take the divine omnipotence as the fundamental principle, to set God over against the world he had created, and to regard the order of that world as deriving not from any sort of participation in the divine reason but rather from the inscrutable mandate of an autonomous divine will. Such a tendency was evident already in the primacy over the divine intellect that Duns Scotus (reversing Aquinas's emphasis) accorded to the divine will. It became dominant in the thinking of the nominalist school, which, despite its diversity, still owed its basic inspiration to the scholastic writings of William of Ockham.

But while the driving concern was with the freedom and power of God in the order of creation, the very strength of that concern necessarily generated cognate impulses in theological discussions about the order of redemption, thus sparking renewed and anxious questioning about the power and freedom of man in the economy of salvation. The circuitry was complex, however, the connections were not always direct, and the energy thus liberated discharged itself along two paths that led in very different directions—the first, in effect, to an ultimate denial of that human freedom, and the second to its affirmation. We will pursue each of them in turn to its appointed destination.

However startling the destination of the first of these paths, there is nothing paradoxical about it. The emphasis on the omnipotence of God and his freedom in the creative process provided, on the one hand, the best basis for a defense of human freedom against the renewed pressure of deterministic views, yet on the other hand, as the Jewish and Muslim traditions both make very clear, it posed to that belief a threat of a different but no less potent kind. Could the deeds of man, no matter how worthy, really hold any mortgage on the freedom of a truly omnipotent God? And if God's power were really unfettered, could any created will be said to escape the enveloping domination of his own uncreated will? To the first of those urgent questions the Jewish Bible could be taken to have responded in the negative, and to the second the Islamic Koran. When Job, after all, had sought some justification, comprehensible in human terms, for the disasters that Yahweh had brought down upon him, Yahweh's only reply had not been a rational vindication of the justice of his dealings with man but rather a terrifying evocation of his omnipotence: "Can you bind the chains of the Pleiades, or loose the cords of Orion? . . . Shall a fault-finder contend with the Almighty?" (Job 38:31); 40:2). And when the Koran admonished the believer: "Ye shall not will except as God wills," [11] members of the early-medieval Muslim school known as the Jabariya deduced that the movement of the divine will must necessarily be present even in the evil men do: "We are told that Ghailan asked: 'Does God will that sins should be committed?', to which Maimun retorted: 'Are they committed against His Will?' Whereupon Ghailan was silenced." [12]

Such considerations had by no means been irrelevant to the Augustine who taught divine predestination *ante praevisa merita* and the irresistibility of grace—no more so, indeed, than they were later to the Luther who urged against Erasmus the widespread sense that we

11. Koran 81:29; trans. A. Y. Ali, p. 1697.
12. Watt, pp. 40–41.

must be "under necessity if the foreknowledge and omnipotence of God are accepted."[13] But they were certainly much less central to the thinking of either of those men than they were to the Muslim predestinarians or even to some of the late-medieval scholastics. In Chaucer's "Nun's Priest's Tale" the narrator, having told us that

> . . . what that god forwoote must nedes be
> After the opinioun of certeyn clerkis,

and having referred by name to "Augustyn," "Boëce," and "the bishop Bradwardyn," adds:

> That in scole is gret altercacioun
> In this matere, and greet disputisoun.[14]

Indeed, in the *De causa dei* (1344), the long polemic that Thomas Bradwardine wrote against those thinkers of his own day whom he denounced as *pelagiani pestiferi*, while clearly reacting against the determinism of some of the Aristotelians and frequently referring to the condemnations of 1277, he "concentrates his attack on the proud self-conceit of those who think that it is possible to maintain human autonomy under the eyes of the sovereign God."[15] Moved less, it seems, by the weakness of man as a *fallen* creature than by his natural dependency simply as a *creature* (that is, simply as one who has been created), he was led to stress the "omnicausality" of God, and, *as a result*, to argue that men are justified not through their works but through the prevenience of grace and are predestined to eternal life, therefore, *ante praevisa merita*.

Bradwardine presents us with a forceful illustration of the degree to which the heightened preoccupation with the divine freedom and omnipotence so characteristic of fourteenth- and fifteenth-century theology possessed the potential to undercut the freedom and autonomy of man. In this, however, he represents something of an extreme, even when ranged alongside such theologians as Duns Scotus,

---

13. Luther, *De servo arbitrio*; in *Werke*, 18:719.
14. *The Nonne Preestes Tale*, p. 259.
15. Oberman, *Bradwardine*, p. 95. These brief remarks on Bradwardine are grounded in the analyses both of Oberman and of Leff, *Bradwardine and the Pelagians*.

Gregory of Rimini (ca. 1300–1358), and Johann von Staupitz, all of whom similarly taught the doctrine of predestination *ante praevisa merita*, though on very different grounds.

Far more characteristic of the period as a whole is the stance adopted by so many theologians of the nominalist school, such men as Ockham himself, Holcot, Pierre d'Ailly, Gabriel Biel, and Bartholomaeus von Usingen (1465–1532), Luther's teacher at Erfurt. These men were no less concerned than was Bradwardine to vindicate the freedom and omnipotence of God, but they were nudged by that concern along the second of the two paths referred to above and led by it to a destination very different from his. So different, indeed, that he himself would have felt compelled to rank all of them among the "modern Pelagians" against whose detestable influence he felt it his mission to struggle.

Although of course differences and variations in thinking existed among these men, recent studies have made it clear that on the particular questions of justification and predestination their attitudes were very similar and that in general they were animated by a common spirit. Crucial to that spirit was not merely their responsiveness to the Old Testament vision of Yahweh as a god of power and might but, more specifically, their fidelity to another fundamental biblical theme: that of God's promise and covenant. The significance of this differentiating factor should not be overlooked. The only force, after all, that is capable of binding omnipotence without thereby denying it is the omnipotent will itself. Conversely, if that will were incapable of binding itself, it could hardly be regarded as truly omnipotent. Whereas God, therefore, cannot be said to be bound by the canons of any merely human reason or justice, he is certainly capable by his own decision of binding himself to follow a certain pattern in dealing with his creation, just as an absolute monarch can bind himself in his dealings with his subjects. Nor is that analogy improper or misleading. It is a commonplace in the medieval texts themselves.[16] More fascinatingly, recent investigations have uncovered the fact that the analogy

16. There is a good example in Gabriel Biel's sermon, "On the Circumcision of the Lord" (ca. 1460), a translation of which is printed in Oberman, *Forerunners*, pp. 165–74. See p. 173 for his parable of the "lenient king."

has firm foundations in the text of the Bible itself; for it has been argued, and on very compelling grounds, that Israel took as a model to describe Yahweh's pact with her and her own peculiarly covenantal relationship with him the ancient Near Eastern treaty form, especially that very one-sided form whereby a powerful suzerain conceded his terms and freely pledged his loyalty to a faithful vassal.[17]

In the thinking of these nominalists, and especially in that of Holcot, d'Ailly, and Biel, the covenantal theme finds its expression in their extensive employment of that crucial distinction between the absolute power and the ordained power of God to which reference was made in the last chapter. That distinction, though present in the thirteenth century—Albertus Magnus (ca. 1200–1280) implies that in his own day its use was already customary[18]—rose to prominence only in the fourteenth century. The terms *potentia dei absoluta* and *potentia dei ordinata* occur frequently enough in the writings of the nominalists, but scholars disagree, unfortunately, on the precise meanings to be attached to them. All would agree that God's absolute power meant God's *ability* to do anything that does not involve a contradiction—that is, his omnipotence considered apart from the chosen natural, moral, or salvational order of things made known in revelation or apparent in the operations of nature itself. The disagreement concerns whether that ability is relevant only to "the total possibilities *initially* open to God" before his creation of the established order or whether it continues to remain open to realization. And that disagreement involves, in turn, a comparable lack of consensus about what was meant by God's ordained power.

Thus, at one extreme, it has been argued that if the absolute power refers only to the possibilities initially open to God, the ordained power must accordingly denote "the total ordained will of God, the

17. George Mendenhall was the first to perceive this; see his *Law and Covenant* (1955). See also McCarthy and Hillers.
18. See *Summa Theol.*, vol. 1, Tract. 19, qu. 78, membrum 2: "Ad hoc *dici consuevit*, quod potentia Dei potest accipi absolute, et potest accipi ut disposita et ordinata secundum rationem scientiae et voluntatis," etc. (italics mine), in Borgnet, ed., *Opera omnia*, 31:832. Cf. the valuable discussion of the distinction in Miethke, pp. 142–56.

complete plan of God for his creation." Everything that happens, however unusual or even miraculous, must reflect God's ordination, and the ordained power, therefore, is not to be identified "with the particular laws by which the established order normally operated."[19] At the other extreme, it is precisely the latter identification that is endorsed, and the absolute power is understood accordingly as an ability to transcend those laws—an ability so potentially active, indeed, as to threaten "the entire foundation of His [God's] ordained law" and to transform it into "the most fleeting of contingencies, ever liable to be dispensed with."[20] This is confusing enough, no doubt, to us, but it was confusing already, it should be noted, to some of the late-medieval thinkers who used the distinction—not excluding Ockham himself, who ruefully warns of the ease with which anyone who "has not been excellently instructed in logic and theology" can fall into error in this matter.[21]

The confusion can be dissipated, however, if we are prepared to acknowledge with Pierre d'Ailly and Francisco Suárez (1548–1617) that the expression *potentia ordinata* could be (and in fact was) used in *both* ways. It was used, that is, to denote both the ordination whereby God has externally willed that certain things are to be done and the ordinary power by which he acts in accord with the order—natural, moral, salvational—that he has in fact established and ordained and apart from which he can act only *de potentia absoluta*. Aquinas and Ockham favored the first usage, d'Ailly thought the second "more ap-

19. Thus Courtenay (speaking of the thirteenth-century usage, with which he aligns that of Ockham), "Nominalism and Late Medieval Religion," in Trinkaus and Oberman, eds., pp. 26–59 at 37–43; cf. his "Covenant and Causality," p. 95, n. 4: "The distinction . . . means that according to [the] absolute power God, inasmuch as he is omnipotent, retains the *ability* to do many things which he does not *will* to do, has never done, nor will ever do." Courtenay, it should be noted, acknowledges with reference to d'Ailly, Gabriel Biel, and Gregory of Rimini that the distinction was sometimes given the second of the two meanings under discussion here.
20. Thus Leff, *Bradwardine and the Pelagians*, p. 132; cf. Iserloh, *Gnade und Eucharistie*, pp. 67–79. Leff has since moved to distance himself from Iserloh's interpretation and has indicated his wish to distinguish the use made of the distinction by Ockham himself from the more radical use to which his "followers and successors" put it; see his *Ockham*, especially pp. 15–16, 450, 470–71.
21. Ockham, *Opus nonaginta dierum*, chap. 95, in Bennett and Offler, eds., 2:728. Cf. *Tractatus contra Benedictum*, chap. 3, in ibid., 3:234.

propriate" (*magis proprius*), and Suárez described the second as "more common" (*magis usitatus*).[22] Certainly, it was the usage that Duns Scotus and Aegidius Romanus (ca. 1246–1316) followed as early as 1302, and Luther and Sir Thomas More as late as 1516 and 1533 respectively. It was the usage that alone made sense of the theological analogy drawn by jurists when they distinguished between the ordained or ordinary power of the pope (or emperor or king), whereby he was bound by the provisions of the established law, and the absolute power, whereby he transcended those provisions and could dispense with them. It was, conversely, the usage that corresponded with the juridical analogy drawn by so many of the theologians—including Ockham himself, who wavered enough in his thinking to illustrate the theological distinction by referring to the fact that the pope can do "absolutely" some things that he cannot do "according to the statute of the law."[23]

However they understood it, it was the concern of those who used the distinction to underline the fact that God was indeed omnipotent and free, that the established order in the realms of nature and morality and in the economy of salvation was not grounded in any necessary or essential nature of things capable even of binding God, but was instead an order that simply reflected God's free and inscrutable choice, that it was, accordingly, radically contingent. This stress on contingency is more marked in the nominalist theologians than it had been in Aquinas, especially so in view of the fact that they tended to follow the second meaning of *potentia ordinata*. At the same time, however, it was not their intention to suggest that God is prone to act

22. D'Ailly, *Quaestiones*, I, qu. 13, art. 1 D, fol. 159r; Suárez, *Disp. Metaph.*, XXX, sect. xvii, § 32–36, especially at p. 141. Suárez, like some others, uses the word *ordinaria* rather than *ordinata*. Dr. Johannes Eck (d. 1543) gives a particularly clear formulation of the second usage; see *In primum librum Sententiarum*, dist. 42, ed. Moore, p. 123.
23. Thus Scotus, *In Quatuor libros Sententiarum*, 1, dist. 44, qu. 1; 1, 443–44. Aegidius, *De eccl. pot.*, III, chap. 2, 3, 7, and 9; ed. Scholz, pp. 149–59, 181–82, 190–95. Luther, *Vorlesungen über 1 Mose*, chap. 19, 14–20, chap. 20, 2; in *Werke*, 43:71–82, 106. (He uses the expressions *potestas ordinaria* and *potestas ordinata* interchangeably.) More, *Confutation*, 4:Y3v; ed. Schuster et al., p. 569. Ockham, *Quodl.*, VI, 1, fol. 91r. On the relationship between juristic and theological usages, see Oakley, "Jacobean Political Theology."

in an arbitrary or despotic way. If God has freely chosen the established order, he *has* so chosen, and while like an absolute monarch he can dispense with or act apart from the laws he has decreed, he has nonetheless bound himself by his promise and will remain faithful to the covenant that, of his kindness and mercy, he has instituted with man.

So far as the order of salvation is concerned, this meant that the nominalist theologians were able to protect the freedom and omnipotence of God without being led thereby to assert a doctrine of predestination *ante praevisa merita*. By his absolute power, of course, God *can* justify men by grace alone and predestine them to eternal happiness regardless of their deeds. He is no man's debtor; of themselves, and without the conjunction of grace, human actions, however worthy, are incapable of meriting salvation. Of his ineffable mercy and by his ordained power, however, God has chosen to accept men as partners in the work of their salvation. He has done so in such a fashion that if, of their natural powers, they freely do the best they can (*faciunt quod in se est*), he will confer upon them that habit of sanctifying grace by which alone, in the presently established dispensation, acts that are morally good can be transformed into acts that merit an eternal reward. If he is not bound to do this by any simple or absolute necessity, for that has no place with God, he is so bound by what Chaucer's Nun's Priest accurately designates as a "necessitee condicionel"—an "unfailing necessity . . . appropriate to God," as Holcot tells us, "because of His promise, that is, His Covenant, or established law [*ex promisso suo et pacto sive lege statuta*]."[24] Accordingly, while these thinkers can still speak of God's predestination of the elect, it is very much a predestination *post praevisa merita*, one grounded, that is, in God's foreknowledge of man's meritorious deeds.

However much Luther may have been influenced earlier by this doctrine of the *facere quod in se est*, from 1516 onward at least he rejected it as presupposing an essentially Pelagian overemphasis on the

---

24. Holcot, *Super libros Sapientiae*, lect. 145B; I cite the translation by Nyhus in Oberman, ed., *Forerunners*, p. 149.

capacities of the human will unaided by divine grace. About the rectitude of that charge modern commentators continue to disagree. Most would now concede, however, that the nominalist theologians of the late Middle Ages themselves believed the use they made of the notion of covenant and dialectic of the two powers provided an adequate bulwark against what they, too, condemned as the errors of the Pelagians.[25] Like so many medieval theologians before them, what they sought to do was simply to proffer an "authentic" interpretation of Augustine's magisterial doctrine of grace. Accordingly, Heiko Oberman—who has asserted that in its "inner structure" the doctrine of justification taught by Ockham, Ailly, Biel, and Usingen is "to be characterized as at least semi-Pelagian"[26]—has nevertheless been properly careful to insist that "the Reformation period is not marked by an unprecedented ascendance of the authority of St. Augustine nor by the sudden discovery of the radical anti-Pelagianism of Augustinian theology."[27] He has argued further for the influence of "the Scotist-Nominalist tradition" on the final doctrinal formulations of the Council of Trent and concluded that "the popular representation of the Tridentine decree on justification as the *via media* between the extremes of a Pelagian nominalism and a Lutheran Augustinianism stands [now] in need of correction."

If, then, as we saw in the last chapter, the customarily alleged continuities of certain modes of piety from the late-medieval period to the era of Protestant Reformation are neither as direct nor as evident as has often been supposed, we must now be prepared to conclude that in the realm of theologies of grace the customarily alleged doctrinal *dis*continuities between the "nominalism" of that period and the theology of

25. Thus, for Ockham, *Quodl.*, VI, 1, fol. 91r, it was Pelagius's error to have argued that man could actually win merit by the exercise of his own natural powers *de potentia dei ordinata*, whereas he himself would argue that that would be possible only by *de potentia dei absoluta*.

26. Oberman, *Harvest*, p. 426; cf. pp. 177 and 181, where he describes Biel's doctrine as "essentially Pelagian" and Usingen's as "clearly Pelagian." For an opposed point of view, see Vignaux, *Justification*, pp. 137, n. 2, 185–93 (with reference to Ockham), and his *Luther*, pp. 89–92 (with reference to Biel, too).

27. The further remarks of Oberman quoted here and below are from his *Forerunners*, p. 131, and his "Das tridentinische Rechtfertigungsdekret," p. 282.

the age of Catholic or Counter-Reformation are not necessarily any more obvious.

Scripture and Tradition

Something similar may be said in relation to the second area of theological concern that rose to prominence during the course of the fourteenth and fifteenth centuries and was destined to become central to the Reformation debates of the following century—namely, that which focused on the sources of Christian doctrine.

In the older view, the sixteenth-century debate was characterized by the clash between Protestant appeals to "the Scripture alone" and Catholic appeals to "Scripture and Tradition." The late-medieval thinkers were classified in a similar fashion, with such men as Wycliffe and Hus, Wessel Gansfort and John Pupper of Goch lauded as forerunners of Protestant biblicism. Karl Ullmann gave standard expression to this view over a century ago when he asserted that among the things "these men made to be more clearly and generally understood" was "the necessity of appealing to Scripture as the pure Word of God in opposition to all human doctrine and tradition."[28] Such a view was grounded, of course, in what was at the time a pardonably inadequate comprehension of the richness and complexity of late-medieval theology, and before the century was out it had been subjected to some harsh criticism. The subject remained, nevertheless, somewhat less than fashionable among scholars. As recently as twenty years ago, when Paul de Vooght addressed himself to it, he still found reason to deplore the lack of scholarly attention paid to the views of the fourteenth-century scholastic theologians concerning the sources of Christian doctrine; and he ventured the opinion that the continuing inadequacies in our knowledge of the theologians of the period in general helped account for the disparate and disappointingly tentative nature of our attempts to comprehend the views of Wycliffe and Hus in particular.[29]

28. Ullmann, *Reformers before the Reformation*, 1:10.
29. De Vooght, *Sources*, p. 13.

In the years since de Vooght wrote, however, there has been something of a surge of interest in medieval explorations of the relationship between Scripture and tradition. It has been stimulated in part by a renewed preoccupation with the lineaments of the sixteenth-century debates on the subject and by an unexpected challenge to the interpretation that historians and theologians alike had given for centuries to the Tridentine decree on Scripture and the apostolic traditions. It had been customary to assume that in opposition to the "Protestant principle" of *scriptura sola* (Scripture alone) the Council of Trent had endorsed the teaching that the Gospel was to be found only partly in Scripture and partly, therefore, in the unwritten traditions the apostles had received from Christ and handed down to their episcopal successors (the so-called *partim . . . partim* formula). Such a teaching had been widely received in the years immediately before the assembling of the council; it was to become a cliché of Counter-Reformation theology, and the text of the decree itself, admittedly, can quite readily be interpreted in such a way as to support it. Close scrutiny of the actual debates at Trent, however, has made it clear that the fathers of the council, in response to vehement minority protest, had actually excised a *partim . . . partim* formula from the draft decree. Joseph Geiselmann and others have argued that this step indicated the council's desire not to impugn the orthodoxy of the minority view urged by Agostino Bonuccio (d. 1553), superior general of the Servites, to whom "tradition" was "essentially an authoritative interpretation of Holy Writ, not its complement," Scripture itself containing "all truths necessary for salvation."[30] And, if this is so, then Trent did not teach the material insufficiency of the Scripture taken alone and the concomitant necessity for an authoritative extrascriptural tradition.

Although Geiselmann's view has not gone unchallenged, its effect upon late-medieval studies has been such as to suggest the impropriety of trying to stretch the views of late-medieval theologians to fit the Procrustean alternatives of Scripture alone or Scripture and tradition.

---

30. Jedin, *History*, II, 75. Jedin draws on Geiselmann. Oberman is among those who disagree with Geiselmann's claim; see *Harvest*, p. 407, n. 136. There is a balanced discussion of the controversy in Moran.

The striving for alternative modes of classification is already evident, therefore, in the literature. It has not yet generated a great deal of confidence in the ways in which individual thinkers are being classified. It is hard to generalize without a craven superfluity of qualifications when a thinker of Ockham's stature can be represented in turn as a precocious advocate of the Protestant appeal to Scripture alone, as undecided between that position and the rival claim that the divine relevation had also been mediated by the apostolic tradition, as one who actually leaned toward this latter "two sources" theory, and as one who definitely embraced it.[31] Generalize we must, however, and it is fair to say that whatever the hesitations and complications evident in the scholarly literature, the outlines of a less anachronistic classificatory schema have definitely begun to emerge.

The basic difficulty is that the church fathers, like the theologians of the early and High Middle Ages, had been content to join together what so many (though by no means all) of their late-medieval and sixteenth-century successors felt moved to put asunder—namely, the Scripture, tradition, and the magisterial authority of the church in relation to both. For the early fathers, the *kerygma*, the revealed "good news," was understood to be communicated in its entirety in the Scripture, and "tradition" was understood in the active sense as a handing down (*trahere*) of that scriptural revelation and of its authoritative interpretation within the community of the faithful. Bonuccio's stance at Trent reveals the tenacity of this general point of view. And if, by his day, it seems to have become something of a minority position among Catholic theologians, that development was comparatively recent. Until the fourteenth century one sees few signs of any inclination to distinguish clearly between the "truths of the Catholic faith" taught by the church and the scriptural revelation itself. The prevailing attitude was very matter-of-fact. Extrascriptural creedal statements tended to be understood as formulating or summarizing scriptural truths; there was little disposition to confront the

31. Thus, in order, Denifle, 2:382; cf. Grabmann, p. 111; de Vooght, *Sources*, pp. 161–67; Van Leeuwen; Oberman, *Harvest*, pp. 365–66, 378–82; Tierney, *Origins*, pp. 221–26.

problem raised by such points of doctrine as the *filioque* clause in the Latin version of the Nicene Creed or the form of several of the sacraments, which could not clearly be grounded in the Scriptures. All the truths of the faith were seen as "deriving" at one remove or another from the Scriptures and there was no hesitation about describing Scripture as the "sole source" of Christian doctrine—though such expressions clearly did not possess the "exclusive and literal" meaning accorded to them in later centuries.[32] Even in the fourteenth and fifteenth centuries, when some had begun to canvass the notion that revelation had been communicated in part by an extrascriptural tradition, such theologians as Guido Terreni (d. 1342), Bradwardine, Wycliffe, Hus, and Wessel Gansfort continued to espouse the older view. Indeed, it is rather as latter-day defenders of that older view than as precocious proclaimers of any proto-Protestant notion of *scriptura sola* that Wycliffe and Hus must properly be understood.[33]

Defenders, then, they were, but self-conscious defenders, deliberate affirmers of an older understanding of tradition and of an older unity that could no longer quite be taken for granted. For the newer understanding of tradition that rose to prominence during this period laid a special stress on John 20:30: "Now Jesus did many other signs in the presence of the disciples which are not written in this book." It separated, therefore, what had previously been united, and solved the problem posed by doctrines that appeared to lack any direct scriptural grounding by affirming the existence of a second source of revelation, an extrascriptural oral tradition stemming from Christ and handed down to their episcopal successors by the apostles.

Of the existence of such a notion there is little secure evidence earlier than the fourteenth century. It is true that in relation to certain established liturgical practices, and in a text later to be included in Gratian's influential *Decretum*, St. Basil (d. 370) had asserted: "We

---

32. See de Vooght, *Sources*, p. 254: "En réalité ces *solum* et ces *sola* n'avaient pas, chez les théologiens de l'époque, sans en excepter Wiclif, ce sens exclusif et littéral que nous leur accordons aujourd'hui."
33. De Vooght, *Sources*, especially pp. 233, 259–60. Hurley, especially pp. 276–79, 337–52, has dissented from his view of Wycliffe's position, but see the pertinent reply in Oberman, *Harvest*, p. 375, n. 41.

accept some of the ecclesiastical institutions from the Scriptures, others indeed, from apostolic tradition."[34] It is true also that that text cannot simply be dismissed as irrelevant on the grounds that it deals with liturgical practices rather than truths of the faith, for patristic and medieval theologians were by no means averse to drawing doctrinal conclusions from the existence of liturgical practices. It is true, again, that Gabriel Biel, in defending the newer two-sources theory, made a point of citing St. Basil's statement, so that it has been possible to claim that it was now "firmly grafted onto the theological tradition."[35]

But since, in the same text, St. Basil went on to accord the same respect to postapostolic tradition as he had previously accorded to Scripture and apostolic tradition, it hardly seems likely that he was concerned to state an opinion about the sources of divine revelation. Nor does the available evidence suggest that in bending it to that purpose Biel was following any path particularly well trodden by earlier theologians.[36] Least of all should the mere fact that the text was included in Gratian's *Decretum* be taken to justify the claim that "for the canon lawyer . . . the two-sources theory has been established."[37] The context in which Gratian introduces the text reveals that his concern in so doing was with ecclesiastical tradition conceived as no more than human custom, and the later decretist glossators were no more inclined than was he to stretch that tradition to include revealed truths of faith. In fact, contextual matters apart, it would have been very odd indeed had they been tempted to do anything of the sort. For

34. St. Basil, *De spiritu sancto*, 66; in Migne, *PG* XXXII, 188. As rendered in Latin in the *Decretum* the text runs as follows: "Ecclesiasticarum institutionum quasdam scripturis, quasdam vero apostolica traditione per successores in ministerio confirmatas accipimus; quasdam vero consuetudine roborata approbavit usus, quibus par ritus et idem utriusque pietatis debetur affectus" (D. 11, c. 5; ed. Friedberg, 1:24).

35. Oberman, *Harvest*, p. 406.

36. Though the English theologian William of Woodford (d. ca. 1400), charged with the task of refuting the errors of Wycliffe at a synod in London, also made some use of the text; see de Vooght, *Sources*, pp. 203–4.

37. Thus Oberman, *Harvest*, p. 369; cf. Tavard's similar ascription to the canonists of a new (though different) understanding of the meaning of *Tradition*, pp. 37–40, 47–48. Rather than Oberman and Tavard, I follow here Tierney, "'Sola Scriptura'"; cf. his *Origins*, pp. 15–31.

if their own thinking on the subject of Scripture and tradition was not really very extensively developed, it does appear to have moved almost entirely within the confines of the older commitment to the material sufficiency of the scriptural revelation and the older understanding of tradition as the church's handing down and interpretation of that revelation.[38]

In general, then, it is the theologians rather than the canonists, and, more particularly, the late-medieval theologians rather than their patristic or scholastic predecessors, who must be credited with the development of the two-sources theory that was destined to become so prominent in the theology of the Counter-Reformation era. On this matter, as on so many others, the contribution of William of Ockham was crucial. For in "his *Dialogus* he presented a classical formulation of the problem which influenced the whole course of late medieval ecclesiology."[39] In that work, acknowledging that there were "diverse and contrary" views on the subject, he described two principal positions. According to the first, "only those things which are asserted explicitly or implicitly in the canon of the Bible are to be reputed as Catholic truths and believed to be necessary for salvation." According to the second, many such truths are "neither explicitly contained in the divine Scriptures nor can be inferred from its contents alone."[40] In the course of subsequent discussion it becomes clear that here, as in other of his earlier writings, his own sympathies lie with the second position. Ockham therefore emerges as an advocate of the two-sources theory, and in this he was followed, though with subtle fluctuations, by a whole series of late-medieval theologians, most of them, like him, of nominalist persuasion. Among them must be listed Marsilius of Inghen (d. 1396), William of Woodford (d. ca. 1400), Henry Totting of Oyta (d. 1397), Pierre d'Ailly, Jean Courtecuisse (d. 1423), and Ambrosius of Speier (late fifteenth century).

---

38. In the course of the controversy over apostolic poverty, John XXII reaffirmed this understanding. His statement was included in the *Extravagantes Joannis XXII* (Tit. 14, c. 4 and 5; ed. Friedberg, 2:1230, 1236) and "no major canonists of the fourteenth century dissented from it"; see Tierney, "'Sola Scriptura,'" p. 350.
39. Tierney, *Origins*, p. 219.
40. Ockham, Dialogus, Lib. II, c. 2; in Goldast, 2:410–12.

Among them must also be listed Gabriel Biel, who in his formulation of the two-sources theory, Oberman has argued, comes "closer than any of his predecessors to the formulation of the Council of Trent: Scripture and Tradition should be held in equal esteem."[41]

Omitted from this listing is a name that one might expect to find and that others would certainly be willing to include: that of Jean Gerson, d'Ailly's distinguished pupil. The omission is deliberate. The fourteenth and fifteenth centuries witnessed the questioning of older unities and the appearance of a division between those who affirmed the single-source theory (the material sufficiency of Scripture and the older understanding of tradition) and those who espoused the newer two-sources theory. That much is certain, though disagreements still persist about the alignment of particular thinkers with one or other of the respective camps.[42] Only a little less certain, however, is the impossibility of aligning with either of those two camps every theologian who addressed the topic. Gerson is a case in point, and it has recently been argued that in one of his works he went beyond the two-sources theory, with which his name has certainly been linked, in that he took the radical step of assigning "to the Spirit-governed Church . . . the authority to judge and declare what the *literal* sense of Scripture is." As a result, for him, in contradistinction to the advocates of the two-sources theory, "the Bible itself has no theologically authoritative literal meaning," and "the possibility of argument from Scripture against the [ecclesiastical] *magisterium* is . . . programmatically and theoretically eliminated."[43]

The correctness of this appraisal is doubtless debatable. But it is a valuable one if only because it suggests the existence at that time of a third position distinct from the two preceding. Whereas the advocates of the two-sources theory had shattered the older unity by understanding tradition not simply as the handing down and authoritative

---

41. Oberman, *Harvest*, p. 406.
42. For Ockham, see above, n. 31. Similarly with Guido Terreni: de Vooght, *Sources*, pp. 132–37, and Tierney, *Origins*, pp. 251–59, align him with the older single-source position, whereas B. M. Xiberta, "Scriptura, Traditio et magisterium juxta antiquos auctores ordinis Carmelitarum," in Balić, pp. 253–73, and Tavard, pp. 31–34, represent him as the advocate of a two-sources theory.
43. See Preus, pp. 79–81 and n. 23.

interpretation of the Scriptures but as an extrascriptural oral tradition constituting a second source of revelation, the representatives of the third position tended in the direction of a further and more radical step. For they laid a wholly new emphasis on the active teaching role of the church, loosening the bonds that had previously limited the *magisterium* to the faithful elucidation of the Scriptures or of Scripture and tradition alike, freeing it to create "new tradition," attributing to it, in effect, the final authority to determine—even through novel dogmatic formulations—what the tradition *must* originally have contained. And in so doing they broke with Vincent of Lérins's (d. *ante* 450) time-honored definition of what constituted orthodox tradition —namely, what had been believed "everywhere, always, by all."[44] All in all, a not too remote anticipation of the view that Möhler and the members of the Tübingen school taught in the nineteenth century and which has since become so prominent in Roman Catholic theology—the view of tradition, not as a set of passive historical "monuments" but as a living thing, one that finds its definitive expression in the faith of the church today and is crystallized not only in the lives of the faithful but also, and more precisely, in the authoritative pronouncements of the *magisterium*.[45]

Not all Franciscans were advocates of this position. Ockham himself certainly was not; he specifically insisted that the determinations of the church could not in themselves constitute a distinct source of Catholic truth. Nor were all who sympathized with the view Franciscans; both Gerson and John Pupper of Goch so stressed "the metaphysical priority of the Church over Scripture" as to insist "that the Church can even declare the grammatically less probable meaning of the text to the true literal sense."[46] Nevertheless (though here one must perforce speak very tentatively), it would appear that the vogue of a specifically Franciscan doctrine, and the problems attendant upon it, did much to sponsor the crystallization of this third position. For the doctrine of the absolute poverty of Christ and the apostles and the

44. Vincent of Lérins, *Comminatorium*, chap. 2; in Moxon, p. 10.
45. See the useful brief discussion in Moran, pp. 38–42.
46. Steinmetz, "Libertas Christiana," pp. 204–5.

insistence that the renunciation of property, whether held individually or in common, lay at the very heart of Christian perfection had as
little unambiguous foundation in apostolic tradition as it had in the
Scripture itself. It reflected a new understanding of the Christian message; it was, in effect, as their enemies alleged and as prominent Franciscans themselves admitted, a "new tradition," one that could be
firmly grounded only in the teaching authority of the church itself.
Hence the insistence of such distinguished Franciscan theologians as
St. Bonaventure and Duns Scotus that "Catholic truth was not what
the church had demonstrably always proclaimed but what the church
was proclaiming then and there, in their own time."[47] Hence, too,
the assertion of the general chapter of the Franciscan order at Perugia
in June 1322 that articles of faith derived "either from sacred Scripture
or from the determination of the church," thereby affirming the belief
that "the church was a second source of divine revelation supplemen-
tary to Scripture."[48] Hence, finally, though this time by way of reaction to Franciscan claims, John XXII's evocation of the older view,
and his insistence in Cum inter nonnullos that to ignore the explicit
scriptural base of doctrine would be "by taking away its proof" to render "the Catholic faith doubtful and uncertain."[49]

John XXII's reaction is interesting. In modern Roman Catholic
theology the position closest to the one he rejected—the notion of the
church as itself a "living tradition"—has often been linked with the
doctrine of papal infallibility. In the fifteenth century, however, the
position cognate to it could be espoused by a conciliarist (Gerson) and
a man traditionally portrayed as a "Reformer before the Reformation"
(John Pupper of Goch). Similar perplexities attend upon any attempt
to chart the subsequent careers of the other two positions outlined

47. Tierney, Origins, pp. 144, 222. Among the texts that Tierney cites in support of
this claim are Bonaventure, De perfectione evangelica, qu. 1, art. 2, in Opera, 5:153,
and Scotus, Reportata parisiensia, IV, dist. 11, qu. 3, n. 13, in Opera, 24:120, where
he says (though with reference, admittedly, not to the doctrine of apostolic poverty
but rather to that of transubstantiation): "Hoc principaliter teneo propter auc-
toritatem ecclesiae, quae non errat in his, quae sunt fidei et morum."
48. Tierney, Origins, p. 193. The texts of the encyclical letters approved at Perugia
are printed in Baluzius and Mansi, 3:208–13 (see especially pp. 209–10).
49. Extra. Joann. XXII, Tit. 14, c. 4; ed. Friedberg, 2:1230.

above. Thus the first and older position is not simply to be identified with the later Protestant appeal to *scriptura sola*. It was taught, after all, by Bonuccio at Trent and had been embraced during the fourteenth and fifteenth centuries by men of as different sympathies as John XXII, the condemned heretics Wycliffe and Hus, and Guido Terreni, the proponent of papal infallibility. And if the second or two-sources theory did indeed feed into the mainstream of Counter-Reformation theology, it must nevertheless be remarked that it numbered among its adherents conciliarists as well as papalists. All of which might well lead one to suspect that the truly important ecclesiological disagreements of the era centered less on the specifically magisterial power of the church than upon its jurisdictional power in general. That suspicion would not be misplaced.

The Nature of the Church

The thirteenth century has been characterized as belonging still to "the *prehistory* of ecclesiology," and James of Viterbo's *De regimine christiano* (1301–2) has been called—not without justice—"the oldest treatise on the Church." [50] In the *Liber sententiarum*, which became the standard textbook for medieval students of theology, Peter Lombard devoted no separate section to the topic *De ecclesia*; the same approach is evident in the theological works of Aquinas a century and more later. Only in the fourteenth and fifteenth centuries did ecclesiology become a focus of intense concern among theologians. That shift in interest therefore calls for explanation.

It has been argued that the shift was due in part to the nominalist preoccupation with divine omnipotence and the understandable concern of nominalist theologians, therefore, with the historical institutional arrangements a covenanting God had actually chosen *de potentia ordinata* to make. This argument may be plausible, but it is not readily susceptible of either proof or disproof. A more concrete argument has pointed to the trials and tribulations that the ecclesiastical institu-

---

50. Lagarde, 5:4; Arquillière. There is room, of course, for some disagreement about the accuracy of that designation; see Thils, pp. 243–44; Hendrix, pp. 348–49, n. 5.

tion was forced to endure during these centuries and to the flood of publicistic literature they helped engender. Among those trials three stand out: first, the conflicts between Boniface VIII and Philip IV of France and between John XXII and Lewis of Bavaria; second, the long dispute over the Franciscan doctrine of apostolic poverty, which had surfaced during the conflict between mendicants and seculars at Paris in the 1250s and racked both the order and the church at large for the better part of the century following;[51] third, the unprecedentedly grave split in the Latin church from 1378 to 1418, which has gone down in history as the Great Schism of the West.

The first of these disastrous trials led to an outpouring of publicistic literature concerning the proper relationship between temporal and spiritual authorities, one paralleled in importance during the Middle Ages only by the earlier outburst during the Gregorian era. Critical though this issue was, it cannot concern us here. More significant for our purposes is the simple fact that the initial conflict between Boniface VIII and Philip IV spawned the first group of important treatises devoted specifically to the church or to aspects of its power: the *De regimine christiano* of James of Viterbo, Aegidius Romanus's *De ecclesiastica potestate* (1302), and John of Paris's *De potestate regia et papali* (1302–3). These tracts already manifest the anxious scrutiny of church structures and far-reaching speculation concerning the nature and location of ecclesiastical authority that were to characterize the publicist and theological writings connected with the two other great challenges to the church's traditional order. Taken as a whole, then, along with the canonistic commentaries on which they so often drew, the writings produced by all three crises confront us with a body of thought on matters ecclesiological at once more extensive, more varied, more developed, and more systematic than anything emerging from the centuries preceding.

51. The question of apostolic poverty did as much as that of papal privileges to mold Franciscan thinking concerning scriptural and ecclesiastical authority in general and papal authority in particular. Tierney, *Origins*, pp. 65–66, asserts that "the main lines that this whole theoretical controversy [concerning papal privilege] followed were determined by the first exchange of polemical treatises at Paris in the years 1255–1256."

In its most radical and extreme manifestations, this body of thought measured the institutional church of its day against a would-be historical understanding of the conditions prevailing in the primitive Christian communities of the apostolic era and, finding that church understandably wanting, pursued its own beckoning ideals across the shadowy and fluctuating border that separated prophetic criticism from outright heresy. More commonly, however, it erected its own varying but imposing structures upon the extensive foundations laid by the theological controversies and canonistic formulations of earlier centuries.

Among these foundations, two stand out as central, one theological, the other canonistic. The theological foundation is the position that Augustine had adopted in his conflict with the Donatists, which was consciously challenged during the Middle Ages only by those hardy spirits susceptible to the lures of heresy. The canonistic foundation is the practice whereby the medieval canonists had come to treat the universal church as a single corporate entity akin to other corporations, a practice that helped shape the single most important ecclesiological debate of the era. The first pertained to the nature of the holiness that was to be required of the church; the second to the nature of the unity that the church could be said to possess. We will take them up in turn.

Of the four marks of the church designated in the Nicene Creed— one, holy, catholic, apostolic—the mark of holiness appeared earlier and more often in the various creeds than did the other three. It was also the characteristic that gave rise to some of the earliest ecclesiological controversies. All agreed that the church—the body of Christ, the body wherein, via the sacraments, the saving grace of God was mediated to sinful man—*had* to be holy. Already in the third century, Cyprian, bishop of Carthage (d. 258), had become embroiled in disputes concerning the way in which that holiness was to be defined and what it implied for the sacraments of baptism and penance. On this issue, however, as on so many others, the later contribution of Augustine proved determinative.

The birthplace of Donatism was the North African province of the

Roman Empire. There, by Augustine's lifetime, it had split the Christian community into bitterly opposed orthodox and schismatic churches. Its point of departure had been the great persecution of Diocletian (285–305), under the pressure of which some of the clergy had apostatized. After that persecution a group of zealots had challenged in particular the authority of the bishop of Carthage (on the grounds that he had been ordained by one who had repudiated his faith and thereby lapsed into mortal sin), had questioned in general the validity of sacraments administered by clergy of immoral or unworthy behavior, had adopted the position that the church had forfeited its claim to be holy if it tolerated within its ranks members guilty of the cardinal sin of apostasy or clergy morally unworthy of their high office, and had insisted, in effect, on making "the unity and the catholicity of the church contingent on its prior holiness."[52] For these Donatists, that holiness was to be judged solely in terms of the moral rigor with which its individual members conducted their lives. The church was for them to be a body of the elect, its members, clerical as well as lay, restricted to the ranks of the righteous—it was, in Ernst Troeltsch's categories, to be a sect. This being so, the Donatists were eventually willing to make the startling claim that their own church, limited though it was to the North African province, and schismatic at that, alone possessed the sacraments, the primary instrumentalities through which grace was mediated, and alone could claim to be the one and true Catholic church.

If the Donatists made the unity of the church contingent upon its holiness, Augustine, by way of reaction, went a long way toward making its holiness contingent upon its unity. For him, it was schism far more than the individual unworthiness of its ministers that struck at the very life of the church. Cut off, indeed, from "the unity of the body of Christ," and, as a result, from the grace that, by divine ordination, the church and its sacraments mediate to man, nobody could attain true holiness. For the holiness of the church did not reside in the subjective righteousness of its individual members but rather in its own institutional sanctity as the locus of the regenerative working of

52. Pelikan, 1:309.

divine grace. "The church is one, and its holiness is produced by the sacraments," Optatus, another anti-Donatist, had said. "It is not to be considered on the basis of the pride of individuals."[53] The emphasis, therefore, was on the objective and the sacramental, and the authenticity and holiness of the sacramental channels of divine grace were seen to depend upon the personal moral worthiness neither of minister nor of recipient. So that while Augustine, in his confrontation with Pelagianism, was led to state his belief in predestination in a particularly uncompromising form, thus identifying the true church not with any institution or visible fellowship of men but with the invisible body of the elect foreknown to God alone, in his writings against the Donatists he was led to identify the visible, institutional church, with its saints and sinners, hierarchy and sacraments, as the one true Catholic church and the sole ark of salvation. If the membership of that church is more inclusive, strictly speaking, than that of the "essential" or "invisible" church, it is not God's will that we, like the Donatists, should presume to do what he himself will not undertake to do before the Last Judgment—namely, to separate the wheat from the chaff, the saints from the sinners.

In an even more direct and thoroughgoing fashion than his doctrine of grace, Augustine's teaching on the church succeeded in defining the terms of medieval orthodoxy and in establishing the boundaries within which ecclesiological discussion, if it aspired to be orthodox, had necessarily to be conducted. It also laid the requisite foundation on which the scholastic theologians were able to develop a sacramental theology and the canonists to erect an analysis of hierarchical and ecclesiastical power. By the fourteenth century, both of these bodies of thought had undergone very considerable elaboration, but it is the latter—the canonistic investigation of the structures of ecclesiastical power—that must concern us here. For it funneled directly into the great late-medieval debate concerning the nature of the church's unity.

To say that, however, is not to deny the impropriety of too insistent a separation between the concerns of the theologians and those of the

53. Optatus, *Donat.*, 2:1; *CSEL*, 26:32. Cf. Pelikan, 1:311.

canonists. In the twelfth- and thirteenth-century definitions of the church, it was still customary to give a prominent place to the sacraments, especially to the Eucharist. Was not the church, after all, itself the body of Christ, a prolongation of Christ's presence in the world, one that incorporated the faithful in a mysterious community of salvation? During those same centuries, nevertheless, the diminution in the sense of the organic connection between Christ's self-immolation and the priest's eucharistic act, which we noted in discussing medieval liturgical developments, was paralleled by and linked with a comparable diminution in the sense of organic connection between Christ and his church. In the patristic era, those connections had been so deeply felt that the church could be referred to as the "true" body of Christ (*corpus Christi verum*) and when, during the Carolingian era, the term "mystical body of Christ" (*corpus Christi mysticum*) became prominent in theological literature, it had been used to denote not the church but the Eucharist. From the mid-twelfth century onward, however, something of a reversal took place.[54] Perhaps under the impact of the great controversy of the previous century concerning the nature of Christ's presence in the Eucharist, theologians became anxious to emphasize the *real*—as opposed to a mystical or merely spiritual—presence of Christ in the sacrament. As a result, it became common to designate the Eucharist not as "the mystical" but as "the true body of Christ," and the term *corpus Christi mysticum*, applied now to the church in the manner familiar to us today, fell victim to a progressive secularization.

In St. Bonaventure, and, more frequently, in Aquinas, we may find the analogy of the church as a mystical body being drawn not from the sacramental body of Christ but from natural bodies or bodies in general, so that Aquinas can speak of "the mystical body of the church" (*corpus ecclesiae mysticum*).[55] This is an expression almost devoid of sacramental associations and one already on the way to acquiring those juristic connotations that were fully exploited during the fourteenth and fifteenth centuries by canonists and publicists alike. Already in

54. See Lubac, especially pp. 117–37. Cf. Ladner.
55. See Lubac, pp. 129–30.

the thirteenth century, Innocent IV had identified the *aggregatio fidelium* with the *corpus Christi*, and Tierney has commented that "in assuming that the Church, defined as the *corpus Christi*, was an entity capable of the quite prosaic function of property ownership, Innocent was apparently regarding it not only as a *corpus mysticum* but as something akin to a legal corporation."[56] By the early fifteenth century, when Pierre d'Ailly expressed sentiments almost identical with those of Innocent IV, the equation had become a commonplace: the church had come to be "interpreted as a polity like any other secular corporation," and "the notion *corpus mysticum* itself," charged now "with secular political contents," had come to be almost a synonym for "moral and political body" (*corpus morale et politicum*).[57]

The importance of this development is not to be gainsaid. In the first place, it accelerated the process (already well advanced among the canonists) whereby categories and concepts drawn from secular legal and political thinking were applied to the church. Of the traditional categories of ecclesiastical power, indeed, it was the power of jurisdiction and in particular the *potestas jurisdictionis in foro exteriori*—its public, coercive, most unambiguously nonsacramental and *political* subdivision—that was classified as pertaining to the *corpus mysticum*.[58] In the second place, by opening up a certain distance between the sacramental and governmental aspects of the church, it made possible (without any challenge to the traditional Augustinian teaching on the church's holiness) the initiation of a great debate concerning her unity. Indeed, not only did it make such a debate possible, it positively invited one. For the notion that the church as a mystical body was an entity akin to a legal corporation suggested conclusions of several types. And during the century and more preceding the onset of

56. Tierney, *Foundations*, pp. 140–41.
57. Kantorowicz, pp. 203, 211–12. Thus d'Ailly, *Tractatus de ecclesiastica potestate*, in Dupin, 2:942: ". . . et ita intellinguntur esse oblata Christo, id est Communitati Fidelium, quae est Corpus Christi."
58. The sacerdotal or sacramental power (*potestas ordinis*) was said to pertain to the *corpus Christi verum*. There was some disagreement about the degree to which the *potestas jurisdictionis in foro interiori* was to be regarded as truly jurisdictional in essence or aligned with the *potestas ordinis*. On these points, see Oakley, "Figgis," pp. 380–82, and the literature referred to therein.

the Great Schism, the canonists, in their attempts to rationalize the structure both of the individual churches of Christendom and of the universal church itself, had been led to develop two separate doctrines concerning the church's unity. "The more conspicuous one, which has usually been regarded as the canonistic doctrine *par excellence*, insisted that the unity of the Church could be secured only by a rigorous subordination of all the members to a single head." Hence the doctrine of absolute papal monarchy that dominated most of the canonistic glosses of the fourteenth century and attained its least inhibited expression in the works of such high-papalist publicists as Aegidius Romanus, Augustinus Triumphus (d. 1328), Alvarus Pelagius (d. 1352), and John of Turrecremata (d. 1468).

> But side by side with this [doctrine] there existed another theory, applied at first to the single churches and then at the beginning of the fourteenth century, in a fragmentary fashion, to the Roman Church and the Church as a whole, a theory which stressed the corporate association of the members of a Church as the true principle of ecclesiastical unity, and which envisaged an exercise of corporate authority by the members of a church even in the absence of an effective head.[59]

This theory, along with an older strand in canonistic thinking going back to the twelfth- and early-thirteenth-century commentaries on Gratian's *Decretum* (and especially to their discussions of the case of the heretical pope), laid the essential foundations for the pattern of conciliarist thinking that was to attain mature expression during the schism and its aftermath in the writings of such men as Conrad of Gelnhausen, d'Ailly, Gerson, Francesco Zabarella (d. 1417), and Nicholas of Cusa.

The ambivalence of the canonistic heritage blocked the crystallization of a coherently constitutionalist understanding of the church's unity until the imperative necessities of a protracted schism called such an understanding into being. That ambivalence also did something to impede the development of a rival doctrine of unity hinging upon papal absolutism, but did not ultimately prevent it. Indeed, to us, the curialist insistence on the pope's sovereign authority over the

59. Tierney, *Foundations*, p. 240.

church is surely the most familiar feature of late-medieval ecclesiological discourse. According to the anonymous papalist author of the
pamphlet known as the *Determinatio compendiosa* (1342):

> Especially is he, the pope, above every council and statute . . . ; he
> it is, too, who has no superior on earth; he, the pope, gives dispen-
> sations from every law. . . . Again, it is he who possesses the pleni-
> tude of power on earth and holds the place and office of the Most
> High. . . . He it is who alters the substance of a thing, making
> legitimate what was illegitimate . . . and of a monk making a canon
> regular, . . . he it is who by absolving on earth absolves [also] in
> heaven, and by binding on earth binds [also] in heaven. . . . Again, it
> is to him that nobody may say: "Why do you do that?" . . . He it is for
> whom the will is reason enough, since that which pleases him has the
> force of law (*ei quod placet, legis vigorem habet*); . . . he is not bound by
> the laws . . . *etc* (*solutus est legibus*). Indeed, the pope is the law itself
> and a living law (*lex viva*), to resist which is impermissible. This then
> is the Catholic and orthodox faith, approved and canonized by the holy
> fathers of old, from which all justice, religion, sanctity and discipline
> have emanated. If anyone does not believe it faithfully and firmly, he
> cannot be saved, and without doubt will perish eternally.[60]

An extreme statement, perhaps, but one familiar enough in its claims
to dull the apprehension of what precisely is involved and to blunt the
perception of what is not. Three caveats, therefore, may be in order.

In the first place, this high-papalist doctrine made no special claims
for the pope in relation to sacerdotal or sacramental powers; in that
respect he was but a bishop among bishops and it was conceded that
Christ had bestowed the "power of order" equally upon all the apostles, those first prelates in whose lineage later prelates stood. The doctrine was concerned, rather, with the distribution among the ranks of
the hierarchy of the "power of jurisdiction in the external forum."
This power, it was asserted, Christ had bestowed in superior and

60. Scholz, *Unbekannte kirchenpolitischen Streitschriften*, 2:544. Extreme though it
may seem, the anonymous author's list of papal prerogatives is not unrepresentative
but follows closely a comparable list given by Gulielmus Durandus (the Speculator),
itself derived, it seems, from the *glossa ordinaria* to the Decretals, the author of which
had taken it from an earlier gloss by Tancred (d. 1235). The claims involved are
explicitly juridical: "They referred to the legislative and dispensatory powers of the
pope within the framework of positive ecclesiastical law" (Tierney, *Origins*, pp. 26–
27).

unique measure upon Peter, so that the plenitude of power that was claimed for the pope as successor to Peter was a plenitude of jurisdictional power *in foro exteriori*—in effect, a fullness of public, coercive, governmental power. Further, from the time of Innocent III until the completion of the full-fledged doctrine in John of Turrecremata's great *Summa de ecclesia*, it was claimed with increasing frequency and growing elaboration that the pope was not only superior in jurisdiction to other prelates in the church but also the immediate *source* of the jurisdiction wielded by all those lesser prelates. As Augustinus Triumphus argued (with reference to Matt. 16 : 19):

> When Christ, therefore, granted the power of jurisdiction, he spoke not in the plural but in the singular, saying to Peter alone, "I shall give thee the keys of the kingdom of heaven," as if clearly to say: although I shall have given the power of order to all the apostles, I give thus to you alone your power of jurisdiction, to be dispensed and distributed through you to all the others.

And because it is not Christ but the pope as successor to Peter who "thus confers the power of jurisdiction on the other prelates of the Church, in the same way he can take it away from them." [61]

In the second place, despite the understandable antipathy aroused by such a doctrine among the local ordinaries, the independent basis of whose jurisdictions it directly challenged, papal lawlessness was not its necessary corollary, nor was a doctrine of arbitrary despotism intended. For the papalists, canonists and publicists alike, invoked by way of analogy the covenantal pattern that, as we have seen, was so marked a feature of the theology of the day. Some of them distinguished between the pope's absolute and ordained or ordinary powers. They directed the pope's attention to the fact that God, his omnipotence notwithstanding, "nearly always" condescends to observe the laws that he has imposed upon the natural world, "producing the effects of secondary agents through the mediation of secondary agents." They argued (as did Aegidius Romanus) that the pope likewise, his plenitude of power notwithstanding, ought to govern the church in line with the laws he himself has established, permitting "chapters to

61. Augustinus Triumphus, *Tractatus brevis*; in Scholz, *Publizistik*, p. 492.

carry out their elections, and prelates to discharge their duties, and other churchmen to perform their tasks, in accordance with the form given them."[62]

If those who wished to extend the reach of the pope's authority might well be tempted to invoke the intervention of his absolute power (as, ironically enough, Henry VIII of England did on the divorce question), it was also possible for those who wished to oppose what they took to be such an extension to resist. They had grounds in that the action involved, though undoubtedly possible *de potentia absoluta*, was not permissible by his ordained power, regulated as it was by the provisions of the written law (*de regulata et secundum jura scripta ordinata potestate sua*).[63]

In the third place, if, by his absolute power, the pope could clearly transcend the law, he was sovereign in relation to the positive canon law of the church. He was not superior to the limits imposed by natural law or freed on matters of faith from the bonds of the scriptural revelation. Nor is it to be supposed that this doctrine of papal sovereignty entailed necessarily or even usually a belief in papal infallibility. It is true that the medieval canonists, unlike some of their modern successors, were content to treat the magisterial power as an aspect of jurisdiction. It is also true that they certainly regarded the pope's jurisdiction as embracing the right to render decisions in disputes pertaining to matters of faith. Christ's promise to Peter that his faith would not fail (Luke 22:32) they took, however, to be a guarantee of the indefectibility of the universal church rather than of Peter himself, and certainly not of the infallibility of his papal successors. The *Decretum*, after all, contained allegations that past popes had fallen into error on matters of faith. It also contained a crucial and

62. Hostiensis, *Lectura*, *ad* X, 5, 31, 8 *in v*. Ita, and *ad* X, 3, 35, 6 *in v*. nec summus Pontifex; fols. LXXIr and CXXXr. Aegidius Romanus, *De eccl. pot.*, III, chap. 9; ed. Scholz, pp. 191–92.
63. For Henry VIII, see "Instructions to Sir Francis Bryan and Peter Vannes, sent to the Court of Rome," in Brewer et al., IV, pt. 2, 2158 (no. 4977). For an example of the opposing usage, see "Appelation deutscher geistlichen von dem executor des von papste geforderten zehntens an den päpstlichen stuhl 1352–60," ed. Winkelmann, 2:843 (no. 1182). Further examples of the canonistic use of the distinction in Oakley, "Jacobean Political Theology," especially pp. 330–32, and Wilks, pp. 291, n. 2; 294–96; 319, n. 5; 349–50.

much-glossed text (Dist. 40, chap. 6) indicating that if the pope were "caught deviating from the faith" he was not immune to human judgment. This ground would seem too stony to be hospitable to any notion of papal infallibility. When, indeed, that doughty canonist John XXII encountered the doctrine in 1324, although he did not meet it head on, he did contrive to brush it aside as a "pestiferous doctrine." [64]

That he should have lost so little time in doing so appears to reflect his deeply felt sense that simply to admit the doctrine of papal infallibility would be to undercut the traditional doctrine of papal sovereignty. For if popes were infallible in their pronouncements on matters of faith, then the pronouncements of his predecessors on such matters were irreformable and he himself was bound by them. And that is precisely what at least the Franciscan proponents of infallibility were out to suggest. The doctrine was something of a late-medieval novelty, first explicitly proposed, it has recently been argued, by Franciscan propagandists eager to defend the inviolability of Nicholas III's bull *Exiit qui seminat* (1279), which endorsed the Franciscan doctrine of apostolic poverty as a matter of revealed truth. The doctrine grounded the irreformability of such decrees in the infallibility of their papal authors and entailed the corollary that any pope who (like John XXII) attempted to abrogate the teachings of a predecessor could be recognized for what he was: a pontiff "only in name and appearance," a pseudopope who had been separated *ipso facto* from his papal office.

The doctrine of papal infallibility was a novelty designed, at least in its inception, "to limit the power of future popes, not to loose them from all restraints." [65] Understandably, despite the existence of a small group of "curial infallibilists" surrounding John XXII, the doctrine did not find much resonance even among papalist writers prior to

64. In the bull *Quia quorundam: Extravag. Joann. XXII*, Tit. 14, c. 5; ed. Friedberg, 2–1230.
65. Tierney, *Origins*, p. 130. Taking note of the further nuances indicated by Turley, I follow in this Tierney's illuminating and provocative treatment, judging its central thesis to have survived intact the onslaughts of even such distinguished critics as Stickler, Dempf, and Congar, as well as the distressingly personal attack launched by

John of Turrecremata in the fifteenth century. It was not destined to rise to prominence in Catholic theology until the sixteenth and seventeenth centuries.

Had it been powerful earlier, of course, the alternative, or conciliarist, understanding of the church's unity would doubtless not have constituted so prominent a threat to the hegemony of the papalist position during the fourteenth and fifteenth centuries as it did. Indeed, the unexamined assumption that the doctrine of papal infallibility was widely held even in that period may well explain the frequency with which the conciliarist position has been misrepresented as an unorthodox ecclesiology of revolutionary vintage foisted upon the church by those dangerous radicals Marsilius of Padua and William of Ockham. Whatever the influence exerted on the conciliar thinkers by Ockham's arguments, he was not, according to the usual general understanding of the term, a conciliarist at all. As he was something less than a conciliarist, Marsilius was something more. Marsilius denied the divine foundation of papacy and hierarchy, portraying the church as a merely spiritual community of believers linked solely by the common bond of a sacrament and creed, and denying to its members, accordingly, the exercise of any coercive jurisdictional power at all, any *potestas jurisdictionis in foro exteriori*. Marsilius's views left some mark on the thinking of Dietrich of Niem (d. 1418) and Nicholas of Cusa, but were too radical to make their way into the mainstream of conciliar theory during the age of the great councils. For that theory was in fact an essentially moderate doctrine of ecclesiastical constitutionalism, with unimpeachably orthodox foundations in the cozy respectabilities of the pre-Marsilian era.[66]

Remigius Bäumer. For this last, see Bäumer, "Um die Anfänge der päpstlichen Unfehlbarkeitslehre"; Tierney's reply (and Bäumer's rejoinder): "On the History of Papal Infallibility." For the most instructive exchange in English, see Stickler, "Papal Infallibility," Tierney, "Infallibility and the Medieval Canonists"; Stickler, "Rejoinder to Professor Tierney."

66. For this and what follows, I draw upon the extensive discussion of these and related issues in Oakley, *Political Thought of Pierre d'Ailly; Council over Pope?*; "Almain and Major"; "Conciliarism at the Fifth Lateran Council?" and "Conciliarism in the Sixteenth Century."

In the extensive canonistic discussions concerning *Decretum Gratiani*, Distinction 40, Chapter 6, and the possibility of a pope "caught deviating from the faith," two main schools of thought had emerged. According to one, a pope who lapsed into heresy ceased *ipso facto* to be pope. Only if he contumaciously persisted in his heresy would recourse be had to a judicial superior and then only to make it clear that he was guilty of heresy and to proclaim a merely *declaratory* sentence of deposition. According to the other school, however, an heretical pope did not cease *ipso facto* to be pope; he had instead to be subjected to trial, judgment, and deposition. And the body possessing the requisite superior authority enabling it to stand in judgment was the general council, since, even acting in opposition to the pope, it possessed a superior jurisdiction in matters pertaining to the faith. It is in the combination of this second theory of papal liability with the later canonistic understanding of church unity as residing in "the corporate association of the members" that we find the foundations of the strict conciliar theory. That theory received a precociously complete formulation in the *Tractatus de potestate regia et papali* of John of Paris but rose to prominence only in the years after the outbreak of the Great Schism.

The strict conciliar theory has often been misunderstood. It possessed no monolithic unity. One must avoid the fatal trap of confusing it with the type of conciliar thinking espoused earlier by Marsilius of Padua. And the version dominant at Constance and Basel was given more than one form by the various conciliar thinkers, who, in accordance with their differing temperaments, vocations, and circumstances, wove theories of differing dimensions and textures. They did so, nevertheless, around a shared pattern of belief.

Their basic assumption, which of course they shared with the papalists, was that of the divine institution of all ecclesiastical power. This power they divided, again like the papalists, into a power of order and a power of jurisdiction. About the former they had very little to say, for the pope did not base his claim to preeminence in the church on his possession of orders. His claims to invulnerability rested upon the nature of his jurisdictional power, and, more precisely, upon his power of jurisdiction in the external forum. It is this type of jurisdictional power alone that the conciliar theorists of the era of Constance and Basel had in mind when they asserted the superiority of council to pope. Upon an analysis of this jurisdictional power and of the precise manner in which it was distributed throughout the ranks of the faithful these men bent their efforts.

Against the claims of the high papalists they denied that Christ gave the power of jurisdiction to Peter alone and not to all the apostles and that the jurisdiction of inferior prelates must therefore be derived from the pope and not immediately from God. Against those claims, accordingly, they also denied that the plenitude of jurisdictional power can reside in the pope alone. They did not wish thereby to deny the divine origin of the papal primacy. But if the office itself is of divine institution, its bestowal upon a particular individual is the work of men. And when the cardinals elect a pope, they do so not in their own right but as representatives of the community of the faithful. For the final authority in the church, as in other more particular congregations, resides in the whole body of its members.

The authority of the whole body is not exhausted by the mere act of electing a head. Even after a papal election the fullness of power still resides in some sense in the church as well as in the pope. So that, as Zabarella put it, the plenitude of power is fundamentally in the whole church as in a corporate body, and only derivatively in the pope as the "principal minister" of that corporation. Or, in d'Ailly's version, the plenitude of power must be said to belong *inseparably* to the body of the church, *representatively* to the general council, but only *separably* to the pope, who is the subject who receives it and the minister who exercises it.[67] Thus, although the fullness of power may be ascribed to the pope by virtue of his superiority to any other single ecclesiastic and his normal exercise of it, he is not superior to the universal church or to the general council representing it, and he must exercise that power for the good of the whole church. It follows that, like any other corporation in relation to its head, the council has the right to set limits to

67. Zabarella, pp. 559–60; d'Ailly, *Tractatus de ecclesiastica potestate*, in Dupin, 2:945–46, 950–51.

his exercise of the *plenitudo potestatis* in order to prevent his abusing it to the destruction of the church.

That right is conceived of as being exercised both under emergency conditions and on a more continuing basis. The emergency situation most readily envisaged (though by no means the only one) is that which occurs when a pope lapses into heresy, or, by being the occasion of schism, endangers the faith of the whole church. Under such conditions, the church—which, unlike the pope, possesses the gift of doctrinal inerrancy—possesses also the power to prevent its own ruin. Infallibility is not necessarily to be ascribed to the doctrinal decisions of a general council (to d'Ailly, for example, that was no more than a matter of pious belief).[68] Yet, in the determination of orthodoxy, the council certainly does possess an authority superior to that of the pope and can therefore stand in judgment over him, correct him, and even, if need be, depose him.

The conciliar theorists were a good deal less precise concerning the exercise of this inherent ecclesiastical authority under nonemergency conditions. Some—notably Zabarella, d'Ailly, and Nicholas of Cusa —in response to the "oligarchic" views long since current among the canonists and at the papal curia (and given explicit theoretical expression by the canonists Hostiensis and Johannes Monachus) regarded the college of cardinals as sharing with the pope in the exercise of the reduced plenitude of power they allotted to him and as functioning, therefore, as a continuously operating institutional restraint on the abuse of that power. But some sort of continuing role was also envisaged for the general council in matters concerning the faith, and also, it seems, in decisions affecting the general state or well-being of the church. And for d'Ailly, Dietrich of Niem, Gerson, and Nicholas of Cusa, at least, regularly assembled general councils were to become a permanent rather than an exceptional part of the structure of church government, an innovation that would have involved a substantial shift in the church's constitution.

Such was the theory that permitted the councils of Pisa and Constance to take the drastic steps necessary to end the schism and that

68. See Oakley, "Pierre d'Ailly and Papal Infallibility."

found clear expression in the Constance decrees *Haec sancta synodus* and *Frequens*. The theory was predicated on a perfectly orthodox insistence that the unity of the church resided ultimately in the association of its members with one another and with Christ, their "principal" and "essential" head, rather than in its domination by the pope, its subordinate and "accidental" head. It involved, therefore, an essentially moderate insistence on the ministerial nature of papal authority, and only in the latter phase of the Council of Basel was it used to justify what amounted to an attempted seizure of the central administrative machinery of the church, and then with the result that some of its most distinguished advocates went over to the pope's camp.

It has long been customary to suppose that the ignominious ending of Basel and the failure of the conciliar movement marked also the demise of conciliar theory. But though the late fifteenth century saw a great recovery in the prestige of the high-papalist ecclesiology, that ecclesiology still had to compete with its conciliarist rival for the loyalties of the faithful. Just as recent historical studies (notably those of Tierney) have made it abundantly clear that the conciliar theory was not so recent or revolutionary in its origins as it was once assumed to be, Jedin, Klotzner, Bäumer, and others have proved that its demise was neither so sudden nor so final as we had been led to suppose.[69] Scotland, Italy, England, Germany, France, all produced their latter-day supporters of conciliar theory, especially the Parisian theologians John Major (d. 1550) and Jacques Almain (d. 1515), who gave the theory a classic expression right on the eve of the Reformation. Nor is it to be supposed that they did so as spokesmen for an alien ideology clearly branded as heterodox, destined for preservation only in the discredited propaganda of Gallican circles, or recognizable in retrospect as pointing in a Protestantizing direction.

Pius II's bull *Execrabilis* (1460) condemned as "erroneous and detestable" appeals from papal policies or decisions to the judgment of a

69. See especially Bäumer, *Nachwirkungen* (a very useful synthesis of the literature), and "Die Konstanzer Dekrete 'Haec sancta' und 'Frequens' im Urteil katholischer Kontroverstheologen des 16. Jahrhunderts," in Bäumer, *Von Konstanz nach Trient*, pp. 547–74.

future general council, and it has been said of the decree *Pastor aeternus*, promulgated in 1516 by the Fifth Lateran Council, that "to the papal prohibition of appeal to a Council was now added a condemnation of the [conciliar] theory itself." [70] But *Execrabilis* represented the views of only one faction in the church and the crucial phrases of *Pastor aeternus* are too restricted in meaning to constitute any unambiguous condemnation of conciliar theory. In particular, it should be noted that *Pastor aeternus* does not spurn the superiority decrees of Basel, nor is there any mention of Constance or any rejection of *Haec sancta*. Such a move would not have been regarded as redundant at the time, for Ferdinand the Catholic, in the instructions to his representatives at the council, had explicitly suggested the need for a formal repudiation of *Haec sancta*. But then, even Ferdinand did not think the notion of papal superiority to the council extended to an heretical pope or to one whose title was in doubt. [71] Without the marked persistence of such ecclesiological hesitancies into the Age of Reformation, it would be hard to explain the failure of the Council of Trent, despite the challenge laid down by the novel Protestant ecclesiologies of the day, to promulgate any dogmatic decree on the nature of the Christian church.

70. Jedin, *History*, 1:133.
71. See the text in Doussinague, app. 50, p. 539: "Porporneys ante Su Santidad en el concilio que aquellos dos decretos se revoquen expresamente y se haga nuevo decreto que declare que el Papa es sobre el concilio *excepto en el caso de la eregia como dize el canon Si Papa XL dis. y en el caso que dos o tres son elegidos en cisma por Sumos Pontifices que solo en estos dos casos el Conçilio pueda conosçer y sea juez de la causa del Papa y no en mas*" (italics mine).

CHAPTER 4 · DIRECTIONS OF HERESY: THE COMPLEXITIES OF DEVIATION

[Hus] writes [in his *De ecclesia*] that "the dissension has arisen because priests of Christ have preached against the pestiferous crimes of the clergy." But this is not true, for long ago, when Hus was still in his father's loins, there were sound and weighty [*autentici et sollempnes*] preachers in the realm of Bohemia who preached against the simoniacal heresy and against . . . the avarice, sensuality, pride, and luxury of the clergy. But they did not mix the errors of Wyclif's forty-five articles into their sermons, and they taught the people to hold and believe what the Roman church held and believed . . . and therefore dissension did not arise among the clergy of Bohemia then as it has today.

—STEPHEN PÁLEČ

The word "heresy," which denotes an individual choosing, is older than Christianity, and the religious phenomenon it has been used to denote is almost as old. Only during the doctrinal debates of the patristic era did the word come gradually to acquire the definition current in theological circles throughout the Middle Ages—namely, the pertinacious maintenance of doctrinal error by a Christian in defiance of ecclesiastical authority. Thus defined, it clearly possessed a disciplinary as well as a doctrinal dimension; what was involved was not simply error but rather the stubborn choosing to persist in error in the teeth of correction by the appropriate magisterial authority. And, as such, heresy posed a continuing threat to the medieval church from as early as the twelfth century.

175

Any attempt to come to terms historically with the nature and reality of that threat must surmount unusually difficult obstacles. In common medieval usage, and amid the intricate intermingling of the religious and political that was characteristic of the era, the strict theological definition of heresy was not necessarily adhered to. Controversialists were not always very discriminating in hurling accusations of heretical depravity at their opponents; nor, as the case of Joan of Arc so well attests, were powerful enemies necessarily squeamish about bending such accusations to purely political ends. Even when the theological definition did prevail, the doctrinal issues involved were often very intricate and the perception of error was to a remarkable degree in the eye of the beholder. Historians today are still debating the reality of John Hus's alleged heterodoxy. And anyone interested in the heresy of the Free Spirit must perforce face some startling facts. The *Mirror of Simple Souls*, the work from which were drawn the erroneous propositions for which Marguerite Porete, a Beguine from Hainault, was burned in 1310, was approved in the fourteenth century by the distinguished scholastic Godfrey of Fontaines (d. ca. 1306), and in the fifteenth by Pope Eugenius IV. It was copied many times in late-medieval monastic circles, was translated from the original French into Italian, Latin, and Middle English, and was rendered into modern English and published under the aegis of the English Benedictines in 1927, complete with official *nihil obstat* and *imprimatur*.[1] It is symptomatic of the continuing difficulty of interpreting such materials that whereas the historian responsible for attributing the work to Marguerite Porete regards it as clearly heretical, three more recent accounts portray it, respectively, as an orthodox manifestation of mysticism of the Dionysian, transformational type, as perhaps marginally heretical, and, more puzzlingly, as "both orthodox and 'of the Free Spirit.'"[2]

---

1. Romana Guarnieri, who in 1946 identified the book as the work of Marguerite Porete, gives its history and provides an edition of the original French text in her "Il movimento del libero spirito" (see especially pp. 513–635). The modern English version is that of Kirchberger.
2. Thus Orcibal, pp. 55–60; Lerner, *Heresy*, pp. 200–208; McLaughlin, p. 40.

That these two examples are drawn from the late Middle Ages should not be taken to signify that the phenomena they serve to illustrate were restricted to the fourteenth and fifteenth centuries, even though (or perhaps because) the evidence available for this period is much more extensive than that surviving from earlier centuries. The explanation lies in the nature of much of that additional evidence. The very growth of the threat posed by heresy had led at the end of the twelfth century to the supersession of the traditional (and frequently merely reactive) role played by the bishops in containing it, first, by that of papal legates charged ad hoc with the task of detecting and combating doctrinal deviation, and then, during the pontificate of Gregory IX (1227–41), by the machinery of the Inquisition, organized and operating as an independent institution staffed by the friars and directed by the papacy. The Inquisition, which had a continuous history beginning in the early thirteenth century, did not operate in every European country or in any given country all of the time. But wherever and whenever it did operate, it tended to detect the presence of heresy and accordingly left a body of inquisitorial records tempting to the historian in their volume and their apparent precision.

The seeming objectivity of such records, however, should not blind us to the fact that the "confessions" they preserve were frequently elicited under torture and usually in response to stereotyped patterns of questioning set forth in the inquisitorial manuals. The manuals themselves owed much to the memory of the classical heresies of the ancient church and something also to the condemnations of positions later identified as erroneous.[3] As a result—and nowhere, it seems, more obviously than in relation to the heresy of the Free Spirit—the polemics directed against heresy and the records themselves tend to assimilate the individual example to the textbook case, and to suggest, accordingly, a uniform program or a coherent organization where none perhaps existed. Thus the specific instance is treated less as an isolated outburst than as the momentary surfacing of an as-

3. On the nature and importance of these manuals, see Dondaine.

sumedly continuous stream of heretical depravity flowing underground across the centuries.[4] These tendencies suggest the desirability of approaching the heresy of the late Middle Ages from more than one angle, addressing it first in descriptive historical terms, but measuring it then, in more theological vein, against the inner logic and internal coherence of the body of medieval Catholic belief.

From Waldensians and Joachites to Lollards and Hussites

"The point of departure for the development of mediaeval sects was the Gregorian reform and revolution within the Church. In both directions its influence was decisive; in the sphere of the development of the Church this influence was direct; in the sphere of sect-formation it was indirect."[5] The flood of scholarly work on medieval ecclesiastical and religious history that has been rising steadily during the half century and more since Ernst Troeltsch made this classic assertion has done little to question and much to vindicate the fundamental accuracy of his central insight. More recent work has underlined the fact that medieval heresy as such did not originate in the eleventh century. It has not, however, challenged the claim that heresy first emerged as a truly important element in medieval society only during the late eleventh and twelfth centuries, amid the turbulence spawned by the Gregorian onslaught against clerical corruption and in the wake of the general quickening of monastic and religious life that distinguished that era. "Piety produced heretics as well as saints,"[6] and the heightened spirituality and zeal for moral regeneration that led some to become prominent reformers within the church led others to meet their lonely destiny outside its boundaries.

Of the multiple heterodoxies that appeared during these centuries, two stand out as having attained the status of truly major heretical movements. The first, the dualistic heresy of the Cathars—or Al-

4. See the comment in Lambert, pp. 106–7, 170–71.
5. Troeltsch, 1:349.
6. Wakefield and Evans, eds., p. 7.

bigenses, as they came later to be called—need not detain us here. Long before the end of the thirteenth century, the Albigensian crusade and the strenuous efforts of the inquisitors had broken its back. By the early fourteenth century it had been well-nigh eliminated from France, and the scattered remnants in Lombardy were of negligible importance.[7] The second of these movements, however, was of some consequence. The Waldensians continued to expand until they became possibly the largest group of heretics. They put down roots in most parts of southern, central, and western Europe (with the exception of England), found their way across the era of Protestant Reformation, and survived into the modern era as an independently organized church.

The heresy had its origin in the teaching and example of Valdes, a rich merchant of Lyons. Moved by a version of the life of St. Alexius, he consulted a master of theology and at some time around 1170 underwent a religious experience apparently akin to that of Francis of Assisi later on. He divested himself of family and wealth, sought a better acquaintance with the Scriptures and the teaching of the fathers, and began to preach a life "of poverty and evangelical perfection like that observed by the apostles."[8] His preaching proved something of a success and he quickly drew followers, women as well as men. But although their vow of poverty received the approval of the ecclesiastical authorities, their desire to preach, which impinged upon clerical prerogatives, did not. Valdes made a profession of orthodox faith in 1180 or 1181 at a diocesan council at Lyons.[9] But the "Poor of Lyons," as they began to call themselves, continued their preaching in defiance of directives to the contrary, incurred excommunication at the hands of the archbishop of Lyons, and were driven out of the territory subject

7. It was in 1321 that the last Cathar bishop whom we know to have worked in western Europe was captured in Tuscany. See Lambert, p. 140.
8. In the words of the inquisitor Bernard Gui; Mollat, ed., *Bernard Gui*, 1:35. There is a translation of the account of his conversion in the anonymous chronicle of Laon in Wakefield and Evans, pp. 200–202. The name "Peter" is unhistorical and was attached to Valdes only in later Waldensian legend; see Gonnet and Molnár, pp. 43–44, and Lambert, pp. 156–57.
9. Translation in Wakefield and Evans, eds., pp. 204–8.

to his control. The decree *Ad abolendam* issued by the Council of Verona in 1184, anathematizing among others "the Humiliati or Poor of Lyons," accelerated this process of rejection.[10] Although its enforcement was at first sporadic, and although Valdes himself and his original followers from Lyons sought to keep the door open to reconciliation with the authorities, the next few decades witnessed a gradual slide from schism into outright heresy. During that period, nonetheless, they succeeded in spreading their message into the Dauphiné and Piedmont (always to remain their particular strongholds), as well as into Provence, Germany, and Lombardy, where they entered into the legacy of other groups similarly moved by the ideal of the apostolic life and a concomitant inclination to antisacerdotalism. Although their earlier appeal had extended to the lower clergy as well as to the laity and appears also to have transcended the distinctions of social class, they came to draw their adherents almost exclusively from the ranks of the laity and, after about the mid-thirteenth century, from the ranks especially of artisans and peasants, perhaps predominantly from the poor and unlettered. Being "the religion of the small man," clinging to the simplicity of the Gospel message as the Waldensian preachers intuited it, the Waldensian sect enjoyed "the distinction of being the one international medieval heresy to attract wide support from the peasantry."[11]

The reverence of the Lyons group of Waldensians for the person of Valdes had proved early on to be too much for their Lombard confrères and, along with the latter's Donatism, had led to a split between the two groups, French and Italian. An attempt at reconciliation in 1218 had proved abortive. Nevertheless, the individual characters of the two groups did not preclude a common loyalty to the ideal of the evangelical life of preaching and poverty that Valdes had held up before them. Something similar may also be said about the differences in

10. See Lambert, pp. 71–73.
11. Lambert, pp. 158, 161. For the social origins of the Waldensians, see also Gonnet and Molnár, pp. 163–85. It is worthy of note that the Hussites who encountered surviving Waldensians in Bohemia, while honoring them as fellow evangelicals, were also somewhat disillusioned by their poor intellectual caliber; see Lambert, pp. 153–54. For an account of Waldensian-Hussite contacts, see Gonnet and Molnár, pp. 211–82.

prevalent beliefs and practices that gradually became evident between the Waldensians of Germany and Central Europe and those of Italy and southern France. Unlike the former, the latter came into contact with ideas of Catharist provenance, and, if the records of the inquisitions held in the Piedmontese valleys during the fourteenth and fifteenth centuries are to be believed, Catharist influence may be seen in some of their rites and beliefs.[12] Nevertheless, behind these and other regional accretions and variations, and behind analogous fluctutions across time, can be detected the lineaments of a body of common commitments—not so much a shared *doctrinal* corpus as the familiar consequences of a certain fundamental disposition common to all.

Basic to that disposition was the stubborn insistence on living the life of the Gospel as they themselves directly apprehended it, a life of rigor, simplicity, and poverty, at the heart of which lay the struggle to maintain the exacting moral ideal that Jesus himself had taught. The established church, with its hierarchy and harlotry, its qualifications and compromises, its stress on "institutional" rather than subjective holiness, had long since submerged that ideal (or so they believed, though with varying degrees of intensity) in a "Pharisaical" tradition that could no longer be regarded as fully Christian. Hence their eventual rejection of the authority, the priesthood, the sacraments, and the ritual of the Roman church, the worldly church that had sold out to Constantine. Hence their insistence that purity of spiritual and moral life was the true condition for the exercise of ecclesiastical authority and that they alone, therefore, could validly administer the Eucharist, hear confessions, and remit the sins of their fellow believers. Hence, too, their radical simplification of the religious life, their refusal to take oaths, their rejection of the doctrine of purgatory, of prayers for the dead, of saints' days and the intercession of saints, of so many of the ritual observances characteristic of Latin Catholicism. Hence, finally, despite their public attendance at the regular parish mass, their private sectarian aloofness. "Everywhere pressure welded together the rank and file, and transformed the earlier movement of awakening within the Church of Valdes's day into a heretical

12. See Lambert, pp. 161–62, for a skeptical appraisal of these records.

counter-Church"—though one held together, it must be admitted, less by any formal organizational structures (which tended to weaken across time) than by the commitment and tenacity with which the superiors (or *perfecti*) pursued their lives of missionary preaching, bringing their simple Gospel message to schools, homes, and places of work.[13]

Their energetic missionary spirit and the quality of moral and religious life characteristic of their preachers best explain, perhaps, their enduring vitality and extraordinary staying power—leading the German Waldensians more than once in the fifteenth century to put out feelers for union with the Hussites of Bohemia, and enabling their southern brethren in Burgundy, Piedmont, and the Dauphiné to withstand over the course of two centuries repeated inquisitorial and military attacks, culminating in the crusade launched against them by Innocent VIII in 1488.

In their longevity, as in so many other things, they contrast sharply with "the brothers and sisters of the sect of the Free Spirit and voluntary poverty" (as they called themselves on one occasion), who, during the course of the fourteenth and early fifteenth centuries, attained much notoriety and a certain prominence, at least in the hostile chroniclers and in the records of the Inquisition. Even on the basis of the most uncritical and credulous reading of the available evidence the Free Spirits cannot be said to have constituted an organized movement or cohesive sect. And the most recent accounts, the authors of which have clearly absorbed Grundmann's warnings about the danger of taking the Inquisition records at face value, reflect a critical, somewhat skeptical, handling of the sources and have been enriched by the discovery that (contrary to earlier assumptions) some Free Spirit writings have in fact survived.[14]

---

13. Lambert, pp. 156, 163–64. For a different assessment of the importance of Waldensian organization in securing the survival of the sect, see Leff, *Heresy*, 2:463–64.
14. I refer here and in what follows to the important study by Lerner, *Heresy*, and to McLaughlin's article, "Free Spirit." Cf. Grundmann, "Ketzerverhöre," especially pp. 519–23. Leff's treatment of the Free Spirit marks something of an exception to the trend and has accordingly come in for criticism; see the reviews by H. Grundmann in *Deutsches Archiv für Erforschung des Mittelalters*, 24 (1968):284–86, and by H. S. Offler in *English Historical Review*, 84 (1969):572–76.

What we see, then, is a heresy that can no longer be assumed to be connected with the pantheistic views for which Amaury of Bene was condemned at Paris in 1210, or with the views of Ortlieb of Strassburg later on. Instead, the Free Spirit made its first appearance in Swabia in the latter part of the thirteenth century and was attributed by the decree *Ad nostrum* of the Council of Vienne to the Beghards and Beguines of Germany. That decree depicted it as a heresy involving no less than eight erroneous propositions, the gist of which is as follows: that in this earthly life a man can attain to such perfection that he is incapable of sin; that such a man, having attained to a degree of perfection in which sensuality is completely subjected to reason, no longer needs to fast and pray and can permit his body whatever pleases it; that such a man is no longer subject to human obedience or to any precept of the church; that he can attain final blessedness in this life, does not require the light of glory to be raised to the vision and enjoyment of God, and has no need of the acts of virtue necessary to imperfect men; that the sexual act is no sin when nature inclines one to it, and that there is no need to show any sign of reverence before the elevated host.[15]

Charges framed on the model of these condemned propositions were periodically leveled throughout the fourteenth century, usually against Beghards and Beguines, and in east-central Europe as well as in more westerly localities such as the Strassburg region, Thuringia, and the Low Countries. It has been claimed that "it was in Hussite Bohemia that the Free Spirit . . . reached its highest medieval development"—indeed, that without it "the [Hussite] revolution might not have taken place." But the evidence supporting this claim has been controverted, as have also the Free Spirit connections with (and, indeed, the very existence of) the fanatical "Adamites," those intriguing advocates of "ritual nudism and sexual emancipation" whom the Hussite general John Žižka allegedly destroyed in 1421.[16] In any case, charges of Free Spirit sympathies in general trail off in the

---

15. The text of *Ad nostrum* is printed as *Clem*. V, 3, c. 3; ed. Friedberg, 2:1183–84.
16. *Pro*: Kaminsky, "The Heresy of the Free Spirit in the Hussite Revolution," in Thrupp, ed., pp. 166–86 (at pp. 166 and 168); also idem, *History*, pp. 351–60, 418–33. *Con*: Lerner, *Heresy*, pp. 119–24. Cf. the judicious mediating comment of Lambert, pp. 323–24.

earlier part of the fifteenth century; by the latter part of that century
we begin to lose sight of the Free Spirit altogether.

What, then, of their views? The allegations of *Ad nostrum* may have
been based on the list of "errors" plucked rather clumsily from Marguerite Porete's *Mirror of Simple Souls*.[17] Despite those charges, the
picture that emerges is a cautious and nuanced one, far removed from
the older sensational evocations of a movement of antinomian liber-
tines, advocates of a mystic eroticism, of "promiscuity on principle."
That exotic interpretation of the Free Spirit has been given renewed
currency in recent years by the pertinent sections of Norman Cohn's
splendid book.[18] It reposes, however, on evidence of dubious veracity;
it tells us less about the actual beliefs and practices of the Free Spirits
than about the darker fantasies of their hostile contemporaries and the
unwitting incomprehension of their clerical interrogators. Despite
all the suspicions, rumors, and actual charges, the alleged antinomianism of the Free Spirit remains a *quaestio disputata*. If it did
indeed occur, it was clearly very much at odds with their well-attested
commitment—shared with the adherents of so many other late-
medieval religious movements—to the pursuit in poverty and self-
abnegation of the apostolic ideal. The picture is one of a spiritual
orientation that was "closely related to the orthodox mystical movement of the later Middle Ages and grew out of a concern for a life of
spiritual perfection." That spiritual orientation was, in effect,

> far more typical of the late medieval search for God and godliness than
> has commonly been supposed. Free Spirits believed that they could
> attain union with God on earth, but they thought that they could only
> reach this state by means of bodily austerities and spiritual abnegation
> and that attainment of the state resulted in detachment from daily
> concerns rather than in radical engagement in them.[19]

This stress on the final state of union with God and the concomitant
detachment from the externalities of religious life helps account for

17. Lerner, *Heresy*, pp. 82–83, makes this case; cf. Guarnieri, p. 416. Lambert, p.
179, points out prudently that the loss of much of "the documentation of the Council
of Vienne" has rendered "exact reconstruction of the historical context of *Ad nostrum*
impossible."
18. Cohn, chaps. 7 and 8: "An Elite of Amoral Supermen," pp. 149–94.
19. Lerner, *Heresy*, p. 3.

the recurrent charges of antinomianism and libertinism levied against
the Free Spirits. A similar stress is to be found in the writings of unquestionably orthodox mystics who warned their own charges against
the seductions of a false and heretical freedom of the spirit. It seems
clear that the Free Spirits, by too unqualified an affirmation that the
perfected soul might in this life be absorbed wholly into God, did indeed go beyond those mystics. Their affirmation exceeded even that of
Meister Eckhart, to whom their writings were sometimes attributed,
who was accused of a series of heresies, including autotheism (identification of self with God), but of whose "radical traditionalism and
orthodoxy," Dom David Knowles has said, "there is no longer any
doubt."[20] Few ventured so far as to profess formal pantheism, but the
charge of autotheism, and with it the circumvention or minimizing of
the sacramental mediations of the church, seems fully justified. In an
arresting formulation that has often been cited, Sister Katherine is
depicted as having said to her confessor: "Rejoice with me, I have become God." Less strikingly, but still rather dangerously, Marguerite
Porete in the *Mirror of Simple Souls* depicts the "annihilated" soul as
"joined and united to the Holy Trinity," indeed, as God "by right of
Love." Even more dangerously, she goes on to stress the consequent
freedom of that "annihilated" soul (united already as it is with God)
from all externalities, for it no longer needs to "seek God by penance,
nor by any sacrament of Holy Church, nor by thoughts, nor by words,
nor by works."[21]

Although those who argue for a link between the heresy of the Free
Spirit and the views espoused by the radical chiliastic enthusiasts of
the Hussite revolution (the Taborites) envisage an ultimate blending
between the antinomianism attributed to the Free Spirits and the millenarianism associated with the Joachist tradition, few of those who

20. Knowles, "Denifle and Ehrle," p. 4.
21. See the partly heretical tract "Daz ist Swester Katrei Meister Ekehartes Tohter
von Strâzburc," in Pfeiffer, 2:464–65; *Mirouer des simples ames*, chaps. 68, 21, 85, in
Guarnieri, pp. 572, 541, 586. The last statement (p. 586) in its totality reads: "Ceste
[Ame], qui telle est, ne quiert plus Dieu par penitance ne par sacrement nul de Saincte
Eglise, ne par pensees ne par paroles ne par oeuvres, ne par creature d'ycy bas ne par
creature de lassus, ne par justice ne par misericorde ne par gloire de gloire, ne par
divine cognoissance ne par divine amour ne par divine louange."

can be identified with any certainty as Free Spirits seem to have been moved by millenarian yearnings, or, indeed, by historical theories of any sort, and the Joachist tradition was itself of very different provenance.

The Joachist tradition can be traced quite explicitly to two Italian authors of the twelfth and thirteenth centuries. The Joachists are usually linked with the rigorist, or "Spiritual," wing of the Franciscan order, which by the end of the fourteenth century had come increasingly to comprehend its own tribulations as champion of the doctrine of apostolic poverty in terms of the Joachite prophetic tradition. The doctrines that came to form that tradition were variations on, harmonics of, or even derivations from the works of Joachim of Fiore (ca. 1135–1202), the famous Calabrian monk who had been abbot of the Cistercian house of Curazzo before becoming the founder of the Order of San Giovanni in Fiore, which eventually included more than thirty houses. He was an exegete rather than a theologian, or perhaps a poet of sorts rather than either (Marjorie Reeves dubs him "a poet of the meaning of history").[22] His thinking, largely symbolic, was complicated by a penchant for numerological speculation. In two great works, the *Liber Concordie* and *Expositio in Apocalypsim*, he elaborated along trinitarian lines a temporal schema embracing the whole history of mankind. He saw human history as falling into three great epochs, each divided into seven ages, associated with the seven angels of the Apocalypse, or forty-two generations, each of approximately thirty years' duration. The first age was that of the Father, aligned approximately with the Old Testament era; the second was that of the Son, aligned with the era of the New Testament and destined to endure if each of the generations was still to last thirty years (that was unclear) until around 1260; the third age was to be the era of the Holy Spirit. Each age had its own distinguishing characteristics. The first, which had had married men as its leaders, had been an age of the flesh, of fear and suffering, of servitude, law, and knowledge. The second, led by clerics, was an age of flesh and spirit, of faith and action, of filial

22. Reeves, p. 132.

obedience, of grace and *partial* wisdom. The third, of which St. Benedict had been the precursor and for which a new order (or new orders) of religious would prepare the way, was to be led by monks. It would be the age of the spirit, of charity, of contemplation, the age of liberty and of ever greater grace, the age not of knowledge or merely partial wisdom but of revelation—the age, indeed, in which the "everlasting gospel" (*evangelium aeternum*), mentioned in the Apocalypse (Rev. 14:6), and which Joachim associated with the angel of the sixth seal, would finally be disclosed.

Whether Joachim himself actually envisaged the supersession in the coming "third era" of the traditional sacramental order, the emergence of a new "spiritual" church, and the appearance of a new revelation has remained a subject of scholarly controversy.[23] He may merely have intended to suggest the spiritualization of sacramental practice, the revivification of the church, and the unfolding to the faithful of the old Gospel in its full spiritual significance. "Today," Marjorie Reeves has said, with "the distinction between what Joachim taught and what certain crazy Joachites proclaimed" well established, "we no longer consider seriously the accusation that Joachim expected a third Testament to supersede the first two." But, while exculpating him from heresy and affirming that "his intention was entirely faithful to the Church," even she admits that "when his imagination took eagle's wings it swept him far, and sometimes beyond the bounds."[24]

As a result, he left plenty of room for the "crazy Joachites" who came later to exploit his arresting vision in very different and clearly heretical ways. And none did so more strikingly or more influentially than the young Franciscan Gerard of Borgo San Donnino, who in 1254, while residing in his order's house of studies at Paris, wrote his *Introductorius in evangelium eternum*. In effect he identified the "everlasting gospel" with the writings of Joachim himself; claimed that that

---

23. See Bloomfield, pp. 267–71, and Reeves, pp. 126–32, both of which contain rich bibliographical data. On Joachite prophecy and the Spiritual Franciscans there are valuable short accounts in Leff, *Heresy*, 1:51–255, and Lambert, pp. 182–206. Cf. Tierney, *Origins*, pp. 58–204, for some important new arguments.
24. Reeves, pp. 129, 132.

gospel and (therefore) those writings would in the third age supersede the traditional and familiar Gospel of the Son; insisted that the Age of the Holy Spirit was destined to dawn in the year 1260; announced that the angel of the sixth seal who introduced the everlasting gospel had been none other than St. Francis of Assisi himself; and identified the spiritual monks who were to preach that gospel and to usher in the new dispensation as none other than the members of his own order of friars minor.

Although the identification of Francis as the angel of the sixth seal was not condemned and was accepted by many a moderate Franciscan, including St. Bonaventure himself, the general thrust of Gerard's version of the Joachite vision was clearly heretical, and, like himself, it was branded as such. Elements of his version were nevertheless accepted by disgruntled Franciscan "Spirituals" of Provence and Italy, especially by those under the leadership of Pierre de Jean Olivi (1248–98), Angelo Clareno (1247–1337), and Ubertino da Casale (1259–1328), all of whom in one degree or another espoused Joachite ideas. The later Spirituals were finally nudged by John XXII into the outer darkness of heterodoxy. Along with members of other dissident Franciscan groups who had come to be known as *Fraticelli*, and sometimes in common with non-Franciscan sympathizers or fellow travelers, they came to blend elements drawn from the Joachist tradition with their own rigorist interpretation of the Franciscan teaching on poverty. Thus they came to distinguish between the "carnal church" and the "spiritual church," identifying the former with Rome and portraying it as composed of the minions of Antichrist, but regarding themselves as composing the latter, and therefore living with impatient longing for the vindication of their doctrine of evangelical poverty and the dawning of the new and purified order of things in which they would fulfill their destiny of restoring the whole church to Christ. In time groups of them were also accused of more radical deviations: of refusing all spiritual jurisdiction to the Roman church, of denying, in Donatist fashion, the validity of sacraments administered by priests in mortal sin, of prophesying the coming reign of Antichrist. And so on. The stream of accusations and condemnations runs strong throughout much of the fourteenth century, enters the fifteenth as a rapidly dwindling trickle, and, like the heresy of the Free Spirit, peters out in the latter half of the same century.

About this denouement there was something not uncharacteristic. Throughout the heartland of western and central Europe the fifteenth century witnessed a decline in the vigor and lasting power of heretical dissent. But the triumph of the forces of orthodoxy in those regions was shadowed by the emergence of new and powerful heterodoxies in lands on the eastern and western peripheries to which heresy had previously been foreign.[25] And the heresies in those peripheral regions, those of the Wycliffites in England and the Hussites in Bohemia, have been seen as inspired directly by the heterodox teachings of a single man, in each case a theologian and prolific author with strong academic roots and powerful political affiliations as well.

In the case of the English Wycliffites, at least, that interpretation is substantially correct. Having drifted into political as well as ecclesiastical radicalism and been driven underground by the combined forces of church and state, the Lollards were destined to see the fifteenth century out as fragmented, localized groups.[26] They were composed largely of tradesmen and artisans, lacking national organization and betraying the type of variation in belief that one could expect such circumstances to produce. Shorn of the last remnants of their academic tradition and deprived of influential leadership in the years after 1414, when Sir John Oldcastle organized a disastrous Lollard march on London, dead as a political force after 1431, when one of their plots came to the attention of the authorities, the Lollards ended by stressing above all moral and practical issues. The Bible should be made available in English to all, they urged, even the unlearned; clerics should concern themselves with preaching rather than with the sacraments; sinful priests were not to be credited with the power to

25. Though there had been some movement of Waldensians into Bohemia; see Gonnet and Molnár, pp. 211–82.
26. Or "mumblers," as the bishops came to call them as early as 1387, using a Middle Dutch term of abuse that had long since been applied in the Netherlands to Beghards and Beguines.

perform the sacraments; images were not to be worshiped—as John Morden of Chesham said to his (orthodox) son-in-law: "[They] be but stockis and stonys for they cannott helpe themself; how can they helpe the[e]? And the worshipping of them is but idolatrie."[27] And so on. Much in this Lollard preoccupation with the apostolic ideal and evangelical simplicity suggests an affinity with the Waldensians.

Their distinctive and continuing rejection of the doctrine of transubstantiation, however, signals that the links with Wycliffe's own more theoretical theological commitments were never entirely broken. Those links become more evident if we push back to the early years of the fifteenth century, or the last years of the fourteenth—to the teachings of William Sawtrey (d. 1401), the first Lollard to be put to death under the provisions of the new antiheretical statute *De haeretico comburendo*, or to the "Twelve Conclusions" circulated in Westminster by Lollard partisans while Parliament was sitting in 1395. At that time two successive archbishops of Canterbury, William Courtenay (d. 1396) and Thomas Arundel, were laboring hard to root out the Wycliffites from the University of Oxford, "the church's principal recruiting ground in England" and "the platform from which their opinions could be disseminated among the higher clergy in each new academic generation."[28] Indeed, had not their efforts been so effective, there is little reason to think that the Lollard movement, graced by the type of educated clerical leadership it was in fact denied, would not have succeeded in maintaining a more coherent and thoroughgoing commitment to Wycliffe's own theological views.

What, then, were his views? They were, in the first place, those of an aging, disappointed, angry, and increasingly frenzied man, most of them committed to writing during the last eight years of his life (1376–84). Wycliffe was a priest with a distinguished academic career at Oxford who had entered the royal service as a propagandist during one of the recurrent border conflicts between crown and papacy over the division of ecclesiastical spoils. Academic prominence and zealous political service notwithstanding, he had somehow failed to

27. Thomson, *Later Lollards*, p. 91.
28. McFarlane, p. 114.

secure the type of ecclesiastical preferment that one might have expected his industry and talents to have assured him. Not that he was not reasonably well provided for with benefices—too well, indeed, to enable him to avoid the characteristic clerical vices of absenteeism and pluralism, though not well enough to shield him from the temptation of saving a little money at the cost of becoming a negligent pluralist. Nor well enough, it may be, to enable him to engage in (unsuccessful) litigation at the papal court to recover the position he had lost as Warden of Canterbury College without engaging also in the practice that ecclesiastical reformers often denounced as "chop-churching."[29] It is possible that during the period 1373–75 he was the candidate of the royal council for the bishopric of Worcester (again unsuccessful); it is certain that in 1375 he was insulted by Gregory XI's failure to redeem a repeated promise to appoint him to a prebend at Lincoln; it is certain, too, that around this time he began to harbor feelings of persecution.

These details are worth mentioning because they have been adduced, along with other factors, to explain the deepening radicalism of his later years, when he succeeded in alienating so many of his former supporters by denying the divine institution of the papacy and by challenging the church's official eucharistic teaching. Other factors include the mounting clerical criticism of his radical reliance upon the authority of Scripture and of his views on ecclesiastical property—the growing threat, therefore, of actual persecution—and his own revulsion at conditions at Rome after the onset of the Great Schism, as well as the arrogance and irascibility of his native temperament. Similarly nontheological factors have been invoked to explain the vehemence and radicalism with which he struck out right and left at the papacy, the bishops, the lower clergy, the sacraments—indeed, the whole traditional structure of the medieval church—during his last

29. McFarlane, p. 29, suggests that it was in order to raise the necessary money for the lawsuit that Wycliffe in November 1368 exchanged his rectory at Fillingham in Lincolnshire for the less valuable one of Ludgershall in Buckinghamshire, receiving from the brokers who arranged the transaction a cash payment reflecting the differing values of the two benefices. See also McFarlane, p. 26, for Wycliffe's failure to meet his responsibilities as an absentee incumbent in relation to his canonry and prebend in the collegiate church of Westbury-on-Trym.

two years, after he had withdrawn from Oxford to his parish of Lutterworth in Leicestershire. He has been depicted as exhibiting during these years a "senile fanaticism," as the possible victim of high blood pressure, as goaded on by "disappointed ambition" or "swept along by resentment."[30] Even a biographer as fundamentally sympathetic as Workman was led, indeed, to admit that it was "difficult to decide whether we have here signs of a growing fanaticism, the result of conscious defeat, or proofs of the ill effects of his [first] stroke."[31]

Although it would be hard to overestimate the importance of such factors, it would certainly be possible to do so. Ill health, temperament, disappointed hopes, changes in the ecclesiastico-political temperature and pressure undoubtedly do help to explain why Wycliffe was moved to advance some very radical propositions in theological matters. They throw but little light, however, on the process that led him to the *particular* positions he actually did adopt. Those positions—on the church, the priesthood, the sacraments, the Eucharist—become comprehensible only against the background of a series of commitments, philosophical as well as theological, matured over the course of a lifetime's study, teaching, and deliberation. Though intellectuals often (but oddly) overlook the fact, ideas exert their own logical pressures on the minds that think them; premises yearn for their congruent conclusions.

Nowhere, it has been claimed, is this more fully evident than in relation to the difficult teaching on the Eucharist that Wycliffe set forth in 1379–80 in his *De apostasia* and *De eucharistia*. After 1379 he began to deny the official teaching that at the consecration of the mass the bread and wine are transubstantiated, remaining bread and wine only as accident or in appearance, their substance having been transformed into the body and blood of Christ. He was nudged in that direction at least in part by his ultrarealism in metaphysics. For that ultrarealism involved the insistence that intelligibility and being are to be identified, that whatever the human mind conceives as an entity corresponds not merely to an external reality but to a divine archetype

30. Thus Delaruelle et al., 2:978; McFarlane, pp. 84–85.
31. Workman, 2:311.

(*esse intelligibile*) that is possessed of being, eternal and indestructible: "Hence bread once in being could not be annihilated; even when transubstantiated its own essence continued to coexist with the new substance which had been engendered."[32] And with this "remanetism" went the insistence that the consecrated host "is not the Lord's body but its efficacious sign," and that when we see the host "we ought to believe not that it is itself the body of Christ, but that the body of Christ itself is in a sacramental manner concealed in it."[33]

Leff has argued cogently for a comparable congruence between Wycliffe's metaphysical commitments and the views concerning the Bible and the church that he expressed in *De veritate sacrae scripturae* (1378), *De ecclesia* (1378), and elsewhere. With all his well-attested stress on the sovereign authority of the Bible, Wycliffe cannot be regarded as an advocate of *scriptura sola*; he was quite willing to admit that a full comprehension of its meaning might often depend on the interpretation hammered out by the church fathers and saints, notably by his beloved St. Augustine. But he did approach a certain fundamentalism that led him to make "the Bible the touchstone of all knowledge and conduct," a means whereby he could stand in judgment on the false claims of the hierarchical Roman church. His ultrarealism led him to view the Bible in a manner suggestive less of Christian tradition than of Muslim attitudes toward the Koran—to regard it, that is, as "a metaphysical entity eternally in being with every word denoting an everpresent reality."[34] At the same time, he regarded the church as in its essence "independent of time and place,"

32. Following here the perceptive discussion of Leff, *Heresy*, 2:500–558 (at 502, 551–52). In relation to Wycliffe's eucharistic views, McFarlane (pp. 158–59) adopts a very different approach, but the fact that the Hussites could later adopt his ultrarealism in metaphysics without thereby embracing also his eucharistic teaching should not blind us to the logical congruence between the two positions.
33. Wycliffe, *De eucharistia*, chap. 1; ed. Loserth, pp. 14–16.
34. Leff, *Heresy*, 2:513, 515. Muslims, it should be noted, are a "people of the book" in a way that Christians are not, and the New Testament is no more to be aligned with the Koran than is Muhammed with Jesus. Whereas it is through the Incarnation that Christians claim to encounter the divine, at the base of Muslim belief lies the divine law of righteousness, preexisting in God as an eternal archetype and entering history in the revelations that Muhammed received from the angel Gabriel and committed to writing in the book known as the Koran. See Smith, pp. 17–18.

reducing the "true" church to the archetypal reality, which, being eternal, predates the flawed historical reality the constitutes the visible church. Hence his inclination to take in very literal fashion, and indeed to absolutize, St. Augustine's classic distinction between the heavenly city and the earthly city. For Augustine himself, although both were transtemporal and transspatial societies—that of the company of the elect, the saved, on the one hand, that of the damned on the other—both were destined, nevertheless, to remain inextricably intermingled in the historical reality of the visible church. For Augustine it is not God's will that we, like the Donatists, should presume to separate the wheat from the chaff, the saints from the sinners.

In a sense, however, though he agreed that in this life we could never know with certainty who was of the saved, the predestined, and who of the damned, the foreknown (praesciti), Wycliffe was prompted by his metaphysical commitments to essay in his De ecclesia what at one level at least amounted precisely to a separation of the wheat from the chaff. He defined the church simply as "the congregation of all the predestined"; this alone is "the universal or catholic church."[35] It is the true but invisible church of which Christ, "the chief abbot," is the sole head and the elect the sole members. And there is no guarantee that popes, bishops, or priests, simply by virtue of their office in the visible church, or ordinary believers, simply by virtue of their membership in that body, actually belong to the true church.

By their deeds, however, he more than once implied, ye shall surely know them. Hence the sparks that understandably flew when he brought into contact his attitude toward the Bible and his doctrine of the church. Measured against what he took to be the timeless veracities of the Scriptures, the historically conditioned complexities of the visible church and the humanly flawed performances of so many of her ministers could hardly be found as anything but wanting, as damnable declensions from the apostolic ideal. The logic of his position, it is true, could have led him, had he consistently pursued it, to deny any efficacy at all to the ministrations of the visible church.

35. Wycliffe, Tractatus de ecclesia, chap. 1; ed. Loserth, pp. 2, 7.

And that he certainly did not do. But we are left, at least, with little ground for surprise at the radical nature of the conclusions he actually did draw. He periodically refused to accord efficacy to the ministrations of the sinful priest. More consistently he depreciated the function of the priesthood itself. He minimized the importance of the sacraments. He attacked the bases of the ecclesiastical hierarchy; he rejected the traditional claims of the papacy. He generally questioned, indeed, the mediatory function of the institutional church in the economy of salvation, and ascribed to the royal government a predominant role in the direction of that part of the visible church militant that he came to identify with the realm of England.

Despite the obvious appeal of the last point to John of Gaunt, close adviser to Edward III and Wycliffe's loyal protector, it was outweighed by the extreme and unpalatable nature of his other positions. So it was in Bohemia rather than England that his memory was honored and so many of his writings preserved. That his fellow countrymen spurned his heretical views is not too difficult to understand; that those views found so welcome a reception at the other end of Europe, calls, however, for a more strenuous effort at explanation and the identification of a complex combination of factors.

The first factor was the establishment of a crucial link between Wycliffe's Oxford and the University of Prague, a link that should not simply be taken for granted. It was only after the outbreak of the Great Schism in 1378 and the concomitant alignment of France with the Avignonese obedience and England with the Roman that substantial numbers of Czech students began to forsake the University of Paris for Oxford. Contacts increased with the negotiations leading up to the marriage in 1382 of Richard II to Anne of Bohemia, sister of Wenceslas IV, king of Bohemia, Holy Roman emperor, and the man who later became Hus's protector. The strength of those contacts is indicated by the fact that in 1388 a scholarship was founded at Oxford to maintain a Czech student there.[36]

The second factor is the reception at Prague of Wycliffe's

---

36. Kaminsky, *History*, p. 24.

philosophical realism. At Oxford the admiration for his strictly philosophic views had survived the condemnation of his theological deviations, and by about 1390 Czech students returning to Prague had begun to acquaint their compatriots with his philosophical writings. The metaphysical ultrarealism informing those writings enjoyed a favorable reception in part because the members of the Dominican College, transferred in 1383 from Paris to Prague as a result of the schism, had prepared the ground for it by their own vindication of a Thomistic moderate realism. But the warmth of the reception may also be attributed to the fact that most of the German masters, with whom the growing number of Czechs at the university were in constant conflict, were advocates of the nominalist *via moderna*. Thus, long before Wycliffe's theological works had begun to appear at Prague, his reputation as an eminent and provocative thinker was well established among the Czech masters. Hus had made copies of four of Wycliffe's philosophical tracts for his own use, and someone later inserted in the margins of one of them, *De universalibus*, such approving comments as "May God grant Wyclif the kingdom of heaven" and "Wyclif, Wyclif, you will unsettle many a man's mind!"[37]

His prior reception as a philosopher clearly paved the way for the reception of his theological views when, from the beginning of the fifteenth century—probably after the return of Jerome of Prague from Oxford in 1401—his theological works, too, began to appear in Prague. Their appearance, at least in bulk, resulted from the conscious efforts of two Czech scholars who visited Oxford in 1406–7 and there made contact, it seems, with some of the English Lollards.[38] So positive a degree of interest reflects a well-established Czech tradition of ecclesiastical reform. To men formed by such a tradition Wycliffe

37. In Czech the latter statement reads: "O Viklef, Viklef, nejednomu ty hlavu zvykleš!" and Spinka, *Biography*, p. 38 on n. 33, comments that "the word zvykleš is an obvious play on Wyclif's name." Smahel, p. 19, n. 2, notes (and *pace* Spinka) that "according to a paleographical analysis by V. Vojtíšek the glosses were not written by Hus."
38. For these contacts see Betts, "English and Czech Influence on the Hussite Movement," in *Essays*, pp. 132–59 at 141–42. Also Smahel, especially pp. 20–25.

was more than a fashionable academic luminary—a kindred religious spirit, perhaps, a fellow advocate of a reformed and purified Christianity, of a return to the primitive simplicity of the apostolic church.

The Czech reform movement long predated Hus and had long exhibited some characteristics that were destined to endure: a stern moralism directed especially toward an improvement in the lives of the clergy, a stress on preaching and the study of the Scriptures as the principal duty of the priesthood, an anxious concern to bring the teachings of the church directly to the faithful in the vernacular, a marked devotion to the Eucharist with an emphasis on very frequent reception. This last characteristic set significant limits to the subsequent reception of Wycliffe's doctrines. The reform had been set in motion when the emperor Charles IV and Ernest of Pardubice, archbishop of Prague, summoned to Prague the Austrian preacher Conrad of Waldhausen (d. 1369). Conrad had launched a mission of popular preaching that was continued by his successors, Milič of Kroměříž (d. 1374) and Matthew of Janov (d. 1394). Matthew, a scholar of note succeeded in linking the reform movement with Czech university circles at Prague.

The famous Bethlehem Chapel at Prague had been founded by followers of Milič with the explicit intention of ensuring the continuation of the popular reform preaching in the Czech language that he had initiated. The appointment of its rector was placed, nevertheless, in the hands of the three most senior Czech professors. These were the men who in March 1402 appointed John Hus, then a candidate for the doctorate of theology at Prague, as rector of the Bethlehem Chapel and its preacher. Hus took his duties with the utmost seriousness. During the twelve years of his ministry there he preached some three thousand sermons, assaulting moral corruption in general and the corruption of the clergy in particular with a vehemence and a vituperative energy that can sometimes be quite breathtaking. During those years he rapidly became the outstanding spokesman and leader of the popular phase of the reform movement. And with the defection in 1408 of his theological colleagues, Stanislav of Znojmo and Stephen Páleč, the erstwhile leaders of the movement's academic phase who had been accused of Wycliffite tendencies and had recanted, he was pushed into the forefront of the whole movement.[39]

By that time Hus had begun to make the acquaintance of Wycliffe's theological works. In the next half-dozen years, by his borrowings from those works, his propensity for expressing some of his own views in Wycliffite language, and his willingness even to defend in public some of the condemned Wycliffite propositions, he set his feet on the path that led to his condemnation by the Council of Constance in 1415 and his subsequent burning as a heretic. Wycliffe, Loserth claimed almost a century ago, was "the man for whose doctrine Hus went to the stake."[40] The claim can hardly be contested. It was explicitly as "a disciple not of Christ but of the heresiarch John Wyclif," as a man who had "taught, asserted and preached his [Wycliffe's] many errors and heresies," that Constance sentenced him to degradation from the priestly order and relinquished him to the secular power.[41] Loserth, however, claimed a good deal more. "Hus in reality appears as a genuine Wiclifite," he said, and *De ecclesia* (1413), his most important work, "contains in its dogmatic portions hardly a line which does not proceed from Wiclif." Although de Vooght and others have intimated that this assessment may owe more to German condescension toward a Slav *Untermensch* than to a truly judicious appraisal of the sources, a Czech historian has recently concluded that "Hus's doctrine in its final, ripened form is essentially identical with the doctrine of Wyclif."[42]

---

39. Note, too, that with the promulgation in 1409 by King Wenceslas of the decree of Kutná Hora, most of the German masters seceded from the University of Prague, thus opening up new opportunities for advancement to Czech scholars. In 1409, Hus was elected rector of the university. For Kutná Hora and its background in the politics of the schism, see Kaminsky, *History*, pp. 56–75.

40. Loserth, *Wiclif and Hus*, pp. 177, xvi. The first German edition of the book appeared in 1883.

41. I cite the translation of the sentence in Spinka, *Constance*, pp. 295–98. The original may be found in Novotný et al., 8:501–3.

42. In order of citation: Loserth, *Wiclif and Hus*, p. 156; de Vooght, *Hérésie*, p. ix (cf. Betts, especially pp. 146–48, where he notes that Loserth was one of the German minority residing in Bohemia and ascribes to him "strong anti-Czech prejudices");

The weight of accumulated evidence, however, clearly favors a more qualified conclusion. The editor of the critical edition of *De ecclesia*, of all Hus's writings the one that counted most heavily in the minds of his prosecutors, has estimated that in composing that tract Hus took about one-twelfth of the text from Wycliffe's works, mostly from the latter's own *De ecclesia*. More important, for the problem is not one that can be settled by any mere appeal to textual statistics, the editor states that "the borrowed material . . . is so selected and ordered as to make it clear that the argument and convictions behind it are Hus' own property. . . . [H]e has drawn upon Wyclyf's many treatises for substantiation and elaboration." [43] And even in this tract, the product of his most Wycliffite phase, those convictions, it must be insisted, fall somewhat short of Wycliffe's.

Hus does take over from Wycliffe the definition of "the holy catholic, that is universal, church" as "the totality of the predestined" [*omnium praedestinatorum universitas*], or "all the predestined, present, past, and future." That definition, which had appeared in some of his earlier writings in the context of the competing view of the church as the congregation of the faithful, he treats as the sole, proper, and determinative one. That is to say, he now makes predestination rather than faith the principle of the church's unity and excludes the reprobate (*praesciti*) from her ranks. [44] It is true, too, that he concludes, again with Wycliffe, that "Christ alone is the head of the universal church," and argues that "no pope is the head of that catholic church besides Christ." Since no man can know whether he or anyone else is of the predestinate, "it follows that no one without revelation may rea-

---

Robert Kalivoda, *Husitská ideologie* (Prague, 1961), p. 159, cited from Kaminsky, *History*, p. 37 and n. 110, who notes that "Kalivoda acknowledges Hus's verbal modifications of Wyclif's doctrine, but tends to regard these as inessential."

43. Thomson, *Hus*, p. xxxiii; cf. de Vooght, *Hussiana*, pp. 1–6, for a subsequent summary of the status of the Wycliffe-Hus question, especially in the light of the work of the Czech historian Sedlák.

44. Hus, *Tractatus de ecclesia*, chaps. 1 and 3; ed. Thomson, pp. 2, 14–16. Wycliffe, *Tract. de eccl.*, chap. 1; ed. Loserth, pp. 2, 5. Cf. the extended analysis by de Vooght, *Hussiana*, pp. 11–101, where he compares Hus's views with both Augustine's and Wycliffe's.

sonably assert of himself or of another that he is the head of a particular
holy church, though if he lives well he ought to hope that he is a
member of the holy catholic church, the bride of Christ." All that he
is willing to concede to papal claims, then, is that if the pope's works
do not gainsay it, we may assume that he is "the superior in that particular [that is, Roman] church."[45]

These are radical statements indeed, and Hus was to pay the price
for them. But they should not be taken to reflect his endorsement of
Wycliffe's entire ecclesiology. Even in *De ecclesia* he fails to maintain
his initial commitment to predestination as the principle of the
church's unity. A good deal of the work presupposes, in fact, his failure fully to relinquish the competing view of the church as the congregation of the faithful. His concerns emerge very much in the tradition of the earlier Czech reform as focused overwhelmingly on moral
and practical issues, and he certainly stops short of Wycliffe's radical
conclusions concerning the status of the sacraments, the role of the
priesthood, and the invalidity of the sacramental ministrations of the
sinful priest.

Elsewhere, of course, he repeatedly made it clear that his sympathy
with Wycliffe's philosophical realism in no way entailed any comparable sympathy with his heretical eucharistic teaching. On this matter
Hus was entirely orthodox, and at Constance he struggled hard to
convince his judges of that fact and also that he had never held any of
the forty-five articles of Wycliffe's condemned in 1412 and again in
1415. In relation to some of those articles, however, his responses were
less than candid, and the intricate qualifications he appended to the
final thirty erroneous articles drawn from his own writings (notably to
article 1 on the definition of the church and article 9 on the papacy)
were too ambivalent to persuade his judges of the orthodoxy of his
intentions.[46]

Of Hus's reliance on Wycliffe's words and ideas it has well been

45. Hus, *Tract. de eccl.*, chaps. 4 and 13; ed. Thompson, pp. 20, 107. Cf. the detailed analysis of this tract in Spinka, *Concept*, pp. 252–89.
46. The Latin text of the thirty articles along with Hus's responses printed conveniently in interlinear fashion may be seen in Spinka, *Concept*, pp. 401–9. English
translation in Spinka, *Constance*, pp. 260–69.

said that "in almost every case they underwent modification which changed their original import," the change being "almost invariably from extremism to greater moderation, from theory to practice, from metaphysics to morals."[47] Nevertheless, that reliance was overt enough and seemingly so heavy as to secure his condemnation. His judges at Constance had been conditioned by the German masters expelled from Prague in 1409 to think of Bohemia as a hotbed of Wycliffite heresy and were not reassured on that score by Hus's ambiguous formulations. They were alarmed by reports of the vituperative nature of his preaching against the evils of the ecclesiastical establishment and bemused by the bitter enmity shown toward him even by a fellow Czech such as Stephen Páleč. They were misled also by Páleč's charge that Hus had written: "If I should happen to abjure, understand that I do it only with my lips but do not consent to it in my heart."[48] Those judges, themselves no fanatics, clearly found it impossible to believe that Hus was not a more thoroughgoing Wycliffite than he would have them believe. They saw him, in effect, as a revolutionary rather than a reformer, a subversive rather than a saint, and, acting accordingly, they made him a martyr.

Although a tragic misjudgment perhaps, in a way it was a misjudgment shared by the radicals who had come to the fore at Prague since Hus's departure for Constance—such men as Jakoubek of Stříbro and Nicholas of Dresden, who were destined to lead the "Hussite" movement into open revolution, heresy, and schism. The very passion of Hus's reforming leadership and the overt nature of his flirtation with Wycliffite ideas, which meant for him dishonor, degradation, and death, eased the way for others to a readier transition from reform to revolution and to a more thoroughgoing assimilation of Wycliffite ideas—especially his ascription to the temporal authorities of sweeping powers in ecclesiastical matters, a point of view not native to the Czech reform tradition. If the martyred Hus was to serve the

47. Leff, *Heresy*, 2:676.
48. For this see Peter of Mladaňovice, "An Account of the Trial and Condemnation of Master John Hus in Constance," trans. Spinka, *Constance*, pp. 96–98. The original is printed in Novotný et al., 8:25–120.

Hussite movement as symbol and inspiration, it was not Hus "as he claimed to be—carefully and fundamentally orthodox in his writings —but . . . Hus as the Council of Constance judged him to have been: turbulent, seditious, subversive."[49]

Turbulent enough, indeed, that movement was destined to be. Hus's death, and the subsequent condemnation and burning at Constance of his friend and fellow reformer, Jerome of Prague, aroused a veritable storm of resentment in Bohemia that culminated in a revolt against the Romanist clergy who had denounced Hus and Emperor Sigismund, who had betrayed him. Around the markedly non-Wycliffite cause of Utraquism, the demand for giving to the laity communion under both kinds (*sub utraque specie*)—a demand Hus himself had endorsed only in the last months of his life—the reformers at the University of Prague, their sympathizers among the townsfolk, and their powerful supporters among the Czech nobility and gentry came to unite. As a result, they were able to agree in 1420 on the common religious platform that Jakoubek of Stříbro formulated in the Four Articles of Prague. These articles demanded (1) the free preaching of the Word of God; (2) that the Eucharist be freely administered under both kinds, bread and wine, to all the faithful; (3) that all priests, including the pope, should give up all superfluity of temporal possessions and live as models to all; (4) that the realm be cleansed of all public mortal sins.[50]

Their ability so to agree, however, reflected an uncharacteristic surge of national unity in face of German invasion, and the common platform proved incapable of healing the split between the three main groups into which the Hussite movement had already splintered, each in turn racked by its own internal tensions. The platform itself best represented the views of the centrist wing of the Utraquists led by Jakoubek, but it was already too radical for the more conservative wing that included in its ranks such men as John of Jesenice and Peter of Mladaňovice, who had been friends of Hus. But it was not radical

49. Kaminsky, *History*, p. 6.
50. For the Articles and the role of Jakoubek, see de Vooght, *Jacobellus de Stříbro*, especially pp. 234–36.

enough for the Taborites, the millenarian enthusiasts strong in south-eastern Bohemia, who (among other more extreme proclivities) combined Wycliffe's remanentism and depreciation of the sacraments with an eager expectation of the imminent coming of Christ and of his kingdom on earth.

The story of the interaction and subsequent careers of these groups, of the struggles of Hussite armies against the forces of Sigismund, and of the general maelstrom of fifteenth-century Bohemian politics is exceedingly complex and cannot be pursued here. The abandonment of the Taborites by the more moderate Utraquists and the willingness of the Council of Basel to make the concessions to Utraquist liturgical practice and organizational separatism embodied in the *Compactata* of 1433 made possible the return of Sigismund to Prague and an uneasy reconciliation of the moderate Utraquists with their Roman Catholic fellow countrymen. But it succeeded in ending neither religious dissension nor political unrest. When the century drew to a close, the legacy of Hus's reform was embodied not only in the quasi-separatist but officially recognized Utraquist church but also in the independent sectarian grouping known as the Unity of the Czech Brethren. That body drew its ultimate inspiration from the teachings of Peter Chelčicky (d. ca. 1460), which owed something to Wycliffe but had much more in common with Waldensian views and were clearly heretical.

Three Themes: God, Revelation, Church

The contrasting fates of Wycliffe and Hus and the differing destinies of the movements associated with their names reflect in classic fashion the intricate interplay of religious commitment, ecclesiastical authority, and political loyalty that did so much to shape the career of medieval heresy. Not all heresies, however, were as exposed to the molding impact of political factors (one has only to think of the Brothers and Sisters of the Free Spirit), nor is even an approximate alignment between social situation and sectarian allegiance to be taken for granted. Certainly, violence is done to the variety and complexity of medieval heretical movements by Marxist attempts to portray them as "forms of consciousness," whereby on the ideological level particular groupings of men give expression to the class struggles generated by more fundamental changes in the social and economic temperature and pressure. Whatever the interplay between religious commitment and socioeconomic factors—and it differed from heresy to heresy—the fundamental driving force appears to have been religious. Similarly, the doctrinal positions adopted are best understood as anxious attempts to confront, in the terms suggested by Christianity, the basic religious questions with which men must struggle. Not that such a task of understanding is at all easy. In its full theological development the structure even of orthodox medieval belief was not simple, and the pluralism of medieval deviation presents us with a degree of complexity sufficient to defy any optimistic attempt to reduce it to unity. What we can hope to do—though at the price of a degree of schematization that some may find coercive—is to reduce it to order. And here, once again, Augustine must serve as both initial point of departure and subsequent point of reference.

Central to Augustine's vision of things and the very pivot upon which the whole structure of medieval religious belief turned was his firm appropriation, in the teeth of Gnostic and Manichaean claims, of the biblical visions of God as transcendent Lord of History, sovereign God of might and power, Creator of the universe. He was at constant pains to clarify just what those last words mean and what they imply both for man in particular and for the universe at large. If God made man in his own image and likeness, he made him, nevertheless, as he created the entire universe, not out of preexistent materials or out of his own substance, not working "as a human artificer does, forming one thing out of something else," but creating out of nothing. Between the Creator and all created being there lies, as a result, a difference not merely of degree but of kind—in Kierkegaard's telling phrase, "an infinite qualitative difference."[51]

By the late Middle Ages this fundamental apprehension of things had become very much a part of the day-to-day intellectual baggage of

51. Augustine, *Conf.*, 11:5; ed. Rouse, 1:218; Kierkegaard, p. 257.

those concerned with theological and philosophical questions. It was thus harder for them, perhaps, than it is for us today to perceive its essential novelty; harder, too, to see the gulf that divides it from antique and especially Neoplatonic modes of comprehending the divine and the relationship of the divine to the world in general and to man in particular. Whereas Catharist dualism marked a conscious and far-reaching recession on this point from the purity of Augustine's fundamentally biblical commitments, the radical mysticism of the Free Spirits, it may be suggested, marked an unwitting recession of a different, less extreme but no less significant, kind. The deviation central to the heresy of the Free Spirit was precisely the loss of that sense of "infinite qualitative difference" between God and man involved in the belief that the perfected soul, even in this life, could be absorbed entirely into God on the analogy, for example, of the drop of water in a jug of wine.[52] Given that deviation, the affiliated Free Spirit bracketing of the ecclesiastical and sacramental apparatus whose purpose it was, after all, to bridge the gulf between man and God was no more than an obvious, logical concomitant; and orthodox suspicions of Free Spirit antinomianism, however overblown, were not altogether incomprehensible.

Although the more radical Joachites also came to challenge the efficacy of the "carnal church's" machinery of salvation—and did so not simply for the perfected—their grounds for so doing differed greatly from the rapturous sense of mystic autotheism moving the Free Spirits. To them, as bearers of a prophetic message, the vision of God as sovereign Lord of History was central, and there was no disposition to bridge the gap between transcendent creator and contingent creature. They were driven, instead, by a differing understanding of the way in which God, of his incomprehensible wisdom and mercy, had extended across that gap a loving hand to man.

Augustine had absorbed much from the Neoplatonists. In their books, he tells us, he had even encountered the doctrine of the

---

52. As we have seen, an image with a long tradition in mystical literature and one employed in differing ways and with varying degrees of heterodoxy; see Lerner, "Image of Mixed Liquids."

preexistent *Logos*, the Word of whom we read in the prologue to the Gospel according to St. John. What he had not found there, however, was the vital teaching that in the person of Christ Jesus "the Word became flesh and dwelt among us" (John 1:14), suffering and dying for our sins. That saving teaching he had found only in the Scriptures, which, unlike "the books of the Platonists," identify not merely the goal that men must reach but also the road by which they are to reach it.[53] The Joachites, of course, would have denied none of this. And yet the more radical among them proclaimed the advent of a new age with its own unique testament and the supersession, accordingly, of the Gospel of Christ by a new and everlasting gospel. They thus undermined the uniqueness as well as the finality of the scriptural revelation, the centrality of the incarnation in the whole schema of salvation history, and, as a result, the traditional role of the hierarchical and sacramental church, the Body of Christ, and the prolongation of his presence on earth, as the critical focus of man's anxious attempts to encounter the divine.

Viewed from this perspective, the heresies of the Waldensians, of Hus, and even of Wycliffe, however corrosive of the traditional ecclesiastical order, are focused on what in the logic of theology are more subsidiary issues, and so appear in much less radical light. Wycliffe found no problem with the traditional doctrine of divine transcendence or, despite his intense biblicism, with the traditional teaching on divine revelation. His difficulties, rather, were soteriological, and sprang less from any challenge to the theology Augustine had bequeathed to the medieval church than from a too faithful stress on one particular strand in that theology.

In the last chapter, I treated Augustine's doctrine of grace and his doctrine of the church in separate sections, without doing much to relate one to the other. That procedural choice was deliberately made in order to respond to the historical actualities of Augustine's own intellectual development. He had developed the two doctrines independently of each other and at different points in his career. By 411–

53. Augustine, *Conf.*, 7:9, 20–21; cf. 11:2; ed. Rouse, 1:364–70, 392–98, 2:214.

12, when he wrote the first of his treatises against the Pelagians, he had long since developed his anti-Donatist doctrine of the church. Early in 411 it had been proclaimed the official teaching of the church, and he made little reference to it in his anti-Pelagian writings. And yet when the two doctrines are brought into mutual contact, they are clearly in tension. Pushed to its logical conclusion, his affirmation of predestination and the irresistibility of grace would have had the effect of depriving the sacramental ministrations of the visible hierarchical church of all importance in the economy of salvation. If salvation was entirely dependent upon the free choice of an inscrutable God, not even the most assiduous exploitation of the sacramental channels of grace could do anything to promote the chances of a single individual. Augustine, of course, had not pushed that position to its logical conclusion. But whereas in the context of his writings on grace and salvation he was moved to define the church as the invisible body of the elect, foreknown to God alone, in the context of his writings against the Donatists he had been led to identify the visible church, with its saints and sinners, hierarchy and sacraments, as the true Catholic church and the sole ark of salvation.

The medieval church did not attempt to reconcile these two positions. Whereas Augustine's anti-Donatist teaching on the church became the prevailing orthodoxy, his views on grace and predestination were admitted, as we have seen, only with modifications. But those modifications, it should now be noted, served (though they were not necessarily consciously intended to do so) to bring them into line with that teaching on the church. What emerged was a modified version of Augustinianism that, while affirming man's inability to engineer his own salvation, attributed to him the power, and burdened him with the responsibility, of cooperating with the workings of divine grace. Affirming also the necessity of grace, this version went a long way toward confining its dispensation to those channels of grace called sacraments, the possession of which was the foundation of the church's holiness, and which, to be efficacious, had in most cases to be administered by the priesthood. And it was this version of Augustinianism, packaged and popularized in the Latin West by the influential writings of Pope Gregory the Great (590–604) and under-pinning the power and prestige of the sacerdotal hierarchy, that was to form the bedrock of medieval orthodoxy.

Wycliffe challenged that version of Augustinianism by appropriat-ing Augustine's own doctrine of grace in all its uncompromising fullness—with its insistence on predestination *ante praevisa merita* and on the irresistibility of grace, along with its concomitant implication that the church must properly be defined as the invisible body of the predestinate. And once he had done so, such was the rigidity of his commitment to the doctrine that he was nudged under the pressure of attack into a line of doctrinal development directly opposed to that taken by the church itself in the fifth and sixth centuries. Whereas the church in effect subordinated Augustine's anti-Pelagian doctrine of grace to his anti-Donatist doctrine of the church, Wycliffe went a long way toward subordinating his doctrine of the church to his doctrine of grace. Hence, having identified divine predestination as the principle of the church's unity, he was unable to ascribe any effective unity to the visible, institutional church. And having identified divine predestination as the principle of the church's holiness too, he was pushed in the direction of refusing it any objective holiness in virtue of its sacramental ministrations. By an indirect route (the identification of the reprobate by their deeds) he was also forced into sporadic de-nials, Donatist fashion, of any efficacy to the sacraments administered by a sinful priest.

Hus's explicit refusal to endorse such a denial shows the degree to which he himself stopped short, even in his *De ecclesia*, of any com-plete appropriation of Augustine's doctrine of grace and of any com-parable subordination to that doctrine of his anti-Donatist doctrine of the church. As a result, Hus failed to bring his theology under any single controlling principle. To the degree, then, that the perplexity of his judges at Constance was really the outcome of theoretical doc-trinal considerations, it is altogether understandable. For it was grounded in Hus's own theological confusion.

We are left, then, with the Waldensians. Despite their woes and suffering, their stiff-necked and obdurate resistance to ecclesiastical authority, their alleged willingness in Italy even to stand up and resist their persecutors by force,[54] from our present perspective they emerge as the least radical heretics of all. Not for them any questioning of the traditional understanding of the divine, or of the status of revelation, or of the delicately poised balance between human initiative and divine grace. Their heretical preoccupations, inspired by a divergent reading of the gospels and fueled by the compelling vision of an apostolic purity long since betrayed by the pharisaical church of Rome, were focused on problems pertaining to the mediation of grace. Those preoccupations led them to an essentially Donatist rejection of the jurisdiction, hierarchy, and sacraments of that "Constantinian" church and to a congruently sectarian stress on subjective rather than "institutional" holiness.

Of course, in such rejections of the official church and its traditional claims there is a marked convergence among many of the heretical tendencies that surfaced during the late Middle Ages.[55] But it takes no more than a glance at the startlingly disparate doctrinal affirmations that often lay behind such negations to realize that a convergence of attitudes toward religious practice should not always prompt us to expect any harmony of underlying spirit, let alone any identity of fundamental commitment. And that realization is not irrelevant to the enormous amount of attention paid in the past to the continuity of medieval heretical movements into the Age of Reformation.

The Question of Continuity

That continuities existed is beyond question. The swing of historiographic fashion away from "forerunners of the Reformation" should not blind us to that fact. What is in question, however, is the meaning and significance to be attached to those continuities. In this

---

54. Thus abandoning their own prohibition of killing; see Lambert, p. 336; Leff, *Heresy*, 2:482–83.

55. Thus in fifteenth-century Bohemia there certainly appears to have been a genuine blending of older Waldensian with later Hussite views, perhaps also (though the claim is more arguable) with Joachite and Free Spirit tendencies; see Kaminsky, *History*, pp. 171–80, 349–60; Lambert, p. 296; Gonnet and Molnár, pp. 211–82.

connection, the schematic presentation of the last section, whatever its inadequacies, will have proved its value if it serves to remind us of two very basic points: first, that the structure of Christian belief has its own internal logic, that comparable choices of fundamental theoretical emphases tend to entail comparable shifts in more practical religious attitudes; second, the partially countervailing point already signaled—that the structure of Christian belief is so complex that shared attitudes toward religious practice may well spring from widely divergent doctrinal premises. Therefore, we should be fortified against assuming any necessarily *historical* connection between late-medieval heresy and the ideas of the Protestant reformers, whatever their similarities and whatever their shared hostility toward the traditional Catholic system.

It seems appropriate, then, to evince a certain reserve toward claims that some sectarian groups in Switzerland and Germany, usually classified as Anabaptists, reveal the survival in those areas of the heresy of the Free Spirit, or that the view of the Eucharist ultimately adopted by Zwingli was in direct continuity with a tradition of "sacramentarianism . . . endemic for centuries" in the Netherlands.[56] Similarly, the recrudescence of chiliastic views among, for example, the Anabaptists of Münster during the apocalyptic years 1533–35 need not be taken to require the postulation of a continuous stream of revolutionary millenarianism stretching back into the Middle Ages. Nor should there be any disposition to exaggerate the contributions of surviving groups of Hussites, Lollards, or Waldensians to the development of Protestantism. The Unity of Czech Brethren, the Lollards, and the French (though not the Italian) Waldensians ultimately threw in their lot with the churches of the Reformation and forfeited thereby their historic separate identities. But the doctrinal inspiration of the Reformation churches was of quite distinct provenance, and the contribution of the surviving heresies was rather that of having promoted, in the regions in which they were prevalent, a certain receptiv-

56. Such claims are advanced in Clasen and in Williams, pp. 26–37.

ity toward the newer Protestant ideas or of having provided fertile soil
for reforming evangelization.

Thus the French Reformer Guillaume Farel (d. 1565) deliberately
set out to evangelize the Waldensians in his native Dauphiné and was
able to induce them in 1530 to dispatch to the Lutherans two representatives charged with seeking doctrinal sustenance and concord. On
the other hand, it was the Bohemian Utraquists themselves who initiated contacts with Luther, and the less conservative among them,
along with the Brethren of Czech Unity, welcomed the introduction
into Bohemia of at least some of Luther's teachings.

Something similar must be said of the role played by the Lollards
during the course of the English Reformation. Whether because of
intensified attempts to suppress it or because of an actual rise in its
level, there is increasing evidence of Lollard activity from about 1490
onward. By the late 1520s contacts with the Lutherans had been established; by the early 1530s, when William Tyndale's translation of
the New Testament was circulating in England, the older Lollard and
the newer Protestant ideas had begun to merge. Thus it is proper to
see the Lollards as "the allies and in some measure the begetters of the
anticlerical forces which made possible the Henrician revolution."
Further, it is reasonable to assert that "the successes of Protestantism
seem not wholly intelligible without reference to this earlier ground-
swell of popular dissent." Though in some regions Lollardy "demonstrably provided reception-areas for Lutheranism," in others it survived into the reign of Mary Tudor (1553–58) and beyond, resisting
complete absorption into Anglican varieties of Protestantism. So
that, "in various parts of East Anglia and south-eastern England, even
in the North at Halifax, a strong Puritan or dissenting tradition seems
to show continuity of growth from local mid-Tudor radicalism based
mainly on Lollardy." [57]

57. Dickens, pp. 35–36. Dickens's last remark lends support, therefore, to McFarlane's claim (p. 187) that the "feeble protest" of the Lollards "was ultimately drowned
in the louder chorus of protestant nonconformity. Their heirs were, in short, not the
Anglicans, but the Brownists and the Independents." Similarly, Thomson, *Later Lollards*, especially pp. 249–53. See also Aston.

Continuities, then, indeed there were. But it may help us to keep them in proportion if we note, by way of conclusion, how very much they pale in comparison with the continuity manifested so dramatically in the deepening frenzy of the witchcraft craze. The witchcraft phenomenon gathered momentum throughout the fifteenth century, peaked in the sixteenth, and continued on well into the seventeenth. Such fifteenth-century popes as Eugenius IV, Nicholas V, and Innocent VIII doubtless helped fix the categorization of witchcraft as a heresy, but it was clearly a heresy persecuted with no less enthusiasm by the Protestants than by the Catholics. Even in the Age of Reformation, the ideas about it that were codified in the *Malleus maleficarum* of 1486 (the infamous inquisitor's manual that was prefaced by Innocent's bull against witches) seem to have succeeded in exerting a continuing, widespread baneful but serenely ecumenical influence on Protestant and Catholic alike.

CHAPTER 5 · MOVEMENTS OF REFORM: STRUCTURAL, MONASTIC, MORAL, EDUCATIONAL

"A rotten pestilence spreads today throughout the whole body of the Church; the more extensive it becomes the more irremediable it is; the more deep-seated the more perilous. . . ." If these things were said by the Blessed Bernard, so much the more can they be said now; for since then the Church has gone from bad to worse.
—PIERRE D'AILLY (1350–1420)

I cry out, therefore, and publicly affirm . . . that of all the evils, divisions, schisms, errors, deformities and so on pertaining to and following from the matters I have been touching upon, the cause and origin, and indeed the root, has been and remains today the neglect and disregard of general councils.
—JOHN OF RAGUSA (1395–1443)

"From the sole of the foot to the crown of the head there is no health in it," said Nicholas of Oresme in a sermon of 1363, applying the old biblical saw to the church of his own day. "Everyone knows," added the preacher at Constance in 1417, "that the reform of the Church Militant is necessary—it is known to the clergy, it is known to the whole Christian people. The heavens, the elements, . . . and, with them now, even the very stones cry out for reform."[1] Certainly, by the

---

1. Matthew Roeder, "Oratio in Concilio Constantiensi," in Walch, ed., 1: fasc. 2, 27–49 at 34. Walch dates it to December 30, 1414, but Haller, p. 4, n. 3, argues for October 1417.

end of the fifteenth century, in the wake of the great councils that had done so much to publicize its cause in circles wider than that of the episcopal hierarchy, more or less everyone who wrote on ecclesiastical matters does indeed appear to have become convinced that reform of some sort was vital.

From the path-breaking reform tract *De modo concilii generalis cele-brandi*, which William Durandus, bishop of Mende, wrote for the Council of Vienne (1311–12), to the program of reform set forth two hundred years later during the Fifth Lateran Council (1512–17) by the two Camaldolese monks Tommaso Giustiniani and Vincenzo Quirini in their *Libellus ad Leonem X*, the same note is insistently struck. Again and again during those centuries—and in the writings of poets as well as of publicists, of prelates no less than of propagandists—we hear of the evils of pluralism and of nonresidence, of clerical ignorance and lay superstition, of elections distorted by simony, of the neglect of pastoral duties promoted by episcopal involvement in temporal af-fairs, of jurisdictional confusion sponsored by papal preferments and exemptions, of the relaxation of monastic discipline encouraged by too ready a concession of compromising privileges by the officials of the papal curia. The concubinous clerk and the venal friar, the indo-lent monk and the ambivalent nun, the corrupt cardinal, the lux-urious prelate, the profligate or power-hungry pope—these are types altogether too familiar from the literature to call for extended exem-plification.

That such persons existed there can be no doubt; to be convinced one need only recall the careers of Alexander VI and Julius II and con-sult the records of the episcopal and legatine visitations or the canons enacted by the provincial synods of the period. But if the evidence for the presence of a good deal of corruption and debilitating confusion is clear enough, that for their steady growth across these centuries and for a concomitantly continuous decline in general moral fervor and religious zeal is much less compelling. If such is the despairing sense conveyed by so many of the publicistic accounts of the period, the caveat sounded by Haller over half a century ago in connection with those writings retains its validity today. Such accounts, he argued, are of great value in so far as they give us "a picture of the prevailing mood," but they cannot be relied upon to give us an accurate picture of the religious and ecclesiastical conditions of their day.[2] The strictures they heap upon the clerical life of the era may reflect rising standards of expectation as much as declining levels of performance. The constant repetition of those strictures may also reflect the thoughtless repetition of propagandistic stereotypes as much as the stubborn persistence of the alleged abuses being condemned.

Something of this sort, indeed, is suggested by the discovery that the treatise on clerical corruption presented by Matthew Ménage in 1433 to the Council of Basel was nothing other than a plagiarized version of a similar tract written by William Lemaire 120 years earlier for the Council of Vienne.[3] Similarly, although Pierre d'Ailly, like so many other publicists of the conciliar epoch, quoted with approval Bernard of Clairvaux's lamentations about clerical corruption, it should be remembered that the church over whose decay the saint was lamenting was that of the *twelfth* century. Moreover, d'Ailly's further sense that things since then had gone from bad to worse was itself something of a convention, fostered by the myth of a golden age of apostolic purity. It was subsequently to gain strength in the formulations of such humanist reformers as Giles of Viterbo (1469–1532), whose thinking reveals the influence of that "metaphysics, or metahistory, of decline" whereby the actual conditions of contemporary religious life were comprehended in terms of "the principle that all reality becomes increasingly weaker and more corrupt the further it departs from its source."[4]

The marked tendency among the reformers and publicists of the day to represent the religious and ecclesiastical life of the fourteenth and fifteenth centuries as a pitiable story of progressive decline and to universalize its defects accordingly, with scant regard for the particularities of time and place, should be avoided by the historian. The

2. Haller, pp. 6–12. Cf. the general comments of Hay, pp. 72–73, and of Duggan, pp. 19–26.
3. Delaruelle et al., 1:320 and n. 3.
4. O'Malley, pp. 2, 184.

available evidence, with all its intimations of confusion and decay, suggests instead the outlines of a picture at once more uneven and more nuanced, and understandably, not fully accessible to those living at the time.

Thus, studies of areas as widely separated as Germany and the diocese of Narbonne convey for the fifteenth century a sense not of further decline but of heightened fervor among the people and a deepening intensity of religious commitment. Similarly, the standard of education among the clergy appears to have been rising—though not as rapidly as it was among the inhabitants of the larger towns.[5] Even among the monastic and religious orders, perhaps the single segment of church life in which symptoms of decay are most persistently manifest, the more startling cases of decadence and disarray are not to be taken as necessarily representative of the whole. Province differed from province, of course, but one is tempted to conclude that the life of the average monk or friar in the fifteenth century, like that of the Cambridge don in the twentieth, conduced no more to a career of spectacular vice than it did to a life of heroic virtue. Waning convictions, spiritual sluggishness, an unsteady sense of purpose—these, rather than any far-reaching corruption, appear to have been the most widespread defects. Knowles has affirmed that the English monasteries, certainly, "were not notably less observant or more decadent in the fifteenth century than before, but the age was undoubtedly marked by a lack of distinction and by the lack of an absolute standard of excellence."[6]

Some of the more obvious instances of disarray, rather than being generalized, should be correlated with conditions and events specific

5. Moeller, *Spätmittelalter*, p. 43. Binz, pp. 338–50, warns of the danger of overstressing the reports of clerical ignorance so frequently found in diocesan visitation records. After thirty years of service in rural isolation, the priest who at ordination had met the requisite standards could well have become one of those denounced in the records. After all, he asks (p. 350): "Que reste-t-il, aux historiens non statisticiens, des connaissances mathématiques exigées d'eux au baccalauréat?" Cf. Duggan, p. 25.
6. Knowles, *Religious Orders*, 2:364. Heath comes to analogous conclusions concerning the condition of the parochial clergy in England on the eve of the Reformation; *English Parish Clergy*, especially pp. 187–96.

to particular places and times—for example, with the ravages caused by war and foreign occupation in north-central France during the early decades of the fifteenth century, with the more widespread havoc wrought by the Black Death in the middle years of the fourteenth century, with the dislocation and administrative confusion engendered by the schism in the latter years of the same century. This last, indeed, as we have already seen, had a very deleterious effect—throwing into turmoil those dioceses that lay athwart the unstable frontier between the two obediences; shattering the unity of the great international religious orders; emboldening individual religious to pursue, especially at the hard-pressed Roman curia, petitions for privileges that could not but promote the loosening of monastic discipline; and, as it progressed and financial pressures mounted, encouraging that curia to issue such privileges with increasing disregard for their consequences. Thus, lumping together the two privileges "that cut at the roots of the religious life—appointment as papal chaplain and permission to hold a benefice," only 3 such were granted to English religious during the pontificate of Gregory IX (1371–78). That number rose to 17, however, during the eleven years of Urban VI's reign (1378–89), and under Boniface IX (1389–1404) the privileges totaled more than 260 in a period of fifteen years.[7]

If this general increase reflects the desperate financial plight of the Roman pontiffs during the years of schism, its distribution across time reflects also a further deterioration in the administrative standards and moral climate of the Roman curia that was specific to the pontificate of Boniface IX. To that deterioration we have a powerful witness in the person of Dietrich of Niem (ca. 1340–1418), a veteran curialist who had begun his career in happier Avignonese days. A professional administrator who had no illusions about Urban VI's faults, he contrasts nevertheless that pontiff's willingness to make do with the ancient fiscal prerogatives of the apostolic camera and his refusal to

---

7. These figures are those calculated by Knowles, *Religious Orders*, 2:170–71. He notes that with the ending of the schism, at least so far as England was concerned, the practice more or less came to an end. In the fourteen years of his pontificate Martin V (1417–31) issued only two such privileges.

permit "sharp financial practices" with Boniface IX's systematic resort to what amounted to open simony.[8]

Dietrich finally turned his back in disgust on the whole administrative machinery he had helped to service, threw in his lot with the conciliarists, and became a vehement propagandist for a program of reform in head and members designed to negate much of the jurisdictional centralization of the century and a half preceding and drastically to curtail the debilitating curial involvement in the traffic in benefices. "The conversion of such an experienced administrator," as E. F. Jacob has said, is indeed "too striking an event to be passed over."[9] Even more striking, however, is Dietrich's inability, experienced though undoubtedly he was, to see beyond the abuses promoted by the papal traffic in genefices to the more fundamental evils attending the very existence of the benefice, with its corrupting confusion of the notions of office and property. Its time-hallowed quality, the centrality of its position among the ecclesiastical institutions of the Latin church, the importance of the role it had come to play in the economy of higher education, the indispensable nature of the contribution it had come to make to the financing of royal and princely as well as papal government—all of these factors blinded reformers to the fact that the institution itself lay at the heart of so many of the corruptions they deplored. They focused their complaints instead upon the abuses and inequities apparent in the prevailing modes of preferment, their attention diverted in fact, from what in retrospect appears to have been the obviously questionable nature of the benefice system itself to what they took to be the culpable and remediable defects in its current operation.[10]

---

8. See the fine essay "Dietrich of Niem" in Jacob, *Essays*, pp. 24–43, especially 35–36. Cf. Dietrich, *De schismate*, chap. 8, 9, 10, 11; in Niem, pp. 82–87. Note the telling comment (chap. 9, p. 84): "Haec eo tempore omni timore Dei et veracundia hominum post posita in tam frequenti erant usu, quod Curiales pro majori parte affirmabant talia licite fieri, cum Papa in talibus, ut dicebant, peccare non posset."
9. Jacob, *Essays*, p. 25.
10. Though Nicholas of Clémanges (d. 1437) came closer than most; see his *Tractatus de ruina et reparacione ecclesie*, chap. 2; ed. Coville, p. 115, where he says: "Nulla prorsus hodierna die, in assumendis pastoralibus sarcinis in curaque animarum subeunda, de servicio divino, de subditorum salute aut edificacione mencio est; de proventuum ubertate tantum modo et quantitate queritur."

Given the Avignonese policies of fiscal and jurisdictional centralization, the attention of reformers was focused remorselessly upon the center, upon the administrative mechanisms of the papal curia. And with the onset of the schism and the deepening economic malaise of the late fourteenth and early fifteenth centuries, the reformers pressed with tiresome and increasing insistence. Agrarian depression, social unrest, successive debasements of coinage, monetary crises— these things had led by then to a marked decline in the revenues from the landed possessions of ecclesiastics as well as noblemen and to a "disequilibrium," perhaps even a "crisis," in the whole benefice system.[11] Benefices had now frequently to be combined in order to produce an income capable of supporting an incumbent, pluralism mounted accordingly, and the weight even of such ancient papal imposts as the annates levied on benefices reserved to the apostolic provision became well-nigh insupportable.

Under such circumstances, a failure to perceive the underlying economic forces at work in no way, of course, dispensed one from experiencing their deleterious effects. The overwhelming tendency was to blame the whole sorry mess on the papacy, to hold the fiscal excesses and voracious needs of the curia "responsible for the economic crisis itself," and even, in the most shortsighted way, to identify reform of the church with reform of the operation of the benefice system.[12] Thus in a very real sense the institution of the benefice was the obstacle on which late-medieval attempts at churchwide reform "in head and members" came to grief.

Reform in Head and Members

The call for reform in head as well as members had emanated from the provincial churches and had been bruited already in 1245 and 1274 at the first and second councils of Lyons. But only in the opening

11. Some areas were very badly hit. Thus by 1419 the revenues of the monastery of Saint-Sernin at Toulouse had fallen from 16,000 to 1,000 florins; see Ourliac in Delaruelle et al., 1:318.
12. Thus Ourliac in Delaruelle et al., 1:306. The whole chapter (pp. 295–313) devoted to "la question bénéficiale" is worthy of attention.

years of the fourteenth century did it begin for the first time to achieve so widespread a credibility and to assume so hostile a tone as to call into question the whole postion of jurisdictional supremacy that the papacy had come to occupy in the universal church. To that position the papacy had attained by virtue of the effective leadership given by popes of the late eleventh and twelfth centuries to both the reforming and crusading movements. By the beginning of the fourteenth century, however, that type of leadership it had long since ceased to be able to give. The clamor of criticism that William Lemaire, bishop of Angers, and William Durand, bishop of Mende, raised at the Council of Vienne constituted something more than a straw in the wind.

When the Franciscan Gilbert of Tournai had written his reform tract for the Second Council of Lyons, he had shown considerable circumspection in addressing himself to the role of the papacy. "The supreme pontiff, the successor of Peter, the anointed of the Lord," he contented himself with saying, "we leave to the Supreme Judge. . . . He himself has his own Book of Deuteronomy in the *De consideratione* which the Blessed Bernard wrote."[13] Less than forty years later, however, when William Durand came to draw up his *De modo concilii generalis celebrandi* for the Council of Vienne, no similar restraint was evident. Concerned to vindicate the rights of the provincial churches against curial encroachment—and especially against the burgeoning system of papal provisions—William was at pains in acknowledging the divine foundation of papal authority to affirm the similarly divine foundation of the church's whole episcopal organization. If it was the responsibility of the Roman church, as "head and mother of all the churches," to give a lead in reform that the others would follow,[14] it was also its duty to respect the rights of local churches, and to restrain within the narrowest of bounds those damaging privileges and exemptions from the jurisdiction of the ordinary that were undermining the authority of the bishops within their dio-

13. Gilbertus Tornacensis, *Collectio de scandalis ecclesiae*, §2, 36. Cf. Jedin, 1:7 (where, as elsewhere in the English edition, the translator has rendered Jedin's paraphrase of the text as if it were intended to be a quotation).
14. *Tractatus Guilielmi Durandi Speculatoris de modo generalis concilii celebrandi*, Tertia pars., rub. 1; in *Tract. Illust. jurisconsult.*, XIII, pars 1, fol. 173r.

ceses. In so arguing, William clearly felt himself simply to be demanding of the pope that he, too, should observe the church's ancient law. He may well have felt, though mistakenly, that he was doing no more than that when he went on to assert that, since "what touches all by all should be approved," a general council should be assembled "whenever a new law was to be established or anything was to be ordained concerning matters that affect the common state of the church (*communem statum ecclesiae*)." [15] But even he must have been aware that he was introducing something of a novelty when he went on to urge that general councils should be assembled regularly at ten-year intervals.

It is important to be clear as to what precisely was involved here. Only a few years earlier John of Paris—drawing together ideas that had long since become commonplaces in the canonistic literature—had argued that a general council, by virtue of the fact that it represented the universal church, could depose an incorrigible pope guilty of abusing his authority. In other words, he had come up with an early and succinct formulation of what we have called the strict conciliar theory. Of this, however, we hear nothing in William Durand's tract—no more, indeed, than we hear anything about reform in John of Paris's *Tractatus de potestate regia et papali*. If it were not anachronistic to do so, we might think of William's position as looking forward only to the Constance decree *Frequens*, whereas John's position looked forward to the more radical *Haec sancta synodus*. Anachronistic, however, it would be—and in a highly misleading fashion, for in the minds of those who at Constance engineered their passage, *Haec sancta* and *Frequens* were clearly related. Nevertheless, we ourselves would be ill-advised to take for granted the association of the demand for reform in head and members with the call to establish the general council as a regularly functioning constitutional mechanism within the structure of church government. Still less should we take for granted the further combination of those two notions with the claims advanced on behalf of the council's authority by those who subscribed to the strict concil-

15. Ibid., Secunda pars., rub. XLI, fol. 165v.

iar theory. For the reforming agitation at Vienne came to nothing. The half-century and more that followed witnessed the energetic consolidation and extension of the pope's fiscal prerogatives and jurisdictional powers. It was only with the onset of the Great Schism in 1378 that an effective cry was raised once more for the assembly of a general council, and with it for a renewed attempt on the problem of church-wide reform. Moreover, only the stubborn persistence of the schism persuaded many among the tentative supporters of the *via concilii* to be truly committed advocates of the strict conciliar theory. As Jedin has said, "It required the pitiful situation created by the Schism to bring about the alliance of conciliar theory with the demand for reform which determined the fate of both at the close of the Middle Ages."[16]

At the start of the schism the overriding concern was to agree upon the precise forum capable of adjudicating the disputed papal election. According to one school of opinion, which came to be represented most powerfully by the cardinals of Clement VII, the college of cardinals, as successor to the original apostolic "college," was the competent judge. To many others, however, including St. Vincent Ferrer, the three Italian cardinals who had remained with Urban VI when the others defected, and also (or so it has been alleged) Pedro de Luna, the future Benedict XIII, the general council was the proper court of judgment.

Endorsement of the latter position, however, did not necessarily mean commitment to any full-fledged version of the strict conciliar theory or to the "alliance" Jedin had in mind. Thus Pierre d'Ailly's cautious advocacy of the *via concilii* in his *Epistola diaboli Leviathan* (1381) is simply that; and although Conrad of Gelnhausen, in his desire to vindicate the right of a general council to pass judgment on the disputed election, firmly invokes the central conciliarist principle of the superiority of council to pope, he is not concerned in the *Epistola concordiae* (1380) with the problem of reform. That concern, however, is central to the *Epistola concilii pacis* (1381) of his fellow countryman

16. Jedin, *History*, 1:9.

Henry of Langenstein, who affirms that even without the schism "there has still for a long time been the need for a general council to reform the universal Church in many other transgressions and deviations," and even speculates that God may have permitted the schism in order that the clergy "might as it were be awakened, so that in a council, assembled because of it, the Church . . . might be reformed."[17] But then Langenstein, though a firm proponent of the *via concilii*, made no more of the conciliarist superiority principle than was strictly necessary to meet the objections of those who claimed that the general council did not possess the requisite authority to decide a disputed papal election.

It is not really until the opening years of the fifteenth century, in the wake of growing disillusionment about the intentions of the rival pontiffs, that we encounter the thoroughgoing combination of the strict conciliar theory with the call for a churchwide reform that would erect permanent constitutional barriers to the pope's abuse of his jurisdictonal power. That combination, which bore fruit in the Constance superiority decrees, found notable expression in the writings of d'Ailly, Jean Gerson, Dietrich of Niem, and Francesco Zabarella, as well as in those of Nicholas of Cusa later on at Basel.

Despite the differences in their thinking, all of these men were advocates of what amounted to a constitutional revolution in the church, in accordance with which the papal plenitude of power would be qualified and limited by that more fundamental and extensive jurisdictional power that resided in the universal church itself and was to be exercised on its behalf by regularly assembled general councils representing it. And, as we have seen, d'Ailly, Zabarella, and Nicholas of Cusa added a further twist by responding to the "oligarchic" views defended so forcefully by some of Clement VII's cardinals and assigning to the sacred college the constitutional role of serving as a more continuously functioning institutional brake on the pope's abuse of his power.

17. *Ep. conc. pacis*, chap. 13; in Dupin, 2:809–40 at 825. Gelnhausen's *Epistola concordiae* is printed in Bliemetzrieder, pp. 111–40, d'Ailly's *Epistola diaboli Leviathan* in Tschackert, app. V, pp. [15]–[21]; English translation in Crowder, pp. 41–45.

This complex combination of ideas was likely to retain its stability only to the degree it could give reasonable promise of opening the way out of the cul-de-sac into which the church of the early fifteenth century, divided and unreformed, had stumbled. That promise, certainly, must have seemed well on the way to fulfillment in April 1418, when the Council of Constance drew to a close. Without the widespread currency to which conciliarist ideas had attained, it would be hard to imagine the council's willingness in 1415 to pass the controversial decree *Haec sancta*, which cleared the way for the judgment and deposition of the rival claimants and the subsequent election of Martin V as an undoubtedly legitimate pope. Without the currency of those ideas, too, it would be hard to imagine the council's similar willingness in 1417 to endorse the decree *Frequens*, which, by legislating the assembly of future councils at stated and regular intervals, appeared to guarantee both the shift in the balance of the church's constitution for which the conciliarists argued and the completion of the program of reform in head and members upon which Constance itself had already made a start.

The careers of Pavia-Siena and Basel, the two subsequent councils that were assembled in accordance with the provisions of *Frequens* after intervals of five and seven years respectively, were to prove such hopes illusory. In retrospect, indeed, the forces that clashed then can be seen to have been active already at Constance, at least from mid-1417 onward, when the council fathers, having finally disposed of the rival papal claimants, began to wrangle over their own future priorities. From one point of view, the first priority had to be the energetic prosecution of the matter of reform, with which two successive reform commissions at the council had busied themselves since 1415, and the enactment, before the election of a new pope, of legislation designed to eliminate abuses at the curia and to limit the pope's exercise of fiscal and jurisdictional powers—especially in the area of reservations and provisions. On this last point, however, the zeal of many of the reformers was undercut somewhat by the fact that they were university

18. See Ourliac in Delaruelle et al., 1:310 and n. 1; 249, n. 13.

men whose very careers had depended on the system of papal provisions.[18] Their ranks, moreover, were split by the very organization of the council and its practice of voting by "nations," which also exposed them to national pressures in a highly concentrated form. Of the temporal rulers, finally, only the emperor Sigismund, who had to cope with the Hussite problem, really appears to have felt that he had a practical stake in reform.

Ranged on the other side, then, were the rulers of France and eventually of England, who had succeeded in coming to more or less favorable terms with the papal system of taxation and preferment and who, though they might want later to tilt the system still further in their own favor, clearly felt that they had nothing to gain and much to lose by destroying it. Hence their decision to support those at the council whose first priority it was to proceed to the election of a new pope. The outcome was an English-sponsored compromise whereby in October 1417, before the papal election, the council promulgated the five reform decrees to which the conciliar "nations" had already given their approval. Of those decrees, *Frequens* was clearly the most important; the others enacted certain provisions for the avoidance of future schisms, required in the future a profession of faith from every newly elected pope, forbade "except for great and reasonable cause" the translation from church to church of higher prelates, and decreed the abolition of "spoils" and procurations. In accordance with the terms of the compromise, it was also decreed that the pope who was to be elected "must reform the church in [its] head and the Roman curia" before the Council of Constance was dissolved, calling for action on a list of eighteen items ranging from the composition of the sacred college, via annates, reservations, and collations, to simony, dispensations, and indulgences.[19]

This represented a promising, if modest, start on the work of reform, but the subsequent negotiations between the newly elected Martin V, the council's third reform commission, and the several conciliar nations (whose concerns differed widely) produced general

19. For these decrees, see Alberigo, pp. 414–20. For further reform decrees passed subsequently at Constance, see pp. 423–26.

agreement only on a few further not very sweeping decrees concerning exemptions, dispensations, simony, and the like. The council also produced the concordats that Martin had negotiated separately with the five individual nations, but those concordats, as we have seen, amounted fundamentally to a division of ecclesiastical spoils between pope and nation. The completion of the work of reform was to await, therefore, the assembly of the next council, which, before dissolving Constance, the pope had decreed was to meet in five years' time at Pavia, in accordance with the provisions of *Frequens*.

But even had the newly elected pope been a convinced reformer, the enormous difficulties confronting him and the political and fiscal fragility of his position militated against reform. Because of the depredations of the *condottiere* Braccio of Montone, Martin was unable to enter Rome until 1424. A year earlier, when the five-year limit had run out on all the concordats except the one with the English, such was his indigence that he went back to the earlier arrangements governing provisions and reservations in so far as the nations involved were complaisant and the reform decrees of Constance permitted. Although he struggled hard to reestablish order in the operations of the curia, sponsoring administrative reforms to that end, he clearly hoped to restore the papacy to the position it had occupied before the disastrous years of schism, and he did not sympathize with conciliar reform or the conciliarist sentiments that tended to go with it. The pressure of public opinion within the church obliged him to assemble the Council of Pavia in 1423 and, after the lapse of the stipulated seven years, to summon the next council to meet at Basel. But he never went to Pavia, transferred the council to Siena, and then, frightened perhaps by the radical nature of the reforms proposed in the *Avisamenta* of the French nation (which wildly underestimated the financial needs of pope and curia)[20] or by the threat of collusion between the conciliarist faction and his enemy, the king of Aragon, hastily dissolved the council before it had passed any significant legislation at all.

20. See Brandmüller, 1:150–52.

When the Council of Basel got under way, then, in July 1431, it was burdened by an enormous freight of reforming expectations—all the heavier because the expiration of Martin V's concordats had made the question of annates and the papal powers of collation and reservation a matter of renewed debate among reformers and governmental officials alike. All the heavier, too, because demands for reform were included in the electoral capitulation that the cardinals drew up after the death of Martin V in February of that same year and imposed upon his successor. It was also burdened by having as a successor Eugenius IV, who shared all of Martin V's hostility to conciliar reform but none of the judgment and ability that had enabled Martin to cope with it. Thus his ill-judged, hasty, and abortive attempt to dissolve the council in December 1431 before it had accomplished anything in the way of reform alienated the majority of the council fathers altogether. It set in train the convoluted and sorry sequence of events that led to the pope's convocation of the rival council of Ferrara-Florence, the renewal of schism, and the creation thereby of a state of affairs that was to render impossible the achievement at the council of truly significant and permanent churchwide reform.

In its early phases the council did succeed, however, in decreeing some very sweeping measures—including the abolition of annates, the prohibition of reservations of bishoprics, and the endorsement of *Haec sancta*, *Frequens*, and the "constitutionalist" vision that those decrees embodied. In modified form, some of these reforms were put into force, spasmodically at least, in France and Germany in accordance with the terms of the Pragmatic Sanction of Bourges (1438) and the *Acceptatio* of Mainz (1439). The credibility of the council itself, however, was progressively eroded—by its own internal disagreements, by its arrogation to itself of judicial and administrative functions that properly belonged to the Roman curia, by its eager immersion, therefore, in the traffic in benefices, by its one-sided interpretation of reform in head and members to mean reform in head alone, by its according willingness to deprive the papacy of such traditional sources of revenue as annates without approving any subsidies to replace them, by the increasingly radical nature of its policies in general, and by its growing dependence on the princes in those policies. In 1449 the Carthusian Jacob of Jüterbog, a one-time partisan of the council, could conclude from the fate of the reform councils that "the doctrine of the Pope's supremacy is only a shield behind which the Italians and their party shelter from reform."[21] But as early as 1438 Cardinal Cesarini himself, who as papal legate had lent strong support to the council's reforming efforts, had abandoned it and gone over to Eugenius IV. In doing so, moreover, he had indicated his own sad conclusion that "the multitude" had prevailed at Basel, opening the way for scandal, schism, and the triumph of the princes, who "will control the pope via the council and subordinate him to their wills."[22]

This is precisely the judgment, of course, that is rendered in his *Summa de ecclesia* by the theologian John of Turrecremata, who had also participated in the council. But he had done so as a staunch supporter of Eugenius IV and there is no mention of reform in his work.[23] It is undoubtedly a much more telling sign of the council's ultimate bankruptcy that convinced conciliarists and advocates of reform such as Cesarini and Nicholas of Cusa (not to mention the future Pius II) abandoned it and rallied to Rome. Under the guidance first of Eugenius IV and then of his successor, Nicholas V (1447–55), the papacy was now able to evade the threat of constitutional change posed by conciliarism, to reassert its own authority, and to ignore or blunt the edges of the Basel reforms—though only at the cost of admittedly damaging concessions to the temporal rulers of Europe and the papacy's own transformation into an Italian principality.

Under the stress of this momentous but ultimately disappointing series of conciliar events running from Pisa and Constance to Siena and Basel, the intricately interwoven complex of ideas that, as we have seen, made up the fabric of conciliar thought began now to unravel. Understandably, the first thread to detach itself from that fabric was

---

21. Jedin, *History*, 1:44–45, paraphrasing Jacobus de Paradiso, *De septem statibus ecclesiae*; in Goldast, 2:1567–75, especially 1570–71.
22. See Ourliac in Delaruelle et al., 1:273.
23. Turrecremata, III, chap. 14, fol. 289v.

also the most marginal—the "oligarchic" strand that had ascribed to the cardinals an enhanced constitutional role in the structure of church government. If Pierre d'Ailly's views on the subject were indeed handed on to future generations, it was to generations of curialists, not conciliarists, and they were handed on not by such later conciliar thinkers as Jacques Almain and John Major, who drew so much else from his writings, but by such papalists and curialists as Domenico de' Domenichi and John of Turrecremata himself.[24] The old curialist oligarchic tradition, therefore, found its home in the late fifteenth century where it had found it before—not among the advocates of the strict conciliar theory but in the Roman curia itself, where the cardinals were engaged in a prolonged and bitter struggle to prevent papal encroachment on their traditional rights and privileges. In this struggle their efforts met with little success. The repeated electoral capitulations, with their private demands but ritual public endorsement of the need for reform and the convocation of a council, were, as Jedin has said, "rearguard actions, not offensive strokes."[25] Nevertheless, those capitulations helped keep alive into the sixteenth century the belief that churchwide reform would come only through a council.

The next strand to detach itself was the strict conciliar theory, with its insistence on the superiority of council to pope and its endorsement, in effect, of radical constitutional change in the structure of ecclesiastical government. The disillusionment of many a would-be reformer with the *policies* of Basel did not necessarily mean a total distancing from the conciliar theory itself. Nevertheless, though there were exceptions even in the early sixteenth century, such as the Bolognese jurist Giovanni Gozzadini, as the years wore on and as the appeal to the general council became a merely tactical device in the armory of secular diplomatic weaponry, those who subscribed to the belief that the necessary reform in head and members could be

---

24. Turrecremata never mentions d'Ailly's name, but he reproduces without acknowledgment much of his argument on the topic; see Oakley, "Almain and Major," pp. 687–88.
25. Jedin, *History*, 1:90.

achieved only by recourse to a general council increasingly recoiled from advocacy of the strict conciliar theory. At the same time, the advocates of that theory were not necessarily themselves very interested any longer in reform. When a dissident council finally did assemble at Pisa in 1510, reform is hardly mentioned at all in the tracts of its most prominent apologists. And although in its formal pronouncements the council itself strove to give a different impression, contemporaries did not doubt that it owed its convocation to political considerations, that it existed simply to bring pressure to bear on Julius II and to serve the diplomatic interests of the French king.

What survived of the broader complex of conciliar ideas in the century dividing Basel from Trent was the bruised sense that, while the stipulations of *Frequens* to the effect that councils should now be assembling every ten years were obviously unrealistic, the bland willingness of the Renaissance popes simply to ignore its provisions was no less clearly dangerous and unhealthy. Not, it should be noted, for constitutionalist reasons, but rather because there survived also the stubborn and fundamental commitment to the notion that the longed-for reform in head and members could be achieved only through the instrumentality of a legitimately assembled general council—though one, this time, in which pope and other participants would work together in harmony to promote that end. That commitment was fortified during the years after Pius II's death by the failure of the pope to give any leadership to the work of reform; its strength was made evident after March 1512 by the enthusiasm with which reformers of the caliber of Giles of Viterbo and Giustiniani and Quirini, men who had shunned the unabashedly conciliarist assembly at Pisa, responded to Julius II's convocation of the Fifth Lateran Council. Not even the abysmal failure of that council to impose effective and thoroughgoing measures of reform succeeded in dimming the fervor of that commitment. Had it done so, indeed, it would be hard to imagine the Council of Trent assembling in 1545.

In order for that council to assemble, of course, innumerable obstacles had to be surmounted, not least of which were the sour memories of Basel and the fears of successive popes that a new council would

open the way for the recrudescence of the claim that council was
superior to pope, and with it their own humiliation at the hands of
temporal rulers capable of manipulating that claim. The threat posed
by the dissident Council of Pisa had made it unpleasantly clear that
such fears were not illusory. Only the overriding need to meet that
threat had steeled Julius II, in convoking the Fifth Lateran Council, to
put them aside. During the course of the latter assembly, moreover,
Leo X had expressed his worry that it might try to reduce his own
power and that of his successors to a "merely spiritual" one.[26] And
without the persistence of similar worries in the minds of his successors it would be hard to explain their fateful delay, after the outbreak
of the Protestant revolt, in assembling the general council for which
even the most papalist of reformers repeatedly called.

The Observantine Movement

In the absence of a full-scale reformation of the universal church,
men had long since begun to turn their attention to the possibilities of
reforming particular segments of it. Already at the time of the Council of Pavia-Siena, the Franciscan St. Bernardino of Siena, in a Lenten
sermon at Florence, had urged the advisability of concentrating attention on partial reform. During the Council of Basel, the Dominican
Johann Nider had done likewise, confessing that he himself had lost
hope in "the general reform of the Church either at present or in the
near future," but adding: "On the other hand a partial reform is
possible in many countries and localities. We see it gaining ground
day by day in monasteries and convents, though God knows amid
what difficulties."[27]

That these particular men should see possibilities for partial reform
is wholly appropriate, for neither of them would have been what they
were without the progress that reform of that type was making within

26. He apparently told Bembo and Quirini in 1514 of his fear that "si riducesse l'autorità nostra e di nostri successori ad autorità solo spirituale," cited in Jedin, *History*,
1:135, n. 3.
27. St. Bernardino, sermon entitled "Il Rispetto alle cosa sacre," in Pacetti, ed.,
2:97. Nider, *Formicarius*, cited in Jedin, 1:139.

some segments of their own orders. During their lifetimes the relaxation and decline into which the monastic houses and religious orders had fallen must have been clearly evident. Certainly, it is evident in retrospect to us—in the overall drop in the number of Benedictine houses, in the declining numbers of monks belonging to some of the greatest houses (from 120 to 60 at Cluny itself during the first quarter of the fifteenth century),[28] in the fall-off in vocations that led the Dominicans to open their ranks to "oblates," sometimes no more than children.

Distressing symptoms of this sort should not be taken to indicate, however, that the monastic urge itself was dying. Despite the division into two obediences occasioned by the schism, and despite subsequent persecution at the hands of Turk and Hussite alike, it was during this period that the Carthusians, the most rigorous of all the orders, underwent their greatest expansion. New houses were added at points as far distant from one another as Danzig and Coventry, Pavia and Amsterdam, so that on the eve of the Reformation the order possessed about two hundred houses spread across seventeen provinces, of which the English province was perhaps the most vital. No other order could match that degree of vitality—certainly not the Cistercians, among whom the symptoms of relaxation and decay were widespread. And yet, in contrast with their Benedictine brothers, the Cistercians added a score and more of new houses during the fifteenth century, and the Belgian province, in particular, contrived somehow to flourish right through the late Middle Ages.

The continuing vitality of the monastic urge is more characteristically evident, however, in two other developments of the era: the foundation of new monastic or quasi-monastic groupings and the appearance within the older orders of the "observantine" type of monastic spirit.

No new great religious order was established during this period. New groupings were nearly all regional in scope, and indeed—with the exception of the Birgittines in Scandinavia (1378 onward), the

28. Delaruelle in Delaruelle et al., 2:1039.

Hieronymites in Spain (from roughly the same era), and the Minims in southern Europe (1454 onward)—they all had their beginnings at least as lay confraternities seeking to carve out some sort of middle ground between the forms of life endorsed by the traditional monastic and mendicant orders and the less formal modes of communal life pursued by the old Beghard and Beguine communities. Of those groupings the most famous and influential were, of course, the Brothers and Sisters of the Common Life, who had their origins in the late fourteenth century and whom we have discussed earlier.

Other such groupings that had already appeared included the Alexians in Flanders and the Rhineland during the aftermath of the Black Death and in southern Europe the Jesuates (1360 onward). Like the Brothers and Sisters of the Common Life, these groups tended to link the striving for personal sanctification with an apostolate of good works toward their fellow Christians. Like them, too, they may often have served as way stations or testing grounds for those en route to the cloister. Unlike the brothers, however, all the others were transformed into full-fledged religious orders, most of them adopting some variant of the Augustinian rule. This was not the case with the latecomer on the scene, the Oratory of the Divine Love, which made its appearance only around 1500. Although the Oratory helped spawn a religious order, that of the Theatines (1524), and with it contributed much to the rise of the Catholic reformation of the sixteenth century, it remained, nonetheless, a lay confraternity, and its roots must be sought in the spirit that had already led to the establishment in many Italian cities of confraternities of laymen devoted to charitable works.

The monastic spirit being sufficiently alive during this period to sponsor such authentic new departures, it would have been odd if it had not manifested itself also in the stirrings of a concern for renewal. This sense can be observed in the older established orders, especially in the Dominicans, Franciscans, Augustinians, and even among the Benedictines themselves. The successes achieved, often in the teeth of bitter opposition from the less zealous majority, though real, are no more to be exaggerated than to be ignored. Improvement was piecemeal; the point of departure, in almost every case, was the attempt to identify the ideal of perfection peculiar to the order concerned; the further line of march was the attempt in the particular houses to realize that ideal by the often painful return to the precise and unqualified observance of the rule in all its original rigor. Hence the characteristic preoccupation, among monks and friars alike, with eliminating the inroads made by private possessions on the commitment to personal poverty; hence, too, the concern to restore a truly common life and, among the monks, to reestablish the strict monastic enclosure.

Thus, among the Dominicans, the years of schism saw St. Vincent Ferrer (1350–1419) recalling his religious brethren in the Avignonese obedience to the ideals of apostolic service that had informed the order in its earliest days. In the Roman obedience, the disciples of St. Catherine of Siena, many of whom were Dominicans, did likewise. Of those disciples, the most prominent was her former confessor, Raymond of Capua, who became master general for the Roman obedience and, starting with Colmar in 1389, established in Germany entire convents of "Observants," which he placed under the immediate authority of "vicars of the Observance." In so doing, he hoped that as the friars from the Observant houses were moved around they would disseminate throughout the order a new zeal and commitment to its primitive ideals. Similarly reformed houses were established in Italy by John Domenici, another of St. Catherine's disciples, who in 1393 was himself named vicar general for the Observants in Italy, and who was later followed in that position by a man whom his own preaching had converted. That man we know as St. Antonino of Florence, and it was under his rule that the convent of San Marco in Florence, destined later to harbor both Fra Angelico and Savonarola, became not only a center of the Observance but also, having acquired the library of the savant Niccolo Niccoli, a focus of humanistic learning.

A comparably powerful reform movement took place in the ranks of the Franciscans, among whom in Italy, the Observance had begun in a small way as early as 1368. Its expansion, however—reaching eventually into France, Spain and Portugal, England, Burgundy, Germany, and even Poland and Hungary—was very much bound up with the efforts of the great preaching friars St. Bernardino of Siena and John of Capistrano. Given the extremes to which the Spiritual wing of the order had gone, it is understandable that the spirit of the Franciscan Observance was distinguished by a careful moderation designed to avoid friction with the "Conventual" majority. This spirit comes out very clearly in the *Constitutiones Bernardini*, which St. Bernardino, as vicar general of the Italian convents of the Observance, gave to them in 1440.

The point of departure of the *Constitutiones* was complete acceptance of the relevant papal decrees as the norm for the Franciscan life; they stated that the evangelical counsels were not to be taken as obligatory; they avoided any statement that might be construed as a censure of their Conventual brethren. At the same time they eschewed dispensations, prohibited the use of money, and evoked the simplicity of St. Francis's own dedication to holy poverty. It was all very much in the spirit of views that Bernardino himself had been expressing for years—as, for example, in 1425, when he had said that the true hardship involved was not so much the physical privations imposed by "the joyous life of the Friars Monir" as the call to suppress one's own personality. "One must *appallotolarsi*"—roll oneself up into a ball— he said,

> like a beetle's little ball of dung, which rolls now this way and now that. If you are a proud man, you must become humble; if with a melancholy one, you must be gay. Always, if you see the scales weighted down on one side, put your weight on to the other, to make it even—and this from obedience. You must bear with everyone, as others must bear with you—for we are not alike. Some eat more, some less; some can fast and others cannot; one is apt at contemplation and another not. . . . And all must be equal. . . . Religion [the life of the professed "religious"] is like a river, in which there are many stones: the stream bears them on.[29]

Similar stirrings of reform of the Observant type made themselves felt among the Cistercians, among the Augustinian canons (the Win-

---

29. See Pacetti, ed., 2:534–37; I cite Origo's translation in *World of San Bernardino*, p. 217.

desheim congregation representing but one grouping of Observants within that order), and among the Augustinian Eremites—to the Observant congregation of which Martin Luther was himself to belong. But the houses most dramatically affected by this type of reform were probably such monasteries as Monte Cassino and Subiaco in Italy, St. Matthias in Trier, and Melk on the Danube, which became centers of renewal within the Benedictine family. For them, as for houses belonging to the other orders, renewal certainly meant an attempt to return to the strict observance of the Rule—but in their case it also meant something further. Until this time, the more individual and affective piety of the type disseminated throughout the church by the Cistercians and Franciscans had found no official foothold in the houses of "black monks" that were still formed within the original Benedictine tradition of "liturgical monasticism." With the coming of the Observance in the late fourteenth and early fifteenth centuries, however, side by side with the Office a place was made for personal prayer, and recourse was increasingly had to more methodical meditative practices of the type that were to be developed so systematically by the practitioners of the *Devotio moderna*.

Moreover, to a reformed house that eventually belonged (not all did) to an Observant congregation within the Benedictine family—to that in Germany centering on Bursfeld, or in Spain centering on Valladolid, or in Italy centering on Mount Oliveto near Siena or Santa Giustina at Padua—the coming of the Observance meant the ending of the absolutism that had once characterized the office of abbot and the definitive loss by the individual houses of the local autonomy that had been the tradition of the order, though already much eroded. In this, however, the Observant congregations were simply reviving and extending in modified form the program of grouping individual houses into provinces subject to the jurisdiction of "visitors" elected by triennial chapters, which the Cistercian pope, Benedict XII, had sought to impose on the Benedictines in 1336 as part of his own (largely abortive) attempt at churchwide reform of monastic and religious orders.

This fact deserves emphasis. If the keynote of the various movements of the Observance was the spontaneous stirring of the reforming spirit within the orders, it must not be supposed that they owed nothing to the efforts of external authorities. Thus, for example, it was the Council of Basel that appointed John Rode, abbot of the Observant house of St. Matthias, as visitor of the Benedictine houses of southwest Germany and charged him with the task of reform. And it was to Martin V, again, that Rode owed his position as abbot of St. Matthias, for, at the petition of the archbishop of Trier, Martin had relieved him of his vows as a Carthusian and placed him in charge of the Benedictine house. Similarly, it was because of the initiative taken by Albert V, Duke of Austria, that the Observance came to Melk, making that monastery a center of renewal not only for Austria but also for Bavaria.

Councils, popes, secular rulers can all claim some part, direct or indirect, in the spread of the reform among monastic and religious orders during the late fourteenth and fifteenth centuries. Their efforts, however, like those of the individual reformers themselves, were fragmentary and piecemeal. It was doubtless the creation with papal consent of Observant congregations that was to assure for the monastic and religious life an honored place within the boundaries of the pruned and purified Catholicism of the era of Counter-Reformation. But it is also the conspicuous absence of the type of consistent central leadership that could have come only from Rome that helps account for the uneven geographical distribution of Observant houses and for the sorry fact that no one order succeeded entirely in reforming itself before the onset of the Reformation. And that despite persistent and sometimes heartbreaking reforming efforts in the teeth of opposition emanating from the unreformed houses. Rather than being the leaders or consistent supporters of such reforming efforts, the popes took the more typical role of adjudicator between the competing claims of Observant congregations and Conventual or unreformed provinces. Thus it was characteristic of the papacy's indirect type of involvement in the reform that the squabble among the Augustinian Eremites, which brought Luther to the Roman curia as representative of the German Observant congregation, should have been occasioned by the attempt of that zealous reformer Giles of Viterbo to unify all twenty-six Conventual provinces and ten observant congregations under his own direct jurisdiction as prior general of the order. And it was characteristic of the degree to which the Observants still felt their rigorous way of life threatened by the laxity of the Conventual majority that Luther (ironically enough) did not go to the curia to support that unification, which one might have thought held promise of leading to the permeation of the whole order with the reforming Observant ideal, but was rather empowered by his congregation to oppose it.

Reforms on the National and Provincial Level: Cusa, Savonarola, Ximénez

It is sufficient to recall the great preaching missions undertaken by St. Vincent Ferrer, St. Bernardino of Siena, and John of Capistrano, all of them friars of the Observance, or the pastoral labors as archbishop of Florence of that other Observant friar St. Antonino, to realize that the stirrings of reform within the religious orders had an impact on the larger and less cloistered world inhabited by the laity and secular clergy. Some products of the Observance, indeed, we find involved in reforming efforts on the local or national level: in France, Standonck of the Windesheim Congregation; in Italy, Savonarola, a Dominican Observant; in Spain, Ximénez, a Franciscan Observant. Such efforts punctuate the history of the late Middle Ages, can be seen in progress at points as far distant as Bohemia and France, and particularly reveal the increasing role that the temporal authorities, for good or ill, were coming to play in the life of the church. Thus, as we have seen, the movement in Bohemia to raise the level of Christian living among secular clergy and laity alike long predated Hus and owed its initiation to the collaborative venture of Emperor Charles IV and the archbishop of Prague. Similarly, in France it was King Charles VIII who assembled the Reform "consultation" of Tours in 1493, at which Jean Standonck set forth his program for reforming the secular clergy. On the other hand—as Renaudet's account makes clear—religious renewal was not notably advanced under his successor, Louis XII, by the willingness of Georges d'Amboise to resort to military force to impose his reforms, despite wholly extraordinary powers over the French church wielded by Amboise as the king's chief counselor and papal legate.[30]

From among the numerous attempts at various kinds of local or national reform—institutional, jurisdictional, moral, educational —we must content ourselves with selecting for brief examination only three. The three, it must be admitted, are of clearly divergent focus, very different provenance, and vastly differing effect, but are chosen precisely for these reasons. The first, an example of papally sponsored reform, is connected with Nicholas of Cusa's legatine mission to Germany and the Netherlands in 1451–52. The second is that sponsored at Florence by Girolamo Savonarola (1452–98) during the last decade of the same century, a striking illustration (in its weaknesses as well as its strengths) of the type of moral and spiritual regeneration that under certain conditions an inspired and prophetic preacher might prove able to promote. The third, testifying to the supportive contribution to reform concerned and sympathetic monarchs could make, is the great renovation of the Spanish church in the late fifteenth and early sixteenth centuries, in which Cardinal Ximénez de Cisneros (1436–1517) came to play a distinguished role. All three cases illustrate, though in differing fashion, the growing dominance of the political factor in the arena of religious and ecclesiastical reform.

Coming after the triumph of the papacy and the demise of the Council of Basel, Nicholas of Cusa's mission is of particular interest. It was the most sweeping of several that the newly elected pope, Nicholas V, initiated in 1450. The papacy had turned back the threat posed to its prerogatives by the conciliarist program of reform in head and members; now it remained to be seen what credence could be

---

30. Renaudet, especially pp. 290–365, 437–62. Even less fruitful for reform was the similarly dictatorial authority wielded by Cardinal Wolsey over the English church from 1518 to 1529 by virtue of his combined offices of papal legate and lord chancellor of England.

given to its own alternative conception of the manner in which reform should be achieved—namely, "as an effect of papal power operating through legislative acts, such as papal Bulls, or through the decrees of papal legates and visitors *in partibus*." [31]

On the face of it, it seemed, quite a lot could be expected from that approach to reform. Among other things, the pope charged Nicholas with responsibility for "the reformation of individual churches . . . secular as well as regular, exempt and non-exempt alike," in Germany, the Netherlands, and Bohemia. [32] And in order to facilitate the discharge of this onerous task, the pope conferred upon him the high rank of *legatus a latere*, urging him to proceed with prudence, employing such traditional instrumentalities as visitations, sermons, the issuing of reform decrees at provincial councils, but permitting him also, in extreme need, to call upon the coercive sanctions at the disposal of the temporal power.

Armed with these instructions, Nicholas set out from Rome on December 31, 1450; by April 1452, when his mission officially ended, he had made his way through the sprawling ecclesiastical provinces of Salzburg, Magdeburg, Mainz, Cologne, and Trier, holding four provincial councils and several diocesan synods, issuing some thirteen reform decrees (including an outright prohibition of the traditional cult of the "bleeding hosts" at Wilsnack), conducting more than eighty visitations, preaching more than fifty sermons, attempting to mediate jurisdictional squabbles, persuading, admonishing, suspending, deposing, and increasingly, as the legation wore on and local resistance stiffened, resorting to omnious threats—of excommunication, of interdict, of the sanctions wielded by the secular arm. All in all, an extraordinary effort, which took him in fifteen months over an itinerary of some 2,800 miles and all the way up to the North Sea coast of the Netherlands and back.

Because of the heroic scope of the mission and the stature of the man who undertook it, there has been an understandable tendency among historians to attribute to it much more success than the available evi-

31. Jedin, *History*, 1:118.
32. See Sullivan, p. 391.

dence appears to warrant.[33] Undeniable successes there were, especially in the realm of monastic reform, where Nicholas was able to make skillful use of the energies contributed by supportive representatives of the Windesheim, Bursfeld, and Melk reforms. Against these successes, however, must be set not only several specific failures, such as his inability even to initiate reform within the province of Trier or the bishopric of Liège, but also the discouraging degree to which his reform decrees and the sanctions he imposed on simoniacs, unruly monks, and concubinous clerics turned out, after his departure, to be dead letters.

For these failures Nicholas must himself in some small part be blamed. There are curious disjunctions between the sublimely spiritual vision of reform conveyed in the pages of his *De concordantia catholica* (1433) or the later *Reformatio generalis* (1459) and the narrowly legalistic nature of so much of his practical reforming activity, between his decrees against abuses in the benefice system and the fact that he was himself a pluralist drawing revenues at that very time (however legally) from as many as twenty benefices, between his own exhortations to moderation in the work of reform and the increasing resort to intimidation and threat of armed force that marked the latter stages of his mission and was later to render his reforming efforts as bishop of Brixen (1452–61) largely abortive.[34]

This deepening and misjudged severity, however, may have been only an understandable reaction to the obstacles and disappointments Nicholas repeatedly encountered during the course of his wearying mission. Over those he had had no control; for them he can be required to take no blame. Some, indeed, were rooted in the conditions of life in late medieval Germany, in the quirk of history that had transformed the leading German prelates into great territorial princes,

33. Perhaps the most widely known of the positive appraisals of the legatine mission is that in Pastor, 2:105–37. I follow here the somewhat less enthusiastic appraisal of Vansteenberghe, pp. 87–139, and the more negative recent account of Sullivan.
34. Aubenas, in Aubenas and Ricard, p. 282, speaks of his "ardeur extrême" and "sévérité excessive," and adds: ". . . il y a apporté un grand zèle, certes, mais déparé par une excessive rudesse, et non sans maladresse." Cf. Vansteenberghe, especially pp. 143–53.

often more prone to use their spiritual authority to promote their temporal interests than the reverse, occasionally bellicose warriors willing to use armed force as well as the penalties of excommunication and interdict in order to collect their debts or harass their dynastic rivals.[35] Other obstacles and disappointments experienced by Nicholas, however, reflect the degree to which it is simply unrealistic, under the turbulent conditions still prevailing in the wake of Basel, to expect the popes to exert the kind of sustained pressure on the clerical leadership that was clearly required to achieve enduring reform. Thus, though he undoubtedly was concerned to promote reform, Nicholas V had to face the fact that the very notion of a papally imposed reform was bitterly opposed even by some of those most convinced of the need for thoroughgoing reform. Thus, in Germany, such a hard-core conciliarist as Carthusian Vincent of Aggsbach could snort that "the loss of a thousand talents caused by the neglect of the Council is to be made good with a gratuity of threepence," and could call instead for a new withdrawal of obedience and the spontaneous assembly of the new general council that alone would be capable of sponsoring a thoroughgoing reform in head and members.[36] Or again, in a reaction specifically to Cusa's mission, the author of the anonymous memorial that was given to him at Mainz claimed that the reform of the members would follow readily enough when once the head had been reformed, and, pointing out the similarity between some of Cusa's reform decrees and those of Basel, argued that if they were accepted on his authority as legate, then that authority "would seem to be higher than that of a general council. Which would not conform to the truth."[37]

At the same time, Nicholas V was caught up, like Eugenius IV before him, in the disabling process of attempting to establish a secure base for the papacy by transforming the papal states into a consoli-

---

35. Hence the decree promulgated by Nicholas at Magdeburg forbidding bishops to use the interdict in order to collect their personal debts; see Sullivan, p. 402; cf. pp. 405, 413.

36. Jedin, *History*, 1:43–44, 117–20 (here again, despite his translator, paraphrasing, not quoting; cf. Jedin, *Geschichte*, 1:95).

37. The memorial is printed in Walch, ed., I, fasc. 1, 103–110; see pp. 103–4.

dated Italian principality, while trying to reassert an increasingly tenuous papal authority in the church at large—at the price, if need be, of damaging concessions to the temporal rulers of Europe. And in Germany that meant concessions to the prince bishops, among others. Hence, or so it must be surmised, his crippling exemption of the archbishops and bishops from Nicholas of Cusa's legatine authority, despite the fact that their total cooperation was essential if Cusa's mission was to succeed. Hence, too, his repeated unwillingness, once appeals from those affected were lodged at Rome, to stand behind his own legate's sentences and condemnations—as, for example, in the case of Cusa's prohibition of the Wilsnack cult, which the bishop of Havelberg had simply refused to enforce.

For Nicholas of Cusa himself, therefore, it was in many ways a "no-win" situation. If his legatine mission can be taken to represent the type of papally sponsored reform envisaged and (less frequently) engaged in by the popes of the era of restoration, it was a reform hampered by the entanglement of pope and church in the political life of the day. It was also a reform that turned out to depend, for whatever limited success it enjoyed, less upon the vigorous exercise of papal leadership than upon the conscientious cooperation and support provided in the localities by such men as Archbishop Frederick of Magdeburg or the members of the Bursfeld and Windesheim congregations, who were already committed to the work of partial reform.

Though it also reveals the degree to which the complex interplay of political and religious factors could be determinative even in matters pertaining to morality and spirituality, the story of the brief ascendancy of Savonarola at Florence forty years later is vastly different; it is treated less often, in fact, as a striking phase in the history of late-medieval religious reform than as a bizarre episode in the history of Renaissance culture—the inexplicable conversion of a worldly city to a moment of puritanical zealotry, or, at best, a classic manifestation of the phenomenon to which Burckhardt referred as "the periodical upheaval of the Italian conscience."[38] And yet Savonarola began his reli-

38. Burckhardt, 2:450.

gious life in the Dominican priory of San Domenico in Bologna, a house that, even within the Observant congregation of Lombardy to which it belonged, enjoyed a reputation for strict observance of the rule. During the years of his ascendancy at Florence, moreover, the only official positions he held were those of prior of San Marco (1491–98) and, from 1493 on, of vicar general of a new congregation centering on San Marco and separated from the Lombard congregation in order to facilitate that even stricter observance to which he was committed. During those years Savonarola strove also to impart the urgencies of his reforming zeal to those outside the cloister, excoriating in his sermons the corruption of clergy and curia alike. And if, for a while, he succeeded in converting Florence to his vision, that city itself succeeded before the end in converting him into a powerful exponent of the Florentine millennial myths and civic religion.[39]

The point of departure of Savonarola's reform was the Observantine movement of monastic reform that had earlier achieved considerable success in Italy and within his own order. By his time something of a falling off from earlier high standards had again occurred, probably within the Lombard congregation as a whole and certainly at his own priory of San Marco. For that house, after the plague of 1448 had reduced its numbers, no less zealous a person than St. Antonino had found it necessary to obtain papal permission to own property and enjoy a regular income, as the priory could no longer subsist on the alms of the faithful. Savonarola's initial rise to prominence was as the compelling and ascetic reformer who restored strict observance first to San Marco, which quickly began to attract a growing membership, and then to the convents at Fiesole, Pisa, Sasso, and Prato, which were now attached to his new congregation; a reformer who strove always, as a contemporary admiringly wrote, "to introduce into their studies and way of life an almost divine order."[40]

Savonarola's success in reforming San Marco, to which the sons of leading Florentine citizens were now beginning to flock, and the de-

---

39. This is the thesis advanced with sustained force and a wealth of detail by Weinstein. Much of what follows depends on his fascinating account.
40. Cited by Ridolfi, p. 76.

gree to which the convent was becoming a focal point in the artistic and literary life of the city (Accademia Marciana, it came to be called) served to enhance his reputation and to heighten the respectful and fearful attention large numbers of Florentines were already paying to the prophetic sermons he had been preaching, first at San Marco and then, from Lent 1491 on, at the cathedral itself. The burden of the message he preached to the Florentines was at first traditional enough. A good deal harsher in tone, it does not appear to have been altogether unlike the message conveyed in the eschatological preaching of St. Vincent Ferrer, whose memory was venerated at San Marco, where Fra Angelico had left a portrait of him. He made a sweeping attack on the corruption of the church and of society and gave a terrifying apocalyptic warning that "the sword of the Lord" was poised over the earth.[41] God was preparing a "mighty scourge" that would cleanse the church in Italy amid universal tribulations before the onset of the last days, he warned; now was the time, before it was too late, for them to repent of their sins and purify their lives.

In all of this there was nothing, Weinstein has argued, about any unique, providential role to be allotted to the city of Florence. That was to come later, during the critical months of November and December 1494, when Florence trembled before the approach of the victorious army of Charles VIII of France, which had crossed the Alps and, advancing on the city, was scattering all opposition before it. In a sermon two years earlier, it seems, Savonarola may have linked the tribulations whose impending arrival he consistently prophesied with the descent from the Alps of a new conquering Cyrus whom none would be able to resist. And now, to the horror of his trembling listeners, he sought to remind them of that fact, identifying Charles with that Cyrus and the French army with the divine scourge he had foretold and urging them with redoubled fervor to repent. The apparent vindication of his prophecies gained for him enormous authority among the Florentines; after the collapse of the Medici regime, his further success as one of the chief negotiators of the treaty with Charles

41. "Ecce gladius Domini super terram, cito et velociter": see Ridolfi, pp. 48–49.

VIII that secured not only the safety but also the freedom of Florence won for him the reputation as savior of his city.

On those grounds alone, one might well expect the grim appeal of his message of repentance to have grown. During those same critical months, however, Savonarola began to sound in his sermons a new and more optimistic note, envisaging himself "as the man sent by God, not only to warn Italy of the tribulations which had now come, but also to lead her out of the abomination of desolation." And Florence he now heralded as the "city of God," the "beloved of Christ," "the center and the heart of Italy," the city that, having reformed and reconstituted itself as a truly Christian republic, would become even "more glorious, richer, more powerful than ever before," for she was destined by God to be the New Jerusalem, the center from which the reform of the church and the regeneration of social and political life would spread out across the whole of Italy.[42]

Though it was remarked neither by himself nor by his eager hearers, the new note betrays a fundamental shift of emphasis in Savonarola's prophetic discourse. He moved from a more universal message of repentance and doom to a millenarian vision focused specifically upon Florence, echoing "the particular variety of millenarian fantasy" that was very familiar to the Florentines, who had long since cultivated "the myth that celebrated Florence both as the New Jerusalem and the New Rome in a dual mission of spiritual and political leadership." The atmosphere of public piety and fervor that characterized the years of his ascendancy, the realignment of festivals, the burning of vanities, the great processions led by the public organization of younger boys (the *fanciulli*) at once both "propitiative and celebratory," the very collective nature of so much of the frenzied religious activity— these things reflect the degree to which Savonarola, "celebrating the city as the Lord's chosen . . . , had penetrated to the religious core of Florence's civic patriotism." He thus released energies untapped by the eschatological preoccupations that informed so much of the popu-

42. Weinstein, pp. 116–17, 146–47, 167–70.

lar preaching of the day and had shaped his own original message.[43]

It may be argued that the adjustment of Savonarola's previously universalist religious vision to the urgencies of the Florentine civic religion and millennial myth accounts for the momentary triumph of his reform at Florence. It must also be noted, however, that the depth of his own engagement in the political destinies of Florence accounts also for his own downfall amid the wreckage of that reform. For his great offense in the eyes of Alexander VI (or of those who surrounded him) appears to have been less an unambiguous challenge to the spiritual authority of the papacy than his crucial role in aligning Florence with Charles VIII and against the anti-French league that the pope had formed with Milan, Venice, Aragon, and the Emperor Maximilian. Even in his own hour of direst need, after all, Savonarola—Thomist and papalist to the core—decided against the appeal for a general council that, for a while at least, he had considered making to the secular rulers of Europe. Before his death at the stake, he accepted the pope's benediction and plenary indulgence. After his death, his writings were admired and he himself was venerated by such stalwarts of Catholic Reformation spirituality as St. Philip Neri (1515–95), founder of the Oratorians, and the Dominican Observant Luis of Granada (1504–88), author of "the most important manual of prayer which Spain produced in this era," the *Libro de la oración y meditación*, which appeared in 1544.[44]

In Spain, however, the entanglement of church reform with political life had already proved to be at once more direct and more benign in its effects than in either the Germany of Nicholas of Cusa or the Italy of Savonarola. The long-drawn-out crusade to drive the Muslims from the Iberian Peninsula had promoted an identification of religious

43. See Weinstein, pp. 114–17, 146–47, 168–69, 238–39. For the ritual significance of the *fanciulli* and their processions, see Richard C. Trexler, "Ritual in Florence: Adolescence and Salvation in the Renaissance," in Trinkaus and Oberman, eds., pp. 200–264, and especially 250–64.

44. See Bataillon, *Erasmo y España*, pp. 592–97; cf. his "De Savonarole à Louis de Grenade." Louis was only the most illustrious product of the extremely rigorous Dominican reform that drew clear and direct inspiration from Savonarola.

and national ideals to a degree unparalleled in Latin Christendom. After the union of the crowns of Aragon and Castile in 1479, Ferdinand and Isabella had been able to bring the national church effectively under royal control. Already in 1478 Sixtus IV had permitted the establishment of a new inquisitorial tribunal in Spain, which, unlike its forerunners, was a strictly national institution under royal control. In 1482 the two monarchs had secured from the same pontiff the right to nominate to the most important ecclesiastical offices in their kingdoms, thus establishing their control over the hierarchy. That control they certainly used to advance the process by which their royal power was being extended, but they used it also to promote the cause of reform in the church.

This is clearly evident in the positive way in which Ferdinand responded to the convocation of the Fifth Lateran Council, appointing a committee of bishops, theologians, and diplomats to draw up a reform program to be submitted to that council, and himself, while calling for the formal repudiation of the Constance decree *Haec sancta*, urging nevertheless that it was in the interest of the universal church that the principle behind *Frequens* be respected and that general councils be assembled every ten to fifteen years.[45] The same concern with reform, but on the national level, is evident in the support both monarchs gave to the forces of renewal within the Spanish church itself.[46]

Those forces are not simply to be identified with Cardinal Ximénez de Cisneros or those immediately associated with him. The Spanish church of the period produced more than one able and energetic bishop, and reform of the Observantine mold gained ground among the Benedictines, Augustinians, Franciscans, and Dominicans—in the last case, it seems, partly under the inspiration of Savonarola's reformed Congregation of San Marco. In all of this monastic reform, the evidence currently available permits us to ascribe a definite role to Ximénez only in connection with the Franciscans.[47] But there the

45. Doussinague, app. 50, p. 539.
46. See Ricard's useful discussion in Aubenas and Ricard, pp. 299–311.
47. Bataillon, *Erasmo y España*, p. 4, n. 11, stresses: "The study of the reform of the

nature and extent of his contribution is clear, as it also is in relation to the secular clergy. And those contributions justify our ascribing to him the dominant role in the wide-ranging reform of the Spanish church, which placed it in the forefront of the Catholic Reformation as it gained momentum in the mid-sixteenth century.

Ximénez's period of ascendancy came comparatively late in his life and covered the years from 1492, when he became confessor to Queen Isabella, to 1517, when he died. During those years he became successively archbishop of Toledo, primate and therefore chief minister of the queen (1495), cardinal and inquisitor general (1507), and twice served also as regent. He had entered the Franciscans only in 1484, after some years as a secular priest; when he did so, he chose to join the more rigorous branch of the order, which he came in 1494 to head as vicar general for the Observant Franciscans of Castile. When he came to lead the reform of the order, he understandably chose the traditional tactic of trying to spread the Observance—though in pursuing that tactic he displayed a limitless energy, an implacable zeal, and a ready willingness to resort to coercive measures that were far from traditional. His reform has been described as consisting "essentially in taking their monasteries, for good or ill, away from the Conventuals and installing the Observants in them."[48] Confronted with this impending fate, the Conventuals naturally fought a strong rear-guard action, marshaling support among their noble patrons as well as at the Roman curia itself. But Ximénez induced the queen to take a personal interest in the struggle, and as a result by 1497 he had received from the pope the full powers he needed to bring the more outrageously recalcitrant to heel. By 1517, when he died, the Conventuals had lost most of their influence in Spain, though the claim that they had disappeared altogether is incorrect.

---

orders cannot yet be undertaken, in the way it should be, on the basis of the documents from the monastic archives. Those that have remained in the convents are not open to the public. The countless bundles of documents emanating from the monasteries secularized in the nineteenth century . . . are still inaccessible: they constitute in the A[rchivo] H[istorico] N[acional] at Madrid] a non-catalogued holding, belonging to the Ministry of Finance."
48. Bataillon, *Erasmo y España*, p. 5.

Ximénez showed similar vigor and persistence in pursuing the reform of the secular clergy. Even as archbishop of Toledo, he continued to live a life of Franciscan simplicity and poverty, seeking also, though without success, to impose a communal life on the canons of his cathedral. He had greater success in inducing the Catholic monarchs to use their power to appoint to the episcopate men worthy of their high calling and spiritual responsibilities. He convoked synods at Alcalá (1497) and Talavera (1498), at which were promulgated a series of decrees addressed not only to the customary task of rectifying disciplinary abuses such as clerical concubinage but also to the less frequently pursued goal of restoring the dignity and renewing the pastoral ministry of the diocesan priesthood. Thus priests were to be obliged to reside in their parishes, to keep decent parish records of baptisms and the like, to go regularly themselves to confession, to expound to their flocks on Sundays the Gospel of the day, to make sure that the children of the parish were given religious instruction, and so on. To help them with the last task, Ximénez published a simple catechism. Moreover, his establishment in 1502 of a printing press at Alcalá made possible the wide dissemination of other types of instructional religious literature, including St. Vincent Ferrer's *Tractatus de vita spirituali* and a Castilian translation of Ludolf of Saxony's *Vita Christi*. His broader educational activities reflect a related concern to produce for the future a body of clergy better equipped by education than their predecessors for the urgent tasks of doctrinal formation and pastoral care that confronted them.

He used the income of his archbishopric to help endow the new university of Alcalá, the ecclesiastical bent of which is evident in its first constitutions, which were promulgated in 1510. Its central focus was the theological college of St. Ildefonso (founded 1498). There was no faculty of law, and the faculty of arts functioned to prepare the students for a program of theological studies that embraced, in addition to scholastic theology, scriptural and patristic studies in the original languages. There was, accordingly, a strong stress on Greek and Hebrew as well as Latin, and a marked interest in Arabic and Syriac as well.[49] Ximénez's gradual assembly of a distinguished team of linguists eventually included the Cretan Demetrios Doucas, who filled the prestigious chair in Greek; the converted Jew Alfonso de Zamora, who in 1512 began the teaching of Hebrew at Alcalá; and the distinguished humanist Antonio de Nebrija, who conferred considerable renown on the chair of rhetoric.

All three of these men were involved, in varying degrees, in the great project of scriptural research that had long preoccupied Ximénez and that led eventually to the production at Alcalá under his direction of the great six-volume Complutensian Polyglot Bible—an extraordinary achievement in the history both of printing and of biblical scholarship. The volume including the Greek, Aramaic, and Vulgate texts of the New Testament, along with a critical apparatus, was printed in 1514. The remaining five volumes included the Old Testament in parallel Hebrew, Greek, and Latin texts, the Aramaic Targumim, and a triple lexicon for the Hebrew, Greek, and Aramaic. They were completed before Ximénez died, but the whole massive work went into circulation only after 1520, when it received Leo X's approbation. It has been pointed out that in all of this activity Ximénez's concern was comparatively conservative. Unlike Erasmus, he did not set out to make a new Latin translation but rather, through a painstaking comparison and analysis of the Hebrew, Greek, and Latin texts, to reconstruct the correct version of the traditional Vulgate. Nonetheless, the whole project, along with the educational ethos Ximénez imparted to his new univeristy at Alcalá, signals the advent of something new, the fertilization of scriptural and theological studies of the traditional mold by the newer scholarly and educational concerns of the Renaissance humanists. In this respect, therefore, it may be regarded as one particular manifestation of that discrete current of reform already in full flow elsewhere in Europe, which reflected a religious ideal that one may label, though not without a certain nervousness, as distinctively humanistic.

49. And not without reference to the relevant provisions of the Council of Vienne; see *Clem.* V, 1, c. 1; ed. Friedberg, 2:1179.

The Problem of the Humanist Contribution

The way in which one understands the humanist contribution to reform depends very much on the way in which one understands Renaissance humanism itself and the nature of its relationship to the religion and the theology of the day. If one sympathizes with the recent tendency to emphasize rather than to minimize the degree to which the Italian humanists were concerned in their writings with religious questions—to stress, indeed, the importance of their contributions to the history of Christian thinking—then one may well be inclined to understand Renaissance humanism and Ockhamist nominalism as sharing some common tendencies, as being "two parallel modes of asserting a repudiation of preceding thirteenth-century scholastic efforts to forge a unity between revelation and reason."[50] One will tend, as a result, to accord a good deal of significance to the quasi fideism and emphasis on primacy of the will evident in the earlier humanists Petrarch (1304–74), Coluccio Salutati (1331–1406), and Lorenzo Valla (1405–57). One may even be tempted, brooding about the obvious voluntarism of these men, to remark the "pessimistic estimate of the human condition" evident in their writings and in those of other humanists, and, via an intriguing line of argument, conclude with the suggestion that the great Protestant Reformers in general, and Luther in particular, "met the religious needs implicit in the new culture of the Renaissance, and in ways largely consistent with its fundamental assumptions."[51]

No one who feels the urge to probe for underlying unities in late-medieval, Renaissance, and Reformation patterns of thought (and what church historian does not?) is likely to be altogether indifferent to the vistas that open up before such approaches. But it is hard to overlook the formidable obstacles that lie in the way. If one follows the

50. Charles Trinkaus, "The Religious Thought of the Italian Humanists and the Reformers," in Trinkaus and Oberman, eds., pp. 339–66 at 344. This article builds upon views expressed in his *Image and Likeness*.
51. Thus William J. Bouwsma in his provocative paper "Renaissance and Reformation: An Essay in their Affinities and Connections," in *Luther*, ed. Oberman, pp. 127–49 at 149. Cf. the critical response by Bengt Hägglund in ibid., pp. 150–57.

latter suggestion about the affinities between Renaissance and Reformation, one must be prepared to ignore, or to bracket as untypical of the Renaissance, the highly optimistic (indeed, semi-Pelagian) view of the freedom and dignity of man expressed by such later humanists as Gianozzo Manetti (d. 1459) and Pico della Mirandola (d. 1494). Furthermore, despite the centrality of his position in the current of reform to which we are addressing ourselves, we must also be prepared to bracket Erasmus, or at least to ignore the degree to which he himself, fervent moralist but no systematic theologian, left himself open to Luther's charge that he was guilty, willy-nilly, of "Pelagianizing." And yet, according to Huizinga—Erasmus's formal protestations to the contrary—there was something to that charge.[52] And if Huizinga was correct on this matter, we may glimpse therein the underlying theological premise that made it logical enough for Erasmus, with all his prudence and traditionalism, to place his emphasis so insistently on the moral dimension of Christianity, on the formative role of scriptural reading and patristic commentary, on the educative responsibility of an enlightened pastoral ministry, rather than on the sacramental mediation of a sacerdotal hierarchy.

However beckoning the vistas disclosed by these more recent approaches, then, prudence dictates that we pass them by—particularly given the exigencies of our concern with currents of religious and ecclesiastical reform. In that context especially, a particular force attaches to the sobriety of Kristeller's continuing "refusal to define humanism in terms of any particular philosophical or theological doctrines" and his "attempt to define it instead through a set of intellectual concerns or scholarly disciplines." A similar force attaches to his insistence that, whatever their individual predilections, the humanists were not concerned "as a group" with philosophical or theological questions at all, many of them, perhaps, being "nothing but grammarians or rhetoricians."[53] The only qualification called

---

52. Huizinga, *Erasmus*, pp. 162–65.
53. I quote here and below from his recent restatement of the position he has long since made familiar: Paul Oskar Kristeller, "The Role of Religion in Renaissance Humanism and Platonism," in Trinkaus and Oberman, eds., pp. 367–70.

for—if qualification it be—pertains to the words "nothing but," which could well be taken, though improperly so, as intended to evoke the pejorative overtones so often conveyed by the expression "mere rhetoric." For that "pursuit of eloquence," which, it has well been argued, "united humanists of all shades," involved something more than a concern with the elegant manipulation of external rhetorical devices. It involved a concern to match "language and form to subject and ideas," with the object not simply of illuminating the intellect in scholastic fashion by logic but also of moving the will by persuasion, so that men might be actively impelled to live that life of virtue for which, or so they believed, it was the primary duty of education to equip them.[54]

In assessing the humanist contribution to religious and ecclesiastical reform, it would seem appropriate to take as one's point of departure Kristeller's testimony that he finds much of the contribution of humanism to "the religion and theology of its time" to lie "in the style of writing, in the scholarly and critical treatment of religious texts such as the Bible and the Church Fathers, in the critical treatment of Church History," perhaps also (though the point "is most difficult to prove") in "the preference for certain problems." Starting from this point, we can feel little temptation to focus too exclusively on the northern Renaissance. For it was in Italy itself that we first find humanism placed at the service not simply of religious ends in general but of reforming goals in particular. One has only to recall the labors of Ambrogio Traversari (d. 1439), general of the Order of Camaldoli and capable Greek scholar, whose humanist fascination with antiquity, wedded to an ecumenical concern to foster reunion with the Greek church, turned his attention to the Greek fathers and prompted him to translate works of St. John Chrysostom, St. Basil, and Gregory of Nazianzen. Or the layman Gianozzo Manetti, who hoped to contribute to the renewal of theology by producing a new translation of the Bible, becoming in the process the first humanist fully to master

54. Gray, pp. 500, 501, 505, 513–14; cf. Bouwsma, in *Luther*, ed. Oberman, p. 129.

Hebrew. Although he never completed his project, he did produce a new Latin translation of the Psalms from the Hebrew and of the New Testament from the Greek—all in all, enough to justify according him a place among the pioneers of biblical scholarship.

Manuscripts of some of Traversari's translations had made their way in mid-century as far as England;[55] and translations of the Greek fathers by other Italian humanists were later printed by northern presses. But it was not the pioneering efforts of Manetti as biblical translator and commentator that were to exert an influence beyond the Alps but rather the *Adnotationes in Novum Testamentum* of Lorenzo Valla, which Erasmus discovered in 1504, a half-century and more after they were written, and published in 1505. By that time, as we have seen, Ximénez and his associates in Spain were applying the philological skills of the humanists in an effort to purify and restore the text of the Vulgate. Only a few years earlier, John Colet, later dean of St. Paul's in London, though no Greek scholar, had attempted in his Oxford lectures on the Pauline epistles, by breaking with the scholastic techniques of the past and applying the humanist method of historical criticism, to recover a lively sense of the historical circumstances under which Paul had written and to evoke from the text the very spirit that had moved the apostle. A similar intention (though wedded to a piety of more mystical flavor) informed the roughly contemporaneous work of Jacques Lefèvre d'Etaples (d. 1536) in biblical editing, translation, and commentary. Indeed, "the highest ambition of the intellectual elite of the time was to be able to read the Scriptures in the original Greek and Hebrew."[56] With this end in view and while still a layman, the Venetian Quirini, later to become a Camaldolese monk, had set himself the task of mastering both languages. When he and Giustiniani came to address their reform program to Leo X, they endorsed the growing sense that a knowledge of the Scriptures was to be regarded not as an attribute of the professional theologian alone but as a necessary part of the formation of the ordinary priest in the dioce-

55. See Weiss, pp. 93–105.
56. Jedin, *History*, 1:157.

san pastoral ministry; they proposed, accordingly, that ordination be refused to anyone who had not yet made his way through the entire Bible.[57]

It was in Valla's *Adnotationes* that Erasmus found an endorsement of the application of humanist philological skills to the correction and improvement of the biblical text bold and thoroughgoing enough to sustain that protracted endeavor of his own that in 1516 resulted in the publication of his *Novum Testamentum*—or *Novum Instrumentum*, as he entitled the second edition of 1519.

The appearance of that work, containing the first complete edition of the Greek New Testament to be published, along with Erasmus's new Latin translation and accompanying notes, caused a great sensatoin. Although other humanists and many churchmen of more traditional intellectual formation greeted it with enthusiasm, theologians of more conservative bent reacted with indignation and dismay to his implied downgrading of the Vulgate. Though Erasmus can hardly be described as unruffled by the attacks of the latter, he was not moved to modify his position. In the preface to the *Novum Instrumentum*, which he addressed to the "pious reader," he had registered a vehement dissent "from those who do not wish the divine Scriptures to be translated into the vulgar tongue and read by the unlearned, as though Christ taught in so obscure a manner as scarcely to be understood by a few theologians, or as though the safeguard of the Christian religion lay only in its being unknown."[58] In 1519 he expanded the preface into a separate essay entitled *Ratio seu methodus compendio perveniendi ad veram theologiam*. Here he reiterated his position, bolstering it with an attack on the sterile dialectic and impious Aristotelianism of the scholastic theologians and an exhortation to return to the "ancient theology" (*prisca illa theologia*) so deeply informed by Scripture and so nobly expressed in the writings of the Greek and Latin fathers from Origen to Augustine.[59]

57. Ibid., pp. 157–58.
58. In *Novum Testamentum Praefationes*, in Holborn, pp. 139–74 at 142.
59. Printed in Holborn, pp. 177–305.

In this work and in his editions of so many of those fathers, he was pursuing a program of educationally and pastorally oriented reform, in which such other humanists as Colet, Sir Thomas More, Ximénez, Lefèvre, and the German Hebraicist Johann Reuchlin (d. 1522) certainly shared, but which in the fullness of its inspiration was so much his own as to merit the title "Erasmian." That program certainly reflected the enduring humanist pursuit of eloquence as a means of moving the will by persuasion to the active pursuit of the good. Further, it embodied the more recent humanist concern to sponsor a moral and spiritual regeneration of the present by an historically informed penetration of the great documents of Christian antiquity through to their clarity and simplicity of spirit. But the program owed something also to the simple, affective piety focusing on the life and humanity of Christ that we associate quintessentially with the *Devotio moderna*, but which in Erasmus invigorated his pastoral and educational concerns, imparting to them no little of their freshness.

Thus, as the Erasmian program of reform found expression in his biblical and patristic scholarship, it found expression also in the tireless preaching of that gospel which he himself (in what appears to have been a conscious refurbishing of a patristic phrase) labeled the *philosophia Christi*.[60] That gospel received its most complete and influential formulation in his *Enchiridion militis Christiani*, a manual of piety or "compendious guide for living," as he himself described it, written, significantly enough, for the layman. The burden of that particular version of the good news is that the embattled Christian has two fundamental weapons at his disposal with which to fight against "the whole troop of vices" that besiege him. Those weapons are "knowledge and prayer"—knowledge, above all, of Christ as he is mediated to us through an assiduous perusal of the Scriptures, one illuminated by the commentaries of the fathers; prayer that finds ex-

---

60. Spitz, *German Humanists*, pp. 26 and 204, points out that it was a phrase used before him by Peter Abelard and by the German humanist Rudolf Agricola, and that Traversari had referred to the Greek Fathers as "philosophers of Christ." Before him, as Trinkaus notes (*Images and Likeness*, 1: 342–43), Petrarch had used the latter expression of St. Augustine.

pression not in the obsessive pursuit of ceremonial or external religious practices but in a lively inward piety and bears its fruit in the full appropriation of Christ's teaching and the faithful imitation of his example. Overall, the impression conveyed is of a practical Christianity, which, although by no means antitheological or antisacramental in its ethos, is certainly markedly ethical and *un*sacramental in its orientation, hinging less on Christ's ultimate redemptive sacrifice than on his lived moral example.

As such, it turned out to have enormous appeal to the educated and committed laymen of the day, many of whom were convinced that the Erasmian program was destined to bring about at last a renewed Christianity and a reformed church. As a result, during the three decades or so following its publication in 1503, the *Enchiridion* came to enjoy a growing and, in the end, a spectacular popularity, running through no fewer than twenty-three editions in the years 1515–21 alone, and being translated during those decades into Castilian, Czech, Dutch, English, French, Italian, and Portuguese.

The Erasmian program of reform eventually proved too fragile a vessel, however, to ride out the ideological tempest that burst upon Europe in the wake of Luther's revolt. By the time of Erasmus's death in 1536 it was already foundering in troubled waters; by the end of the century, though it had touched the lives of Protestant and Catholic reformer alike, it had long since been smashed upon the rocks of Protestant militancy by the waves of a post-Tridentine Catholicism to whose dogmatism it was fundamentally alien. For a few years after 1525, it is true, it had found calm waters and a receptive harbor in the Spain of Charles V, where the appropriate channels had long ago been buoyed by the reforming works of Ximénez, and where it was well sheltered by the official protection of the imperial court. But Erasmus himself always remembered with wistful affection the formative years he had spent on English soil in the company of Colet and More, Fisher and Mountjoy. And there is congruity as well as justice to the claim that it was there, among the churchmen and humanists who shaped the Henrician religious compromise and in the enduring legacy they

in turn bequeathed to the moderation of the Anglican religious settlement, that Erasmianism was at last to find those permanent moorings
that the drift of the times and the direction of the tides had elsewhere
conspired to deny it.[61]

61. Referring here to the claim so powerfully advanced by McConica.

CHAPTER 6 · VARIETIES OF LATE-MEDIEVAL SPIRITUALITY: THE WITNESS OF SIX LIVES

To blys God bryng us al and sum,
Christe, *redemptor omnium*.

—LATE-MEDIEVAL ANONYMOUS

The choice of the lives to be sketched here is not a particularly artful one. No compelling claims can be made for their representative quality. Each is drawn from a separate region in Europe, and deliberately so, but I do not mean thereby to insinuate that sanctity in the later Middle Ages was a peculiarly Hispanic virtue, reform a singularly French proclivity, or "heresy" a uniquely Bohemian vice. In view of the topic, it is hardly surprising that five of the six subjects are clerics; nevertheless, that all are men, or that the solitary layman is cast in the role of "sinner," is not to be made the premise for any uninhibited deductions. More revealing, perhaps, is the fact that (at least for most of their lives) four of the five clerics were seculars rather than regulars—but less because it reflects any conscious choice on my part than because it does not. Given the nature of the sources and the persistent reticence of medieval writers when, to us at least, genuine self-disclosure would seem called for, the business of putting truly believable flesh on ungrateful medieval bones is never easy; often, indeed, it is altogether impossible. If I make the attempt, I do so simply out of a desire to illustrate the embodiment in concrete particularity of movements, phenomena, and developments already described in more abstract and general terms, and to capture the sometimes surprising interrelations and disjunctions among them. And if I group together in one place the sketches resulting from that attempt, it is precisely because those interrelations and disjunctions so often conspire to render the lives of my chosen subjects unassimilable, without undue coercion, to the confining role of exemplificatory vignette.

Vincent Ferrer (ca. 1350–1419): Saint

> Then I saw another angel flying in midheaven, with an eternal gospel to proclaim to those who dwell on earth, to every nation and tribe and tongue and people; and he said with a loud voice, "Fear God and give him glory, for the hour of his judgment has come; and worship him who made heaven and earth, the sea and the fountains of water." [Rev. 14:6–7]

This apocalyptic reading sets the whole tone of the Dominican office for the feast of St. Vincent, Confessor, in which it forms the centerpiece. Its very words are echoed in Calixtus III's bull of canonization (1455); its choice reflects the view of Vincent's life at that time prevailing and long after dominant. Born at Valencia in 1350, destined early by pious parents for an ecclesiastical career, professed as a Dominican friar at the age of seventeen, first student and then teacher at several of the order's schools, priest, religious superior, chaplain and counselor to Aragonese king and Avignonese pope, Vincent devoted himself to the great missionary journeys associated with his name only from 1399 to 1419, during the last twenty years of his life. Nonetheless, according to the view already prevailing at the time of his canonization, he was to be taken above all as "the preacher of the end of the world." He was seen as a prophetic figure tirelessly crisscrossing France, Spain, northern Italy, and parts of Switzerland, where he delivered around 6,000 lengthy sermons to some 200,000 people, remorselessly focusing their attention on the imminence of the coming of Antichrist, the terrors of the impending *dies irae*, the awful finalities of the Last Judgment. Small wonder, then, that he was remembered as the "angel of judgment," the angel, as it were, of the Apocalypse, crying out with a loud voice, if not, indeed, that Babylon the Great was fallen, at least that a term had finally been set to her grossness and impurity.

The lack of any complete texts of his sermons, the problem posed by credulous interpolations in the *reportata*, or sermon notes, handed down, and the well-attested general difficulties in the way of coming to terms with his literary legacy have all helped to perpetuate the traditional picture. That picture could scarcely have survived, however, had it not possessed at least some firm grounding in reality. The celebrated letter he wrote to Benedict XIII in 1412 certainly attests powerfully to the depth of his preoccupation with the coming of the reign of Antichrist, the Last Judgment, and the end of time, and to the urgency of his conviction that those awful events were fast approaching.[1] That preoccupation is also shown in his marked concern with the evangelization of the Jews in Spain, for he shared the traditional belief that their conversion would be one of the signs of the imminence of the last days.

It is well attested, moreover, that his movements across Europe were accompanied by great manifestations of excitement and public fervor; to his own shock and dismay, the crowds pressing around him frequently tried to seize fragments of his clothing to keep as relics. The moment of his arrival in a town (when all work, apparently, would grind to a halt) must have been very dramatic indeed, for it released a flood tide of emotion that frequently combined with the waves of his own rhetoric to reduce both preacher and hearers to tears. For St. Vincent did his traveling accompanied not only by a few Dominican confrères but also by a growing multitude of men and women assistants, followers, well-wishers, and hangers-on, including an organized band of flagellants (or *disciplinati*) drawn often from great distances by the compelling force of his message. Upon his entry into the town, having been welcomed and escorted by local clergy, magistrates, and crowds of curious onlookers, the whole group would assemble in some central place, the flagellants would bare their backs, and amid the usual scenes of gaping awe and dusty exaltation would

1. For this letter, see Fages, *Histoire*, 1:322–26.

commence their grim pattern of public self-mortification. Under some circumstances, as at Toulouse in 1416, their punitive extremities of self-abasement attracted considerable adverse attention. After that particular episode, Gerson and d'Ailly sent a worried letter counseling Vincent to be on his guard lest his own reputation be compromised by the excesses of his overenthusiastic followers. We do not have Vincent's full reply to that letter, but, via Gerson (whom it appears to have satisfied), we learn that he apparently assured the two churchmen that his *disciplinati* were indeed under discipline, fully submitted to the directives of the ecclesiastical authorities. And we do know independently that as members of "the Company of Master Vincent," they were in fact subjected to an organized regimen in accordance with the rule of life that he himself had drawn up for them.[2]

The incident is revealing: it suggests that behind the sensational public memories and the hints of notorious extravagances lay a somewhat more sober reality. The more reliable collections of sermon notes taken down by his hearers strongly confirm that impression. These collections—notably one emanating from the Freiburg region of Switzerland in 1404 and another from Valencia in 1413[3]—reveal (at least in the numbers of sermons devoted to those specific themes) a much less obsessive preoccupation with the coming of Antichrist and the terrors of the Last Judgment than the traditional view would suggest. The organization of the sermons reveals the working of a highly ordered and logical mind clearly disciplined in the scholastic mold. Their content, however, reflects a reliance less upon the scholastic theology than upon the views of such great teachers as Gregory the Great, Bernard of Clairvaux, and Bonaventure, and less, in turn, upon the word of any commentator than upon the unmediated word of the Scriptures, with which he shows a well-developed and easy familiarity. And if the inspiration is indeed the word, the

2. See Gerson, *Epistola ad Vincentium Ferrarium contra se flaggelantes*, in Dupin, II, 659–60 (it concludes with d'Ailly's endorsement); idem, *Tractatus contra sectum flagellantium*, in Dupin, 2:660–64 (especially 662 C–D).

3. For the former, see Brettle, pp. 173–95, who describes the whole collection and prints a transcription of the four sermons dealing with eschatological themes. For the latter, see Silvera.

focus is very much upon the Word, the incarnate Son, upon the successive phases of whose earthly life he bases repeated moral exhortations geared to the theme of the "imitation of Christ." He likens Christ's daily "gracious visitation" in the Eucharist to the visitation of a doctor who brings to us no ordinary remedy but rather the "precious medicine of his own body and blood." [4]

The notes of the Freiburg collection are in Latin and therefore lack the flavor and immediacy of the versions of the Valencia collection, which are in Vincent's native Catalan. [5] They are nevertheless especially valuable because of their particular provenance and the reassuring credentials of their author: for they were preserved at the Franciscan monastery of Freiburg—in the region, therefore, where the original sermons were delivered—and they were the work of no simple or credulous auditor but of Friedrich von Amberg, a master of theology who at the time of Vincent's missionary visit in March 1404 to the then canton of Freiburg, was the superior of the Franciscan province.

Friedrich begins his transcription with the assurance: "I have reported from his own mouth, as best I could, all the sermons which he preached on that occasion, and . . . have written them down with my own hand." [6] The sermons in question number sixteen in all, delivered in various towns around the canton, sometimes to congregations of religious or of diocesan clergy but most usually to large popular gatherings, normally at the rate of one a day, but rising on March 21 to two and on the day preceding to three. In subject matter they fall into two groups. The first and larger group of eleven are markedly Christocentric, focusing on the fundamental building blocks for a life of Christian perfection; they bear such titles as "Concerning the Eight Ways of Praying," "Christ the Healer," "Concerning the Virtues of Christ in His Passion," "Concerning the Remission of Sins," and "Concerning the Ladder of Salvation." The remaining, smaller group

4. *Sermo de extremo judicio:* [*iv*] *super bonos et malos*; in Brettle, p. 190.
5. Because of this, Gorce criticizes Brettle's reliance upon them and upon other Latin works of St. Vincent's (p. 79).
6. Brettle, p. 175.

of four (the fifth is but a brief recapitulation) reflects the eschatological preoccupations that have often been incorrectly taken to characterize all of his preaching.

Here, as elsewhere, Vincent handles the topic of the Last Judgment in four distinct parts, the focus of which is accurately conveyed by the respective titles of the sermons: (1) "Antichrist," (2) "The End of the World," (3) "The Resurrection of the Body," (4) "[The Fate] of the Good and the Wicked." Here, as elsewhere too, we can see in their organization the workings of a highly ordered and logical mind; the first sermon sets up the line of march subsequently to be followed throughout the series and sets forth in somewhat doctrinaire fashion the points that will be elaborated in greater detail and with varying nuances in the other three. The content of the Antichrist sermons is by no means sensational; in skeleton form they seem mild indeed when compared with what we hear of the terrible *cito et velociter* of Savonarola later on. The thrust of the message conveyed is highly traditional and explicitly biblical. Whereas Vincent himself is clearly moved by the upheavals and tribulations of his own day to believe that the end is almost certainly nigh, he is not unaware that others before him have felt similarly and been proven mistaken. Accordingly, he is careful to avoid speaking of any fixed period of time within which Antichrist will make his dreaded appearance, and he explicitly reminds his hearers that to the disciples who had asked the risen Christ when his kingdom would come Christ had replied: "It is not for you to know times or seasons which the Father has fixed by his own authority" (Acts 1:7).[7] His main concern is less with the precise timing of Antichrist's coming than with the use we make of the period remaining before that coming. For there is a remedy against the tribulation of Antichrist, and it is none other than the remedy that Christ himself urged against all future tribulations: namely, that of being vigilant at all times, praying morning and night, and fleeing the occasions of sin. One thing is truly certain: "The cross of Christ is the gate of salvation and

---

7. *Sermo de extremo judicio:* [*i*] *de Antichristo*; in Brettle, p. 181. He stresses the same point in his letter to Benedict XIII; see Fages, *Histoire*, 1:324.

the key to the grace of God, and thus all entering through it will be safe and secure, and to that security he leads us." [8]

In the vision that preceded the beginning of his great preaching mission in 1399 and his appointment by Benedict XIII as *legatus a latere Christi*, Vincent believed he had received a commission to "go through the world preaching Christ," and that, it seems clear, is exactly what he set out to do: seeking to achieve by his preaching, he said, "the conversion and correction of men before the coming of Antichrist." [9] He mounted an appeal for moral and spiritual regeneration that does not appear to have been particularly unconventional except, indeed, in the compelling force imparted by his bearing, his eloquence, the degree of his preoccupation with the last things, and the very shock of his presence. About his whole missionary enterprise there was something, it may be, of the appurtenances familiar to us from the comparatively sophisticated revivalist campaigns of the mid-twentieth century—including a certain amount of advance work with the local authorities, temporal as well as ecclesiastical, and even, it seems, some follow-up reporting to the responsible ordinaries about the impact of his mission in the localities. [10] Similarly, in his evangelical journeyings he was accompanied by a team of priest-catechists who sought to exploit the momentum generated by his great public sermons in order to impress upon children and adults alike, and even upon the more ignorant among the local priests, the rudiments of the faith they professed.

There was something of the successful evangelist, too, in his relationships with the powerful men of his day. Even before his great missionary journeys made him a figure of international renown, Vincent had come to play a role of some prominence in public affairs, both temporal and ecclesiastical. From the first he had been a staunch

8. Ibid.
9. Gorce, p. 60.
10. Thus we have a letter dated 14 March 1411, from a municipal official of the town of Orihuela, where St. Vincent had preached, describing to the local ordinary the overflowing churches, the increase in the numbers of communicants and of confessions, the decline of sorcery and blasphemy, the reconciliation of enemies, and so on; see Gorce, pp. 96–98.

papalist and had embraced with no apparent reserve the legitimacy of Clement VII's title to the papacy. In support of that claim he had in 1380 addressed his influential *Tractatus de schismate* to Pedro IV of Aragon (1336–87), and, in subsequent years, along with Cardinal Pedro de Luna, the future Benedict XIII, he had striven hard to persuade the rulers and people of the Spanish peninsula to give their allegiance to the Avignonese pontiff. During part of that time he was chaplain to the Aragonese king, and his political prominence reached its peak in 1412, when, as one of the judges struggling to settle the disputed succession to the Kingdom of Aragon, he helped put Ferdinand of Castile on the throne.

By the time of Ferdinand's succession, of course, he had long been embarked on his great preaching mission, but not before spending several years at the papal court in Avignon as counselor to Benedict XIII and from 1395 to 1398 as his personal confessor, too. There, in company with his brother Boniface, the general of the Carthusians, Vincent came into contact with such rising ecclesiastical luminaries as Nicholas of Clémanges and Pierre d'Ailly and became acquainted with the intense diplomatic activity that swirled around the curia and in which those men were deeply involved. But despite this exposure to the harsh and complex realities of ecclesiastico-political life, something touchingly unworldly clung to his deportment—his obvious antipathy not only to the pressures the French king was bringing to bear on Benedict but also to the pope's own understandable willingness under military attack to employ armed force to defend the papal palace; the high hopes he placed in Benedict's willingness, in the interest of church unity, to lay down his high office; the keen and bitter disappointment he obviously felt when those hopes were repeatedly dashed; the frayed and anguished loyalty that kept him nevertheless in Benedict's camp even after John XXIII's deposition and Gregory XII's abdication, right down to the bitter moment in 1416 when finally he broke with him at Perpignan. Thus in 1408, even when a man of such unimpeachably moderate credentials as d'Ailly's had reluctantly abandoned any lingering hopes that the goodwill of the rival pontiffs would bring an end to the schism and approached him in the course of his efforts to marshal support for the Council of Pisa, Vincent held aloof and did not respond. Nor did he intervene later when his brother Boniface launched a singularly intemperate and highly personal attack on d'Ailly and the role he had played in relation to Pisa.

But Boniface's Avignonese loyalties appear to have been a good deal less unqualified than Vincent's, and the physical and spiritual crisis in the latter's life that preceded his decision to embark upon his preaching mission was connected with the unbearable tensions he was beginning to feel between his loyalty to the papacy as the instrument and symbol of the church's unity and his deepening anguish at what was emerging as a papally protracted schism—between his conviction that Benedict XIII was indeed the legitimate pope and his dawning realization that that pope was nevertheless emerging as the single greatest obstacle to the ending of the schism. His crisis, however, was resolved in a way true to his earliest and most fundamental commitments. It was no accident, or so it may be suggested, that the mission allotted to him in his vision should have been one of preaching and teaching or that he believed himself charged with that mission by St. Dominic and St. Francis. If it is sometimes difficult to see Vincent's evangelical preaching and his involvement in the public arena of dynastic and ecclesiastical diplomacy as very much of a piece, the same cannot be said of that preaching and his earliest vocation. He was in many ways the quintessential friar, and the arduous missionary efforts that filled the last twenty years of his life can best be understood in the context both of his own earlier formation within the Dominican order and of the goals (both educational and missionary) for which the order itself had striven ever since the days of its founder.

It was in 1367 in the Dominican house in his native town of Valencia that Vincent began his monastic career. That career took him for nine years through a cycle of studies embracing logic, natural philosophy, biblical studies, and theology, which he pursued at Lérida, Barcelona, and the University of Toulouse as well as at Valencia. He was clearly a young man of no ordinary intellectual gifts, and during those years he not only put in a period as professor of logic at Lérida but also wrote the two treatises *De suppositionibus dialecticis* and *De natura universalis*. After his ordination as a priest in 1379, he was for a few years prior of the Dominican house in Valencia before being called upon to teach theology at the cathedral in that town, where he gave courses of lectures aimed particularly at improving the level of doctrinal and theological formation among the secular clergy of the diocese. It may well be that it was during this phase of his life that he wrote for a group of brethren in the religious life his *Tractatus de vita spirituali*— no work of mystical theology, as the title might be taken to suggest, but a very concrete work of spiritual counsel, possessing much of the clear, balanced, logical, and practical character that distinguished his later missionary sermons. In it he devoted a whole chapter to the topic of preaching, stressing "that the words should appear to proceed not from a proud or angry spirit, but from the very heart of charity and paternal compassion," and that the preacher should be like the mother who nurtures her children and "rejoices at their progress and at the glory of paradise that she hopes for them."[11]

Both in tone and in aspiration, the ties that bind those sentiments and the whole direction of his early career with the great mission of his final years are clear and firm. During his missionary years, despite his own preoccupation with the terrors of the Last Days, he appears to have been well aware that the road to true and lasting repentance was one along which men had to be beckoned by encouragement and hope rather than driven by fear. The nature of that mission, moreover, can best be understood if it is seen in the context of the purpose of the early Dominicans to bring the Gospel in all its rigor and beauty to the comparatively unchurched peoples in the rural areas of southern Europe, to bring the pure nourishment of the Word to the hungry sheep, who, looking up and not being fed were succumbing to heresy. Vincent was surely mindful of that heritage when, often taking the key scriptural texts for his sermons from the Dominican office of the day, he sought to evangelize the heavily Waldensian regions of the Dauphiné and Piedmont.

11. *Tract. de vita spirit.*, chap. XIII; ed. Fages, 1:34.

Both as teacher and preacher, he sought in true Dominican fashion to deliver souls from the darkness of ignorance and the beguiling twilight of sin. It is hard to know what to make of the gift of tongues that men ascribed to him or of his alleged successes as a faith healer. But the words that no less a witness than the king of Aragon described him as being accustomed to use when he placed his hands on the sick may serve as example of a prayer expressive also of his broader and most heartfelt aspirations when he surveyed a poorly catechized, war-ridden, divided, and scandalized Christendom groaning in travail: "May Jesus, son of Mary, who hast led thee into the Catholic faith, preserve thee in that faith, and restoring thee deliver thee from this infirmity."[12]

Francesco di Marco Datini (ca. 1335–1410): Sinner

That we can speak at all about the spiritual life of the merchant Francesco di Marco Datini reflects the characteristic force with which Francesco insisted that his branch managers preserve all their business documents and letters, the conscientiousness with which he did likewise, the foresight that led him to provide in his will for the collecting of all these materials in the house he was bequeathing to his native city, and the fortunate historical accident that kept them preserved intact in that same house for more than four and a half centuries, until in 1870 they were rediscovered bundled together "in sacks in a dusty recess under the stairs."[13]

The house still stands in Prato, the small city in the Tuscan plain not far from Florence where Francesco was born around 1335, one of

---

12. Cited by Gorce, pp. 178–79.
13. Origo, p. vi. These papers, wholly extraordinary in their completeness, include—besides account books, ledgers, deeds of partnership, and so on—no fewer than 150,000 letters, among them the private correspondence between Francesco and his wife and between him and his closest friend, the notary Ser Lapo Mazzei. Guasti published the latter series in his *Ser Lapo Mazzei*; Origo's book, however, is the first to exploit in any systematic fashion the full range of the private correspondence. Unless otherwise indicated, all passages quoted, along with the English translations, are taken from her *Merchant of Prato*, to the pages of which the numbers in parentheses refer.

four children sired by Marco di Datino, taverner, minor landowner, and small businessman. Orphaned by the Black Death and briefly in the care of a foster mother, he made his way via Florence to Avignon and returned to Prato only after he had amassed considerable capital. He came back ready to make a strong entry into the clothmaking trade, upon which the economy of the city depended. There he established the central office of his far-flung and variegated mercantile enterprises and built the great fortune whose vast bulk (along with his house, possessions, and farms) he was to bequeath as a foundation to serve the needs of the city's poor.[14]

Two mementos signal the gratitude felt toward him by his fellow citizens and their wish to celebrate his generosity. Over the door of his house they carved the inscription:

> The Foundation of Francesco di Marco
> Merchant of Christ's Poor
> of which the commune of Prato
> is the dispenser
> Left in the year 1410.[15]

Forty years after his death they commissioned Fra Filippo Lippi to paint the panel that protrays Francesco very much in the manner of "the merchant of Christ's poor," kneeling in rapt adoration at the Virgin's feet, along with the four *buonomini* (elders) appointed by the commune of Prato to administer the charitable foundation he had established.

Generosity and piety are the qualities memorialized, and the careful stipulations he made in his will enhance that impression. The generosity, of course, seems obvious enough, and it is underlined by the ancillary list of specific bequests to individual servants and dependents. Nor is the piety qualified by the explicit insistence that the foundation was in no way to be "under the church or of officials or prelates or any other member of the clergy," or by the eloquently re-

---

14. "For the love of God, so as to give back to His Poor what has been received from Him, as His gracious gift" (368). The will itself, along with its codicils, is printed in Guasti, ed., II, 273–310. The passage cited appears at 290.
15. "Ceppo [lit.: log] di Francesco di Marcho / Mercantante dei Poveri di Xto / del quale il Chomune di Prato / è dispensatore / lasciato nell' anno MCCCCX" (241).

vealing prohibition of the establishment within the house of any "altar or oratory or chapel . . . by means of which the *Casa del Ceppo* might be considered a place belonging to the clergy and evilly disposed men might come in and occupy it, *saying it was a benefice*" (367–68; italics mine).[16] Even the precious and unusually intimate glimpse that the Datini papers provide of the private individual tells us some things about the day-to-day Francesco that are congruent enough with the characteristics publicly memorialized. He is revealed as a son who in the days of his prosperity cherished a deep and abiding affection for his foster mother: "You may do with me and with my possessions," he told her, "as with your own" (24). He is shown reacting with anxious solicitude to the misery of his employees when they were ill, and to the bereavement of their next of kin when they died. He appears as a believer of conventional piety, but one no less assiduous in his sermon-going than he was in his institutional almsgiving, and even willing as an old man to go on pilgrimage with one of the penitential companies known as the *Bianchi*, "all barefoot, and scourging ourselves with a rod and accusing ourselves to Our Lord Jesus Christ of our sins" (362). He is revealed also as a companion capable of retaining the warm and disinterested friendship even of so gentle and upright a spirit as the notary Ser Lapo Mazzei. And he is shown as an attentive host in his later years, welcoming with ingenuous pride to his fine house (not, admittedly, without a certain Toad of Toad Hall quality) such luminaries of state and church as Louis II of Anjou, who visited more than once, and Pierre d'Ailly, who came in 1409 to attend the christening of Francesco's grandchild.

These gleanings reveal little enough on which to base any compelling candidacy for the role of sinner; but despite their beguiling moments, the overwhelming impression of Francesco's character conveyed by the Datini papers is quite at variance with this picture and considerably darker.

The reason for this discrepancy must doubtless be sought in a particular intersection of circumstance and temperament, which, while

16. The passages cited appear in Guasti, ed., 2:289–90 and 300.

it goes a long way toward explaining the dimensions of his success as a merchant, goes some of the way, also, toward explaining the extent of his failure as a man. Despite his later renown as the greatest merchant produced by Prato, one who had returned to his native city in 1383 after having made good at Avignon during the preceding thirty-three years, he had experienced tragedy and stuggle in his early years. Having lost his family (with the exception of one brother) in the Great Plague of 1348, and having spent but a few months as an apprentice in Florence, he had gone, at the age of fifteen, to seek his fortune in the bustling, corrupt, overcrowded, and costly city of Avignon. As none of his private letters before 1371 were preserved, we know little of his early years at Avignon beyond the fact that he dealt chiefly at first in armor. We know that he did not scruple to sell that armor both to the soldiers of fortune who ravaged the south of France during the last two decades before the onset of the great schism and to the communes struggling to defend themselves against the depredations of those adventurers. We can only guess that the qualities that enabled him to claw his way to mercantile prominence must have been those that continued to characterize him in later years—shrewdness, opportunism, greed, remorseless drive, and truly formidable industry.

During those later years, his wife, doctors, business associates, and spiritual advisers all urged him repeatedly to relax a little his grip on affairs, to settle back now and enjoy the fruits he had harvested by dint of so much labor and worry, to value his riches, as Ser Lapo said, "at their true worth, that is, own them as if they were not [his]," or, again, to "put some order in [his] life" (237). This, however, he clearly could not do. Like many another businessman who has made good on his own, he never mastered the art of delegating responsibility. Even in his old age, at the expense of sleep and health, he drove himself to write all the correspondence of his firm. "I am not feeling very well today," he confessed in one of his letters when he was over sixty, "on account of all the writing I have done in these two days, without sleeping either by night or by day, and these two days eating but one loaf" (viii). One gets the impression of a life of harried labor and complusive worry, worry extended without any measure to the petty as well as the portentous. Not that it was a life untouched by pleasure: he liked his wines, he liked his food, he liked his women. Of his description of the pilgrimage he went on, Iris Origo justly comments that "it is difficult not to receive the impression of a nine-day picnic only occasionally punctuated by sermons and prayers" (361).[17] While at Avignon he fathered at least one bastard and after his marriage at least two more, one by a household servant, the other by his slave girl Lucia. In humiliating and destructive contrast, however, his marriage was childless, his relations with his wife sadly acrimonious (as turbulent, indeed, as those with many of his employees), and even in his final years he never quite succeeded in piloting his day-to-day life into anything remotely resembling tranquil waters.

Wine and women, then, but certainly not song. Understandably enough, Francesco was not content with it all. During his later years a note of somewhat mawkish melancholy begins to invade his letters. "Fate," he wrote to his wife in 1395, "has so willed it that, from the day of my birth, I have never known a whole happy day. . . . Yet if my end be a good one, I care little for the rest. But I greatly fear it will not be, and I think of little else" (185). A gloomy exaggeration, no doubt, but his words properly suggest that one must seek his credentials as an appropriately qualified sinner less in any noteworthy achievement of vice than in the gloomy interstices of his everyday miseries.

Anger and greed, the vices against which the preachers of his day

17. The following passage of that description (362) is revealing: "And when the Mass was said, we all scattered in the roads or the fields, to eat bread and cheese and fruit, and such-like things. For during the nine days that the pilgrimage lasted, none of us might eat any meat, nor take off his white clothes, nor lie in a bed. And that we might have what was needful, I took with us two of my horses and the mule; and on these we placed two small saddle-chests, containing boxes of all kinds of comfits, and a great many small torches and candles, and cheeses of all kinds, and fresh bread and biscuits, and round cakes, sweet and unsweetened, and other things besides that appertain to a man's life; so that the two horses were fully laden with our victuals; and beside these, I took a great sack of warm raiment, to have at hand by day and night." It should be noted that the date of Francesco's pilgrimage was 1399; it was the return of the Black Death that had stimulated once more the activity of the penitential movement in which he was participating.

repeatedly railed, these he had in richly overabundant measure, and it would be easy to make much especially of his greed—a professional failing that, by the end of his life, had become almost instinctive with him. From the safety of Bologna, to which he and his family had fled in 1400 to avoid the wave of plague inundating Florence and Prato, he did not hesitate to dun his debtors still resident in those ravaged cities, drawing from Ser Lapo, who had stayed behind and seen two of his children die, the anguished plea to desist, to grasp the fact that "there is a time to chastise, and one to forgive" (373). Nevertheless, it was neither greed nor questionable business practices, nor anger, nor lust, that Ser Lapo focused on when he sought to identify for an anxious Francesco the very roots of his failings; it was rather his coldness of heart and the willfulness of temperament that led him so persistently to assume that his very destiny was his to shape in accordance with the immediacy of his own desires.

That the diagnosis was a shrewd one, even Francesco appears to have admitted. But, the overwhelmingly conventional and propitiatory pieties of his last years notwithstanding, he does not really seem to have been able to do much about it. The coldness is especially marked in his relations with his wife. It is well exemplified in the meanness of spirit that led him to rebuke her lest she waste in reading the time that should be devoted to her household duties—despite the fact that she had just succeeded, at the age of thirty, in painfully mastering the skills of reading and writing in order to be able to conduct her own correspondence with a distressingly and almost continuously absent husband. The willfulness is similarly evident in his unreadiness to let go a little, to find more space in an unnecessarily harried life of getting and spending for the simplicities of human affection and the solace of religious devotion, in the impatient desire to control his eternal destiny with the same degree of imperious mastery as he had exercised over his partners, his employees, and his far-flung commercial enterprises. It is evident, too, in his dying, in which resignation, it appears, was no more manifest than it had been in any of his living. Into "that good night" he had no intention whatsoever of going gently, and we have it on Ser Lapo's authority that despite his advanced years, "it seemed to him very strange that he should have to die, and that his prayers should be of no avail" (384).

If we were to select a motto that would characterize the bold public man, the great merchant of Prato, we could hardly do better than to choose the one that appears as superscript on so many of his great ledgers: "In the name of God and of profit." But the wistful interior discomfort of Francesco di Marco Datini, the uncertain private man who importuned his wife and friends with his anxieties no less than he burdened them with his demands, is better caught by the words he wrote in 1399, when the plague that had orphaned him in 1348 and almost killed him in 1374 was now advancing once again on Tuscany: "May God give me grace, if it be His pleasure, to lead a better life than in the past, for it is a dog's life—and it is all through my own fault" (161).

Jan van Ruysbroeck (1293–1381): Mystic

From the workaday writings spawned in the course of a lifetime's remorseless pursuit of externalities, it is clearly possible to get a lively sense of what Francesco di Marco Datini must have been like to know. His self-revelation, though unwitting, is surprisingly complete. From Jan van Ruysbroeck's eleven authenticated writings, most of them concerned with the interior life of the spirit and revealing enviably developed powers of introspection and self-analysis, however, it is extremely difficult to extract any firm profile of his personality. About himself and what he was he tells us in all that writing next to nothing. One gets the sense of a warm and compelling personality, and this his early biographers confirm. But that is all.

About the external events of his life we are not much better informed, but what we know, at least, is clear. Born in 1293 in the village of Ruysbroeck near Brussels, he was sent at the age of eleven to live in that city with his uncle John Hinckaert, priest and canon of the collegiate church of St. Gudule and a man of more than formal piety.

Educated in Brussels, Ruysbroeck was ordained a priest in 1317 and spent the next twenty-six years serving as vicar of St. Gudule's and pursuing a life of austerity (and probably also of study) in the company of his uncle and another canon of saintly reputation, Francis van Coudenberg. Seeking a more contemplative life of greater solitude, the three men withdrew in 1343, when Ruysbroeck was already fifty, to a hermitage at nearby Groenendael. Joined there by a group of disciples, they organized themselves in 1349 into a community of canons regular, adopting the Augustinian rule. Of that monastery Francis van Coudenberg became the first provost and Ruysbroeck the first prior. There he spent the rest of his long and apparently uneventful life completing some of the writings he had begun as a diocesan priest and contriving to keep in contact with both the reformers and mystics of his day. There he was visited certainly by Geert Groote, perhaps also by Tauler. There he died in 1381 in his eighty-eighth year.

In its externalities, then, a life so provincial and uneventful as to fade into insignificance when placed beside that of either St. Vincent Ferrer or Francesco di Marco Datini, or, indeed of any other of our subjects. In its interior dynamics, however, it was a richly textured life of passion and great drama. And about that interior life, despite the deliberately self-effacing nature of his writings, we can assume ourselves to be more than usually well informed. Not that we can altogether divorce those writings, or indeed his understanding of the interior life, from the external happenings of his region—at least, not from those happenings that pertained to the spiritual life of his day. Much of his writing dates to the years he spent as a diocesan priest and reflects an effort to respond to the thirst for spiritual guidance that was manifesting itself among the comparatively highly urbanized and spiritually demanding populace of the Netherlands. Thus, one of those works, *Van den Kerstenen Ghelove* (*On the Christian Faith*) is a commentary on the creed designed for use by priests. Another, *Van den XII Beghinen* (*The Twelve Beguines*), consists of a series of pious meditations. The latter work, moreover, like such earlier works of his as *Het Rijcke der Ghlieven* (*The Kingdom of Lovers*), *De Gheestelike Bru-*

locht (The Spiritual Espousals),[18] and *Van den Blinckenden Steen (The Sparkling Stone*—though sometimes known as *The Perfection of the Sons of God*), bears the mark of his intense hostility to the "heretical" or "false mysticism" of his day, against which he had preached as a diocesan priest.

The main focus of his attack appears to have been the teachings of Bloemardinne of Brussels, who has been identified as Heylwig of Bloemart, a very influential woman with aristocratic connections who had been active among the Beguines of Brussels. None of her writings has survived, but if the mystical deviations described so explicitly and attacked to frontally in the second book of *The Spiritual Espousals* are indeed based on those writings, it seems proper to see in them an authentic expression of the heresy of the Free Spirit.[19] Noting that "whenever man is empty and undistracted in his senses by images, and free and unoccupied in his highest powers, he attains rest by purely natural means" and "without the grace of God," Ruysbroeck goes on to say that some men fall into the tragic error of mistaking that emptiness for union with God:

> Through the natural rest which they feel and have in themselves in emptiness, they maintain that they are free, and united with God without mean, and that they are advanced beyond all the exercises of Holy Church, and beyond the commandments of God, and beyond the law and beyond the virtuous works which one can in any way practise. . . . And therefore they remain in mere passivity without the performance of any work directed up towards God or down towards man.[20]

Such men, however, "wish to be free, and obedient to no-one, not to pope, nor bishop nor parish priest. Though they may feign it to the

18. Better known, perhaps, as *The Adornment of the Spiritual Marriage*, from the title given to the Latin translation made by Ruysbroeck's disciple Willem Jordaens—*De Ornatu Spiritualium Nuptiarum* (Paris, 1512).
19. This is the view of Lerner, *Heresy*, pp. 190–95. For the relevant passages, see *De Gheestelike Brulocht*, II, 40–43; in Poukens and Reypens, eds., 1:103–249 at 228–34; English trans. in Colledge, *The Spiritual Espousals*, pp. 166–75. Guarnieri, pp. 443–44, notes that the passages in question have the appearance of being a condensation of Marguerite Porete's *Mirror of Simple Souls*.
20. Colledge, pp. 166–67, 170–71.

outside world, in their hearts," he insists, "they are submissive to no-one, neither in will nor in deed, for they believe that they are empty of all matters which Holy Church observes." Hence it is Ruysbroeck's harsh conclusion that though "they believe themselves to be the holiest," they are in fact "the evillest and most harmful men that live."[21]

Similar protestations are broadcast throughout his works, both early and late. They urge the necessity of obeying the church, of receiving her sacraments, of practicing her virtues, of remembering always that we cannot become one with God simply by nature and without his grace, of realizing, too, that in so becoming one with God we must nevertheless remain eternally other than him. Thus in *The Spiritual Espousals*, one of his earlier works, he tells us that the properly humble man will be "humble and reverent before Holy Church and the sacraments," and in the Eucharist will benefit from "the heavenly secret working of Christ" and will experience "the second coming of Christ our Bridegroom."[22] Again, in *The Twelve Beguines*, a later work, he affirms that "we cannot issue out of ourselves into God and lose our created nature; and so we must remain everlastingly different from God and remain created creatures. For no creature can become God nor can God become any creature."[23] In *The Little Book of the Enlightenment* (*Dat Boecsken der Verclaringhe*), one of his last works, he warns once more against those ignorant and prideful men who believe "that out of their own natures they have found within themselves the indwelling of God and who wish to become one with God without His grace and without the exercise of virtue, and in disobedience to God and to Holy Church. And they wish by nature to be the sons of God, as do all those of whom I have spoken who live in error."[24]

21. Ibid., pp. 170–72.
22. *Espousals*, 2:19 and 14; trans. Colledge, pp. 64, 59.
23. *Vanden XII Beghuinen*, in Poukens and Reypens, eds., 4:31: "Want wij en moghen uut ons selven in Gode niet comen ende onse ghescapenhiet verliesen; ende alsoe moeten wij eewelijc een ander van Gode bliven ende ghescapene creatueren. Want gheene creatuere en mach God werden, noch God creatuere" (trans. from Colledge, p. 28).
24. Poukens and Reypens, eds., 3:275–98 at 298; trans. from Colledge, p. 28.

We find indications that he was well aware of the danger of being misunderstood: the very frequency of his protestations; that he had not wanted his difficult early work *The Kingdom of Lovers* to be circulated; his later decision to write *The Little Book of Enlightenment* in order to clarify "with short words" what he had taught in the early works written for those advanced in contemplation.[25] He was misunderstood all the same, and by no less a figure than Jean Gerson. On the basis of the description of contemplative union with the divine in the third book of *The Spiritual Espousals*, Gerson attributed to Ruysbroeck errors similar to those Ruysbroeck himself had attacked earlier in the same work and which we have described as pertaining to the heresy of the Free Spirit.[26] In so doing, Gerson may have been misled by the free and often unfaithful Latin translation by William Jordaens, which he appears to have used.[27] Despite such contingencies, however, it must be admitted that the unguarded nature of some of Ruysbroeck's formulations in that work and the very density of his thought in general conspire to render the possibility of misunderstanding unusually high. Though he was a staunch admirer of Ruysbroeck, Geert Groote, it will be recalled, was nervous about that potential for misunderstanding. Only a close reading of the writings can fully convey both the grounds for that nervousness and the degree to which Ruysbroeck himself strove, especially in his later works, to remove them. But some sense of what is involved and some feeling for the shape of his thinking as it unfolds in two important works can be conveyed by taking a brief glance at *The Spiritual Espousals* and *The Sparkling Stone*—the first an early and comparatively lengthy work, probably his masterpiece, the second a short work written later on his life, both following the same pattern and both happily available in English translations made directly from the original Flemish.[28]

25. Poukens and Reypens, eds., 3:276; cf. Colledge, pp. 13–14.
26. The late André Combes made this whole issue the subject of a massive investigation, resulting in his *Essai sur la critique de Ruysbroeck par Gerson*.
27. For the infelicities of that translation, see Colledge, pp. 12–13.
28. The parenthetical page references to *The Spiritual Espousals* are to Colledge's translation. Those to *The Sparkling Stone* are to the translation printed in Petry, pp. 292–320, which itself is from *John of Ruysbroeck: The Adornment of the Spiritual Marriage*; *The Sparkling Stone*; *The Book of Supreme Truth*, ed. C. A. Wynschenk and Evelyn

Here, as elsewhere in Ruysbroeck's writings, the reader confronts two difficulties related to the charge of quietism or pantheism (or autotheism) sometimes levied against him. In the first place, while insisting on the need for the Christian to cultivate the church's sacraments and to grow in the life of virtue and good deeds, he can also describe the contemplative experience of union with God as pertaining to a higher place of spiritual development than the active life of virtue and can say that for a man to attain to that plane he must be "empty of all outward works, just as though he performed nothing. For if within he is preoccupied with any work of virtue, so he is distracted by images" (*Espousals*, III, 2, p. 181; compare 4, p. 183). In the second place, while insisting that even in the contemplative experience "we cannot wholly become God and lose our created being" (*Sparkling Stone*, 9, p. 309), he can also boldly describe that experience as "a uniting in the essential unity of God" (*Espousals*, III, Prol., p. 179) and as being "embraced in the Holy Trinity," "an eternal remaining in the superessential unity in rest and delectation" (*Espousals*, III, 6, p. 185).

If we keep in mind, however, Ruysbroeck's characteristic exemplarism, though we cannot dismiss the difficulties raised by such formulations, we can at least open some sort of route around them. Thus, if man cannot wholly become God, we must not lose sight of the fact that God has made man's nature "in the image and likeness of Himself" (*Espousals*, Prol., p. 43), that "he has created every man's soul as a living mirror (*levenden spieghel*), upon which he has imprinted the image of his nature." That is to say—for Ruysbroeck can hardly be classified as either a theocentric or a Christocentric mystic—we mirror in ourselves not only God as unity but also God as trinity.[29] And we can be said to do so in two intersecting ways: the one, as it were, dynamic and concerning the movement of our spiritual lives,

Underhill (London, 1951), pp. 181–221. The two works go well together: chaps. 1–9 of *The Sparkling Stone* convey in brief compass the matter of the first two books of *The Spiritual Espousals*, and chaps. 10–14 the matter of its third book. The Flemish text of *The Sparkling Stone* may be found in Poukens and Reypens, eds., 3:3–41.

29. *Een Spieghel der Eeuwigher Salichkeit*, in Poukens and Reypens, eds., 3:129–219 at 202–203.

the other static and concerning the nature of our humanity. We must take them up separately, though by doing so we do some damage to the movement of Ruysbroeck's thought.

Although "in the exalted nature of the Divinity" we can observe "that it is all simplicity and unity," nevertheless "this exalted unity . . . is a living fertile unity. For out of this same unity the Everlasting Word is evermore born of the Father," and from the "mutual contemplation of the Father and the Son in Their eternal illumination, there flows an eternal satisfaction, an unfathomable love, and that is the Holy Spirit" (*Espousals*, II, xvi, xviii, pp. 123, 136). In this "ebbing and flowing" sea which is God (*Espousals*, II, 17, p. 127), this Trinitarian life of flux and reflux, of ecstatic movement from unity to multiplicity, from identity to difference and back again, those chosen to partake of the mystical union are destined somehow to participate. For "the Holy Trinity made us in this everlasting image and in this likness. And therefore God would have us go forth from ourselves in this Divine light, and supernaturally attain to this image, which is our own life, and possess it with Him, operatively and in delectation, in everlasting blessedness" (*Espousals*, III, 7–8, pp. 186–87).

A dark teaching, no doubt. To understand it, Ruysbroeck said, one "must have died to himself and live in God" (*Espousals*, III, Prol., p. 180). But we can perhaps get a fingerhold on what is involved if we take into account the other and more static way in which Ruysbroeck believes us to mirror the trinity and unity of God. All men, he tells us, consist of body, of "spirit," and of the "soul" that joins them. And all men, whether good or bad, possess a threefold unity: in the physical powers of the body, in the "superior powers" of "the spirit or of the mind," and in the soul that "makes the body living and preserves it living." In the lowest of these three unities "man is sensual and animal; in the middle union, man is rational and spiritual; in the highest, man is preserved in his essence." In good men, moreover, these three unities are "supernaturally adorned": the lowest, or physical, through the imitation of Christ in external works of virtue and mortification; the middle or spiritual, "with the inflowing of God's graces and gifts" and the "three divine virtues of faith, hope and love";

the highest, "above our intellectual comprehension," in unity and rest in God "beyond all intention and beyond ourselves and beyond all things."[30]

This doctrine of the threefold unity Ruysbroeck uses to organize the development of his argument—both in *The Spiritual Espousals* and in *The Sparkling Stone*. Thus, in the latter, having disposed of the "hireling," he treats in turn of what he calls the "faithful servants of God" (chaps. 6 and 7; pp. 300–303), the "Secret Friends of God" (chaps. 7–8, pp. 302–6), and the "Hidden Sons of God" (chaps. 8–14, pp. 304–20). He devotes Book I of *The Spiritual Espousals* to the "active life" needful to all men who wish to be saved," Book II to "the interior, exalted, yearning life to which many men attain by virtues and the grace of God," and Book III to "the supernatural life of the contemplation of God, which a few men can achieve" (Prol., p. 44). These two triads should be aligned with each other. Thus the faithful servant of God is none other than the good man making proper use of his lower powers to pursue an active life of external works of virtue and mortification; the secret friend of God is the good man properly exercising his rational and spiritual powers in an inward life of yearning, "of loving and inward cleaving to God" (*Sparkling Stone*, chap. 7, p. 302) through such "means" as faith, hope, and love and without abandonment of selfhood; the hidden son of God is he who has received the Holy Spirit in the spark of his soul, who has transcended selfhood "above every exercise of virtue" and has been "swallowed up above reason and without reason in the deep quiet of the Godhead" (*in die diepe stilheit der Godheit*) (*Sparkling Stone*, chap. 9, pp. 307, 309).

If but few are called to this highest state—the contemplative life of unity with God—it is not to be supposed that those who are called are drawn wholly into God and abandon thereby the active life of outward virtue or the inward life of yearning. For Ruysbroeck, it must once more be insisted, the unity and trinity that we find in God is imaged in the unity and trinity we find also in man—unity of body, "spirit,"

30. *Espousals*, 2:2–4; p. 88. I am indebted also to Colledge's succinct commentary on pp. 19–20.

and "soul," unity therefore of the active, yearning, and contemplative lives. As he says when he begins to discuss the contemplative life, "The inward lover of God [that is, the hidden son of God] possesses God in delectable rest, and himself [that is, his spiritual powers] in a compelling and active love, and all his life [that is, his physical or lower power] in virtues with justness and due proportion" (*Espousals*, III, Prol., p. 179). Or, as he puts in in a simpler (and less complete) formulation in *The Sparkling Stone* (chap. 7, p. 303), those "foolish men who would be so inward that they would neither act nor serve, even in those things of which their neighbor has need," are "neither secret friends nor faithful servants of God, but are altogether false and deceived. For no man can follow the counsels of God who will not keep His commandments."

If but few are called to the contemplative life of unity with God, it must also not be supposed that even those few do so by virtue of any superior penetration of the questing intellect into God or, indeed, by virtue of any activity whatsoever that they can fully call their own. Given Ruysbroeck's pervasive Trinitarianism, I have already suggested, it would be pointless to try to classify him as either a "theocentric" or a "Christocentric" mystic, and to attempt to apply to him the related distinction between speculative and affective mysticism, if not quite so pointless, would be almost as difficult. Although it would be improper to deny the role ascribed by Ruysbroeck to the "higher power" of reason in the movement of man's spiritual life, it has to be noted that it is a role that is limited to the interior life of yearning pursued by the secret friends of God. It is superseded when, as hidden souls of God, we enter the contemplative life of union, going forth "into God with our feeling above reason," following "the brightness above reason with a simple sight, and with a willing leaning out of ourselves," to be caught up in the "storm of love" where "our activity is above reason and wayless" (*Sparkling Stone*, chaps. 9 and 10, pp. 307, 312–13). It is instead "the will, which is the capacity for loving," (*Espousals*, II, 33, p. 158) that presses on when "reason and understanding fail before the Divine clarity" (*Espousals*, II, 21, p. 140), though if it reaches its goal and encounters the divine in ecstatic embrace and "superessential" contemplation, it does so not because of any attribute or exercise of its own but rather because it is God's "good will to have it so" (*Espousals*, III, Prol., p. 179; *Sparkling Stone*, chap. 13, p. 318).

Here once again, it may be suggested, we can appreciate the relevance of the theological distinction between the absolute power and the ordained (or ordinary) power of God to an understanding of the claims being made by the medieval mystics. In *The Sparkling Stone* Ruysbroeck explicitly contrasts the life we lead "in the ordinary state of grace," in which "we carry our works before us as an offering to God" (chap. 9, p. 307), with "the wayless state," in which we feel "the indrawing touch of God," making known to us his "wide-opened good pleasure" and demanding that we should be one with him. And the image Ruysbroeck evokes for this latter state is that of the transfiguration of Christ on Mount Tabor, with the Father saying "to all his chosen in his eternal Word: 'This is my beloved son, in whom I am well pleased" (chap. 12, pp. 316–17). As he puts it in *The Spiritual Espousals* (III, 9, p. 190), "This is the dark silence in which all lovers are lost," a participation in "the rich embrace" of the Trinity's "essential unity," "an eternal resting in a delectable embrace of the flowing-out of love." Were it possible for us to attain it by any exercise of virtue of our own, "we should then," he says, "hasten to divest ourselves of this our mortal flesh, and . . . launch ourselves on the waves of this blessedness, and no creature could ever call us back again." But this, of course, it is not given to us to do—hence the heartfelt and wholly characteristic prayer in which he concludes the work: "That we in delectation may possess this essential unity, and that we may clearly contemplate Unity in Trinity, grant us that love which denies no prayer addressed to its Divinity. Amen. Amen."

Richard Fox of Winchester (1448–1528): Bishop

In its broad outlines Fox's life falls into three clear and easily definable phases. About the first we know next to nothing that is certain. Born in Lincolnshire in 1448 of a family somewhat above the yeoman class, Fox—according to such late accounts as that of Greneway, president of Corpus Christi College, Oxford (written no earlier than 1566)—pursued his grammatical studies at Boston before going in succession to Magdalen College, Oxford, to Pembroke College, Cambridge, and to the University of Paris to complete his education with the study of canon law. His name first crops up in the official record in January 1485, when Richard III indicated that he was abroad in the service of the rebel Henry Tudor. Before that year was out, the tables had been turned. Fox was present on August 22 at the crowning of the victorious Henry VII on Bosworth field, and was appointed (November 10) a councillor to the new king.

With that appointment the second phase in his life began, and about it we are much better informed. In the years after 1485 he rose rapidly in the service of Henry VII, becoming one of the king's closest and most trusted advisers. In February 1487 he was appointed lord privy seal, a position he was to hold for almost thirty years. After Henry VII's death in 1509 Fox effected a smooth transition to the changed conditions and shifting policies of the new reign and worked closely with Thomas Wolsey, who in 1515 became lord chancellor of England.

In the course of his three decades of service to the new dynasty, Fox labored long and hard both to secure its uncertain position at home and to protect its interests abroad. In so doing, he came to discharge a considerable variety of duties—administrative, diplomatic, even military—and in France and Scotland as well as in England. Thus at various points in his career we can catch glimpses of him presiding as master of ceremonies over great events in the royal household and organizing the obsequies for his late sovereign; participating in complex and arduous diplomatic negotiations with the French at Etaples in 1492, with Philip, archduke of Austria, in 1496, and with James IV of Scotland in 1498; supervising the extension of the great hall of Durham castle and the work of the military engineers on the defenses of Norham castle; holding Norham against a besieging Scottish army; organizing the procuring, equipping, and victualing of ships for the king's service; accompanying the army that Henry VIII sent to France in 1514; beseeching Wolsey, even from retirement, "to remembre the bill concernynge the kepers of the Kyngis brewhouses, and gunners of the towne and blokhouse of Portismouthe; which had no wages by a long season. And nedis they must be had."[31]

Fox discharged his multifarious responsibilities with great skill and efficiency and his career was attended by a high degree of success. Writing his life of Henry VII later on, Francis Bacon described Fox as "not only a grave counsellor for war or peace, but also a good surveyor of works, and a good master of ceremonies." He possessed, moreover, the true diplomat's ability to give "the smooth answer, as it was like oil unto the wound, whereby it began to heal." Above all, he was "a wise man, and one that could see through the present to the future."[32] Nor, it would seem, was his manifest success bought at the cost of his humanity or fundamental decency. He eschewed the arbitrary, was careful to give reasons for the demands he made on others, and enjoyed a reputation for fair-mindedness, moderation, and mercy. His sympathy with the poor and the powerless is obvious; long after his retirement, in one of his last interventions in state policy, he did not forget to urge that the military commander on the Scottish border be careful not to burn the green corn. His generosity, equally, is evident in the obvious pleasure he took in commending those who had worked well for him and in helping them to achieve deserved advancement. His dignity and sensitivity are illuminated in the impressive way in which he coped with the younger and less experienced Wolsey's startling rise to a position of dominance, thinking even in his letter requesting retirement to commiserate with Wolsey in his "intollerable labours" and urging him to "laye a part all such busynesses fro vi of the clok in the evening forthward."[33]

Of course, by the time of his retirement in 1516, Fox's own prominence was great and had already drawn him into those endeavors in the

---

31. Letter dated 10 May 1517, in Allen and Allen, eds., no. 58, p. 99; cf. the similar pleas in earlier and later letters to Wolsey during same year: ibid., nos. 57 and 59, pp. 96 and 102–3.
32. Bacon, *The History of the Reign of King Henry the Seventh*, in Spedding et al., eds., 6: 184, 200, 212.
33. Letter dated 23 April 1516, in Allen and Allen, eds., no. 52, p. 84.

field of higher education that were to employ so much of his energy in the third and remaining phase of his life, which won for him a Europe-wide reputation as a patron of learning, and which formed his most enduring legacy to later generations. By that time he had served as chancellor of the University of Cambridge and as master of Pembroke College in that university. At Oxford, meanwhile, he had become official visitor to Magdalen College and New College, had given new statutes to Balliol, and was well on the way to realizing the greatest of his educational achievements, the foundation of Corpus Christi College (1515–16). This college, "the definitive institution of Renaissance education in England" and "an English adaptation of the type of trilingual college already flourishing at Alcalá," provided the first permanent base for the new humanistic learning at Oxford.[34] Provision was made for a public lecturer in Greek and for readers in Latin and theology who were to cover a very broad and Erasmian range of authors and, in the case of theology, to focus on the Latin and Greek fathers rather than the medieval scholastic authorities. Although Fox, unlike Ximénez, made no provision for the teaching of Hebrew, "his was nevertheless the most radical departure from traditional studies yet seen in England," and we have it on the authority of Erasmus that Cardinal Campeggio, Henry VIII, and Wolsey (as well as Erasmus himself) were all deeply interested in the venture. It was indeed through the good offices of Wolsey that humanists of the distinction of Juan Luis Vives, Thomas Lupset, and Nicholas Kratzer came to be associated with Corpus even though they were never fellows of the college.

Fox himself attracted to the new foundation the first fellows, including his own poor kinsman Thomas Fox and the future cardinal Reginald Pole; several of them, such as John Claymond, the first president, were from Magdalen College. Fox's letters to Claymond (which he always signed "your lovying broder") reveal both his affection for the man and the warmth of his concern for the well-being of the college and its members. Thus, having acquired the site, made

34. McConica, p. 82.

arrangements for the building, and chosen the president and fellows, he was active in "endowing them with lands in the counties around, sending up their kitchen stuff from London by river, while yet they 'live upon his purse', collecting splendid books for their library, reading their verses, anxious for their health." [35] Though he was a benefactor also of Magdalen College and of Pembroke College, Cambridge, and though he endowed schools at Taunton and in his own home town of Grantham (the latter of which Sir Isaac Newton was to attend), right up to the time of his death as a blind old man in 1528, it was clearly his cherished foundation of Corpus that won his affection and inspired his pride. Appropriately enough, over the centuries the members of his college have been mindful amply to reciprocate those sentiments.

All in all, Fox had a distinguished, well-rounded, and eminently satisfying public career, and there would have been nothing odd about it, in modern terms, had he not, while serving as a public official and being for some years the most important of Tudor statesmen, been successively priest, bishop, and for some years probably the most powerful of Tudor ecclesiastics. At the time, of course, such a combination of roles was not unique. His successive incumbencies of the bishoprics of Exeter (1487–92), Bath and Wells (1492–94), Durham (1494–1501), and Winchester (1501–28), with their respective annual revenues (appropriately graduated) of approximately £1,560, £1,642, £2,821, and £3,691, served in classically medieval fashion to provide his salary, his expenses, and a suitably handsome reward for his frequently supererogatory labors.[36] A considerable historical interest attaches, however, to the way the performance of his duties was affected by that combination of offices. In regard to his political responsibilities his multiple roles entailed a degree and intimacy of contact with the dynasty he served not readily suggested by the title of lord privy seal: for example, he not only served as the trusted counsellor of Henry VII and Henry VIII, he also buried the former and baptized the latter. In the present context, however, what the combina-

35. Allen and Allen, eds., p. xiv.
36. I draw these figures from Howden, ed., pp. xvii, xxii, xxxi, xxxviii.

tion entailed for the discharge of his duties in ecclesiastical matters calls for a somewhat more extended comment.

For the first seven years of his episcopate he exercised his episcopal duties in absentia, failing even to visit his cathedral churches in the dioceses of Exeter and Bath and Wells, but appointing a vicar general to take care of all administrative tasks and a suffragan bishop to fulfill those sacramental functions that called for episcopal orders. Though Fox was later to express misgivings about the "inumerable sawles wherof I never see the bodyes,"[37] at the time he appears to have felt no qualms about his nonresidence. He appointed capable and conscientious men to the two main surrogate positions. William Sylke, indeed, his vicar general in both dioceses, and later on at Durham too, was a doctor of laws who himself eventually went on to become bishop of Norwich. The episcopal registers for both dioceses do not suggest that nonresidence under such circumstances had any immediately disastrous consequences; the routine work of property management, ordinations, induction into benefices, and so on appears to have gone ahead in a normal and uninterrupted fashion. For all their brevity and formality, however, the registers do reveal that in the absence of a bishop whose diocese was his chief concern, there was a less than active pursuit of tasks beyond the purely routine—the disciplining, for example, of indecorous or nonresident clergy, or the visitation of convents and monasteries and the rectification of abuses in such houses. Certainly, when Hugh Oldham became bishop of Exeter in 1504, he was to find much in the diocese that called for critical scrutiny and vigorous amendment.[38]

It was in 1494, when Fox went to Durham, that he became for the first time a resident bishop. He had been translated to that important bishopric presumably because Henry VII needed an experienced and trustworthy man in the position of prince-bishop, charged with re-

37. Letter to Wolsey, dated 30 April 1517, in Allen and Allen, eds., no. 57, p. 93.
38. All four of Fox's episcopal registers are extant, but only two have been published: that of Bath and Wells by E. R. Batten, *The Register of Richard Fox while Bishop of Bath and Wells* (1889), and that of Durham by Howden. In her lengthy introduction to the latter, however, Howden analyzes (pp. xiii–lvi) the contents of all four registers, devoting the bulk of her attention to the multivolume register for Winchester.

sponsibility for the defense of the border against the Scottish threat. But although it was for political reasons that he now became a resident bishop, and was preoccupied largely with political, administrative, and even military affairs, the Durham register for his episcopate suggests that the very fact of his presence made a significant difference. For the first time in his episcopal career he chose not to appoint a suffragan bishop, and the record indicates that he himself held ordinations in 1496 and twice in 1497. It indicates, too, that his administrative energies extended beyond the vigorous vindication of his property rights. He certainly was at pains to discipline unofficially nonresident priests, and one of his first acts after enthronement as bishop in July 1495 was to conduct a visitation of the collegiate church of Bishop Auckland to impose some reforms there. It is not that he achieved a distinguished performance in his ecclesiastical duties as bishop; he was too burdened with administrative, military, and diplomatic responsibilities for that. But as Howden has said, "By the mere fact of his residence in the diocese and of personal contact with his subordinates, certain minor reforms were made and life was given to ecclesiastical routine." [39]

A similar impression is conveyed, but in much more marked fashion, by the bulky register covering Fox's years at Winchester, the wealthiest see in England and one that then extended eastward to include Surrey as well as Hampshire. Because of its location, which enabled him now to remain readily available to the king while at the same time residing within the diocese, the degree of his control over diocesan affairs depended entirely on the amount of time he was able to wrest from his governmental duties and the energy with which he made use of that time. After his retirement in 1516, though he was nearing seventy, he threw himself wholeheartedly into the work not simply of diocesan administration but of diocesan reform, conducting visitations of parishes, either personally or by deputy, in 1520, 1527, and 1528, and of the religious houses of the diocese in 1521 and 1522. He followed up those visitations with the appropriate reforms,

39. Howden, ed., p. xxix.

admonitions, and, where necessary, the imposition of ecclesiastical discipline—with such energy, indeed, that in 1527 he had to defend himself to Wolsey against charges of excessive rigor.[40] And even before his retirement he had instigated his vicar general to conduct visitations of the religious houses for men in 1501, 1507, and 1510, and in 1508 had commanded the archdeacon in the archdeaconry of Winchester to hold yearly parochial visitations and to make provision for the vernacular instruction of the people in the fundamentals of the faith.[41]

The hard lessons learned in the course of all these efforts at a more systematic supervision of the religious life of his flock are reflected in his decision to exact pledges from new parochial incumbents to remain in their parishes, and in his move to amalgamate some benefices in Winchester in order to alleviate the poverty of the incumbents. They are reflected, too, in his translation of the Benedictine Rule (the first fruit, it seems, of his retirement) "into oure moders tonge, commune, playne, rounde, Englisshe, easy and redy to be understande." He undertook that task at the request of the four convents of Benedictine nuns in his diocese, and his prefatory remarks reveal already a weary recognition of what he was up against. "For as moche as every persone ought to knowe the thyng that he is bounde to kepe or accomplisshe," he begins,

> we the sayd Bisshope, knowing and consideringe the premisses and rememberynge that we may not without like peryll of our sowle suffer the sayd religiouse wemen, of whose sowles we have the cure, to continue in their sayde blindenesse and ignorance of the sayd Rule, to the knowledge and observance whereof they be professed; and especially to thentent that the yonge novices may first knowe and understande the

40. Letter dated 18 January 1527, in Allen and Allen, eds., no. 28, pp. 150–51. In that letter Fox makes the proud claim that "(except for Suthwarke, whiche is under the jurisdiction of tharchdeacon) I trowe there be as litle openly knowen synne or enorme crymes, both in persones spiritual and temporall, as is within any dioces of this realme." In regard to the religious houses for men in his diocese, he also says, "I have never taken procurations of any of theym for all the visitations of my tyme, by the space of xxvi yeres," thus claiming (correctly) that for him visitation was not a right (on the analogy of a benefice) but a solemn duty.
41. Howden, ed., p. xlviii.

sayde Rule before they professe them to it, so that none of them shall mowe afterward probably say that she wyste not what she professed, as we knowe by experience that somme of them have sayd in tyme passed.[42]

If Fox's presence in the diocese of Winchester was clearly beginning to make an impact on the quality of religious life there even before he withdrew from full-time government service in 1516, the letter in which he petitioned Wolsey for retirement reveals that the experience of residence had also had its impact on the bishop himself and had sharpened his perception of the probable cost of his earlier neglect of his dioceses. Revealing that his mind was "trowled nyght and daye with other mens enormities and vices more than I dar write," he now sought license "to be occupied in my cure, wherby I maye doo soom satisfaccion for xxviii yeres negligence."[43] It has been suggested that his anxiety to retire may have reflected in part his disenchantment with the prevailing anti-French foreign policy; but there is no reason to doubt the sincerity of his concern about the sins of omission attendant upon his earlier neglect of his episcopal duties. Some of that concern may simply reflect the shock of an efficient, seasoned, and energetic administrator at the slackness, confusion, and lack of assured direction among the clergy, both secular and regular, that closer and more continuous contact with diocesan affairs had brought home to him. But the ring of passionate unease in the phrases of a later letter to Wolsey suggests that he was moved also by impulses of a much more unambiguously spiritual type. In that letter, written in 1517, begging to be excused from renewed attendance at the royal council, he not only deplores his earlier neglect of his pastoral responsibilities but also expresses his unease of conscience about his earlier involvement in matters pertaining to the war. Given "the many intolerable enormytes

42. Fox's translation was later printed under the title *The Rule of Seynt Benet* (London, 1516). I cite the preface from Allen and Allen, eds., no. 55, pp. 87–88.
43. Letter to Wolsey dated 23 April 1516, in Allen and Allen, eds., no. 52, pp. 82–83. Cf. the letter to Wolsey dated 30 April 1517, in ibid., no. 57, p. 93, where he speaks of his cure "wherein I have be almost by the space of xxx yeres so negligent, that of iii several cathedral chyrches that I have successivly had, ther be too, *scilicet* Excestre and Wellys, that I never see, and innumerable sawles wherof I never see the bodyes."

involved therein," he says, he is led to think "that if I dyd continuall penance for it all the dayes of my lyfe . . . I cowde not yit make sufficient recompense therfor." Indeed, if he were to involve himself again in such matters and came to die, "I thynk I shuld dye in dispeyr." Even to be summoned to treat of such matters has had the effect of troubling "not a littell my spirits"—so much so that "I fere that I shall not by raison thereof be in such quyetnes that I shall dar say masse thies next v or vi dayes" [44]

These are not the words of the confident civil servant—bishop, secure in the knowledge of his abilities and of the value of the duties he was discharging, the younger man whose unruffled temperament and mood of calm acceptance is reflected in the motto *Est Deo Gracia*, which in the great kitchen of Durham castle adorns his device of a pelican vulning herself. But they do express the hopes and fears of the older and more chastened man, whose ambitions were now fixed on goals of a pastoral and educational nature, and who, assuring Wolsey that he sought neither "ease of . . . bodye" nor "quietenesse of mynde" nor "lucre of money," added in all simplicity, "I pray God I may *lucrari animas*." [45]

John Hus (ca. 1370–1415): Heretic

About the external events of John Hus's life I have had much less to say than about the internal structure of his theology. Not much *can* be said about events before his appointment in 1402 as rector of the Bethlehem Chapel at Prague, for his early years are shrouded in obscurity. Born around the year 1370 at Husinec, in southwest Bohemia, he embarked on his studies at the University of Prague with his ambitions directed in wholly conventional fashion toward a career in the church. Or, at least, that is what the later Hus would have us believe; for at some point between 1395, when he received the master of arts degree, and 1400, when he was ordained to the priesthood, he underwent a conversion experience that left him an exponent of the

44. Letter to Wolsey dated 30 April 1517, in ibid., no. 57, pp. 93–94.
45. Letter dated 23 April 1516, in ibid., no. 52, p. 83.

stern commitment, rigorous moralism, and other characteristic emphases of the indigenous Czech reforming movement. And an eloquent and influential exponent he proved to be. While continuing his theological studies (he became master of theology in 1404) and preaching at the Bethlehem Chapel, he rose first to prominence and then to symbolic leadership both of the reform movement at large and of the circle of theologians at Prague sympathetic to Wycliffite views. Though by no means the most radical of the reformers, he became the best known, was excommunicated in 1412, and was nudged out of Prague by the imposition of an interdict on that city. He spent two years of exile preaching and studying under noble protection in southern Bohemia. Then, in an attempt to break the impasse that had developed between Rome and the Bohemian reform movement, he unwisely accepted the safe-conduct proffered by Emperor Sigismund and set off to plead his case and that of reform before the newly assembled Council of Constance. Having once arrived, however, he was soon reduced from the status of an independent theologian free to make his case to that of a suspected heretic, incarcerated first in a Dominican monastery and then in the castle of the bishop of Constance. Sigismund's earlier promises to the contrary, he was subjected to trial, condemnation, and well-intentioned pressure to recant. Finally, on July 6, 1415, he was degraded from the clerical order and burned at the stake as a heretic.

Given the ambivalence of his own doctrinal formulations and the fact that he did not represent the truly radical wing of the Bohemian reform movement, the great puzzle about his life lies in its ending. And the clues that may lead to the solution to that puzzle must necessarily be teased from the tightly woven fabric of a life confusingly overlaid with an appliqué of legend and propaganda, both adulatory and hostile. Because it turns out to be no easy task, it is tempting to seek the explanation for Hus's ultimate martyrdom in the impact of external factors that would have been at work even had he been a very different man. Such factors were indeed powerfully at work in the train of events leading up to his condemnation. The problem is the degree to which they proved in the end to be determinative. Among the various claims that have been made, some are certainly less than convincing. It has been suggested, for example, that John XXIII saw in the trial of Hus "a great opportunity . . . to divert the attention of the council [of Constance] from his own unsavoury past and . . . [to] earn the applause of Christendom for destroying the enemy of the faith."[46] But it is not so much Hus's trial that calls for explanation as its outcome, and that outcome was the work not of John XXIII but of the council that had by then already deposed him. More than one historian has considered this fact itself highly relevant. Thus, pointing out that Hus's judges were advocates of what he calls "the heretical conciliar view," de Vooght has speculated that such men as d'Ailly and Gerson may well have needed "to reassure themselves as to their own orthodoxy," and so "seized the occasion and burned a heretic." But since he wrote on Hus, de Vooght himself has veered toward the conclusion that such a negative view of the conciliar position is of modern ultramontane inspiration. As a result, he would now be prepared, presumably, to admit that it is anachronistic and misleading to depict conciliarist views as the source of any particular uneasiness in the consciences of those who adhered to them in the fifteenth century.[47] Yet again, Zabarella, Gerson, and d'Ailly, the men who dominated the commission that finally condemned Hus, have been portrayed as heavily biased against him—to such a degree, indeed, that "it is obvious that Hus could expect no just treatment from them."[48] That portrayal is grounded very much in the account written by Peter of Mladaňovice, the principal source for Hus's trial but one written, it should be noted, by a partisan of Hus. Nevertheless, even if Peter's account is taken at face value, and even if one concedes an initially negative bias in the commission's leaders, it is still puzzling that the actual course of the trial did nothing to erode that bias.

46. Betts, p. 193.
47. De Vooght, *Hérésie*, pp. 470, 474. For his later conclusions on the conciliar position and the dogmatic status of *Haec sancta*, see his *Pouvoirs du concile*.
48. See Spinka, *Concept*, pp. 350–80 at 356; cf. his *Biography*, pp. 248–90. Spinka has provided us with a convenient translation of Mladaňovice's account and related source materials (both Czech and Latin) in his *John Hus at the Council of Constance*.

All three, after all, possessed deserved reputations as men of prudent temperament and responsible and moderate character. None was a fanatical heresy hunter. In trying to Carmelite William of Hildernissen at Cambrai in 1411, d'Ailly had proved himself gentle enough and willing to discriminate between those errors that were firmly based and those grounded merely in rumor.[49] And at Constance, d'Ailly and Gerson successfully defended against Matthew of Grabow's charges of heresy the Brothers and Sisters of the Common Life, whose founders, Geert Groote and Florens Radewijns, may both have studied at Prague at the time of John Milič, and whose spirituality had something in common with the native Bohemian reform movement of which Hus was himself the product.[50]

If men of this sort finally proved incapable of seeing behind the doomed and apparently devious Wycliffite the man who now appears to have been the real Hus—theologically confused, doctrinally ambivalent, but probably at heart fundamentally orthodox—we must surely ask why. And once again, it is tempting to seek the solution in the impact of factors external to Hus himself. Among them, the war of propaganda waged against him at Constance by the disgruntled German masters expelled from Prague and by his Czech compatriots —notably Stephen Páleč—must claim first place. Presumably because Páleč had been prominent in the leadership of the Bohemian reform movement until 1408, and had finally broken with Hus only in 1411, when the latter attacked the papal bull of indulgences, the judges at Constance appear to have attached particular weight to his adverse testimony. D'Ailly, for example, felt that Páleč had dealt "very kindly" with Hus's books and could easily have extracted from

49. The record of the trial is printed in Fredericq, 1:267–79, no. 249 (12 June 1411). Lerner, who has compared this record with a "far superior [manuscript] version, hitherto unused," gives an account of the incident in his *Heresy*, pp. 157–63.
50. See de Vooght, *Hérésie*, p. 316; and Spinka, *Biography*, pp. 14–15, where he echoes the judgment of the Czech historian F. M. Bartoš that Groote was "a sort of Dutch counterpart of the Czech Milič." Note, however, that Post, *Modern Devotion*, pp. 221–32, while admitting "the similarity between the phenomena in Prague and Deventer" and the residence in Prague of Radewijns and such other devotionalists as Lubbert ten Bosch, questions the claim that Groote himself ever studied there.

them "many more and harsher" erroneous articles than in fact he
did.[51]

How well advised they were to place such weight on Páleč's testimony is, of course, a moot point. To Spinka, Páleč was a depraved
liar, unworthy of credence.[52] To Kaminsky, on the other hand, he was
precisely the man who clearly saw the point at issue, who well knew
"that whatever Hus might prove about the letter of his works, he in
fact led a revolutionary movement."[53] But however one judges his
role as Hus's "principal enemy," and whatever motivations underlay
that role, the form it took and the impact it had upon d'Ailly, Gerson,
and Zabarella would ultimately be inexplicable without the powerfully adverse impression created both at Prague and later at Constance by Hus's own behavior. To say that is to say also that the solution to the puzzle of Hus's martyrdom must ultimately be sought less
in the workings of any external factors than in the character of the man
himself. And there we confront a "profound enigma."[54]

It was Páleč's claim that the fatal flaw distinguishing Hus's stance as
reformer from that of his predecessors in the Bohemian reform movement was not his determination to attack the clerical corruption of the
day but rather his defiance of the teaching authority of the Roman
church and his responsiveness to the doctrinal errors of Wycliffe. The
claim is at once cogent enough and a little simplistic. In the first
place, although he was not the first of the Bohemian reformers to
stimulate the wrath of the offended clergy by his moralizing censures,
there was something notably unrestrained about the outraged invec-
tive he hurled against those whom he so readily identified as simoniacs
or as the luxurious, worldly, and unworthy clerics of his day. In an
analysis of the sermons that he delivered over the course of some years
de Vooght has drawn attention not merely to the violence of his language but also the degree to which, as time went on, that violence

51. Mladaňovice, *Relatio*, I, chap. 4; ed. Novotný, 8:108. Eng. trans. in Spinka,
Constance, p. 221.
52. Spinka, *Biography*, pp. 263, 274. But Spinka perforce admits (pp. 135–36) that
in the disagreement over the actual *contents* of the papal bull of indulgences of 1411, on
which he broke with Hus, Páleč appears to have been correct.
53. Kaminsky, *History*, pp. 38, 52.
54. De Vooght, *Hérésie*, p. 477.

deepened.[55] He has also stressed that there was "something excessive" in Hus's behavior that goaded his critics into an uninhibited fury of opposition. Other commentators, too, have noted his lack of diplomacy, the "daring" nature of his critiques of ecclesiastical authority, the "atmosphere of defiance that developed under his practical leadership," the "streak of exhibitionism" that "led him into gratuitous acts of bravado and . . . further incensed his enemies."[56]

That exhibitionism comes out clearly in his apparent inability to refrain from sprinkling his arguments with statements drawn from Wycliffe or even from employing provocatively Wycliffite terminology when formulating perfectly orthodox positions. And that bravado is particularly evident in the move that cost him the support of so many of his sympathizers, colleagues, and friends at Prague—the decision in 1411 to challenge John XXIII's "crusading" bull of indulgences, despite the fact that there was clearly room for genuine disagreement on one of the central points at issue. He publicized that challenge not only in the university by means of scholastic debate but also among an aroused and excited populace by means of sermons preached in Czech. In this particularly damaging stand there was much both of puritan zealotry and of academic idealism. But in this, again, as in his general stance toward ecclesiastical authority and toward the teachings of Wycliffe, one senses the presence of more troubling qualities sometimes regarded as equally characteristic of the academy.

Notable among these, and despite the degree of his concern with practical moral issues, was the disconcerting ease with which he was willing to reach for his principles, and to do so in situations where men of less abstractly theoretical but perhaps more reflective bent would have shown a more sober appreciation of the density, the complexity, the highly contingent particularity of human affairs. The eagerness with which he took his stand on principle set him on a collision course with the ecclesiastical authorities first at Prague, then at

55. De Vooght, *Hérésie*, pp. 64–71.
56. Ibid., p. 477; Spinka, *Biography*, pp. 151, 139; Kaminsky, *History*, p. 40; Leff, *Heresy*, 2:638.

Rome, and then at Constance, and encouraged such true radicals as Jakoubek of Stříbro and Nicholas of Dresden to pursue the logic of his position to its revolutionary end; yet at the same time he himself wavered, held back, and betrayed the curious streak of submissiveness that eventually proved fatal for him. As de Vooght has put it: "He excited the bull but had scruples about killing it."[57] It is as if in boldly challenging ecclesiastical authority he felt such filial respect for it that he desperately needed its approval for his very challenge. There is something of that submissiveness in his decision to leave Prague in 1412 at the very height of his popularity in order to spare the city the inconveniences of an interdict; there is a good deal more of it in his decision to go to Constance in order to submit his cause to the judgment of the general council.

His disconcerting alternation between defiance and submissiveness at Constance, coupled with the lack of candor or clarity in his responses to some of the erroneous articles attributed to him, help more than anything else to explain the failure of his judges to penetrate the confusing screen of rumor, falsehood, charge, and countercharge. This screen had come to blur for them the outlines of a religious commitment that was certainly not Wycliffite, that was traditionally orthodox in intention, and that was within a hairsbreadth of being orthodox in actual fact. As a result of that failure he was condemned to die. But though the personal qualities that did so much to ensure his condemnation seem destined, now as in his own lifetime, to evoke mixed feelings, the nobility of spirit that sustained him through his last terrible days and saw him safely past the pitfall of recantation to his death as a heretic must surely evoke ungrudging admiration. The enormous courage with which he died must be accorded a full measure of respect, for he cannot really be said to have sought martyrdom. Hus's humble sense of his own frailty was clearly too acute for that, and it is well brought out in the prayer contained in a letter he wrote less than two weeks before his death:

> O most kind Christ, draw us weaklings after Thyself, for unless Thou draw us, we cannot follow Thee! Give us a courageous spirit that it

57. De Vooght, *Hérésie*, p. 478.

may be ready; and if the flesh is weak, may Thy grace go before, now as well as subsequently. For without Thee we can do nothing, and particularly not go to a cruel death for Thy sake. Give us a valiant spirit, a fearless heart, the right faith, a firm hope, and perfect love, that we may offer our lives for Thy sake with the greatest patience and joy. Amen.[58]

Pierre d'Ailly (1350–1420): Reformer

We know next to nothing about Pierre d'Ailly's childhood years. Born in 1350 at Compiègne in the Ile de France, d'Ailly was of bourgeois origins and the family name was drawn from the village of Ailly in Picardy. He entered the University of Paris in 1364 as a bursar at the Collège de Navarre, became a bachelor of arts in 1367, and during the following fourteen years surmounted the successive hurdles of the long course of studies leading to the doctorate of theology, revealing himself in the process as a creative proponent of Ockham's nominalist theology. The closing decades of the century were the years during which he began to manifest the diplomatic skill and capacity for leadership that were later to win for him—especially in connection with the councils of Pisa and Constance—a position of international prominence. It is entirely fitting that when he died on August 9, 1420, at Avignon, he was there as a legate of the new pope, Martin V, still serving in public capacity the church for whose unity he had labored so long.

It was around 1375, during the years when Jan van Ruysbroeck, in seclusion at Groenendael, was coming to the end of his long life, that d'Ailly, still a student of theology at the University of Paris, wrote his commentary on the *Sentences* of Peter Lombard. A little more than a hundred years later, that commentary was printed for the first time, appropriately enough under the aegis of the Brothers of the Common Life, whose peculiar vocation d'Ailly had staunchly defended at Constance. Between 1475 and 1495, while Richard Fox was rising to prominence in the service of Henry VII, other printed editions ap-

58. In a letter to Lord John of Chlum, dated 23 June 1415. Trans. from Spinka, *Constance*, p. 279.

peared; Cardinal Campeggio, who we know was keenly interested in Fox's new foundation at Oxford, appears to have acquired a copy of one of the editions dating to 1500.[59] At the turn of the century, indeed, interest in d'Ailly's literary legacy appears to have run high, and not only among the Gallicans of the theological faculty at the University of Paris, where Jacques Almain and John Major in their own conciliar tracts leaned heavily on his authority. Thus, for example, before his epoch-making trip to the New World in 1492, Christopher Columbus read and annotated what later became, as a result, d'Ailly's most widely known work—the highly derivative geographical treatise written in 1410, entitled *Ymago mundi*. Similarly, in his *Babylonian Captivity of the Church*, Martin Luther indicated that in his student days he had been greatly impressed by d'Ailly's *Sentences*, and especially by the view of the Eucharist expressed in the fourth book of that work.[60] The survival of interest in his geographical, logical, philosophical, theological, and ecclesiological views is also reflected in the printing of works other than the *Sentences*. Among other of his writings, *Ymago mundi, Conceptus et insolubilia*, and *Tractatus de anima* all appeared between 1478 and 1505, and his *Tractatus de reformatione* was to be printed six times in the sixteenth and seventeenth centuries, as well as being later included in such collections as those of von der Hardt and Louis Ellies Dupin.[61]

The enduring popularity of this last work deserves emphasis, for it focuses attention on the aspect of d'Ailly's career that must concern us here. His career was of great richness and range. That he was personally acquainted with all three of our other five subjects who were his contemporaries, men as different as St. Vincent Ferrer, Francesco di

59. The first edition was published at Brussels in 1478. Subsequent editions appeared at Strassburg in 1490 and at Venice and Lyons in 1500. The copy in the Beinecke Rare Book Library at Yale University—*Quaestiones super I, III et IV Sententiarum* (Lyons: Nicolaus Wolff, 1500)—appears originally to have been the property of Cardinal Campeggio.
60. *Imago mundi*, ed. Buron (1930). The editor's introduction (1:1–113) discusses Columbus's interest in the work. For Luther's comment, see *De captivitate Babylonica*; in *Werke*, 6:497–573 at 508.
61. Salembier, *Petrus de Alliaco*, pp. xxii–xliv, gives a complete listing of d'Ailly's works, their locations, and successive printings.

Marco Datini, and John Hus, emphasizes that range. So, too, do the number of times and the variety of contexts in which his name has cropped up in the course of this book. We have already caught glimpses of him in his role as a prominent theologian of the Ockhamist persuasion, a thinker whose views on natural law, justification, predestination, the status of Scripture, the nature of the church, and several other related topics have found their place in the histories of those subjects. Many of the works in which he expressed those views date from his early years as student and teacher at the University of Paris, where he also served successively as proctor of the French nation (1372), rector of the Collège de Navarre (1383), and chancellor of the university (1389). Even had he not gone on to prominence in any broader public arena, it seems safe to assume that as an important university figure and the author of 170 works—books, tracts, letters, poems, sermons, covering an astonishing variety of subjects—he would still have been remembered as a distinguished contributor to the intellectual life of his day.

But go on to more conspicuous activities of course he did, and we have also caught glimpses of him as ambassador at the papal court of Avignon, where at various times he represented both the University of Paris and the French king, as ecclesiastical trouble-shooter trying to drum up support for the impending Council of Pisa, as bishop of the great see of Cambrai, presiding over the trial of a man who appears to have sympathized with the heresy of the Free Spirit. These roles were not unrelated. It was during his successive embassies to Avignon that d'Ailly caught the attention first of Clement VII and then of Benedict XIII, who conferred a series of minor benefices upon him (along with a dispensation to hold them in plurality), and then made him bishop of Puy in 1395 and of the more important see of Cambrai in 1397—an office he retained until John XXIII elevated him to the cardinalate in 1411. The very rapidity of his advancement sponsored some adverse reactions. His successor at Puy, which he had never visited, was critical of his neglect of the diocese, and some of his colleagues at the University of Paris accused him to having permitted Benedict XIII to purchase his loyalty. It is difficult to assess the extent to which such criticisms and suspicions were justifiable; he was bishop of Puy, after all, for only a few months, and his loyalty to Benedict XIII did not in the end prevent his abandoning the pope and incurring thereby the hostility (this time) of Boniface Ferrer. In the meantime, however, d'Ailly certainly courted unpopularity by opposing the French withdrawal of obedience in 1398, was active in bringing about a partial restoration of obedience in 1403, tried to absent himself in 1406 from the Council of Paris, which sought to institute proceedings against Benedict, and, when coerced into attending, insisted courageously in the teeth of opposition on defending that pontiff.

By the end of 1408, nevertheless, he had broken with Benedict in disgust and was actively campaigning to marshal support for the forthcoming attempt at Pisa to end the schism. From the time of that shift in direction we can trace his rise to prominence on the international scene as an ecclesiastical statesman, as a leading conciliarist, and as one of John Hus's judges at Constance. Cutting across these several phases in his career, however, and serving in some degree to bind them together, is an abiding commitment to church reform—on the international as well as the local level, in head as well as in members, in matters constitutional as well as disciplinary, and, in some measure, in matters educational, too. This commitment to reform he had indicated as early as 1381 in two short works, *Epistola diaboli Leviathan* and *Invectiva Ezechielis contra pseudo-pastores*, and he underlined it again in 1388, on the occasion of an embassy to the papal court at Avignon, by taking the opportunity to preach against clerical immorality. But it was as bishop of Cambrai from 1397 on that he first had the opportunity to put some of his reforming ideas into practice on the diocesan level, and also, in his *Tractatus de materia concilii generalis* (1402–3), to set forth proposals for a comprehensive reform of the church at large. Of that work, which also reflects his conciliarist views, the third part he presented with only minor revisions to the Council of Constance in 1416 as the discourse entitled *Tractatus de reformatione ecclesiae*.

The later circulation of that work in Protestant circles,[62] the fact

62. Ibid., p. xxxii.

that Luther cited approvingly his heterodox sympathies concerning the Eucharist, his prominence as a conciliar theorist and the enduring popularity of his conciliarist views in Gallican circles, his firm and open commitment to the nominalist theology of Ockham—all of these things frequently conspired to encourage historians to see him as something of a radical. Until the last half-century or so, he was often portrayed as a "Reformer before the Reformation" or at least as a man of shaky and unsound doctrinal loyalties, at once an anticipator of Luther, an agnostic, a philosophical skeptic, perhaps even an Averroist![63] A perusal of the *Tractatus de materia*, moreover, reveals that he ventilated the possibility that the cardinalate, not being of divine institution, might well be allowed to lapse into disuse, and the place of the cardinals as papal assistants taken by prelates from the several kingdoms and provinces.[64] A further perusal of that work, and of the *Tractatus et sermones*, suggests also, and surprisingly, that d'Ailly was quite taken with some of the views of Joachim of Fiore, whose writings he may have come across in 1385 in the library of the Collège de Navarre.[65]

His own "apocalyptic" sympathies, although not central to his thinking, were certainly real enough. He may affirm that knowledge concerning the timing of Antichrist's coming and of the end of the world has not been revealed to us in the Bible, and, like St. Vincent Ferrer, he may go on to invoke Christ's statement that it is not for us to know the times or seasons the Father has fixed by his own authority;[66] but he also goes on to hedge about the latter statement with qualifications and to hazard the opinion that God could well permit the future revelation to us of knowledge concerning the time of Antichrist's com-

63. For some of these characterizations and comments about them, see Tschackert, pp. 303 ff.; Salembier, *Cardinal*, pp. 297–98; Gandillac, 44.
64. *Tract. de mat.*, pt. III; Oakley, *Political Thought of Pierre d'Ailly*, app. III, pp. 244–349 at 322–24 and 328; in the latter passage he indicates that he himself does not approve of the opinion there expressed to the effect that the cardinalate should be abolished.
65. Or so Salembier, *Cardinal*, p. 313, supposes. See *Tract. de mat.*, pt. III; Oakley, *Political Thought of Pierre d'Ailly*, pp. 314–15. Also "Sermo secundus de adventu domini," in his *Tract. et serm.*, sig. s6v ff.; "Sermo tertius de adventu domini," ibid., sig. t6r; "Sermo de quadruplici adventu domini," ibid., sig. t6r.
66. See Reeves, pp. 422–24.

ing, and could do so not merely *de potentia absoluta* (that goes without saying) but even *de potentia ordinata*.[67] Yet such sentiments, however deeply felt, do not bulk very large in his writings. They appear mainly to reflect a periodic sense of despair over the protracted nature of the schism, and the disarray it was generating in the church, as well as a fluctuating disposition, fueled perhaps by Joachite and certainly by pseudo-Joachite writings, to take the troubles of the time as evidence that the end of the world was fast approaching. Nor was his apparent flirtation with the doctrine of "impanation" any more central to his thinking. It simply reflected his sense that that doctrine presented fewer problems, philosophically speaking, than did transubstantiation, and was coupled, as Luther himself noted, with the affirmation that it was, of course, excluded doctrinally or theologically speaking because the church has "determined otherwise."

With the decline in recent years of the credence historians have been willing to give to those negative appraisals of the nominalist theology that were primarily of neo-Thomist inspiration or to those dismissive judgments of conciliar theory that were ultimately of ultramontane provenance, it becomes more difficult to cast d'Ailly convincingly in the role of radical with reference either to his theology in general or to his ecclesiology in particular. So far as his views on justification and predestination go, he appears to have swum very much with the most powerful theological currents of his day. He was certainly a committed and influential advocate of the strict conciliar theory, and therefore of constitutional reform in the church's government, but we have seen that that theory was itself no radical or heterodox innovation but rather a constitutionalist position, rooted at least as deeply in the canonistic and ecclesiological tradition as was its high-papalist rival. Among the advocates of conciliar theory active in the era of the great councils, d'Ailly emerges as something of a moderate—the more so in that, after becoming a cardinal, he revised the *Tractatus de materia* in such a way as to blunt its more radical edges. He eliminated those passages critical of the cardinalate and in-

67. "Sermo de sancto dominico," in *Tract. et serm.*, sig. C4v; cf. his *De persecutionibus ecclesiae*; ed. Valois, pp. 566–67, 573–74. "Sermo de quadruplici adventu domini"; *Tract. et serm.*, sig. t5v–t6r.

serted language denouncing as erroneous the idea that the cardinalate was useless or not of apostolic origin. As we have seen, he became an influential proponent of the curialist or "oligarchic" view, which saw the college of cardinals as the successor to the "sacred college or senate of the apostles" and ascribed to it the constitutional role of serving as a continuously functioning institutional brake on the pope's abuse of his power.[68]

If it is difficult, then, to cast d'Ailly convincingly in the role of radical either as theologian or as conciliarist, it seems unlikely, whatever use Protestant propagandists later contrived to make of his proposals for reform in head and members, that we should find therein any more persuasive intimations of truly radical leanings. His significance as a reformer lies in the fact that he combined in his thinking, just as he reflected in his career, all the elements that composed the mature conciliarist position of the classical era but that subsequently parted and went their separate ways. Thus his attribution to the cardinals of an enhanced constitutional role in the government of the universal church made its strongest impact on the thinking of such a high papalist as Turrecremata and found its warmest welcome among the curialists of the era of papal restoration. His advocacy of the strict conciliar theory, on the other hand, left its most permanent mark upon the Gallican Catholicism of sixteenth-, and seventeenth-, and eighteenth-century France and reverberated most strongly among such Gallican theologians as Richer, Bossuet, and Louis Ellies Dupin. At the same time, his program for reform of the church in head and members and his sense that this program could best be carried out through the efforts of a general council enjoyed its most obvious vindication in the final assembly and the successful disciplinary legislation of the Council of Trent. A brief glance at the contents of his *Tractatus de reformatione ecclesiae* may serve to illustrate this last point.[69]

---

68. See Oakley, *Political Thought of Pierre d'Ailly*, p. 251, and app. V, pp. 346–57.
69. See *Tract. de mat.*, pt. III; Oakley, *Political Thought of Pierre d'Ailly*, pp. 314–42, and app. V and VI, pp. 346–49, for the changes d'Ailly made when revising it as the *Tract. de ref.* The footnotes include cross-references to the disciplinary legislation of Trent.

Striking the theme of "downhill all the way," which was then fashionable, the tract begins with a rather portentous introduction denouncing the corruption of the church and predicting further calamities if something is not done about it. Six sections follow, in the first of which d'Ailly insists that if the whole body of the church is to be reformed at all it will be necessary to hold both general and provincial councils far more frequently than was customary in the past. Among other things, the badly needed reform of the Roman curia can be undertaken only by a general council, and it is the failure to hold such councils that accounts for the long duration both of the Western schism and of the schism between the Greek and Latin churches and for many other evils as well. He proposes, therefore, that provision be made for provincial councils to assemble at least once every three years, and for general councils to assemble automatically at intervals of thirty or, at most, fifty years, without the necessity of any specific papal convocation or mandate.

In the second section he denounces, among other things, "that detestable abuse from which the present schism drew its origin"—namely, attachment of the papacy to any nation or kingdom for so long a time that the nation could almost claim it as its own. This abuse should be remedied, and it should also be decreed that no two successive popes could be drawn from the college of cardinals, since it is not to be presumed that noncardinals are ineligible. As for the cardinals themselves, the greater part of them should never be drawn from a single nation or kingdom, there should be no more than one cardinal from any single ecclesiastical province, their number should be reduced, and something should be done to eliminate the scandalous pluralism so prevalent among them. In addition, d'Ailly deplores the tendency of the curia to multiply the number of excommunications attached to its penal constitutions and to burden the faithful with an excessive number of statutes and canons obliging on pain of mortal sin.

The third section concerns the plight of the episcopate, pleading that new provision be made to prevent the underaged, the ignorant, and the unworthy from being made bishops and to prevent bishops from involving themselves too deeply in secular affairs. Provision should also be made to cut down the evil of nonresidence, to prevent corruption and the imposition of unfair financial burdens on the faithful, and to improve episcopal administration in general. The multiplication of saints, feast days, images, and devotional novelties should be eschewed; liturgical reforms should be instituted. Finally, an attempt should be made to prevent the collection of any fees for the administration of orders or of the sacraments in general, or of burials, or for the performance of anything pertaining to spirituals.

In the fourth and fifth sections d'Ailly addresses himself to the need for reform among both the monastic clergy and the secular clergy. There are too many monastic orders and religious communities—far more than the available revenues can support or the existing need justify. The activities and numbers of the mendicants should be curtailed and monastic exemptions from episcopal jurisdiction eliminated. It is clear that his sympathies lie with the secular clergy, but here again reform is needed. Widespread clerical ignorance and a deplorable system of promotions have to be remedied—the former by providing theological libraries and teaching in theology at the cathedral churches, the latter by the appointment to major positions of the learned rather than the well-connected and of theologians rather than lawyers.

The final section concerns the need for reformation in the lives of the laity, especially of the princes. It consists of a wholly traditional lecture on the duty of Christian princes to set a good example to their subjects; to eschew immorality, blasphemy, the practice of the magic arts, and heresy; to attack the Saracens and to curb the activities of the Jews; to rule their people, in effect, on behalf of Christ and not merely for their own selfish ends.

Unquestionably it was a comprehensive and largely practical program of reform, but its anticipation, in its detail, of so many of the disciplinary decrees of Trent is indicative less of d'Ailly's prescience than of the persistent nature of the problems plaguing the late-medieval church. Few of his specific proposals for reform were entirely new; many echo the clichés of the reforming literature back to the

Council of Vienne and beyond; some reflect also his own personal experiences as bishop of Cambrai. In that capacity he had worked hard to promote the moral reform of his clergy, both regular and secular, conducting visitations of the religious houses—as, for example, the Cistercian abbey of Epinlieu in 1401, encouraging the activities of the Brethren of the Common Life and renewing the privileges and statutes of the Windesheim Congregation. Like Groote before him, he had battled against clerical incontinence, not hesitating to invoke against prevaricators the canonical penalties of suspension and excommunication. But his concern reached beyond the mere restoration of clerical discipline. He made full use of the instrumentality of the diocesan synod to rally the support and kindle the enthusiasm of his clergy, attacking, in the discourses delivered at those synods, not only simony but also the building of new churches, the canonizing of new saints, the solemnizing of new feasts. He revised the version of the breviary in use in his diocese, strove to improve the level of education among his clergy, and, at Cambrai itself, built a library and saw to it that it was furnished with appropriate books.[70]

In all of this activity, despite his public prominence and the multiplicity of his writings, it is surprisingly difficult to get a sense of the man himself, and the biographical picture one constructs is marred by an irremediable externality. But we are not altogether without clues to the spirit that animated his reforming activities. And those clues point—unexpectedly perhaps, but certainly with no little insistence—to the centrality of his preoccupation with ecclesiastical authority. Even his early theological writings make unambiguously clear how very great an emphasis he was prone to place, in matters religious as well as moral and legal, on will, power, and authority. At its very deepest, according to him, the roots of obligation are engaged, not in the persuasive grounds of reason, but in the executive prescriptions of the will. It is not from the rational ends it serves, however compelling they may be, that every law, divine and natural no less than human, derives its obligating force, but rather from the

---

70. For his activities as Bishop of Cambrai, see Salembier, *Cardinal*, pp. 114–46.

command or prohibition of the competent superior authority.[71] Nor is this emphasis merely a matter of theoretical affirmation. His nervousness about the unilateral French withdrawal of obedience from Benedict XIII in 1398, his subsequent efforts to promote a restoration of obedience at least in the essential spirituals, if not in the accidental *temporalia* that had come to be attached thereto, and his later opposition in 1406 to a renewed withdrawal may all be taken to reflect a genuine worry about the illegitimate intrusion of the temporal power at the expense of the competent ecclesiastical authority. A similar concern is evident in his willingness to accept what was for him the philosophically problematic doctrine of transubstantiation because the magisterial authority of the church stood behind it. The conviction that underlay such worries and concerns, moreover, makes itself felt in the calm confidence with which he was willing, as bishop of Cambrai (and having satisfied himself by appropriate investigatory procedures), to confirm the authenticity of two characteristically late-medieval miracles of the bleeding-host variety, around which popular cults had grown in his diocese, and even to accord indulgences to those who participated in those cults.[72] It is the same conviction that speaks also in the decisive firmness of his manner toward Hus, a man, after all, who shared so many of his own reforming instincts.

What moved d'Ailly as a reformer, then, in some ways most deeply and certainly most consistently, was an almost instinctive concern to protect the integrity of ecclesiastical authority—from the popes and papal absolutists who had long abused or distorted it, from the princes and clerics who continued to bend or flout it, from the heretics who

71. See Oakley, *Political Thought of Pierre d'Ailly*, pp. 172–97.
72. For these cults, the first of which was connected with the church of St. Gudule in Brussels and the second with the chapel of Bois-Seigneur Isaac near Nivelles in Brabant, see Salembier, *Cardinal*, pp. 139–40. In the latter case, a corporal had been stained, allegedly by the blood flowing from the host, and, having kept that corporal for two years and subjected it to various tests, d'Ailly confirmed the authenticity of the miracle in the following terms: "Nous doncque prenant esgard que les choses susdictes soient vrayes, et inclinans à tells supplications par l'authorité apostolique et à nous en cest endroit concédée, confirmons, approuvons et ratifions ledit corporal avec l'hostie et sang et toute autre chose contenue en iceulx et dépendants d'iceulx commes choses sacrées, sainctes et vrayes" (in Vinchant, ed., 6:133).

stubbornly and frontally challenged it. This being so, and given that reticence about himself that has long frustrated his biographers, it may be suggested that the words Peter of Mladaňovice attributes to him while addressing John Hus at a critical moment in the latter's trial are more revelatory of the spirit that moved the man than are any of his wholly conventional prayers that have come down to us. To d'Ailly the issue at stake appears to have been so totally clear that, even on the most favorable and sympathetic of estimates, Hus's obdurate scruples about submitting himself unreservedly to the decision of the council must have smacked of an unhealthy and dangerous scrupulosity. Hence the sternness with which he urged Hus, even as he had successfully urged William of Hildernissen before him, to abjure all the errors that were being attributed to him, even if he could not himself recognize them as his own: "Master John! behold," he said,

> two ways are placed before you, of which choose one! Either you throw yourself entirely or totally on the grace and into the hands of the Council, that whatever the council shall dictate to you therewith you shall be content. And the Council . . . will deal kindly and humanely with you. Or if you still wish to hold and defend some articles of the fore mentioned, and if you desire still another hearing, it shall be granted you. But consider that there are here great and enlightened men— doctors and masters—who have such strong reasons against your articles, that it is to be feared lest you become involved in greater errors if you wish to defend and hold those articles. I counsel you—I do not speak as judge.[73]

73. Mladaňovice, *Relatio*, ed. Novotný, 8:103; trans. from Spinka, *Constance*, pp. 213–14.

EPILOGUE

Before its erosion by the cautious qualifications and reservations evinced so often in the scholarship of the past few decades, the traditionally firm historical profile of religious and ecclesiastical life in the late-medieval centuries was distinguished by three commanding features. In the first place, it betrayed the conviction that in the long history of the Christian church the fourteenth and fifteenth centuries were characterized by a degree of ecclesiastical decadence and religious decline so grievous as to be destined finally to alienate from the traditional pattern of churchly life the most truly committed and the most deeply devout. In the second place, it presupposed the congruent assumption that in certain critical respects the period was in sharp discontinuity with the great age of medieval religion preceding; the degradation of Boniface VIII at Anagni marked a critical turning point in the history of the papacy, signaling the incipient collapse of that whole structure of ecclesiastical governance within the framework of which medieval Catholicism had contrived to flourish. In the third place, it reflected the countervailing recognition, in the seemingly disparate phenomena that we identify as heresy, mysticism, conciliarism, humanism, and so on, of the redemptive stirrings of interrelated movements of reform. Those movements drew their impulse from the common wellsprings of religious vitality, pointed in the direction of the Protestant Reformation, and were destined at the end of the period to converge upon that great upheaval.

Nevertheless, whatever troubles beset the church of the fourteenth and fifteenth centuries (and like those in its day that beset society at large, they were both multiple and various), we have found the doomed sense of continuous and accelerating decline—however revelatory of the mood of ecclesiastics and intellectuals—to be an inadequate index to the varied, fluctuating, but frequently vital realities of late-medieval religious life. We have found, moreover, no less in its weaknesses than in its strengths, that the continuities binding the late-medieval church with that of the earlier period are a good deal more insistent than they have been thought to be. Similarly, the alleged links binding the disparate stirrings of "reform," both with one another and with the later churches of the Reformation, are a good deal more problematic than the traditional picture suggests. Perhaps more worrisome than the inadequacies of the traditional view, given the necessarily rich complexity of whatever picture one attempts to construct in its place, is the continuing, unavoidable problem of relating that picture to the revolutionary religious upheavals of the following century: not, admittedly, the type of problem susceptible of solution in a few concluding comments; but neither is it one altogether to be sidestepped.

What, then, is to be said? Few, I assume, would want to question the presence in varying degrees during the fourteenth and fifteenth centuries of most of the components out of which kings, princes, popes, and reformers (the magisterial reformers, their radical Protestant critics, and their Catholic opponents alike) were to construct over the course of the sixteenth and seventeenth centuries the new religious order of the post-Reformation era. Nor would many want to contest the claim that much about that new order could be anticipated by a scrutiny of late-medieval religious and ecclesiastical life—from the apocalypticism and Donatism of the radical sects, for example, to the dominant role in religious life that national, territorial, and civic governments played in Catholic as well as Protestant Europe; or from the profoundly Augustinian preoccupation with the problems of free will, grace, and predestination to the sharpened focus on the nature, form, and status of divine revelation; or from the type of disciplinary reforms that Trent finally effected to the intensely individualistic nature of the forms of piety prevalent across so much of the Christian world, Protestant and Catholic alike. And so on—to construct a more elaborate and exhaustive list would surely pose few major difficulties.

But little in all of this suggests the inevitability of the process whereby the transition was made to the new religious order, and much, indeed, occasions surprise about the exact configuration assumed by that order. Not even the characteristically late-medieval tension between the deepening piety, enhanced religious expectations, and intense "churchliness" of the populace on the one hand[1] and the increasing calcification of the ecclesiastical establishment on the other, with its inability to respond more than fitfully to the religious aspirations of the day—not even that tension suggests that there was anything *necessary* about the sort of explosive breakthrough that Luther actually succeeded in sponsoring.[2] No good grounds exist for assuming that however grave that tension, it could not merely have endured. Nor are there firm grounds for supposing that the oppressive anxieties it generated in the hearts precisely of the most devout might not in the long run have been dissipated through the gradual transformation of their thinking, perhaps by religious ideals of the Erasmian type, or even by that late-medieval species of Augustinianism that Johann von Staupitz personified so influentially for Luther, but which pointed also (and, perhaps, rather?) in the direction of the theology of grace espoused in the Tridentine era by the cardinals Contarini and Seripando.[3]

What that tension may help account for, admittedly, is the warmth and enthusiasm of the initial reception given to Luther's views, especially among the lower orders in the cities of northern Germany and among those of humanist sympathies. But it throws little light upon the religious formation of Luther himself, who, like his closest followers, was a good deal more than a mere ecclesiastical critic, or upon the roots of those profound and novel views that he propagated with such conviction, passion, and force. Nor does it necessarily throw that

1. See especially Moeller, *Spätmittelalter*, pp. 32–44.
2. Moeller, "Problems of Reformation Research," in *Imperial Cities*, p. 12.
3. On this point and the contribution of "the Augustinian intellectual nexus" to the development of Luther's theology, see the contributions of Heiko A. Oberman and Lewis W. Spitz to Oberman, ed., *Luther and the Dawn of the Modern Era*, pp. 40–116.

much more light on the commitment of those who rallied to his standard. Of seventeenth-century England Keith Thomas has said: "This was no simple unified primitive world, but a dynamic and indefinitely various society, where social and intellectual change had long been at work and where currents were moving in many different directions."[4] Of Luther's Germany it would be possible without impropriety to say something very similar, and recognition of that fact is prone understandably to promote a certain sobriety in one's generalizing. One can set aside those territorial princes and prince-bishops whose enthusiasm for the Lutheran cause would appear to have been proportional to the promise they saw in it for enhanced control over their territorial churches or for the profitable secularization of ecclesiastical lands. But even if one brackets such "political" conversions, a close scrutiny of groups that responded with immediate enthusiasm to Luther's views sometimes reveals how much they simply misconstrued them. More frequently, it reveals how greatly their response was limited to the negative or polemical dimensions of his message, to his bold attack on some prominent features of the old ecclesiastical order or on such traditional religious practices as the traffic in indulgences, and failed to extend to the rich and in some respects profoundly original commitments motivating that attack.[5] Thus, if the doomed and violent effort of the imperial knights led by Ulrich von Hutten and others to recover their former influence in German society was in some measure fueled by an appropriation of Lutheran ideas, it was indeed a very confused appropriation. And the gross misconstruction of his doctrine of Christian liberty by the peasantry during the catastrophic revolt of 1524–25 was a source of great anguish to Luther himself. More startling, however, is the degree to which even those moved more directly by clearly religious concerns missed the radical nature of his message. Thus, the annalist of

---

4. Thomas, *Religion and the Decline of Magic*, p. 5.
5. Thus Moeller, "Imperial Cities and the Reformation," in *Imperial Cities*, p. 74, comments that "in the eyes of the townspeople [who welcomed his views] the parallelism between Luther's antipathy for the Roman church and their own must have seemed clearer and more important than the difference in the foundations on which they built their arguments."

the Doesburg house of the Brethren of the Common Life, in reporting the impact of Lutheran ideas, makes no mention at all of the central doctrine of justification by faith. Indeed, he gives the impression that the main impact of the doctrine of Christian liberty on the Brethren had been to encourage the younger Brothers to refuse the complete shaving of the head customary in the Congregation and to hold out instead for a less thoroughgoing form of tonsure![6] Even more striking, and given Moeller's bold formulation ("No humanism, no Reformation"),[7] a good deal more fateful, is the "constructive misunderstanding," which led the humanists during the critical early years to give Luther their enthusiastic and clamorous support. Thus they took him to be one of themselves, simply a more passionate and providentially effective exponent of their own Erasmian ideals—to such a degree that the young Martin Bucer actually expressed surprise that the Reformer's disputation theses at Heidelberg in 1518 denied the free will of man.

As time went on, of course, Erasmus and many other older humanists came to perceive the gulf that divided Luther from them and to realize (perhaps to their surprise) that their own sympathies bound them rather to the medieval Catholic past than to any future shaped in accordance with his religious vision. Even at the outset, however, not all of his supporters had misunderstood him. And even among those who had, many were younger humanists whose lives were transformed by their encounter with his teaching of a gracious God, who were moved by a process of conversion to embrace his teaching of justification by faith, and from whose ranks were subsequently to be drawn so many of the intellectual leaders of the Reformation. For the appeal of Luther's gospel, and the anguished breakthrough by which he himself had attained to it, were both grounded in that great hunger for the divine that is one of the most striking features of late-

6. Post, *Modern Devotion*, pp. 586–89.
7. For this and much of what follows, see his "German Humanists and the Beginnings of the Reformation," in Moeller, *Imperial Cities*, pp. 19–38 at 36. Cf. his remark (p. 29): "It was a constructive misunderstanding that made the humanists into supporters of Luther, and it is not too much to say that this misconception raised the Reformation from the concern of one man to a revolution in world history."

medieval religious life. Both reflected deeply felt religious needs, and
the one is no more to be explained away than the other.[8] But, because
they are not to be explained away or ultimately "explained" at all, historians must still struggle to shed some light on their origins or antecedents. No easy task, of course. The ending of the fifteenth century, however, coincided with something of a high point in medieval
piety and "churchliness," and Luther was in his critical years himself
shaped by one of the most rigorous of late-medieval monastic reforms.
If, then, we are really to penetrate to any internal understanding of the
man and of the followers who best understood him, we would do well
to seek the wellsprings of their religiosity less in any reaction to the
more obvious shortcomings of the medieval Catholic system at its
weakest and most decadent than in the profound inadequacies they
sensed in it even at its strongest and most pure.[9] Luther's strength, it
has been argued,[10] and the very heart of his appeal, lay in the fact that
he succeeded in giving new, "nonmedieval" answers to the essentially
medieval religious questions that still troubled him and so many
others in his day. More than any of the traditional solutions proposed
by the late-medieval church his novel answers possessed, at least for
some, a compelling measure of authenticity, the power to convince,
and the force to assuage the persistent yearnings of the religious spirit.
At one level, but arguably at the deepest level of all, the matter may
have been no more complex than that.

8. See the comments of Ozment, *Reformation in the Cities*, pp. 43–44; Moeller,
"Probleme des kirchlichen Lebens in Deutschland vor der Reformation," in Jedin et
al., *Probleme der Kirchenspaltung*, pp. 26–30. Cf. for the origins of the Reformation in
France the similar comments of Febvre, especially p. 41.
9. Note, in this connection, their attack on sacramental confession. Having earlier
expressed some reservations about Ozment's argument in *Reformation in the Cities*, I
must here acknowledge its force in relation to Luther's closest followers.
10. Following here Moeller, "Probleme des kirchlichen Lebens in Deutschland vor
der Reformation," in Jedin et al., pp. 29–30.

BIBLIOGRAPHY

I. Bibliographies

Extensive bibliographical data may be found in the following works: G. Mollat, *Les Papes d'Avignon*, 9th ed., Paris, 1949; E. Delaruelle, E.-R. Labande, and Paul Ourliac, *L'Eglise au temps du Grand Schisme et de la crise conciliaire*, 2 vols., Paris, 1962–64; Roger Aubenas and Robert Ricard, *L'Eglise et la Renaissance (1449–1517)*, Paris, 1951 (the two last are vols. 14 and 15, respectively, of *Histoire de l'Eglise*, ed. A. Fliche and V. Martin, 26 vols., Paris, 1934–; Hans-Georg Beck et al., *From the High Middle Ages to the Eve of the Reformation*, trans. Anselm Briggs, Freiburg and Montreal, 1970 (vol. 4 of *Handbook of Church History*, ed. Hubert Jedin and John Dolan, 7 vols., Freiburg and Montreal, 1965–). A good shorter bibliography appears in Francis Rapp, *L'Eglise et la vie religieuse en Occident à la fin du Moyen Age*, Paris 1971. Mention should also be made of some useful historiographic and bibliographic essays and listings on particular topics: John W. O'Malley, "Recent Studies in Church History," *Catholic Historical Review* 55 (1969–70):394–437; William J. Courtenay, "Nominalism and Late Medieval Thought: A Bibliographical Essay," *Theological Studies* 33, no. 4 (1972):716–34; W. D. J. Cargill Thompson, "Seeing the Reformation in Medieval Perspective," *Journal of Ecclesiastical History* 25, no. 3 (1974):297–308; Lawrence G. Duggan, "The Unresponsiveness of the Late Medieval Church: A Reconsideration," *The Sixteenth-Century Journal* 9, no. 1 (1978):3–26; Herbert Grundmann, *Bibliographie zur Ketzergeschichte des Mittelalters (1900–1966)*, Rome, 1967; Gordon Leff, *Heresy in the Later Middle Ages*, 2 vols., Manchester, 1967, 2:739–77. More recent works are listed in the comprehensive classified bibliographies of new works published on a continuing basis in *Revue d'histoire ecclésiastique*.

II. General Accounts.

The standard general accounts are those by Mollat, by Delaruelle et al., and by Aubenas and Ricard cited above. Though of uneven coverage, *Handbook of Church History*, ed. Jedin and Dolan, vol. 4, is also useful. Two able shorter accounts are Rapp, *L'Eglise et la vie religieuse en Occident* (cited above), and Bernd Moeller, *Spätmittelalter*, vol. 2, installment H (pt. 1), of *Die Kirche in ihrer Geschichte: Ein Handbuch*, ed. Kurt Schmidt and Ernst Wolf, Göttingen, 1966. The last, a brief sketch, is bibliographically very rich. Two older general accounts in English are not fully adequate: A. C. Flick, *The Decline of the Medieval Church*, 2 vols., London, 1930; and L. Elliott-Binns, *The Decline and Fall of the Medieval Papacy*, London, 1934.

III. Works Cited

Ailly, Pierre d'. *Quaestiones super I, III, et IV Sententiarum.* Lyons: Nicolaus Wolff, 1500.

————. *Tractatus et Sermones*, Strassburg, 1491.

————. *Imago mundi*. Ed. Edmond Buron. 2 vols. Paris, 1930.

Alberigo, Joseph, et al. *Conciliorum Oecumenicorum Decreta.* Basel and Rome, 1962.

Ali, A. Y., ed. *The Holy Qur'an: Text, Translation, and Commentary.* Washington, D.C., 1946.

Allen, P. S., ed. *Opus epistolarum des. Erasmi Roterodami.* 12 vols. Oxford, 1906–58.

———— and Allen, H. M., eds. *Letters of Richard Fox, 1486–1527.* Oxford, 1929.

Argentré, C. du Plessis d'. *Collectio judiciorum de novis erroribus.* 3 vols. Paris, 1728–36.

Arquillière, H. X. *Le plus ancien traité de l'église: Jacques de Viterbo, De regimine christiano (1301–1302).* Paris, 1926.

Aston, M. E. "Lollards and the Reformation: Survival or Revival." *History* 49, no. 2 (1964): 149–70.

Aubenas, Roger, and Ricard, Robert. *L'Eglise et la Renaissance (1449–1517).* Vol. 15 of *Histoire de l'Eglise*, ed. A. Fliche and V. Martin. Paris, 1951.

Bainton, Roland. *Here I Stand: A Life of Martin Luther.* Nashville, 1950.

Baldwin, Marshall W. *The Mediaeval Church.* Ithaca, N.Y., 1953.

Balić, C., ed. *De scriptura et traditione.* Rome, 1963.

Baluzius, Stephanus. *Vitae Paparum Avenionensium.* New ed. Ed. G. Mollat. 4 vols. Paris, 1914.

Baluzius, S[tephanus], and Mansi, J. D. *Miscellanea.* 4 vols. Lucca, 1761–64.

Baronius, C.; Raynaldus, O.; and Laderchius, J. *Annales ecclesiastici*. 37 vols. Paris, 1864–83.

Barraclough, Geoffrey. *Papal Provisions*. Oxford, 1935.

————, ed. *Mediaeval Germany, 911–1250: Essays by German Historians*. 2 vols. Oxford, 1948.

Bataillon, Marcel. *Erasmo y España: Estudios sobre la historia espirituel del siglo xvi*. Trans. Antonio Altorre. Mexico City and Buenos Aires, 1966.

————. "De Savonarole à Louis de Grenade." *Revue de Littérature Comparée* 16 (1936): 23–39.

Bäumer, Remigius. *Nachwirkungen des konziliaren Gedankens in der Theologie und Kanonistik des frühen 16. Jahrhunderts*. Münster, 1971.

————. "Um die Anfänge der päpstlichen Unfehlbarkeitslehre." *Theologische Revue* 69 (1973): 441–50.

————. "Antwort an Tierney." *Theologische Revue* 70 (1974): 193–94.

————, ed. *Von Konstanz nach Trient: Beiträge zur Geschichte der Kirche von der Reformkonzilien bis zum Tridentinum*. Munich, Paderborn, and Vienna, 1972.

Beck, Henry G. J. "William of Hundleby's Account of the Anagni Outrage." *Catholic Historical Review* 32, no. 2 (1946–47): 190–220.

Bennett, H. S. *The Pastons and their England*. Cambridge, 1922.

Bennett, R. F., and Offler, H. S., eds. *Guillelmi de Ockham: Opera Politica*. 3 vols. Manchester, 1939–63.

Betts, R. R. *Essays in Czech History*. London, 1969.

Binz, L. *Vie religieuse et réforme ecclésiastique dans le diocèse de Genève pendant le Grand Schisme*. Geneva, 1973.

Blakney, R. B. *Meister Eckhart: A Modern Translation*. New York and London, 1941.

Bliemetzrieder, Franz. *Literarische Polemik zur Beginn des grossen abendländischen Schismas*. Vienna and Leipzig, 1910.

Bloomfield, Morton W. "Joachim of Flora: A Critical Survey of his Canon, Teachings, Sources, Biography and Influence." *Traditio* 13 (1957): 248–311.

Bonaventure, St. *Doctoris Seraphici S. Bonaventurae: Opera omnia*. 10 vols. Quaracchi, 1882–1902.

Borgnet, Auguste, ed. *B. Alberti Magni: Opera omnia*. 38 vols. Paris, 1890–99.

Bouyer, Louis. *The Spirit and Forms of Protestantism*. Trans. A. V. Littledale. Cleveland and New York, 1964.

Boyle, L. E. "The *Oculus Sacerdotium* and Some Other Works of William of Pagula." *Transactions of the Royal Historical Society*, 5th ser., 5 (1955): 81–110.

Bradwardine, Thomas. *De causa dei contra Pelagium*. London, 1619.

Brandmüller, Walter. *Das Konzil von Pavia-Siena: 1423–1424*. 2 vols. Münster, 1968–73.

Brettle, P. Sigismund. *San Vincente Ferrer und sein literarischer Nachlass*. Münster, 1924.

Brewer, John S., et al., eds. *Letters and Papers Foreign and Domestic of the Reign of Henry VIII*. 22 vols. London, 1862–1932.

Burckhardt, Jacob. *The Civilization of the Renaissance in Italy*. Trans. S. G. C. Middlemore, 2 vols. New York, 1958.

Capes, W. W. *The English Church in the Fourteenth and Fifteenth Centuries*. London, 1900.

Chaucer, Geoffrey. *The Canterbury Tales*. Oxford and London, 1906.

Clasen, Claus-Peter. "Medieval Heresies in the Reformation." *Church History* 32, no. 4 (1963): 392–414.

Cohen, Kathleen. *Metamorphosis of a Death Symbol: The Transi Tomb in the Late Middle Ages and the Renaissance*. Berkeley, Los Angeles, and London, 1973.

Cohn, Norman, *The Pursuit of the Millennium*. Rev. ed. London, 1970.

Colledge, Eric, trans. *Blessed Jan van Ruysbroeck: The Spiritual Espousals*. London, 1952.

Combes, André. *Essai sur la critique de Ruysbroeck par Gerson*. 3 vols. Paris, 1945–59.

————, ed. *Joannis Charlerii de Gerson: De mystica theologia*. Luccani, 1958.

Constable, Giles. "Twelfth-Century Spirituality and the Late Middle Ages." Ed. O. B. Hardison, Jr. *Proceedings of the Southeastern Institute of Medieval and Renaissance Studies*, 5th Session, 5 (1971): 27–60.

Courtenay, William J. "Covenant and Causality in Pierre d'Ailly." *Speculum* 46, no. 1 (1971): 94–119.

Coville, A., ed. *Le Traité de la ruine de l'église de Nicolas de Clamanges*. Paris, 1936.

Cox, John E., ed. *The Works of Thomas Cranmer*. 2 vols. Cambridge, 1844–46.

Crowder, C. M. D. *Unity, Heresy, and Reform: 1378–1460*. London, 1977.

CSEL. Corpus Scriptorum Ecclesiasticorum Latinorum. 85 vols. Vienna, 1866–1974.

D'Ailly, Pierre. See Ailly, Pierre d'.

Delaruelle, E.; Labande, E.-R.; and Ourliac, P. *L'Eglise au temps du Grand Schisme et de la crise conciliaire: 1379–1449*. 2 vols. Paris, 1962–64.

Denifle, Heinrich. *Luther und Luthertum in der ersten Entwicklung*. 2 vols. 2d ed. Mainz, 1904–1909.

Denzinger, H. *Enchiridion Symbolorum definitionum et declarationum de rebus fidei et morum*. Ed. A. Schönmetzer. 33d ed. Rome, 1965.

Dickens, A. G. *The English Reformation*. London, 1964.

Dix, Dom Gregory. *The Shape of the Liturgy*. 2d ed. London, 1960.

Doebner, Richard, ed. *Annalen und Akten der Brüder des gemeinsamen Lebens im Lüchtenhofe zu Hildesheim*. Hanover and Leipzig, 1903.

Dondaine, A. "Le Manuel de l'inquisiteur (1230–1330)." *Archivum Fratrum Praedicatorum* 17 (1947): 85–194.

Doussinague, José M. *Fernando el Católico y el cisma de Pisa*. Madrid, 1946.

Duggan, Lawrence G. "The Unresponsiveness of the Late Medieval Church: A Reconsideration." *The Sixteenth-Century Journal* 9, no. 1 (1978): 3–26.

Dupin, Louis Ellies, ed. *Joannis Gersonii: Opera omnia*. 5 vols. Antwerp, 1706.

Eck, John. *In primum librum sententiarum annotatiunculae D. Johanne Eckio praelectore*. Ed. Walter L. Moore, Jr. Leiden, 1976.

Ehler, S. Z., and Morrall, J. B., eds. *Church and State through the Centuries*. London, 1954.

Fages, P. H. O. *Histoire de Saint Vincent Ferrier*. 4 vols. New ed. Louvain, 1901–5.

————, ed. *Oeuvres de Saint Vincent Ferrier*. 2 vols. Paris, 1909.

Favier, Jean. *Les Finances pontificales à l'époque du Grand Schisme d'Occident*. Paris, 1966.

Febvre, Lucien. "Une question mal posée: Les origines de la réforme française et le problème des causes de la réforme." *Revue historique* 161 (1929): 1–73.

Ferrer, Vincent. See Fages, P. H. O., ed.

Fink, K. A. "Zur Beurteilung des grossen abendländischen Schismas." *Zeitschrift für Kirchengeschichte* 73 (1962): 335–43.

Finke, Heinrich. *Acta Concilii Constanciensis*. 4 vols. Münster, 1896–1928.

Franzen, A. "The Council of Constance: Present State of the Problem." *Concilium* 7 (1965): 29–68.

———— and Müller, W. *Das Konzil von Konstanz: Beitrage zu seiner Geschichte und Theolgie*. Freiburg, 1964.

Fredericq, P. *Corpus documentorum inquisitionis haereticae neerlandicae*. 5 vols. Ghent, 1889–1902.

Friedberg, E., ed. *Corpus juris canonici*. 2 vols. Leipzig, 1879–81.

Gandillac, M. Patronnier de. "Usage et valeur des arguments probables chez Pierre d'Ailly." *Archives d'histoire doctrinale et littéraire du Moyen Age* 8 (1933): 43–91.

Geiselmann, Josef. "Das Missverständnis über das Verhältnis von Schrift und Tradition in der katholischen Theologie." *Una Sancta* 11 (September 1956): 131–50.

Gerson, Jean le Charlier de. See Combes, André, ed.; Dupin, Louis Ellies, ed.

Gilson, Etienne. *The Spirit of Mediaeval Philosophy*. Trans. A. H. C. Downes. New York, 1936.

————. *History of Christian Philosophy in the Middle Ages*. New York, 1955.

Goldast, Melchior, ed. *Monarchiae S. romani imperii*. 3 vols. Frankfurt, 1614.

Gonnet, Jean, and Molnár, Amadeo. *Les Vaudois au Moyen Age*. Turin, 1974.

Gorce, M. M. *St. Vincent Ferrier: 1350–1419*. Paris, 1935.

Grabmann, M. *Die Geschichte der katholischen Theologie seit dem Ausgang der Väterzeit*. Freiburg, 1933.

Gray, Hanna H. "Renaissance Humanism: The Pursuit of Eloquence." *Journal of the History of Ideas* 24, no. 4 (1963): 497–514.

Grundmann, Herbert. *Religiöse Bewegungen im Mittelalter*. 2d ed. Hildesheim, 1961.

————. "Ketzerverhöre des Spätmittelalters als quellenkritisches Problem." *Deutsches Archiv für Erforschung des Mittelalters* 21 (1965): 519–71.

Guarnieri, Romana. "Il movimento del libero spirito: Testi e documenti." *Archivio italiano per la storia della pietà* 4 (1965): 351–707.

Guasti, Cesare, ed. *Ser Lapo Mazzei: Lettere di un notario a un mercante del seculo XIV con altre lettere e documenti*. 2 vols. Florence, 1880.

Guillemain, B. *La Politique bénéficiale du pape Benoît XII*. Paris, 1952.

————. "Punti di vista sul Papato avignonese." *Archivio storico italiano*, no. 111 (1953), 181–206.

————. *La Cour pontificale d'Avignon: 1309–1376*. Paris, 1962.

Haller, J. *Papsttum und Kirchenreform*. Berlin, 1903.

Hay, Denys. *The Church in Italy in the Fifteenth Century*. Cambridge, 1977.

Heath, Peter. *English Parish Clergy on the Eve of the Reformation*. London, 1969.

Hefele, C. J., and Hergenröther, J. *Conciliengeschichte*. 9 vols. Freiburg, 1855–90.

Hegler, Alfred. *Geist und Schrift bei Sebastien Franck: Eine Studie zur Geschichte des Spiritualismus in der Reformationszeit*. Freiburg, 1892.

Hendrix, Scott H. "In Quest of the *Vera Ecclesia*: The Crises of Late Medieval Ecclesiology." *Viator* 7 (1976): 347–78.

Herlihy, David. *Women in Medieval Society*. Houston, 1971.

Hillers, Delbert R. *Covenant: The History of a Biblical Idea*. Baltimore, 1969.

Hodgson, Phyllis, ed. *The Cloud of Unknowing and the Book of Privy Counselling*. Early English Text Society, no. 218. London, 1944.

————, ed. *Deonise Hid Divinite and Other Treatises on Contemplative Prayer*. Early English Text Society, no. 231. Oxford, 1955.

Holborn, Hajo, ed. *Desiderius Erasmus Roterodamus: Ausgewählte Werke*. Munich, 1933.

Holcot, Robert. *Super libros Sapientiae*. Hagenau, 1494.

Hostiensis (Henricus de Segusia). *Lectura in quinque decretalium Gregorianarum libros*. Paris, 1512.

Howden, Marjorie Peers, ed. *The Register of Richard Fox, Lord Bishop of Durham: 1494–1501*. London, 1932.

Huizinga, Johann. *The Waning of the Middle Ages*. Trans. F. Hopman. London, 1924.

————. *Erasmus and the Age of Reformation*. Trans. F. Hopman. New York and Evanston, 1957.

Hunt, William. *The English Church in the Middle Ages*. London, 1885.

Hurley, Michael. "'Scriptura Sola': Wyclif and His Critics." *Traditio* 16 (1960): 275–352.

Hus, John. See Thomson, S. Harrison, ed.

Iserloh, Erwin. *Gnade und Eucharistie in der philosophischen Theologie des Wilhelm von Ockham*. Wiesbaden, 1956.

————. "Der Wert der Messe in der Diskussion der Theologen vom Mittelalter bis zum 16. Jahrhundert." *Zeitschrift für katholische Theologie* 83 (1961): 44–79.

Jacob, E. F. *Essays in the Conciliar Epoch*. 3d ed. Manchester, 1963.

————, ed. *Italian Renaissance Studies*. London, 1960.

Jankofsky, Klaus. "A View into the Grave: *A Disputacion betwyx the Body and Wormes* in British Museum MS Add. 37069." *Taius* 1 (October 1974): 137–59.

Janssen, Johannes. *Geschichte des deutschen Volkes seit dem Ausgang des Mittelalters*. 8 vols. Freiburg, 1879–94.

Jedin, Hubert. *Geschichte des Konzils von Trient*. 2 vols. Freiburg, 1949–57. Trans. Ernest Graf, *A History of the Council of Trent*. 2 vols. London, 1957–61.

———— et al. *Probleme der Kirchenspaltung im 16. Jahrhundert*. Regensburg, 1970.

———— and Dolan, John, eds. *Handbook of Church History*. 7 vols. Freiburg and Montreal, 1965–.

Jungmann, Joseph A. *The Mass of the Roman Rite: Its Origin and Development*. Trans. F. A. Brunner. 2 vols. New York, 1950.

Kaminsky, Howard. *A History of the Hussite Revolution*. Berkeley and Los Angeles, 1967.

————. "The Politics of France's Subtraction of Obedience from Pope Benedict XIII, 27 July, 1398." *Proceedings of the American Philosophical Society* 115, no. 5 (1971): 366–97.

Kantorowicz, Ernst H. *The King's Two Bodies: A Study in Mediaeval Political Theology*. Princeton, 1957.

Kettel, Gerhard, and Friedrich, Gerhard, eds. *Theological Dictionary of the*

New Testament. Trans. Geoffrey W. Bromiley. 9 vols. Grand Rapids, Mich., 1964–74.

Kierkegaard, Søren. *Fear and Trembling and the Sickness unto Death*. Trans. Walter Lowrie. Princeton, 1968.

Kirchberger, C. *The Mirror of Simple Souls*. London and New York, 1927.

Klauser, Theodor. *A Short History of the Western Liturgy*. Trans. John Halliburton. London, 1969.

Knecht, R. J. "The Concordat of 1516: A Reassessment." *Birmingham University Historical Journal* 9 (1963): 16–32.

Knowles, Dom David. *The Religious Orders in England*. 3 vols. Cambridge, 1950–59.

————. *The English Mystical Tradition*. New York, 1961.

————. "Denifle and Ehrle." *History* 54, no. 1 (1969): 1–12.

————, and Obolensky, Dmitri. *The Christian Centuries: A New History of the Catholic Church*. Vol. 2, *The Middle Ages*. London and New York, 1968.

Küng, Hans. *The Church*. Trans. Raymond and Rosaleen Ockenden. New York, 1968.

Ladner, Gerhard B. "Aspects of Medieval Thought on Church and State." *Review of Politics* 9 (1947): 403–22.

Lagarde, Georges de. *La Naissance de l'esprit laïque au déclin du Moyen Age*. New ed. 5 vols. Paris and Louvain, 1956–70.

Lambert, Malcolm. *Medieval Heresy: Popular Movements from Bogomil to Hus*. New York, 1976.

Larkin, Emmett. "The Devotional Revolution in Ireland, 1850–75." *American Historical Review* 77, no. 3 (1972): 625–52.

Larson, Gerald J. "Mystical Man in India." *Journal for the Scientific Study of Religion* 12, no. 1 (1973): 1–16.

Leclercq, Jean; Vandenbroucke, François; and Bouyer, Louis. *La Spiritualité du Moyen Age*. Paris, 1961.

Leff, Gordon. *Bradwardine and the Pelagians: A Study of His "De causa dei" and Its Opponents*. Cambridge, 1957.

————. *Heresy in the Later Middle Ages: The Relation of Heterodoxy to Dissent c. 1250–c. 1450*. 2 vols. Manchester, 1967.

————. *William of Ockham: The Metamorphosis of Scholastic Discourse*. Manchester, 1975.

Léonard, Emile G. *Histoire générale du Protestantisme*. 3 vols. Paris, 1961.

Lerner, Robert E. *The Heresy of the Free Spirit in the Later Middle Ages*. Berkeley, Los Angeles, and London, 1972.

————. "The Image of Mixed Liquids in Late Medieval Mystical Thought." *Church History* 40 (December 1971): 397–411.

Lortz, Josef. *How the Reformation Came.* Trans. Otto M. Knab. New York, 1964.

————. *The Reformation in Germany.* Trans. Ronald Walls. 2 vols. London and New York, 1968.

Loserth, Johann. *Wiclif and Hus.* Trans. M. J. Evans. London, 1884.

————, ed. *Johannis Wyclif: Tractatus de ecclesia.* London, 1886.

————, ed. *Johannis Wyclif: De eucharistia tractatus maior.* London, 1892.

Luard, Henry R. *Matthaei parisiensis chronica majora.* Rolls Series, no. 57. 7 vols. London, 1872–84.

Lubac, Henri de. *Corpus Mysticum: L'Eucharistie et l'église au Moyen Age.* Paris, 1944.

Lunt, William E. *Papal Revenues in the Middle Ages.* 2 vols. New York, 1934.

————. *Financial Relations of the Papacy with England.* 2 vols. Cambridge, Mass., 1939–62.

Luther, Martin. *Weimarer Ausgabe D. Martin Luthers Werke.* 90 vols. Weimar, 1883–.

McCarthy, Dennis J. "Covenant in the Old Testament: The Present State of the Inquiry." *Catholic Biblical Quarterly* 27 (1965): 217–40.

McConica, James Kelsey. *English Humanism and Reformation Politics under Henry VIII and Edward VI.* Oxford, 1965.

McFarlane, K. B. *John Wycliffe and the Beginnings of English Nonconformity.* London, 1952.

McKisack, May. *The Fourteenth Century: 1307–1399.* Oxford, 1959.

McLaughlin, Eleanor. "The Heresy of the Free Spirit and Late Medieval Mysticism." *Medievalia et Humanistica*, n.s. 4 (1973): 37–54.

Mendenhall, George. *Law and Covenant in Israel and the Ancient Near East.* Pittsburgh, 1955.

Miethke, Jürgen. *Ockhams Weg zur Sozialphilosophie.* Berlin, 1969.

Migne, J.-P., ed. *Patrologiae cursus completus: Series Graeca.* 161 vols. Paris, 1857–87. (*PG* in notes.)

————, ed. *Patrologiae cursus completus: Series Latina.* 221 vols. Paris, 1884–1904. (*PL* in notes.)

Moeller, Bernd. "Frömmigkeit in Deutschland um 1500." *Archiv für Reformationsgeschichte* 56 (1965): 3–31.

————. *Spätmittelalter.* Vol. 2, installment H (pt. 1), of *Die Kirche in ihrer Geschichte: Ein Handbuch*, ed. Kurt Schmidt and Ernst Wolf. Göttingen, 1966.

————. *Imperial Cities and the Reformation: Three Essays.* Ed. and trans. H. C. Erik Midelfort and Mark V. Edwards, Jr. Philadelphia, 1972.

Molho, Anthony, and Tedeschi, John A., eds. *Renaissance Studies in Honor of Hans Baron.* Florence and De Kalb, 1971.

Mollat, G., "Jean XXII et le parler de l'Isle de France." *Annales de St. Louis des Français* 8 (1903): 89–91.

———. *The Popes at Avignon (1305–1378)*. Trans. Janet Love. New York, 1963.

———, ed. *Bernard Gui: Manuel de l'inquisiteur.* 2 vols. Paris, 1926–27.

Moran, Gabriel. *Scripture and Tradition: A Survey of the Controversy.* New York, 1963.

More, Thomas. *The Workes of Sir Thomas More . . . wrytten by him in the Englysh tongue.* London, 1557.

Moxon, R. S., ed. *The Comminatorium of Vincentius of Lérins.* Cambridge, 1915.

Mulder, Willelmus, ed. *Gerardi Magni Epistolae.* Antwerp, 1933.

Mundy, J. H., and Woody, K. M., eds. *The Council of Constance.* London and New York, 1961.

Niem, Dietrich of. *Theodorici a Niem: Historiarum sui temporis Libri IIII.* Strassburg, 1609.

Novotný, Václav, et al. *Fontes rerum Bohemicarum.* 8 vols. Prague, 1873–1932.

Oakley, Francis. *The Political Thought of Pierre d'Ailly: The Voluntarist Tradition.* New Haven and London, 1964.

———. "Pierre d'Ailly and Papal Infallibility." *Mediaeval Studies* 26 (1964): 353–58.

———. "Almain and Major: Conciliar Theory on the Eve of the Reformation." *American Historical Review* 70, no. 3 (1965): 673–90.

———. "Jacobean Political Theology: The Absolute and Ordinary Powers of the King." *Journal of the History of Ideas* 29, no. 3 (1968): 323–46.

———. "Figgis, Constance, and the Divines of Paris." *American Historical Review* 75, no. 2 (1969): 368–86.

———. *Council over Pope? Towards a Provisional Ecclesiology.* New York and London, 1969.

———. "Conciliarism at the Fifth Lateran Council?" *Church History* 41, no. 4 (1972): 452–63.

———. "Conciliarism in the Sixteenth Century: Jacques Almain Again." *Archiv für Reformationsgeschichte* 68 (1977): 111–32.

Oberman, Heiko. *Archbishop Thomas Bradwardine: A Fourteenth-Century Augustinian.* Utrecht, 1957.

———. *The Harvest of Medieval Theology: Gabriel Biel and Late Medieval Nominalism.* Cambridge, Mass., 1963.

———. "Das tridentinische Rechtfertigungsdekret im Licht spätmittelalterlicher Theologie." *Zeitschrift für Theologie und Kirche* 61, no. 3 (1964): 251–82.

————, ed. *Forerunners of the Reformation: The Shape of Late Medieval Thought*. New York, 1966.

————, ed. *Luther and the Dawn of the Modern Era*. Leiden, 1974.

Ockham, William of. *Quodlibeta septem una cum tractatu de sacramento altaris*. Strassburg, 1491.

O'Connor, Daniel, and Oakley, Francis, eds. *Creation: The Impact of an Idea*. New York, 1969.

O'Malley, John W. *Giles of Viterbo on Church and Reform: A Study in Renaissance Thought*. Leiden, 1968.

Orcibal, J. "Le 'Miroir des simples âmes' et la 'secte' du Libre Esprit." *Revue de l'histoire des religions* 176 (1969): 35–60.

Origo, Iris. *The Merchant of Prato: Francesco di Marco Datini*. New York, 1957.

————. *The World of San Bernardino*. New York, 1962.

Ozment, Steven E. *Mysticism and Dissent: Religious Ideology and Social Protest in the Sixteenth Century*. New Haven and London, 1973.

————. *The Reformation in the Cities*. New Haven and London, 1975.

————, ed. *The Reformation in Medieval Perspective*. Chicago, 1971.

Pacetti, Dionisio, ed. *S. Bernardino da Siena: Le prediche volgari inedite*. 2 vols. Siena, 1935.

Pantin, W. A. *The English Church in the Fourteenth Century*. Cambridge, 1955.

Partner, Peter. *The Papal State under Martin V*. London, 1958.

Pastor, Ludwig. *The History of the Popes from the Close of the Middle Ages*. 40 vols. London, 1889–1953.

Pelikan, Jaroslav. *The Christian Tradition: A History of the Development of Doctrine*. 5 vols. Chicago, 1971–.

Petry, Ray C., ed. *Late Medieval Mysticism*. Philadelphia, 1957.

Pfeiffer, Franz, ed. *Deutsche Mystiker des vierzehnten Jahrhunderts*. 2 vols. Leipzig, 1845–57.

Picotti, G. "La pubblicazione e i primi effeti della 'Execrabilis' de Pio II." *Archivio della Società Romana di storia patria* 37 (1914): 33ff.

Pohl, Michael J. *Thomae Hemerken a Kempis Opera Omnia*. 7 vols. Freiburg, 1910–22.

Post, R. R. *The Modern Devotion: Confrontation with Reformation and Humanism*. Leiden, 1968.

————. *De Moderne Devotie, Geert Groote en zijn stichtingen*. Amsterdam, 1940; repr. 1950.

Poukens, J. B., and Reypens, L., eds. *Jan van Ruusbroec: Werken*. 4 vols. Malines and Amsterdam, 1932–34.

Přerovský, O. *L'elezione di Urbano VI e l'insorgere dello scisma d'Occidente*. Rome, 1960.

Preus, James S. *From Shadow to Promise: Old Testament Interpretation from Augustine to the Young Luther*. Cambridge, Mass., 1969.

Raynal, Wilfrid, ed. *Of the Imitation of Christ by Thomas à Kempis as translated out of Latin by Richard Whytford anno MDLVI*. London, 1908.

Reeves, Marjorie. *The Influence of Prophecy in the Later Middle Ages: A Study in Joachimism*. Oxford, 1969.

Renaudet, Augustin. *Préréforme et Humanisme à Paris pendant les premières guerres d'Italie: 1494–1517*. 2d ed. Paris, 1953.

Renouard, Yves. *The Avignon Papacy: 1305–1403*. Trans. Denis Bethell. Hamden, Conn., 1970.

Ridolfi, Robert. *The Life of Girolamo Savonarola*. Trans. Cecil Grayson. New York, 1959.

Rouse, W. H. D., ed. *St. Augustine's Confessions*. 2 vols. London and New York, 1912.

Rüchlin-Teuscher, Gertrud. *Religiöses Volksleben des ausgehenden Mittelalters in den Reichstädten Hall und Heilbronn*. Berlin, 1933.

Russell, Jeffrey B. *A History of Medieval Christianity: Prophecy and Order*. New York, 1968.

Ruysbroeck, Jan van. See Poukens, J. B., and Reypens, L., eds.

Sacral Kingship. The Sacral Kingship: Contributions to the Central Theme of the VIIIth International Congress for the History of Religions, Rome, 1955. Studies in the History of Religions, vol. 4. Leiden, 1959.

Salembier, Louis. *Petrus de Alliaco*. Lille, 1886.

———. *Le Cardinal Pierre d'Ailly*. Tourcoing, 1931.

Scholz, Richard, ed. *Unbekannte kirchenpolitischen Streitschriften aus der Zeit Ludwigs des Bayern (1327–1354)*. 2 vols. Rome, 1911–14.

———, ed. *Die Publizistik zur Zeit Philipps des Schönen und Bonifaz VIII*. Stuttgart, 1913.

———, ed. *Aegidius Romanus De ecclesiastica potestate*. Weimar, 1929.

Schuster, Louis A.; Marius, Richard C.; Lusardi, James P.; and Schoeck, Richard J., eds. *The Confutation of Tyndale's Answer*. Vol. 7 of *The Complete Works of St. Thomas More*, ed. Richard S. Sylvester. 8 vols. New Haven and London, 1963–.

Scotus, Joannes Duns. *In Quatuor libros Sententiarum*. 2 vols. Antwerp, 1620.

———. *Joannis Duns Scoti: Opera omnia*. Ed. L. Vivès. 13 vols. Paris, 1891–95.

Seidlmayer, M. *Die Anfänge des grossen abendländischen Schismas*. Münster, 1940.

Silvera, S. *Quaresma de Sant Vincent Ferier predicada a Valencia l'any 1413*. Barcelona, 1927.

Šmahel, František. "'Doctor evangelicus super omnes evangelistas': Wyclif's Fortune in Hussite Bohemia." *Bulletin of the Institute of Historical Research* 43 (1970): 16–34.

Smith, Wilfred Cantwell. *Islam in Modern History*. Princeton, 1957.

Sohm, Rudolf. *Kirchengeschichte im Grundriss*. 3d ed. Leipzig, 1889. Trans. May Sinclair, *Outlines of Church History*. Boston, 1958.

Southern, R. W. *Western Society and the Church in the Middle Ages*. Harmondsworth, 1970.

Spedding, James, et al., eds. *The Works of Francis Bacon*. New ed. 7 vols. London, 1879.

Spinka, Matthew. *John Hus' Concept of the Church*. Princeton, 1966.

———. *John Hus: A Biography*. Princeton, 1968.

———, ed. *Advocates of Reform: From Wyclif to Erasmus*. London, 1958.

———, ed. *John Hus at the Council of Constance*. New York, 1965.

Spitz, Lewis W. *The Religious Renaissance of the German Humanists*. Cambridge, Mass., 1963.

———, ed. *The Reformation: Material or Spiritual?* Boston, 1962.

Steinmetz, David Curtis. *Misericordia Dei: The Theology of Johann von Staupitz in Its Late Medieval Setting*. Leiden, 1968.

———. "Libertas Christiana: Studies in the Theology of John Pupper of Goch (d. 1475)." *Harvard Theological Review* 65, no. 2 (1972): 191–230.

Stickler, Alfons M. "Papal Infallibility—a Thirteenth-Century Invention." *Catholic Historical Review* 60, no. 3 (1974): 427–41.

———. "Rejoinder to Professor Tierney." *Catholic Historical Review* 61, no. 2 (1975): 274–77.

Strauss, Gerard. "Success and Failure in the German Reformation." *Past and Present* 67 (May 1975): 30–63.

Stubbs, William. *The Constitutional History of England in its Origin and Development*. 6th ed. 3 vols. Oxford, 1893.

Stutz, Ulrich. *Die Eigenkirche als Element des mittelalterlich-germanischen Kirchenrechts*. Berlin, 1895.

Suarez, Francesco. *Metaphysicarum Disputationum*. 2 vols. Mayence, 1605.

Sullivan, Donald. "Nicholas of Cusa as Reformer: The Papal Legation to the Germanies, 1451–1452." *Mediaeval Studies* 36 (1974): 382–428.

Tavard, George H. *Holy Writ or Holy Church: The Crisis of the Protestant Reformation*. New York, 1959.

Tentler, Thomas N. *Sin and Confession on the Eve of the Reformation*. Princeton, 1977.

Thils, G. "Le 'Tractatus de Ecclesia' de Jean de Raguse." *Angelicum* 17 (1940): 219–44.

Thomas, Jules. *Le Concordat de 1516*. 3 vols. Paris, 1919.

Thomas, Keith. *Religion and the Decline of Magic*. London, 1971.

Thomson, John A. F. *The Later Lollards: 1414–1520*. Oxford, 1965.

Thomson, S. Harrison, ed. *Magistri Joannis Hus: Tractatus de ecclesia*. Boulder, Colo., 1956.

Thrupp, Sylvia, ed. *Millennial Dreams in Action: Studies in Revolutionary Religious Movements*. New York, 1970.

Tierney, Brian. *Foundations of the Conciliar Theory*. Cambridge, 1955.

————. "'Sola Scriptura' and the Canonists." *Studia Gratiana* 11 (1967): 347–66.

————. *Origins of Papal Infallibility: 1150–1350*. Leiden, 1972.

————. "On the History of Papal Infallibility: A Discussion with Remigius Bäumer." *Theologische Revue*, 70 (1974), 185–94.

————. "Infallibility and the Medieval Canonists: A Discussion with Alfons Stickler." *Catholic Historical Review* 61, no. 2 (1975): 265–73.

Tornacensis, Gilbertus. *Collectio de scandalis ecclesiae*. Ed. A. Stroick. *Archivum Franciscanum historicum* 24 (1931): 34–62.

Toussaert, Jacques. *Le Sentiment religieux en Flandre à la fin du Moyen Age*. Paris, 1963.

Toynbee, Paget, ed. *Dantis Alagherii Epistolae*. 2d ed. Oxford, 1966.

Tract. ill. juris. Tractatus illustrium jurisconsultorum. 22 vols. Venice, 1580–86.

Trinkaus, Charles. *In Our Image and Likeness: Humanity and Divinity in Italian Humanist Thought*. 2 vols. Chicago, 1970.

———— and Oberman, Heiko, eds. *The Pursuit of Holiness in Late Medieval and Renaissance Religion*. Leiden, 1974.

Troeltsch, Ernst. *The Social Teaching of the Christian Churches*. Trans. Olive Wyon. 2 vols. New York, 1960.

Tschackert, Paul. *Peter von Ailli*. Gotha, 1877.

Turley, Thomas. "Infallibilists in the Curia of Pope John XXII." *Journal of Medieval History* 1, no. 1 (1975): 71–101.

Turrecremata, Johannes de. *Summa de ecclesia*. Venice, 1561.

Ullmann, Karl Heinrich. *Reformatoren vor der Reformation vornehmlich in Deutschland und den Niederlanden*. 2 vols. Hamburg, 1841–42. Trans. Robert Menzies, *Reformers before the Reformation*. 2 vols. Edinburgh, 1855.

Ullmann, Walter. *Origins of the Great Schism*. London, 1949.

Underhill, Evelyn. *The Mystics of the Church*. London, 1925.

Valois, N. "Un Ouvrage inédit de Pierre d'Ailly: Le *De persecutionibus ecclesiae*." *Bibliothèque de l'école des chartes* 65 (1904): 556–74.

Van der Pol, Willem Hendrik. *World Protestantism*. Trans. T. Zuydwijk. New York, 1964.

Van Leeuwen, A. "L'Eglise, règle de foi dans les écrits de Guillaume d'Occam." *Ephemerides Theologicae Lovanensis* 11 (1934): 249–88.

Vansteenberghe, Edmond. *Le Cardinal Nicolas de Cues (1401–1464)*. Paris, 1920.

Vignaux, Paul. *Justification et prédestination au xive siècle: Duns Scot, Pierre d'Auriole, Guillaume d'Occam, Grégoire de Rimini*. Paris, 1934.

———. *Luther: Commentateur des sentences*. Paris, 1935.

Vinchant, François, ed. *Annales de la province et comté du Hainault*. 6 vols. Brussels and Mons, 1848–53.

Vooght, Paul de. *Les Sources de la doctrine chrétienne d'après les théologiens du xive siècle et du début du xve* . . . Bruges, 1954.

———. *L'Hérésie de Jean Hus*. Louvain, 1960.

———. *Hussiana*. Louvain, 1960.

———. *Les Pouvoirs du concile et l'autorité du Pape au Concile de Constance*. Paris, 1965.

———. "Les Controverses sur des pouvoirs du concile et l'autorité du pape au Concile de Constance." *Revue Théologique de Louvain* 1 (1970): 45–75.

———. *Jacobellus de Stříbro: Premier théologien du hussitisme*. Louvain, 1972.

Wakefield, Walter L., and Evans, Austin P., eds. *Heresies of the High Middle Ages*. New York, 1969.

Walch, Christian, ed. *Monumenta medii aevi*. 2 vols. Göttingen, 1757–63.

Walsh, James, ed. *The Revelations of Divine Love of Julian of Norwich*. London, 1961.

Watt, W. M. *Free Will and Predestination in Early Islam*. London, 1948.

Weinstein, Donald. *Savonarola and Florence: Prophecy and Patriotism in the Renaissance*. Princeton, 1970.

Weiss, R. *Humanism in England during the Fifteenth Century*. 2d ed. Oxford, 1957.

Wilks, Michael J. *The Problem of Sovereignty in the Later Middle Ages*. Cambridge, 1963.

Williams, George H. *The Radical Reformation*. Philadelphia, 1962.

Winkelmann, Eduard, ed. *Acta Imperii Inedita*. 2 vols. Innsbrück, 1880–85.

Wood-Legh, K. L. *Perpetual Chantries in Britain*. Cambridge, 1965.

Workman, Herbert B. *John Wyclif: A Study of the English Medieval Church*. 2 vols. Oxford, 1926.

Wycliffe, John. See Loserth, Johann, ed.

Zabarella, Francesco. *Acutissimi Jurisconsulti . . . Francisci Zabarellis Cardinalis Florentini . . . de ejus temporis Schismate Tractatus*. Strassburg, 1609.

INDEX

Abelard, Peter, 257n
Absenteeism, clerical. *See* Pluralism and nonresidence.
Accademia Marciana, 245. *See also* San Marco, Convent of.
Acceptatio of Mainz, 73, 227
Act in Restraint of Appeals, 16
Ad abolendam, 180
Adamites, 183
Ad conditorem canonum, 45
Ad nostrum, 183–84
Adnotationes in Novum Testamentum (Valla), 255–56
Aegidius Romanus, 145, 158, 164, 166
Agricola, Rudolf, 257n
Ailred of Rievaulx, 86
Albergati, Niccolò, 114
Albert V, duke of Austria, 237
Albertus Magnus, 143
Albigenses. *See* Cathari.
Albornoz, Cardinal Gil, 41
Alcalá, University of, 250–51, 288
Alexander III, pope, 29, 63
Alexander VI, pope, 75–76, 214, 247
Alexians, 233
Alexius, saint, 179
Almain, Jacques, 173, 229, 303
Amaury of Bene, 183
Amberg, Friedrich von, 264
Ambrosius of Speier, 153
Anagni, outrage of, 17, 23–26, 37, 56, 313
Angelica (Angelus Carletus de Clavasio), 126
Angelico, Fra, 234, 245
Angevin rulers and papacy, 33–36, 56
Annates, 50, 70, 219, 225, 227

Anne of Bohemia, queen of England, 195
Antichrist, 188, 261–65, 305
Antipapal legislation, 16–17, 53, 72
Anti-Semitism, 116, 262
Antonino, saint, 113, 234, 238, 264
Apostolic poverty, Franciscan doctrine of, 35, 44–46, 132, 153n, 155–56, 168–69
Aquinas, Thomas, saint, 94, 97, 139, 144–45, 157, 162
Aragon, 34, 72, 226, 247–48, 261, 267
Aristotle, 97, 141, 256
Ars moriendi, 117
Arundel, Thomas, archbishop of Canterbury, 190
Assisi, 40
Augustine of Hippo, saint, 81, 96, 104, 133–38, 140–41, 147, 159–61, 193–94, 204–8, 256. *See also* *Confessions*; *De libero arbitrio voluntatis*.
Augustinian canons, 87, 90, 91, 94, 102, 110, 233, 235, 246
Augustinian Eremites, 236–37
Augustinianism, 207–8, 315
Augustinian Rule, 86, 233, 277
Augustinus Triumphus, 146, 166
Austria, 70, 115
Autotheism, 93, 185, 205, 281
Avignon, 17, 29, 38, 40–41, 54, 56–57, 59, 61–62, 271, 273–274, 301, 303–4

"Babylonian Captivity," 38, 302
Balliol College, Oxford, 288
Barcelona, 268
Basel, Council of, 68–71, 73–75,

335

Library of Congress Cataloging in Publication Data

OAKLEY, FRANCIS.
 The Western church in the later Middle Ages.

  Bibliography: p.
  Includes index.
  1. Church history—Middle ages, 600–1500.   2. Europe
—Church history.   I. Title.
BR252.015   282'.09'.023   79–7621
ISBN 0-8014-1208-0